# Unraveling Reading Comprehension

# Unraveling Reading Comprehension

## Behavioral, Neurobiological, and Genetic Components

edited by


**Brett Miller, Ph.D.**
*Eunice Kennedy Shriver* National Institute of Child Health and Human Development
National Institutes of Health
Bethesda, Maryland

**Laurie E. Cutting, Ph.D.**
Peabody College of Education and Human Development
Vanderbilt University
Nashville, Tennessee

and

**Peggy McCardle, Ph.D., MPH**
*Eunice Kennedy Shriver* National Institute of Child Health and Human Development
National Institutes of Health
Bethesda, Maryland



PAUL H. BROOKES PUBLISHING CO.®

Baltimore • London • Sydney

·P A U L·H·
BROOKES
PUBLISHING CO.®

Paul H. Brookes Publishing Co., Inc.
Post Office Box 10624
Baltimore, Maryland 21285-0624
USA

www.brookespublishing.com



Typeset by Cenveo Publisher Services, Columbia, Maryland.
Manufactured in the United States of America by
Sheridan Books, Inc., Chelsea, Michigan.

The following were written by a U.S. Government employee within the scope of his or her official duties and, as such, shall remain in the public domain: Introduction, Integrative Summary 1, Integrative Summary 2, and Next Steps. The opinions and assertions contained herein are the private opinions of the authors and are not to be construed as official or reflecting the views of the U.S. Government.

The views expressed in this book are those of the authors and do not necessarily represent those of the National Institute of Health, the *Eunice Kennedy Shriver* National Institute of Child Health and Development, or the U.S. Department of Health and Human Services.

**Library of Congress Cataloging-in-Publication Data**

Unraveling reading comprehension : behavioral, neurobiological, and genetic components / by Brett Miller, Ph.D., Laurie E. Cutting, Ph.D., and Peggy McCardle, Ph.D., MPH.
pages cm. – (The extraordinary brain series ; XIII)
"This volume celebrates the 13th symposium in the Extraordinary Brain Series"–Preliminary pages.
Includes bibliographical references and index.
ISBN 978-1-59857-244-5 (alk. paper)
1. Reading, Psychology of. 2. Reading comprehension. 3. Cognitive learning. 4. Reading disability. I. Cutting, Laurie E. II. McCardle, Peggy D. III. Dyslexia Foundation. IV. Title.

BF456.R2M55 2013
418'.4019–dc23 2013007051

Miller, Brett.
British Library Cataloguing in Publication data are available from the British Library.

2017 2016 2015 2014 2013

10 9 8 7 6 5 4 3 2 1

# Contents

# About the Editors

**Brett Miller, Ph.D.,** Program Director of the Reading, Writing, and Related Learning Disabilities Research Program in the Child Development and Behavior Branch, *Eunice Kennedy Shriver* National Institute of Child Health and Human Development, Bethesda, Maryland

Dr. Miller oversees a research program focused on developing and supporting research and training initiatives to increase knowledge relevant to the development of reading and written language abilities for learners with and without disabilities. This program supports research that includes work with diverse groups and includes a range of ages across the life span.

**Laurie E. Cutting, Ph.D.,** Patricia and Rodes Hart Endowed Chair, Associate Professor, Peabody College of Education and Human Development, Vanderbilt University, Nashville, Tennessee

Dr. Cutting holds faculty appointments in the Departments of Special Education, Psychology, Radiology, and Pediatrics at Vanderbilt, as well as a research affiliate position at Haskins Laboratories and an adjunct faculty position at Johns Hopkins School of Medicine, Department of Neurology. Her research focuses on the area of educational neuroscience, in particular the neurobiological and behavioral underpinnings of reading, oral language, and dyslexia.

**Peggy McCardle, Ph.D., M.P.H.,** Chief of the Child Development and Behavior Branch, *Eunice Kennedy Shriver* National Institute of Child Health and Human Development, National Institutes of Health, Bethesda, Maryland

Dr. McCardle has been a classroom teacher, university faculty member, and hospital clinician. Currently, in addition to leading the branch, she directs the research program on language, bilingualism, and biliteracy, which addresses all aspects of typical language development as well as cross-linguistic and bilingualism research related to typical learning and learning disabilities in bilingual individuals.

# About the Contributors

**Suzanne M. Adlof, Ph.D.,** Assistant Professor, Department of Communication Sciences and Disorders, University of South Carolina, Williams Brice Building, 6th Floor, 1621 Greene Street, Columbia, SC 29208

Dr. Adlof's research examines developmental relationships between oral and written language skills in typically developing children and children with language and reading difficulties. The overarching goals of this research program are to improve the early identification of language and reading difficulties and to develop effective treatments to improve academic outcomes.

**Katinka Beker, MSc.,** Brain and Education Lab, Department of Education and Child Studies, Leiden University, Wassenaarseweg 52, 2333 AK Leiden, the Netherlands

Ms. Beker works as a Ph.D. student under the supervision of Drs. Paul van den Broek and Linda van Leijenhorst in the Brain and Education Lab at the Department of Education and Child Studies at Leiden University and studies the development of cognitive processes that are involved in reading comprehension and learning from text.

**Sabrina L. Benedict, M.Ed.,** Peabody College of Education and Human Development, Vanderbilt University, 230 Appleton Place, Nashville, TN 37203

Ms. Benedict received a B.A. from Boston College and an M.Ed. in special education from the Peabody College of Education and Human Development, Vanderbilt University. As a graduate research assistant in Vanderbilt's Education and Brain Sciences Research Lab she implemented phonics interventions, helped develop a morphological reading assessment, and researched how it predicted decoding ability. She currently works as a special education high school teacher in Los Angeles.

**Allison Broadwater, B.A.,** Peabody College of Education and Human Development, Vanderbilt University, 230 Appleton Place, Nashville, TN 37203

Ms. Broadwater is currently pursuing her M.Ed. in child studies with a focus on cognitive development and education from the Peabody College of Education and Human Development, Vanderbilt University. She works as a research assistant in Vanderbilt's Education and Brain Sciences Research Lab, where she focuses on the behavioral assessment of reading ability in children.

**Paul van den Broek, Ph.D.,** Professor, Department of Education and Child Studies, Leiden University, Wassenaarseweg 52, 2333 AK Leiden, the Netherlands

Dr. van den Broek holds faculty appointments in the Department of Education and Child Studies at Leiden University and the Department of Cognitive Sciences at the University of Minnesota. His research focuses on the cognitive and neurological processes involved in reading comprehension in children and adults.

**Scott S. Burns, M.S.,** Senior Research Imaging Specialist, Kennedy Center, Vanderbilt University, PMB 40, 230 Appleton Place Nashville, TN 37203-5721

Mr. Scott oversees the MRI side of the Education and Brain Science Research Lab (EBRL). He is interested in developing automated methods for processing MR data to reduce human error, increase reliability, and ultimately improve the science produced by the EBRL.

**Kate Cain, Ph.D.,** Reader, Department of Psychology, Fylde College, Lancaster University, Lancaster, LA1 4YF, UK

Dr. Cain's research focuses on the development of reading and listening comprehension in children and, in particular, how language skills, knowledge, and cognitive resources are related to reading and listening comprehension problems.

**Hugh W. Catts, Ph.D.,** Professor and Chair, Department of Speech-Language-Hearing, University of Kansas, 1000 Sunnyside Avenue, Lawrence, KS 66045

Dr. Catts is the past president of the Society for the Scientific Study of Reading and is a member of the Scientific Advisory Board of the International Dyslexia Association. His research focuses on the relationship between language and reading development and disorders.

**James A. Clinton, M.S.,** Department of Psychology, Northern Illinois University, Psychology-Computer Science Building, Room 400, DeKalb, IL 60015

Mr. Clinton is a doctoral candidate in the Cognitive and Instructional Psychology program at Northern Illinois University under the guidance of Joseph P. Magliano. His research interests focus on comprehension processes that differ between narrative text and film adaptations of the same narrative. He is also interested in the perceptual processes that guide the comprehension of visual narratives.

**Donald L. Compton, Ph.D.,** Professor and Chair, Department of Special Education, Peabody College of Education and Human Development,

Vanderbilt University, Peabody College Box 228, 110 Magnolia Circle, 418C MRL, Nashville, TN 37203

Dr. Compton's research involves modeling individual differences in the development of children's reading skills and the identification of children with reading disabilities.

**Carol McDonald Connor, Ph.D.,** Professor and Director, Early Learning Research Initiative Center, Arizona State University, P.O. Box 872111, Tempe, AZ 85287-2111

Dr. Connor's research focuses on children's language and literacy development and the multiple sources of influence that affect this development, including the classroom learning environment. Her research also focuses on children with dyslexia and other learning disabilities and on the efficacy of interventions designed to improve their literacy and language skills. She is also a distinguished research associate at the Florida Center for Reading Research.

**Qiuyun Fan, M.S.,** Research Assistant, Education and Brain Sciences Research Lab, Vanderbilt University, PMB 328, 230 Appleton Place, Nashville, TN, 37203

Ms. Fan received an M.S. in biomedical engineering from Vanderbilt University in 2011. She is currently working toward a Ph.D. under the advisory of Adam W. Anderson, from the Department of Biomedical Engineering, and Laurie E. Cutting, from the Peabody College of Education and Human Development. Her research interests include diffusion tensor MRI, high-angular resolution diffusion imaging, and the investigation of neurocorrelates of reading ability using imaging techniques.

**Stephen J. Frost, Ph.D.,** Senior Scientist, Haskins Laboratories, 300 George, Suite 900, New Haven, CT 06511.

Dr. Frost's research integrates cognitive and neurobiological measures of language processing in individuals across a broad age and skill range to elucidate the network that supports skilled reading, as well as the neurological adaptation associated with developing reading skill.

**Jennifer K. Gilbert, Ph.D.,** Research Associate, Department of Special Education, Peabody College of Education and Human Development, Vanderbilt University, Peabody College Box 228, 110 Magnolia Circle, Nashville, TN 32703

Dr. Gilbert's research involves the application of advanced statistical modeling to reading data.

**Art Graesser, Ph.D.,** Professor, Department of Psychology, University of Memphis, 202 Psychology Building, Memphis, TN 38152-3230

Dr. Graesser is a professor in the Department of Psychology and the Institute of Intelligent Systems at the University of Memphis and is a senior research fellow in the Department of Education at the University of Oxford. His primary research interests are in cognitive science, discourse processing, and the learning sciences. More specific interests include knowledge representation, question asking and answering, tutoring, text comprehension, inference generation, conversation, reading, education, memory, emotions, computational linguistics, artificial intelligence, human–computer interaction, and learning technologies with animated conversational agents.

**Elena L. Grigorenko, Ph.D.,** Professor, Child Study Center, Yale University, 230 South Frontage Road, New Haven, CT 06519

Dr. Grigorenko received her Ph.D. in general psychology from Moscow State University, Russia, and her Ph.D. in developmental psychology and genetics from Yale University. Dr. Grigorenko is currently the Emily Fraser Beede Professor of Developmental Disabilities, Child Studies, Psychology, and Epidemiology and Public Health at Yale, and adjunct professor of Psychology at Columbia University and Moscow State University. Dr. Grigorenko has published more than 350 peer-reviewed articles, book chapters, and books. She has received multiple professional awards for her work and has received funding for her research from the National Institutes of Health, National Science Foundation, U.S. Department of Energy, U.S. Agency for International Development, Cure Autism Now, Foundation for Child Development, American Psychological Foundation, and other federal and private sponsoring organizations. Dr. Grigorenko has worked with children and their families in the United States as well as in Africa (Kenya, Tanzania and Zanzibar, the Gambia, and Zambia), India, Saudi Arabia, and Russia.

**Anne Helder, M.Sc.,** Brain and Education Lab, Department of Education and Child Studies, Leiden University, Wassenaarseweg 52, 2333 AK Leiden, the Netherlands

Ms. Helder is currently a Ph.D. student under the supervision of Drs. Paul van den Broek and Linda van Leijenhorst in the Brain and Education Lab at Leiden University in the Netherlands. She studies developmental and individual differences in neurocognitive processes involved in reading comprehension.

**Fumiko Hoeft, Ph.D.,** Director, Laboratory for Educational Neuroscience, and Associate Professor, Department of Psychiatry, University of California, 401 Parnassus Avenue, Box 0945-F, San Francisco, CA 94143

Dr. Hoeft's research focuses on circuit-based approaches to the understanding of reading and dyslexia. She is particularly interested in the neurobiological basis of different phenotypes/subtypes of dyslexia and early risk factors that predispose and protective factors that prevent children from developing dyslexia.

**Gina R. Kuperberg, Ph.D.,** Director, NeuroCognition Laboratory, Department of Psychology, Tufts University, 490 Boston Avenue, Medford, MA 02155; and Director, Martinos Center for Biomedical Imaging and the Department of Psychiatry, Massachusetts General Hospital (East), Harvard Medical School, Psychiatry CNY-2, Building 149, 13th Street, Room 2629, Charlestown, MA 02129

Dr. Kuperberg directs the NeuroCognition Laboratory, which spans the Department of Psychology, Tufts University, and the Martinos Center for Biomedical Imaging and the Department of Psychiatry at Massachusetts General Hospital, Harvard Medical School. Her lab studies the neural basis of normal and abnormal language processing using multimodal neuroimaging techniques.

**Nicole Landi, Ph.D.,** Faculty Member, Yale Child Study; Director of EEG Research, Haskins Laboratories, Haskins Laboratories and Yale University, 300 George Street, Suite 900, New Haven, CT 06511

Dr. Landi received her doctorate in psychology and cognitive neuroscience from the University of Pittsburgh in 2005. Her research examines the acquisition and development of reading and language as well as individual differences in reading and language skill. She studies these issues using multiple methodologies including functional magnetic resonance imaging and event-related potentials. By examining early school age children, adolescents, and young adults, her research spans a broad range of reading and language development.

**Adam M. Larson, Ph.D.,** Research Associate, Visual Cognition Lab, Kansas State University, 492 Bluemont Hall, Manhattan, KS 66502

Dr. Larson is currently a postdoctoral research associate in Dr. Lester Loschky's Visual Cognition Lab at Kansas State University. His research investigates scene perception and eye movements in order to understand how these early cognitive processes can contribute to our comprehension of dynamic actions and events.

**Linda van Leijenhorst, Ph.D.,** Assistant Professor, Brain and Education Lab, Department of Education and Child Studies, Leiden University, Wassenaarseweg 52, 2333 AK Leiden, the Netherlands

Dr. van Leijenhorst's research focuses on how developmental changes in the ability to control our thoughts and behavior relate to changes in brain function. She examines these questions in children, adolescents, and young adults using behavioral as well as brain imaging methods. Her current research aims to elucidate the development of reading comprehension in relation to brain development.

**Haiying Li, M.S.,** Research Associate, Department of Psychology and Institute for Intelligent Systems, University of Memphis, 202 Psychology Building, Memphis, TN 38152-3230

Ms. Li's primary research interests are in language, reading, discourse processing, cognitive science, and computational linguistics. She is investigating language and discourse in English and other languages, both from the perspective of psychological mechanisms and automated computer analyses. She is currently pursuing her Ph.D. at the University of Memphis.

**Lester C. Loschky, Ph.D.,** Associate Professor, Department of Psychology, Kansas State University, 471 Bluemont Hall, 1100 Mid-Campus Drive, Manhattan, KS 66506-5302

Dr. Loschky studies scene perception and visual cognition, including the interrelationships between eye movements, attention, and memory for real-world scenes. He also studies processes in the comprehension of text, picture stories, and—most recently—film.

**Heikki J. Lyytinen, Ph.D.,** Professor, Department of Developmental Neuropsychology, University of Jyväskylä, 40014 University of Jyväskylä, Jyväskylä, Finland

Dr. Lyytinen is the principal investigator of the Jyväskylä Longitudinal Study of Dyslexia, which has revealed how to identify children in need of support in their reading acquisition. This work motivated him to lead the development process of Graphogame technology, which has now initiated worldwide efforts to provide mobile learning game-based support globally via the Grapholearn Initiative.

**Joseph P. Magliano, Ph.D.,** Presidential Research Professor, Department of Psychology, Northern Illinois University, DeKalb, IL 60134

Dr. Magliano's research interests focus on understanding comprehension processes and the extent to which they are similar and different across modalities of experiences (e.g., text, film, and graphic narratives). He has also focused on understanding how to assess and help struggling college students with respect to academic literacy skills.

**W. Einar Mencl, Ph.D.,** Director, Neuroimaging Research, Haskins Laboratories, 300 George Street, New Haven, CT 06515

Dr. Mencl received his Ph.D. in experimental psychology from Dartmouth College in 1994. His expertise is in experimental design and analysis of functional and brain imaging data and applying techniques such as functional magnetic resonance imaging and magnetoencephalography toward the understanding of reading development and reading disability. Other interests include auditory perception, music perception, and multivariate analysis of brain activation patterns.

**Amanda C. Miller, Ph.D.,** Fellow, Department of Special Education and Child Studies, Peabody College of Education and Human Development, Vanderbilt University, 110 Magnolia Circle, Nashville, TN 37203

Dr. Miller's research explores the cognitive underpinnings of individual differences in reading and listening comprehension.

**Robin D. Morris, Ph.D.,** Regents Professor of Psychology, Department of Psychology, Georgia State University, P.O. Box 5010, Atlanta, GA 30302-5010

Dr. Morris is Associate Provost for Strategic Initiatives and Innovation and Regent's Professor of Psychology at Georgia State University. He holds joint appointments in the Department of Educational Psychology and Special Education and the Neurosciences Institute. His scholarly and clinical work focuses on the biological and environmental factors that influence academic, attentional, and social development in children and adolescents. His current research is focused on interventions for dyslexia and reading disabilities, mitochondrial disease, using technology to assist in reading development, and the neuroimaging of the typical and atypically developing brain.

**Chelsea Myers, B.S.,** Lab Manager, Laboratory for Educational Neuroscience, University of California, San Francisco, 401 Parnassus Avenue, Box 0945-F, San Francisco, CA 94143

Ms. Myers is the lab manager at the Laboratory for Educational Neuroscience at the University of California, San Francisco. She graduated from St. Michael's College in Vermont with degrees in biology and Spanish. She plans to return to graduate school in the near future to further pursue her interest in educational neuropsychology, especially as it relates to the biological, neurological, and psychological underpinnings of developmental and learning disorders.

**Tenaha O'Reilly, Ph.D.,** Research Scientist, Educational Testing Service, Rosedale Road, MS 13E, Princeton, NJ 08541

Dr. O'Reilly's research interests are in assessment, reading comprehension, reading strategies, metacognition, and the role of background knowledge in understanding and learning. He is currently involved in projects aimed at designing and evaluating innovative measures of reading comprehension for students in pre-K–12 settings.

**Charles Perfetti, Ph.D.,** Director, Learning Research and Development Center, University of Pittsburgh, 3939 O'Hara Street, Pittsburgh, PA 15260

Dr. Perfetti's central research interest is in the cognitive science of language and reading processes, including lower- and higher-level processes and the nature of reading ability. His current research program addresses several related issues, including the nature of reading skill, the role of word knowledge in comprehension, comparative studies of reading across writing systems, and second-language learning, including studies of adults and children and using behavioral, electrophysiological, and functional magnetic resonance imaging methods.

**Stephen A. Petrill, Ph.D.,** Professor, Department of Psychology, The Ohio State University, 1830 Neil Avenue, Columbus, OH 43210

Dr. Petrill's research focuses on the genetic, neurobiological, cognitive, and environmental underpinnings of dyslexia, language impairment, and math disabilities. In particular, he examines how these approaches explain the comorbidity and independence among different types of learning difficulties and their relationship to the typical range.

**Jonathan L. Preston, Ph.D.,** Research Scientist, Haskins Laboratories, 300 George Street, Suite 900, New Haven, CT 06511

Dr. Preston is a speech-language pathologist with clinical and research expertise on speech–sound disorders, neuroscience, and the phonological bases of literacy. He conducts basic and applied research on speech, language and literacy development, and disorders.

**Kenneth R. Pugh, Ph.D.,** President and Director of Research, Haskins Laboratories, Yale University and University of Connecticut, 300 George Street, Suite 900, New Haven, CT 06511.

Dr. Pugh holds academic appointments as professor of psychology, University of Connecticut; associate professor of linguistics, Yale University; and associate professor of diagnostic radiology, Yale University School of Medicine. He is also director of the Yale Reading Center. His research program falls primarily in two broad domains: cognitive neuroscience and psycholinguistics. A fundamental interest continues to be research into the neurobiology of typical and atypical language and reading development in children.

**Erik D. Reichle, Ph.D.,** Professor of Psychology, Centre for Visual Cognition, University of Southampton, Highfield, Southampton SO17 1BJ, UK

Dr. Reichle's research uses computational modeling and eye-movement experiments to understand how word identification, attention, and visual and oculomotor constraints jointly determine when and where readers move their eyes.

**Jay G. Rueckl, Ph.D.,** Senior Scientist, Haskins Laboratories; Associate Professor of Psychology, University of Connecticut; Head of the Psychology

Department's Perception-Action-Cognition Division; Inaugural Director, University of Connecticut Cognitive Science Program, 300 George Street, Suite 900, New Haven, CT 06511

Dr. Rueckl was trained as an experimental psychologist, and his research combines behavioral methods with both neuroimaging and computational modeling. His primary research focus concerns word reading and its neural bases, and its main goal is to understand how linguistic experience and a universal learning mechanism jointly determine the commonalities and differences that are observed both between and within linguistic communities.

**John P. Sabatini, Ph.D.,** Principle Research Scientist, Research and Development Division, Global Assessment Center, Educational Testing Service, Rosedale Road, MS 13E, Princeton, NJ 08541

Dr. Sabatini's research interests and expertise are in reading literacy development and disabilities, assessment, and educational technology. He is lead editor of two books on innovation in reading comprehension assessment and is currently the principal investigator of a grant to develop pre-K–12 comprehension assessments. He also serves as co-investigator on projects that explore the reading processes of adolescents, English language learners, and students with reading-based disabilities.

**Michael Solis, Ph.D.,** Project Director, The Meadows Center for Preventing Educational Risk, University of Texas, 1 University Station Drive D4900, Austin, TX 78712

Dr. Solis recently completed his Ph.D. in special education at the University of Texas at Austin. He is a former special educator and reading specialist/coach. His research focuses on vocabulary and reading comprehension interventions for students in Grades 4–8. Dr. Solis serves as project director for the Meadows Center for Preventing Educational Risk, where he leads the implementation of randomized controlled trials and single-subject and qualitative studies.

**Joseph Z. Stafura, B.A.,** Graduate Student Researcher, Learning Research and Development Center and Center for the Neural Basis of Cognition, University of Pittsburgh, 413 LRDC, 3939 O'Hara Street, Pittsburgh, PA 15260

Under the supervision of Dr. Charles A. Perfetti, Mr. Stafura uses electroencephalogram methods to investigate processing of associatively and semantically related words, as well as the on-line word-to-text integration processes involved in reading connected sentences.

**Laura M. Steacy, M.Ed.,** Department of Special Education and Child Services, Vanderbilt University, 110 Magnolia Circle, Nashville, TN 37203

Ms. Steacy is a doctoral student in high-incidence disabilities in the Department of Special Education at Vanderbilt University. Her research interests include early predictors of reading achievement and early interventions for students at-risk for reading disabilities. Prior to her doctoral studies, Ms. Steacy was a classroom teacher with experience teaching kindergarten through sixth grade.

**Sharon Vaughn, Ph.D.,** Executive Director, The Meadows Center for Preventing Educational Risk, Sanchez Building, Austin, TX 78712

Dr. Vaughn is H.E. Hartfelder/Southland Corporation Regents Chair in Human Development and Executive Director at The Meadows Center for Preventing Educational Risk, an organized research unit at the University of Texas at Austin. She was the editor-in-chief of the *Journal of Learning Disabilities* and is the recipient of the CEC Research Award, the AERA SIG distinguished researcher award, the International Reading Association Albert J. Harris Award, and the University of Texas Distinguished Faculty Award. The author of numerous books and research articles that address dyslexia, she is also currently the principal investigator for numerous research grants investigating effective interventions for students with dyslexia.

**Jianfeng Yang, Ph.D.,** Associate Professor, Institute of Psychology, Chinese Academy of Sciences, A4 Datun Road, Chaoyang District, Beijing, China 100101

Dr. Yang developed the first large-scale implementation of the "triangle model" of reading in Chinese and has worked on a number of important imaging studies demonstrating stimulus by task interactions in the reading network. Most recently he has been working on methods for analyzing the brain circuitry underlying reading under relatively natural conditions.

**Jason D. Zevin, Ph.D.,** Associate Professor, Department of Psychology, Sackler Institute for Developmental Psychobiology, Weill Cornell Medical College, 1300 York Avenue, Box 140, New York, NY 10065; and Senior Scientist, Haskins Laboratories, 300 George Street, New Haven, CT, 06511

Dr. Zevin is an associate professor of psychology at the Sackler Institute for Developmental Psychobiology at Weill Cornell Medical College and Senior Scientist at Haskins Laboratories. As an undergraduate research assistant, he helped conduct a study in which participants were asked to name words according to spelling-to-sound rules rather than their correct pronunciations (a reversal of the frequency effect was found). Nearly two decades later, he has begun to ask whether the tasks used to study reading in the laboratory might be more generally prone to task-specific phenomena and is considering alternatives.

# The Dyslexia Foundation and the Extraordinary Brain Series

The Dyslexia Foundation (TDF) began in the late 1980s. It was founded by William H. "Will" Baker in collaboration with notable researchers in dyslexia. Through the generosity of the Underwood and Baker families, funds were provided to support the establishment of the first Dyslexia Research Laboratory at Beth Israel Hospital, Harvard Medical School, Boston, Massachusetts; the laboratory opened in 1982, with a goal of investigating the neural underpinnings of dyslexia. Baker became the director of research for the Orton Dyslexia Society and, at the urging of Dr. Albert Galaburda and others, convened top researchers from cognition, neuroscience, and education in a 1987 meeting. That scientific symposium was held in Florence, Italy, under the auspices of the Orton Dyslexia Society, with generous support from Emily Fisher Landau. At that symposium, ideas were presented and discussed, with sufficient time to disagree, to identify research challenges and to brainstorm solutions, and thus the concept of a dyslexia symposium series was born. In spring 1989, the National Dyslexia Research Foundation (later renamed The Dyslexia Foundation) was formed to focus more specifically on research while the Orton Society continued its primary focus on treatment and education. In 1990, the new foundation sponsored the next symposium in Barcelona, Spain. With this second symposium, the first to be held under the foundation's auspices, the Extraordinary Brain Series was born.

This volume celebrates the 13th symposium in the Extraordinary Brain Series. Currently these symposia result in volumes that reflect the papers presented and the discussion that was spurred by those presentations. The series volumes make accessible to all researchers the thoughts of scholars across various disciplines as they tackle various aspects of the behavior, neurobiology, and genetics of dyslexia and of learning to read and write. Below is a listing of TDF symposia and the related volumes.

I. June 1987, Florence, Italy. Symposium Director: Albert M. Galaburda.

   Galaburda, A.M. (Ed.). (1990). *From reading to neurons.* Cambridge, MA: Bradford Books/MIT Press.

II. June 1990, Barcelona, Spain. Symposium Director: Albert M. Galaburda.

   Galaburda, A.M. (Ed.). (1992). *Dyslexia and development: Neurobiological aspects of extraordinary brains.* Cambridge, MA: Bradford Books/Harvard University Press.

III. June 1992, Santa Fe, NM. Symposium Director: Paula Tallal.

Chase, C., Rosen, G., & Sherman, G.F. (Eds.). (1996). *Developmental dyslexia: Neural, cognitive, and genetic mechanisms.* Mahwah, NJ: Erlbaum.

IV. June 1994, Kauai, Hawaii. Symposium Director: Benita Blachman.

Blachman, B.R. (Ed.). (1997). *Foundations of reading acquisition and dyslexia: Implications for early intervention.* Mahwah, NJ: Erlbaum.

V. June 1996, Kona, Hawaii. Symposium Director: Drake Duane.

Duane, D. (Ed.). (1998). *Reading and attention disorders: Neurobiological correlates.* Mahwah, NJ: Erlbaum.

VI. June 1998, Kona, Hawaii. Symposium Director: Barbara Foorman.

Foorman, B. (Ed.). (2003). *Preventing and remediating reading difficulties: Bringing science to scale.* Baltimore, MD: York Press.

VII. June 2000, Crete, Greece. Symposium Director: Maryanne Wolf.

Wolf, M. (Ed.). (2001). *Time, fluency, and dyslexia.* Baltimore, MD: York Press.

VIII. October 2001, Johannesburg, South Africa. Symposium Director: Frank Wood.

*Multilingualism and dyslexia.* No publication.

IX. June 2004, Como, Italy. Symposium Director: Glenn Rosen.

Rosen, G. (Ed.). (2005). *The dyslexic brain: New pathways in neuroscience discovery.* Mahwah, NJ: Erlbaum.

X. June 2007, Campos do Jordão, Brazil. Symposium Directors: Ken Pugh and Peggy McCardle.

Pugh, K., & McCardle, P. (Eds.). (2009). *How children learn to read: Current issues and new directions in the integration of cognition, neurobiology and genetics of reading and dyslexia research and practice.* New York, NY: Psychology Press.

XI. January 2010, Taipei, Taiwan. Symposium Directors: Peggy McCardle, Ovid Tseng, Jun Ren Lee, and Brett Miller.

McCardle, P., Miller, B., Lee, J.R., & Tseng, O. (Eds.). (2011). *Dyslexia across languages: Orthography and the brain–gene–behavior link.* Baltimore, MD: Paul H. Brookes Publishing Co.

XII. June 2011, Cong, Ireland. Symposium Directors: April Benasich and Holly Fitch.

Benasich, A.A., & Fitch, R.H. (Eds.). (2012). *Developmental dyslexia: Early precursors, neurobehavioral markers, and biological substrates.* Baltimore, MD: Paul H. Brookes Publishing Co.

XIII. June 2012, Talinn, Estonia. Symposium Directors: Brett Miller and Laurie Cutting.

Miller, B., Cutting, L., & McCardle, P. (Eds.). (2013). *Reading comprehension: Unraveling its behavioral, neurobiological, and genetic components.* Baltimore, MD: Paul H. Brookes Publishing Co.

# Acknowledgments

First and foremost, the editors of this volume wish to thank The Dyslexia Foundation (TDF) and founder and President William H. "Will" Baker, Jr. Without the many meetings and conversations with Will, we could not have held such a well-planned, well-organized symposium or this volume. He found an ideal venue for working, thinking, and discussing, with both formal and informal gatherings, a setting that let this symposium maximize those strengths that TDF symposia have become known for. We would also like to acknowledge generous contributions from Helen U. Baker, Joan McNichols, Erika and Robin Ray, the Brehm School, the F.L. Chamberlain School, the Summit School, Wilson Language Training, Barbara and Ed Wilson, and other donors who wish to remain anonymous.

We wish to thank Dr. Hollis Scarborough for her valuable scientific input and discussion at the workshop that was held in preparation for this symposium. Many of the Estonia symposium speakers were also at the earlier workshop, but Hollis was unable to participate in Estonia; nonetheless, she was a contributor through her thoughtful comments and challenging questions and ideas that helped to shape the symposium in highly constructive ways.

Special thanks must go to Amelia Baker, Tiffany Ray Ferguson, and Nancy Rhodes for their dedicated work in arranging the details of the conference. Our sincere appreciation must also be expressed to Sarah Shepke and Sarah Kendall for shepherding us through the many potential pitfalls that exist in producing any volume; they provided clear guidance for us to give our authors, were flexible and very helpful in guiding us through the editorial and production processes, and were supportive and encouraging at all times! Thanks too to senior project manager Marcus Johnston and to all those others at Brookes Publishing who worked on this volume, doing copy editing, sending us page proofs, making corrections, and all the other things they did to make this book a reality.

And clearly, this effort could not have happened without the dedication to science demonstrated by those researchers who presented papers at the symposium and their colleagues who coauthored the chapters for this volume.

SECTION I

# Introduction

CHAPTER 1

# Unraveling the Behavioral, Neurobiological, and Genetic Components of Reading Comprehension

## An Introduction

Laurie E. Cutting and Brett Miller

Being able to read is one of the most essential academic skills that an individual needs to attain; how well an individual can read has broad-reaching impacts on educational and job attainment. Nevertheless, despite the importance of reading, many children struggle with it, as evidenced by National Assessment of Educational Progress figures consistently showing that approximately 25%–30% of U.S. children in the 4th, 8th, and 12th grades do not read at adequate levels for functioning in society (National Center for Education Statistics, 2009, 2011). Whereas a great deal of focus and emphasis has been placed on understanding the basic elements of reading—the word-level aspects of reading—until recently, less attention has been focused on reading comprehension—the end goal of reading. Among the various reasons for reading comprehension receiving relatively less attention is the extremely complex nature of the skill, which leads to its being conceptualized differently across researchers in terms of definition, theoretical structure, and practical outcomes. Such differences have thus far represented a significant barrier in moving reading comprehension research forward.

In recognition of the importance of reading comprehension skills to all learners, particularly those with reading disabilities, The Dyslexia Foundation (TDF) hosted the 13th Extraordinary Brain Symposium, titled Unraveling the Behavioral, Neurobiological, & Genetic Components of Reading Comprehension. Consistent with the theme of the symposium series, this symposium integrated viewpoints across a range of perspectives and approaches—behavioral sciences, neurobiology, and genetics—to enrich the scientific discussion and to directly address the challenges facing researchers investigating the origins of reading comprehension skills as well as practitioners working to intervene to address the needs of struggling learners and those with learning disabilities. The symposium series has consisted of very small (approximately 18 researchers), focused meetings with the particular goal of mapping out a 5-year research agenda on a particular topic related to dyslexia. The foundation's conference series has a rich history of yielding many new insights and ideas for research grants and has helped propel the field forward. This conference was the first TDF symposium explicitly focusing on reading comprehension. The topic was chosen because poor reading comprehension can be a significant barrier for individuals with reading difficulties and this difficulty can exist even when word-level decoding difficulties have been remediated. More generally, difficulties with reading comprehension are widespread in a large swath of the general population who may (or may not) have decoding or other reading or language difficulties as well.

The purpose of the TDF's 13th Extraordinary Brain Symposium was to map out a realistic, actionable plan for reading comprehension research. Although most TDF topics are broad and meant to pose challenges to researchers, the 2012 TDF conference was a particularly significant undertaking because of the aforementioned barriers with regard to the complexity of reading comprehension. Reading comprehension is a daunting yet important area of research; the nature of these challenges is apparent from a close read of the research literature and in some previous attempts to reach sufficient consensus within the research community. Given these identified complexities, an incremental approach for the 2012 TDF meeting was taken, with a smaller presymposium that helped to identify and clearly frame the areas of agreement and disagreement in preparation for the 2012 TDF meeting. From this presymposium there emerged several cross-cutting themes, whose identification constituted a first step in the direction of identifying a cogent research agenda. Based on this, the 2012 TDF symposium itself focused on the following emergent themes: the need for an examination of 1) product versus process elements of reading comprehension, 2) text characteristics, 3) inferencing, 4) distinctions between listening versus reading comprehension, and 5) developmental aspects of reading comprehension.

Although each of the aforementioned themes could constitute a meeting in and of itself, speakers were instead asked to contextualize their presentations and discussions in all or at least some of these emergent themes from the presymposia. In addition, the intent of the meeting was expressly *not* to define reading comprehension. Although the definitional issue remains a formidable challenge for the field and is clearly a needed end point, we feel that a consensus definition of reading comprehension will ultimately result from an iterative process of 1) greater understanding of the neurobiological, genetic, and behavioral components of reading comprehension combined with 2) revisiting of the definition for continual refinement as research addressing the first point takes place. Therefore, for this particular meeting, the goal was to focus on how to flesh out an agenda focused on point number one while acknowledging and specifying each individual researcher's differences in construct operationalization.

For this volume, researchers who presented and discussed these themes at the symposium wrote chapters based on their presentations as well as on the subsequent discussions that ensued during the symposium. Those who wrote the integrative summaries for each section have thoughtfully reflected on the chapters in their respective sections in ways that we hope will contribute to moving the field forward in this work.

This volume starts with a chapter that deviates slightly from previous TDF approaches: a reflection on "lessons learned" from past research. This chapter, written by Morris, focuses on the history of word-level processing research and how the field was eventually able to narrow the origin of the deficit to the realm of phonological processing. Although there are still debates as to the underlying processes involved in phonological processing, as well as the potential role of other lower level processes, research in the past few decades has narrowed the scope of potential areas of investigation and has thus resulted in substantial progress in identification, prevention, and treatment of word-level difficulties. Morris's chapter reflects on what has been learned from this successful line of research and offers recommendations for moving forward with reading comprehension research. In particular, he stresses the need for even greater interdisciplinary research, coupled with approaches that continue to build upon previous lessons learned through research that has focused on definition, measurement, theory development, and interventions in dyslexia. After this chapter, the rest of the book is divided into four sections, each of which focuses on a different area related to reading comprehension.

Section I provides an overview of different perspectives of reading comprehension and also presents what can go right or wrong during the reading comprehension process, including across development. The link to reading comprehension by word-to-text integration processes is reviewed by Perfetti and colleagues, who suggest that although we know a lot about word identification processes and have also studied higher level comprehension processes, more focus is needed to understand how the processes integrate a reader's word knowledge with a reader's representation of the text. Graesser and Li review a multilevel theoretical framework that integrates research on discourse processes and the cognitive sciences and then examine implications of how each of the components could affect reading comprehension performance at different levels. Following Graesser and Li's chapter, Helder and colleagues highlight the distinction between the *product* (the coherent mental representation of the text) and the *process* (what happens in a reader's mind while reading) of reading comprehension and argue that understanding the process of reading is what is most central for unpacking reading comprehension difficulties across development. In the next chapter, Cain reviews research on how weaknesses in various processes can give rise to difficulties in reading comprehension and points out that these difficulties are present even in listening comprehension tasks, thus suggesting the importance of processes beyond word decoding; in addition, she highlights the importance of being mindful that multiple complex and interacting factors are likely to be the origins of reading comprehension failure. Then, Catts examines the overlap between oral language impairments and reading comprehension difficulties and explores subtyping of readers based upon the Simple View model. The last chapter in this section provides unique insight into comprehension, with Magliano and colleagues examining the cognitive processes that support narrative processing in both print and visual media, with a particular focus on shared cognitive systems across both types of media. Finally, McCardle integrates these various viewpoints and offers the elegant analogy that the achievement of a full understanding of reading comprehension will be a feat similar to that of having written a musical score for an orchestra. She suggests that when researchers are able to write such a "musical score" for the word-level reading and higher level cognitive processes that must be orchestrated in reading comprehension, we will be able to pinpoint where breakdowns occur and therefore discover how to remediate them. McCardle closes by indicating that substantial progress in writing this "musical score" is possible, given the overall similar goals the researchers in this section have, despite coming from various perspectives and taking different approaches.

Section II focuses on assessment and statistical and computational modeling as related to reading comprehension and offers an overview of state-of-the-art assessments currently under development as well as applications of statistical modeling to understand more about individual differences. Sabatini and O'Reilly focus on the design of a new reading comprehension assessment system based upon six principles, each of which they propose has implications for assessment design and accompanying research agendas. Reichle describes a theoretical framework based upon a computational model of eye-movement control in reading that suggests a potential way to understand age-related differences in reading skill based on the development of oculomotor control, lexical processing, and higher level linguistic processing. Zevin and Yang examine how computational modeling and functional neuroimaging may be combined in order to reveal mechanisms in dyslexia in a much richer, multidimensional way that takes into account both stimulus and task demands. Compton and colleagues present novel ways to examine reading comprehension data, showing that examining person, passage, and question characteristics can provide unique insights. Finally, Miller explains that the synergy of these chapters is that together they attempt to push the field forward in terms of conceptual and theoretically motivated approaches that can be applied to help further our understanding of reading comprehension, noting that considering the application of these approaches will be a critical piece in propelling reading comprehension research forward.

In Section III, neurobiological and genetic approaches and applications to understanding reading comprehension are discussed. Cutting and colleagues examine word- and text-level processing, provide preliminary fMRI data showing both the unique and overlapping aspects of each, and delve into understanding reader–text interactions within a neurobiological framework. Turning toward development of basic brain mechanisms, Pugh and colleagues expand upon their original model of reading to include an integrated account of learning, consolidation, and speech–motor development in reading disability (RD) that now incorporates subcortical mechanisms. Linking nicely to Perfetti's model described in Section I, Kuperberg then focuses on the idea of a proactive predictive system in which semantic and real-world knowledge can be used to generate semantic, phonological, and syntactic predictions about upcoming words and can therefore play a key role in the combinatorial integration of incoming words; in addition, she proposes that breakdowns in this proactive predictive system could lead to poor comprehension. In the last two chapters in this section, the focus is on behavioral and molecular genetics and the potential for integration with neurobiological findings. Petrill reviews findings from quantitative genetic studies that suggest both genetic and environmental sources of variance for the development of reading comprehension skills; he proposes that twin neuroimaging designs would address fundamental questions about the relationships between genes, environments, brain, and behavior. Grigorenko then provides a review of the challenges but great potential for identification of specific genetic mechanisms that underlie RD; she stresses the need to consider developmental context as well as the possibility that the genetic mechanisms that underlie RD may actually be representative of a more general mechanism, such as neural migration anomalies. In the integrative summary for this section, Hoeft and Myers discuss how each of the respective fields of neuroimaging and genetics has the power to contribute important insights into understanding more about reading comprehension, but that combining both approaches within a developmental context, although a challenging research effort, could lead to a "quantum leap" in discoveries about reading comprehension and associated disorders. They suggest that such an integrated approach may ultimately lead to personalized, early, and potentially preventive interventions.

Finally, Section IV focuses on the end target of reading comprehension research: understanding how to intervene with individuals who struggle with comprehension, both at the elementary school level and the middle and high school levels. Connor reviews findings from two elementary school intervention studies, one of which focuses on dialect shifting, and the other on academic knowledge, and examines the direct and indirect effects of oral language on each. Turning to older readers, Vaughn and Solis describe findings from a longitudinal response to intervention study in secondary students and offer considerations for ways to further intensify reading interventions, including integrating explicit reading instruction with strategies that support cognitive processes (e.g., memory and self-regulation). As Lyytinen and McCardle succinctly summarize in their integrative summary, both chapters in this section support a multicomponent and analytical approach to reading instruction. Although the basic skills of decoding and fluency are clearly necessary, these studies indicate they are not sufficient, and therefore it is critical that instruction integrate and consider other higher level aspects of reading, not only in terms of language but also extending to self-regulation, motivation, and goal-directed learning. The complexity of the approach these researchers have taken reflects the many aspects of reading comprehension, but Lyytinen and McCardle leave us with reassurance that approaches such as these indicate significant progress in intervention and provide researchers with the hope of ultimately being able to design and implement interventions that truly address—and ameliorate—the complexity of reading comprehension difficulties.

The final chapter, built from the final discussion of the symposium, provides suggestions for future directions—making use of all that was learned at the symposium and that can be learned from this volume—to tackle the stumbling blocks and push the frontiers of reading comprehension research.

In summary, these many different viewpoints, methods, approaches, and findings in the chapters in this volume collectively offer important current insights and also set the stage for future endeavors in researching reading comprehension. Ultimately, it is clear that success in this arena will necessitate the coordination and integration of many different areas of expertise; in breaking some of these barriers, however, we may produce findings that go beyond even the collective ambitious expectations and hopes of this group of researchers. In closing, we note that each chapter provides an important foundational component toward being able to fully map the "musical score" of reading comprehension, and it is our hope that the reader comes away with a sense of substantial possibilities and hopefulness as we tackle this daunting but complex and intriguing area of research.

## REFERENCES

National Center for Education Statistics (2009). *The Nation's Report Card: Reading 2009* (NCES 2010-458). Washington, DC: Institute of Education Sciences, U.S. Department of Education.

National Center for Education Statistics (2011). *The Nation's Report Card: Reading 2011* (NCES 2012-457). Washington, DC: Institute of Education Sciences, U.S. Department of Education.

CHAPTER 2

# Reflections on Transitions in the Field of Dyslexia

## Learning from the Past to Benefit the Future

Robin D. Morris

The ability to read represents the end point of a long set of complex interactions among a child's developing neurocognitive, language, and learning abilities and the environmental opportunities that provide reading instruction, language opportunities, and access to reading materials. Reading abilities are developed via such brain–environment interactions, and individual differences in each component of this interaction result in a wide range of reading abilities in the general population. Given the increasing importance of reading in our information and text rich world, there is little wonder why we continue to be so interested, even after 100 years, in the concept of dyslexia, a specific type of reading disability that is considered to be "unexpected."

Historically, dyslexia was thought to reflect very circumscribed neurobiological anomalies that would lead to a child's problems in learning to read (Fletcher, 2009). Because of the specificity of dyslexia as a primary reading deficit, in contrast to the more general cognitive deficits that would affect all areas of academic learning and adaptation seen in people with intellectual disabilities, researchers believed that by understanding its unique etiology and proximal causes, whether at the genetic, brain, cognitive, language, or behavioral levels, they could open a unique window into how the brain develops and organizes based on the specific environmental demands involved when learning a complex academic skill. In other words, by using what was considered to be an easily assessed behavior (reading) to identify a group of children with a specific type of learning disability, researchers were able to focus on this more homogenous set of children (or adults) from within the wider range of reading abilities and reading disabilities. Children with dyslexia were thought to be at higher genetic or biological risk for being different in a number of neurobiological and neurocognitive ways when compared with typically developing children. The logic behind this approach was that by understanding such differences in dyslexic children, researchers would be able to broaden their understanding of children's brain learning capabilities and how these were related to their behavioral development. Such knowledge was expected to provide the basis for prevention of such impairments along with improved treatment options for the underlying specific reading problems in children with dyslexia.

Underlying this history has been an inferred hypothesis that dyslexic children and adults, as a group, are different from nondyslexic poor-reading children in some critically important attributes (Fletcher, 2009). They were considered different from the rest of the poor readers who just represented the probabilistic results of the brain–environment interactions that create the entire distribution of reading abilities. Although they were in some ways like other poor readers, they were considered to be different because they did not have the same predictive attributes or backgrounds (low socioeconomic status, emotional disorder, poor school attendance, etc.) that were known to be highly correlated with poor reading. For many years, dyslexia was considered almost a diagnosis by exclusion: If you identified and understood the reason for a child's reading problems, then you could not diagnose dyslexia.

In addition, dyslexia actually represented a classification hypothesis that defined a unique population of children and adults who differed from other readers (Morris & Fletcher, 1988). This model acts by dividing the population's reading variance into more homogeneous subgroups, such as dyslexia, for scientific and predictive value. Such subgrouping could either improve our understanding of the core etiology of the dyslexic group's reading problems, which could possibly lead to prevention of the problems, or differentially inform treatments based on the specific types of reading and reading-related deficits that defined the group. Conceptually, if such subgroup identification does not ultimately lead to a differentiated understanding of the group's etiology or improve prevention or treatment capabilities, then questions should be raised regarding its usefulness and validity as a concept (Fletcher, Morris, & Lyon, 2003).

On the other hand, the related null hypothesis that dyslexic children are really no different from other nondyslexic poor readers on key attributes that could differentiate their prevention or treatment or could provide evidence for different etiologies would raise the question of whether the concept had outlived its usefulness or suggest that our science had not been able to identify those key attributes that are critical to understanding their unique differences. The jury is still out on whether the concept of dyslexia has, or will have, these kinds of validity. Clearly, it has had significant value, particularly over the last 40 years, in focusing a wide range of increasingly sophisticated conceptual and methodological research approaches toward these important questions.

## LESSONS FROM THE PAST

Dyslexia research has a long and complex history. Patient histories from the late 1880s are the first known to describe cases in which children and adults who seemed to have otherwise average sensory, cognitive, and language abilities could not learn to read despite typical classroom instruction (Hinshelwood, 1895). It has been reported that the term *dyslexia* was first used in Germany during this period to describe such patients. The specificity of the patients' impairment in reading was important in that it led the early writers to speculate that their deficit was related to either subtle visual perceptual deficits or problems in their underlying language system resulting from symptoms similar to some alexia deficits seen in aphasic patients. Both of these ideas, that dyslexia was related to core perceptual processing problems and/or to the effects of focal brain lesions, strongly influenced the thinking of the time regarding the brain basis and language system focus of the early researchers. These core ideas about the role of the brain, perceptual processes, and language system functions continue to this day and have resulted in more than a century of research and debate over the nature, validity, and etiology of such a specific reading deficit (Fletcher, Lyon, Fuchs, & Barnes, 2007).

During the early part of the 20th century, the interest in dyslexic patients, and the zeitgeist regarding their perceptual difficulties (i.e., letter reversals) and related left-hemisphere language foundation led researchers on a long, but not entirely fruitful (Bryden, 1988) journey. A major research agenda of the time focused on theories suggesting that children with dyslexia had delayed or poorly developed left-hemisphere dominance for language as its underlying cause (Orton, 1928). This early framework set the foundation for years of research on the impact of atypical development of laterality, cerebral dominance, handedness, and other physical, behavioral, or brain-related asymmetries in causing dyslexia. The concept of maturational lag, that children with dyslexia were behind in the development of these brain-based systems but would catch up over time, was also part of this zeitgeist (Satz, Fletcher, Clark, & Morris, 1981). Although the idea of maturational lag put the concept of dyslexia within a more appropriate developmental framework, longitudinal data have rarely supported the lag concept (Francis, Shaywitz, Steubing, Shaywitz, & Fletcher, 1996).

Laterality research was based in the idea that if we studied the unique patterns of brain-related behaviors (left-handedness, reverse dominance, etc.), these patterns would provide insight into the neurological basis of the disorder, with little regard to the actual reading and reading-related deficits that such children exhibited, with a few notable exceptions (i.e., Bakker, 1979). Unfortunately, although the hypothesis that dyslexia has an underlying neurobiological etiology endures to this day, this historical laterality–related research was not generally fruitful, again with a few exceptions (Bryden, 1988). The problem was that this research repeatedly showed that there were many children with patterns of atypical laterality but no reading problems, and many children presented with reading problems without atypical laterality.

This focus on using patterns of behavior (or profiles) for diagnostic purposes, or to infer underlying brain functions in dyslexia, has been continued by researchers using alternative frameworks based within various research traditions (e.g., subtypes, patterns of processing deficits, intraindividual differences), but with limited evidence of their usefulness or continuing impact on our understanding of dyslexia (Hoskyn & Swanson, 2000; Steubing et al., 2002). In hindsight, this historical research frequently reminds us of the important role of "stupidity" in science (Schwartz, 2008), the idea that what we do not understand is infinite, but that as researchers we need to keep trying to find answers. It also clearly documents how difficult it is for a field to change strongly held beliefs or models or break away from frameworks that time after time have led to the same empty results.

Throughout its history, the term *dyslexia* and its definition have endured many debates and undergone a number of changes. Even during the period when the U.S. government was developing policies and procedures for identifying children with reading disabilities (1969 Children with Specific Learning Disabilities Act, PL-9130), Rutter reports that the "literature on reading difficulties is full of heated exchange about whether or not dyslexia exists" (1978, p. 5). During those years, and unfortunately still today, the term *dyslexia* is frequently used to encompass all types of reading problems and includes many of the correlated deficits that were thought to be either causative or necessary for its accurate diagnosis (i.e., letter reversals, left-handedness, discrepancy between reading and aptitude/IQ).

Probably one of the most long-standing and contentious debates has been the validity of discrepancy criteria in defining a child with dyslexia, even though related definitional concerns have been voiced for over 30 years (Benton, 1978). Although discrepancy criteria have been operationalized in a number of different ways, conceptually the idea was that a child's measured reading ability had to be well below the child's "aptitude," typically assessed by standardized IQ measures, to be considered dyslexic. Such definitions were formed based on the core concept underlying dyslexia, namely, that it was an "unexpected" reading deficit (e.g., not at the expected level based on the child's aptitude/IQ), though what they meant by reading or aptitude was never defined. Although there have been many statistical debates regarding the reduced reliability and increased statistical biases involved when using such difference scores, more recent studies have focused on evaluating the validity of the discrepancy criteria. Most research has done this by evaluating the impact of different approaches to defining a discrepancy, but more important, also by asking critical questions regarding whether children who meet such discrepancy criteria are different in key theoretical and clinical attributes compared to other poor-reading children who do not meet such discrepancy criteria. For years, the research on these questions has consistently shown there to be significant problems in the validity of definitions for dyslexia at many levels: conceptual, measurement, and statistical (Steubing et al., 2002). Children who meet a discrepancy criterion have rarely been shown to differ from children who do not meet a discrepancy criterion on almost any attribute except those highly correlated with the measures used to define the discrepancy. Unfortunately, like laterality research in dyslexia, the lack of evidence-based justification for using discrepancy criteria has not quickly changed a majority of the research or practice (Fletcher, Francis, Morris, & Lyon, 2005). Part of the reason for this has been the lack of alternative models.

## MORE RECENT ADVANCES

Fortunately over the last 20 years, other lines of successful research growing from different theoretical orientations have provided more systematic, theoretically driven data and results that have supported the role that speech sounds, the alphabetic principal, and phonological awareness play in the development of early reading (and written language). This research has increased our recognition that a child must develop a metacognitive understanding that there are core sound units in speech and that these core units are systematically associated with various symbols or combinations of symbols (alphabet). This understanding, developed through various instructional practices, is required in order to learn to decode and read single words effectively (Liberman, Shankweiler, & Liberman, 1989).

Because of this and other research focused on understanding reading development, particularly the key relationship between early reading skills and phonological awareness, the concept of dyslexia has clearly evolved into one today that does not represent all types of reading problems. Dyslexia today is clearly defined as a developmental disorder in which children do not easily learn to accurately decode written words and/or develop fluent single-word recognition when provided quality instruction. Because problems in decoding the sounds within single written words—and possibly other weaknesses, such as in rapid naming or working memory—have an effect on broader reading efficiency, these children frequently have correlated problems in reading fluency and comprehension. Because of these basic struggles at the word level and their influence on reading fluency and comprehension, such impairments have broader impacts on vocabulary, background knowledge development, and children's motivation to read. At the same time, other researchers differentiated children who did not have problems at the word level but struggled with comprehension (Snowling & Hulme, 2011), but such children were not typically called dyslexic.

The core deficit in dyslexia is found to affect most directly the phonological-related abilities in children trying to learn to read, but such limitations in the phonological aspects of language may also negatively affect the lexical representations of written words (Harm & Seidenberg, 1999; Perfetti & Hart, 2001). Whether such specific phonological processing deficits can further be caused by more general processing system deficits (e.g., Tallal, 1980) or attentional deficits (e.g., Sperling, Lu, Manis, & Seidenberg, 2006) has long been debated. Regardless, the clear identification of dyslexia as a word-level problem, as well as the underlying theoretical reading models that have been developed around it, has allowed for a new wave of more systematic and sophisticated research that uses very homogeneous samples of children and adults, thereby providing new data-driven frameworks for understanding dyslexia.

These developmental accounts of learning to read and how it can go wrong led researchers to increase their focus on the rate, sequence, and biological and environmental influences that affect reading and reading-related skill development. As an example, important questions regarding alternative causes for word-level reading disabilities were raised by some researchers in special education and early childhood reading who questioned whether such children were educational casualties (Lyon & Moats, 1997). They expressed concern that by not having been provided with quality, explicit, code-based reading instruction during critical periods, children may not learn word identification skills (Snow, Burns, & Griffin, 1998). At the same time, new and more powerful neuroimaging (i.e., PET, fMRI, MRS, MEG) and genetic analysis methodologies were being developed and utilized that launched another phase of interest in the neurobiological foundations of dyslexia, not at the anatomical level, but at the functional level (Pugh, Mencl, Shaywitz, et al., 2000). In addition, the sophistication and advancement of structural equation modeling and other statistical approaches to understanding complex, multivariate relationships, particularly over time, allowed for new capabilities for evaluating increasingly complex developmental models of change that could actually combine both neurological and environmental factors to provide a more comprehensive understanding of dyslexia (Francis et al., 1996).

A more holistic, brain–environment interactional model for understanding dyslexia started to emerge during the late 1980s and 1990s because of the convergence of these new theoretical models, new measurement methodologies, and the emergence of a "big science" approach that began to focus large, interdisciplinary teams of scientists to work together to address these increasingly complex but important questions.

As a concrete example of these advances, although since the 1880s the unique characteristics of the individual child have been the primary focus in the concept of dyslexia, over the last 10–15 years there has been important attention given to the quality and type of classroom instruction provided to poor readers (National Institute of Child Health and Human Development [NICHD], 2000), along with an increasing focus on the evidence supporting the instruction's effectiveness and the need to consider the intensity of the interventions. The research on instructional quality and type, particularly in reference to children with dyslexia, has recently started to significantly affect the field's thinking, with many researchers now considering the need for clear documentation of evidence-based, explicit, quality instruction as a mandatory component before identifying children with dyslexia.

This requirement is based on an increasing awareness that inadequate instruction in core reading and reading-related skills results in poor word recognition abilities in some children.

With a focus on appropriate, explicit, evidence-based instruction, many such children can develop the word identification and other skills necessary to become age-appropriate readers (see, e.g., Morris et al., 2012). Those children who do not respond are considered to have a higher probability of being dyslexic. Because of this focus on instructional quality and intensity, the emerging concept of dyslexia has become increasingly one of the child with a range of neurocognitive risk factors interacting with environments with differing risk factors related to quality and type of instruction, language and reading experiences, motivation to read, and support. This interactional model has resulted in a more complex, multivariate framework for understanding children with such specific developmental reading challenges but also does not place the entire focus on the child's innate attributes. This increasingly complex set of interacting considerations has resulted in the continued evolution of the concept and definition of dyslexia.

As early treatment modalities and interventions for problems with fluent word recognition have evolved and become more successful, a number of children nonetheless remain treatment resisters (Frijters, Lovett, Sevcik, & Morris, 2013); even in children who do respond positively to quality interventions at the word identification level, reading comprehension problems may continue to occur. Some estimates suggest that less than half of children with dyslexia manage to achieve satisfactory reading skills by adulthood, and it is widely acknowledged that complete reading improvements are rare. A majority of the focus in adult outcome studies is related to the adults' continued poor reading fluency and comprehension abilities, even though their basic word-reading skills are sometimes remediated within normative ranges. The relationship between their basic word-reading skills and their reading comprehension abilities has become of increasing interest and an even more complex challenge to researchers.

It is interesting to note that even early governmental policies and definitions of specific learning disabilities differentiated impairments in "basic reading skill" from those in "reading comprehension" (U.S. Office of Education, 1977), although the theoretical or empirical basis for such differentiation was never specified. This conceptual differentiation of basic reading skills (i.e., decoding, word identification) from reading comprehension and related oral comprehension abilities has a long and interesting history, which has been reinforced by a wide array of supportive as well as nonsupportive research evaluating this "simple view" of reading (Hoover & Gough, 1990; Snowling & Hulme, 2012).

It is interesting to speculate regarding the complexity of the relationship between word identification and reading comprehension, particularly in children who have deficits in either or both (Snowling & Hulme, 2012). As previously noted, it is not difficult to understand that children with dyslexia, with its core deficit in efficient word identification abilities, would have difficulties with reading comprehension. This difficulty is generally thought to be related to the fact that their attentional and cognitive focus is primarily directed toward decoding and word identification needs, in which they struggle, leaving children with dyslexia with fewer resources for memory systems to retain and process the information read, retrieve information from their semantic networks, or allocate comprehension relevant strategies.

One key finding from many intervention studies using some of the best evidence-based instructional programs focused on treating dyslexia is that these programs have frequently been successful in teaching the alphabetic principal, decoding skills, and key word identification strategies and have provided increased opportunities and motivational outcomes that increased the amount of reading participants performed. At the same time, the programs have been less successful in improving reading fluency for connected text and/or reading comprehension, their ultimate goal. Such a pattern of results is seen even in those instructional programs designed and weighted to focus on increasing fluency and teaching vocabulary and reading comprehension strategies. As has been heard from research teachers in intervention studies, there are easily identified groups of students who become very good at word identification but who do not understand the meaning of the words they can easily "read." Speculation about the students' limited oral language capabilities, with apparently poor vocabulary, morphosyntactic understanding, and background knowledge are frequent; but because comprehension is an integrative and contextually sensitive process, such frameworks appear overly simplistic and instructional programs require sophisticated models to yield success (Vaughn & Klinger, 2004). The relationships between word identification, reading fluency, reading and oral comprehension, vocabulary, background knowledge, and other related contextual and cognitive factors are complex. In fact, even a clear understanding of the similarities and differences between oral comprehension and reading comprehension abilities is not well established at this time. Whether these complex interrelationships develop differently in children with dyslexia when compared with other poor readers, or even with typically developing readers, and whether such differences are because of the dyslexic children's initial deficits in word identification that are remediated remain open questions. Nevertheless, these developmental questions relating their specific word identification deficits to their comprehension struggles over time take an important direction for continued research in dyslexia (see Eason, Sabatini, Goldberg, Bruce, & Cutting, in press).

At the same time, there is a corpus of research that has generated an interesting analogue to the historical dyslexia research, although with increased complexity already built in. This research has focused on specific reading comprehension deficits (without word identification impairments) in children and adults. This research has many of the same definitional challenges in operationalizing the concept of reading comprehension deficits as has been described for operationalizing the concept of dyslexia, but the research faces even greater methodological difficulty because of the current, significant difficulty in the measurement of reading comprehension abilities (or comprehension in general, regardless of the format).

In addition, this research has had to address broader questions regarding the oral language and higher order cognitive capabilities of their subjects, namely, how meaning is generated from text, given the multiple levels of analysis possible, the role of context and experience, and the wide range of higher order cognitive processes required. Because the study of specific reading comprehension deficits has a seemingly logarithmic increase in complexity, many researchers in the field of dyslexia have not had the expertise necessary to comprehensively address this area of study, although there are exceptions (see chapters in this volume). The result is a less extensive and less clear knowledge base on which to ground an understanding of reading comprehension deficits in dyslexic children and adults. Researchers have only beginning hints on how best to address the issues.

A parallel track of research in dyslexia over recent years has continued the interest in the neurobiological basis for dyslexic children's struggles in learning basic word identification skills. As the theoretical foundations underlying reading development have become more and more developed, the new neuroimaging methodologies have been linked to such models. At this time, we have a much better descriptive understanding of the brain-based differences underlying the reading systems in dyslexic and nondyslexic readers. Many neuroimaging studies have shown a number of structural and functional differences in left-hemisphere regions when evaluating decoding and word-reading abilities. A "reading circuit" that integrates tertiary association areas and their inputs (temporoparietal, occipitotemporal, inferior frontal), along with various subcortical linkages, has been consistently described using typically developing readers (Pugh, Mencl, Jenner, et al., 2000). At the same time, children with dyslexia have typically been shown to exhibit underactivation of one or more of these parts of the circuit during reading. Because these neuroimaging results are primarily descriptive, speculations regarding the underlying causes of this underactivation are varied.

It would be easy to jump to the historical inference that findings of hypoactivation in dyslexia is de facto proof of the neurological etiology of the disorder, validating this long-standing hypothesis. A number of intervention studies that have used pre–post treatment fMRI or MEG methodologies (e.g., Simos et al., 2002) have shown that in some dyslexic children, there is a level of correction or "normalization" of the previously hypo-aroused reading circuit when they are provided with intense, evidence-based quality instruction focused at the decoding and word identification levels. In such studies, following treatment, in the dyslexic children's brains the reading circuit appears to be similar to that seen for age-matched, typically developing readers. Researchers have focused on the possible genetic and neurodevelopmental influences on this neurocognitive reading circuit, whereas others are interested in the role of environmental and instructional stimulation on its development and functioning.

This brief history and overview of research on dyslexia shows that past focus on definition, measurement, theory development, and interventions has led to a broader and more sophisticated understanding of the disorder. This understanding has resulted in more complex, integrated, and interactional models of brain and environmental risk factors for understanding such children and adults than originally envisioned. Clearly, the concept of dyslexia, its improved definition, and its interdisciplinary research focused on multiple levels of analysis have advanced our ability to understand and intervene with these children in many positive ways even though there were numerous false starts. Many experts have considered the advances made in understanding the core word identification deficit in dyslexia as one of the more important scientific advances made by any field to address the needs of a very prevalent disabling condition.

At the same time, the core causes of the reported brain system functional differences, developing clear theoretical models linking different levels of analysis (genetic, brain, cognitive, language, reading, environment), and an increasing awareness of the multiple factors that may result in the long-term poor reading comprehension outcomes in children with dyslexia remain challenges to the field. Because comprehension is the ultimate goal of reading, it will be important to invite researchers with relevant expertise into the discussions and investigations so that more targeted and theoretically critical questions can be raised about the nature of reading comprehension in the dyslexic child. In many ways, this is the next frontier for dyslexia research—and it is timely, given the currently strong though complex foundation on which the field currently stands.

## REFERENCES

Bakker, D.J. (1979). Hemispheric difference and reading strategies. *Bulletin of the Orton Society, 29*, 84–100.

Benton, A. (1978). Some conclusions about dyslexia. In A. Benton & D. Pearl (Eds.), *Dyslexia: An appraisal of current knowledge* (pp. 453–476). New York, NY: Oxford University Press.

Bryden, M.P. (1988). Does laterality make any difference? Thoughts on the relation between cerebral asymmetry and reading. In D.L. Molfese & S.J. Segalowitz (Eds.), *Brain lateralization in children: Developmental implications* (pp. 509–526). New York, NY: Guilford Press.

Eason, S.H., Sabatini, J.P., Goldberg, L.F., Bruce, K.M., & Cutting, L.E. (in press). Examining the relationship between word reading efficiency and oral reading rate in predicting comprehension among different types of readers. *Scientific Studies of Reading.*

Children with Specific Learning Disabilities Act of 1969. Included in the Education of the Handicapped Act of 1970 (PL 91-230).

Fletcher, J.M. (2009). Dyslexia: The evolution of a scientific construct. *Journal of the International Neuropsychological Society, 15,* 501–508.

Fletcher, J.M., Francis, D.J., Morris, R.D., & Lyon, G.R. (2005). Evidence-based assessment of learning disabilities in children and adolescents. *Journal of Clinical Child and Adolescent Psychology, 34,* 506–522.

Fletcher, J.M., Lyon, G.R., Fuchs, L.S., & Barnes, M.A. (2007). *Learning disabilities: From identification to intervention.* New York, NY: Guilford Press.

Fletcher, J.M., Morris, R.D., & Lyon, G.R. (2003). Classification and definitions of learning disabilities: An integrative perspective. In H.K. Swanson, K.R. Harris, & S. Graham (Eds.), *Handbook of learning disabilities* (pp. 30–56). New York, NY: Guilford Press.

Francis, D.J., Shaywitz, S.E., Steubing, K.K., Shaywitz, B.A., & Fletcher, J.M. (1996). Developmental lag versus deficit models of reading disability: A longitudinal, individual growth curves analysis. *Journal of Educational Psychology, 88,* 3–17.

Frijters, J.A., Lovett, M.W., Sevcik, R.A., & Morris, R.D. (2013). Four methods of identifying change in the context of a multiple component reading intervention for struggling middle school readers. *Reading andWriting Quarterly, 26,* 539–563.

Harm, M.W., & Seidenberg, M.S. (1999). Reading acquisition, phonology, and dyslexia: Insights from a connectionist model. *Psychological Review, 106,* 491–528.

Hinshelwood, J. (1895). Word-blindness and visual memory. *Lancet, 2,* 1564–1570.

Hoover, W.A., & Gough, P.B. (1990). The simple view of reading. *Reading and Writing: An Interdisciplinary Journal, 2,* 127–160.

Hoskyn, M., & Swanson, H.L. (2000). Cognitive processing of low achievers and children with reading disabilities: A selective meta-analytic review of the published literature. *School Psychology Review, 29,* 102–119.

Liberman, I.Y., Shankweiler, D., & Liberman, A.M. (1989). The alphabetic principle and learning to read. In D. Shankweiler & I.Y. Liberman (Eds.), *Phonology and reading disability: Solving the reading puzzle.* Research Monograph Series. Ann Arbor: University of Michigan Press.

Lyon, G.R., & Moats, L.C. (1997). Critical conceptual and methodological considerations in reading intervention research. *Journal of Learning Disabilities, 30,* 577–588.

Morris, R.D., & Fletcher, J.M. (1988). Classification in neuropsychology: A theoretical framework and research paradigm. *Journal of Clinical and Experimental Neuropsychology, 10,* 640–658.

Morris, R.D., Lovett, M.W., Wolf, M., Sevick, R.A., Steinbach, K.A., Frijters, J.C., & Shapiro, M. (2012). Multiple component remediation of developmental reading disabilities: A controlled factorial evaluation of the influence of IQ, socioeconomic status, and race on outcomes. *Journal of Learning Disabilities, 45*(2), 99–127.

National Institute of Child Health and Human Development (NICHD). (2000). *Report of the National Reading Panel. Teaching children to read: An evidence-based assessment of the scientific research literature on reading and its implications for reading instruction* (NIH Publication No. 00-4754). Washington, DC: U.S. Government Printing Office.

Orton, S. (1928). Specific reading disability—Strephosymbolia. *Journal of the American Medical Association, 90,* 1095–1099.

Perfetti, C.A., & Hart, L. (2001). The lexical bases of comprehension skill. In D. Gorfien (Ed.), *On the consequences of meaning selection* (pp. 67–86). Washington, DC: American Psychological Association.

Pugh, K.R., Mencl, W.E., Jenner, A.R., Katz, L., Frost, S.J., Lee, J.R., … Shaywitz, B.A. (2000). Functional neuroimaging studies of reading and reading disability (developmental dyslexia). *Mental Retardation and Developmental Disabilities Research Reviews, 6,* 207–213.

Pugh, K.R., Mencl, W.E., Shaywitz, B.A., Shaywitz, S.E., Fulbright, R.K., Constable, R.T., … Gore, J.C. (2000). The angular gyrus in developmental dyslexia: Task specific differences in functional connectivity within posterior cortex. *Psychological Science, 11,* 51–56.

Rutter, M. (1978). Prevalence and types of dyslexia. In A.L. Benton & D. Pearl (Eds.), *Dyslexia: An appraisal of current knowledge* (pp. 3–28). New York, NY: Oxford University Press.

Satz, P., Fletcher, J.M., Clark, W., & Morris, R. (1981). Lag, deficit, rate & delay constructs in specific learning disabilities: A re-examination. In A. Answara, N. Geschwind, A. Galaburda, M. Albert, & N. Gartrell (Eds.), *Sex differences in dyslexia* (pp. 129–150). Towson, MD: Orton Dyslexia Society.

Schwartz, M.A. (2008). The importance of stupidity in scientific research. *Cell Science, 14,* 1771.

Simos, P.G., Fletcher, J.M., Foorman, B.R., Francis, D.J., Castillo, E.M., Davis, R.N., … Papanicolaou, A.C. (2002). Brain activation profiles during the early stages of reading acquisition [Abstract]. *Journal of Child Neurology, 17*(3), 159–163.

Snow, C. Burns, M.S., & Griffin, P. (Eds.). (1998). *Preventing reading difficulties in young children.* Washington, DC: National Academy Press.

Snowling, M.J., & Hulme, C. (2010). Evidence-based interventions for reading and language difficulties: Creating a virtuous circle. *British Journal of Educational Psychology, 81*(1), 1–23.

Snowling, M.J., & Hulme, C. (2012). Annual research review: The nature and classification of reading disorders: A commentary on proposals for DSM-5. *Journal of Child Psychology and Psychiatry, 53*(5), 593–607.

Sperling, A.J., Lu, Z.L., Manis, F.R., & Seidenberg, M.S. (2006). Motion-perception deficits and reading impairment: It's the noise, not the motion. *Psychological Science, 17*(12), 1047–1053.

Steubing, K.K., Fletcher, J.M., LeDoux, J.M., Lyon, G.R., Shaywitz, S.E., & Shaywitz, B.A. (2002). Validity of IQ-discrepancy classifications or reading disabilities: A meta-analysis. *American Educational Research Journal, 39,* 469–491.

Tallal, P. (1980). Auditory temporal perception, phonics, and reading disabilities in children. *Brain and Language, 9,* 182–198.

U.S. Office of Education. (1977). Assistance to states for education for handicapped children: Procedures for evaluating specific learning disabilities. *Federal Register, 42,* G1082–G0185.

Vaughn, S., & Klinger, J.K. (2004). Teaching reading comprehension to students with learning disabilities. In C.A. Stone, E.R. Stillman, B.J. Ehren, & K. Apel (Eds.), *Handbook of language and literacy: Developmental disorders* (pp. 541–555). New York, NY: Guilford Press.

Section II

# What Goes Wrong When Reading Comprehension Fails?

CHAPTER 3

# Reading Comprehension and Reading Comprehension Problems

## A Word-to-Text Integration Perspective

Charles Perfetti, Joseph Z. Stafura, and Suzanne M. Adlof

Comprehension depends on multiple sources of knowledge and the processes that use such knowledge. In addressing reading comprehension problems, research has naturally focused on the higher level processes that are the object of text comprehension research—making inferences, monitoring comprehension, and so on. In this chapter, we suggest that this approach is incomplete and draw attention to the importance of word-by-word text comprehension processes that integrate a word with the reader's representation of the text.

## READING COMPREHENSION PROBLEMS: WHAT ARE THEY?

The new DSM-5 (*Diagnostic and Statistical Manual of Mental Disorders–Fifth Edition*; American Psychiatric Association, 2013) has a proposed entry for "Specific Learning Disorder" that specifies a comprehension disorder:

> Difficulty understanding the meaning of what is read (e.g., may read text accurately but not understand the sequence, relationships, inferences, or deeper meanings of what is read).

Although having medical and psychiatric specialists defining cognitive and behavioral problems of reading comprehension might be a case of expertise inflation, the proposed DSM is in tune with the reading field's view of the problem. However, the proposed DSM entry is a bit wishy-washy in its constraining condition—specifically an individual with a specific learning disorder "*may* read text accurately." Researchers of comprehension deficits insist that the designation "comprehension deficit" requires accurate (usually described as "adequate") word reading. Otherwise, they could not be sure that the problem is specifically about comprehension and not word reading.

This "exclusion criterion" is parallel to the standard definition of dyslexia, for which adequate general or nonverbal intelligence has been required. Thus, dyslexia is supposed to be about word-reading

Some of the research discussed in this chapter has been supported by National Institutes of Health Grant R01HD058566 awarded to the University of Pittsburgh (Charles Perfetti, PI).

difficulties without general cognitive problems; comprehension disability is supposed to be about text comprehension difficulties without word-reading problems.

## WHAT IS THE MAJOR CAUSE OF READING COMPREHENSION DISABILITY?

If the major cause of word-reading disability (dyslexia) is in the phonological processing system, what is the major cause of reading comprehension disability? The question is worth posing mainly to emphasize that there is likely to be no single answer. The major candidates, reflecting the emphases from research, would be the following:

1. Cognitive system: poor working memory (Goldman & Varma, 1995; Just & Carpenter, 1992); poor cognitive control (Hamm & Hasher, 1992; Hasher & Zacks, 1988; Locascio, Mahone, Eason, & Cutting, 2010).
2. General language problems: deficits in oral language (Nation & Snowling, 1997; also, Cain, 2010; Catts, Adlof, & Ellis Weismer, 2006; Nation, Cocksey, Taylor, & Bishop, 2010; Stothard & Hulme, 1995); problems acquiring semantic relationships (Landi & Perfetti, 2007; Nation & Snowling, 1999); specific language disorders often coincidental with dyslexia (Bishop & Snowling, 2004; Catts, 1991; Catts, Adlof, Hogan, & Ellis Weismer, 2005).
3. Higher level comprehension problems: failures to make inferences (Oakhill & Garnham, 1988); failures to monitor comprehension (Baker, 1984; Garner, 1980).

However, if we take seriously the idea of specific reading comprehension deficits, we would need to apply the exclusionary standards to them. For example, a general cognitive deficit in working memory might limit comprehension processes and reduce inference making or comprehension monitoring. In such a case, it would be misleading to refer to a deficit in inference making or comprehension monitoring in the usual sense of a deficit. Instead, such difficulties would be manifestations of a more basic cognitive problem. Before one can identify a special disability in inference making (or comprehension monitoring or narrative knowledge), word-reading problems must be excluded, as should problems in memory and spoken language.

This approach becomes clearer when the relevant factors are seen as part of the reading system, rather than in a list. Figure 3.1 shows the reading comprehension system, along with pressure points that potentially influence both knowledge structures and processes in the system. Although processes are illustrated, it is the knowledge components that deserve attention in terms of individual differences. Readers differ in their knowledge of words, their spelling, their pronunciation, their meaning, and the conditions of their use—and in their general knowledge. The basic

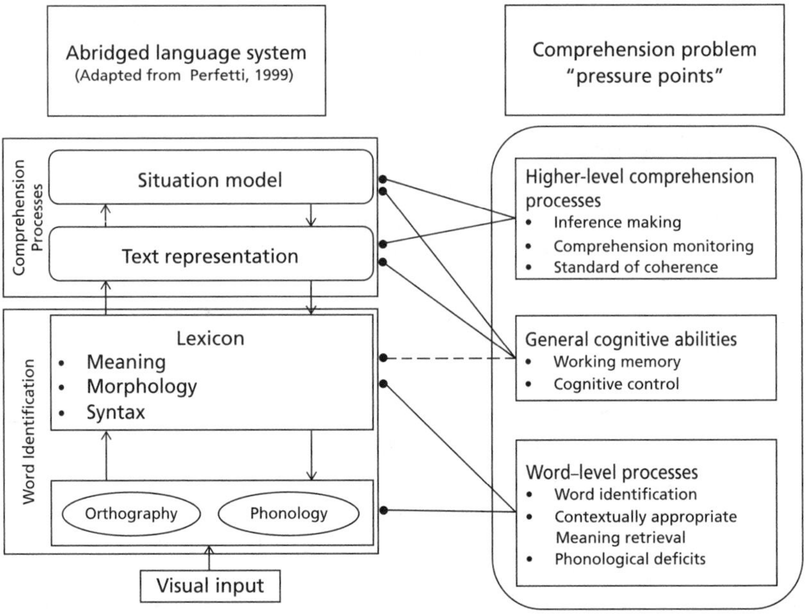


**Figure 3.1.** The comprehension system and its pressure points. The left portion is a simplified, schematic layout of the major knowledge components and processes of the reading comprehension system. The pressure points on the right indicate potential causes of comprehension problems. The connecting lines show hypothesized effects of weaknesses at these pressure points on the major components of the comprehension system. Higher level comprehension processes exert influence on text representations and situation models, whereas word-level pressure points affect the lexical representations that are available for text representations and the situation model. General knowledge, which is omitted from the figure, exerts an influence over most parts of the system. (From Perfetti, C.A. [1999]. Comprehending written language: A blueprint of the reader. In C. Brown & P. Hagoort [Eds.], *The neurocognition of language* [pp. 167–208]. New York, NY: Oxford University Press.)

reading processes (decoding, encoding, retrieval) operate on this knowledge base and may not have as much variability except as affected by the amount of relevant practice they have received. Indeed, the "default" hypothesis for what causes the development of reading skill is relevant knowledge and practice in applying that knowledge in reading. If this sounds too simple, it probably is. But this is the formula for expertise in other domains (Ericsson, Krampe, & Tesch-Romer, 1993), where research has taken the mystery factor out of expertise and supplanted it with explanation based on practice.

The reading field might consider this skill model more seriously. Effective practice at reading text strengthens word knowledge, informational knowledge that supports subsequent reading, and basic and higher level skills in identifying words, retrieving context-relevant word meanings, and making coherence-preserving inferences. The challenge is to make practice effective. Just as component skills in other activities need to be specially tutored (e.g., a backhand in tennis, or chords on the piano), young readers may need help becoming more active readers so that they can monitor their comprehension or draw appropriate inferences. But the real goal, as it is in playing tennis or the piano, is to perform the fully integrated act, in this case the act of reading texts. To perform this act skillfully, much reading is necessary; here, the instructional goal is to provide enough tutoring and scaffolding to support a desire to read (i.e., to practice reading). In this perspective, the goal of trying to find specific comprehension "deficits" that afflict large groups of readers seems misplaced.

## WORD UNDERSTANDING AND TEXT COMPREHENSION

Practice in reading builds word knowledge, and increased word knowledge supports comprehension skill. Our research has partly focused on these reciprocal ideas:

1. Learning words depends on acquiring information about word forms and meanings from word-learning events, and more skilled comprehenders do this better than less skilled comprehenders (Anderson & Freebody, 1981; Balass, Nelson, & Perfetti, 2010; Bolger, Balass, Landen, & Perfetti, 2008; Nagy, Herman, & Anderson, 1985; Perfetti, Wlotko, & Hart, 2005; Stanovich & West, 1989).
2. Text comprehension depends on understanding words and integrating their meaning into a mental model of the text; more skilled comprehenders do this better than less skilled comprehenders (Perfetti, Yang, & Schmalhofer, 2008; Yang, Perfetti, & Schmalhofer, 2005, 2007).

The implications of these twin hypotheses for reading comprehension skill have been explored using various methods. However, "on-line" reading studies are especially important for examining word-learning events and comprehension at a level of detail that can be mapped on to processes and the knowledge stores that they act upon. Here, we focus on the second claim that text comprehension depends on integrating words into a mental model of the text.

### Event-Related Potential Studies of Word-to-Text Integration

The idea of mental model–based integration is illustrated here in two slightly different texts. Text (1) begins thus:

*(1) While Cathy was riding her bike in the park, dark clouds began to gather, and it started to storm.*

Making assumptions about the details of a mental model is tricky. Indeed, the concept of a mental model (Johnson-Laird, 1980), or the more text-specific "situation model" (van Dijk & Kintsch, 1983), has been compelling informally, but aside from inferred spatial relations in the earliest mental models described by Johnson-Laird (1981, 1983; also see Zwaan & Radvansky, 1998), specifications have been ad hoc. In the following example, we illustrate one way to represent a situation model, highlighting that its content is in term of referents and events, rather than the literal text.

<SITUATION: Cathy on bike, in the park, dark clouds>

<EVENT: Storm>

As notated above, the model includes two substructures, *Situation + Event,* to represent the current situation model. The reader has memory access to the situation and can update it through events described in the text. In this case, the situation is updated immediately by the storm event:

<SITUATION: Storm, Cathy on bike in park>

Suppose the next sentence adds to text (1) as shown here:

*(1) While Cathy was riding her bike in the park, dark clouds began to gather, and it started to storm. The rain ruined her beautiful sweater.*

The text is conceptually coherent. Information from the second sentence can be added to the situation model, introducing a new event, the ruination of a sweater. But comprehension proceeds not only sentence-by-sentence, but also word-by-word. The noun phrase that begins the new sentence—*the rain*—is understood immediately in relation to the situation model. It refers to the storm event and can be integrated into the situational representation of the text.

This word-level integration process can be observed through various word-by-word reading measures, including event-related potential (ERP) methods and eye tracking. ERP measures allow for the observation of this integration as it occurs—a comprehension process, rather than a comprehension product. Our experiments, using such sentences as (1) above, measured ERPs initiated by the target word, which is *rain* in the current example. When the target word appeared, the N400 component, an indicator of the fit between the word and its context (Kutas & Federmeier, 2000), was reduced in amplitude, indicating word-to-text integration.

In text (2), which follows the N400 on the word *rain,* there is a more pronounced negative deflection because it does not fit as easily into its context. There is no antecedent for *rain.* Equivalently, the situation model contains no referent to which the new event, the rain, can be attached.

(2) *When Cathy saw there were no dark clouds in the sky, she took her bike for a ride in the park. The rain that was predicted never occurred.*

Experimentally, (2) is a baseline condition against which N400 reductions produced by text manipulations (paraphrase, inference, and explicit mention) are compared. Important is the fact that text (2) is perfectly comprehensible. However, the reader's situation model is different from that in (1)—there is no storm. So, when the word *rain* is encountered, there is no rapid integration process that adds the idea of rain to the situation model; instead, a new mental structure is built around the rain and (finally) its nonoccurrence.

We emphasize the sensibility of text (2) because in most research that uses the N400 as an indicator of semantic processing, something that is sensible is compared with something that is not sensible, or anomalous.

For example, in a classic N400 study, an ERP is recorded on the sentence-final word when it is sensible, given the preceding context, "The pizza was too hot to eat," as compared with the ERP to the anomalous "too hot to drink" (Kutas & Hillyard, 1980). In these situations, the N400 differences are dramatic and appear amenable to explanations based on expectancy violations (Kutas & Federmeier, 2000; Lau, Almeida, Hines, & Poeppel, 2009). The N400 is assumed to be sensitive to poor fit (failures of expectations to be met, or failures to make sense of what occurs). In our case, however, a comparison is made across sensible texts. The texts differ only in the degree to which they invite an immediate word-to-text integration process. (See Brown & Hagoort, 1993, for N400 interpretations based on postlexical integration processes.) It is difficult to imagine what word a reader might predict across a sentence boundary; nearly any grammatical sentence beginning can continue with coherent ties to the preceding sentence.

**The Paraphrase Effect and Comprehension Skill** We refer to the fact that the word *rain* is better integrated with text (1) than with text (2) as the *paraphrase effect*. The ordinary sense of paraphrase, expressing an idea in words different from its original expression, applies only roughly to our use of the term *paraphrase*. A well-written text does not use different words in a new sentence to express the same idea as in the previous sentence as if avoiding repetition. Instead, the textual paraphrase is about the text moving the situation model a bit forward while maintaining coherence. Thus, in text (1), *rain* is not just another way of saying *storm*. Rather, the text moves the mental model forward in a baby step by referring to a correlate or consequence of the storm with the word *rain*.

Thus, the paraphrase effect reflects on-line comprehension, a sensitivity to moment-by-moment updating of the mental model. What we discovered in these experiments was that skilled comprehenders showed the paraphrase effect more robustly than did less skilled comprehenders (Perfetti et al., 2008). We suggested that less skilled comprehenders were showing *sluggish* word-to-text integration. We can imagine that there are some consequences for such sluggishness in maintaining the coherence across sentences, considering the largely incremental processes involved in comprehension (Just & Carpenter, 1980; Tyler & Marslen-Wilson, 1977).

**Paraphrase and Inference** Is this paraphrase effect reflective of a kind of inference? If so, is this another example of less skilled comprehenders being poor at inference generation relative to more skilled comprehenders? We address this question by referring again to our *storm–rain* example. Referring to *rain* after *storm* as a paraphrase is, as we said earlier, a baby step forward in the mental model that maintains coherence. However, the text could also leap forward with a giant step, as it would if instead of text (1) we had text (3). Note that unlike texts (1) and (2), continuation text (3) below is an example only, not text used in our experiments.

(3) *While Cathy was riding her bike in the park, dark clouds began to gather. The rain ruined her beautiful sweater.*

Here, when the reader encounters the word *rain*, there is no storm event in the reader's mental model; so there is nothing to which *rain* gets attached. Instead, the reader constructs a new event: Rain. It's not a big stretch, given the dark clouds, to infer a rain event. And to keep the text coherent, this bridging inference (e.g., Graesser, Singer, & Trabasso, 1994; Singer & Halldorson, 1996) is readily made, although with some detectable cost to processing efficiency. Yang et al. (2007) observed that for texts of this type, the N400 amplitude was not significantly different from baseline. Thus, reading "The rain" in sentence (3) was similar to reading "The rain" in sentence (2) as far as the ERP record was concerned.

There is a way to evade the cost of making this bridging inference in the second sentence if, in the first sentence, the reader makes a forward or predictive inference. Such an inference would have to be generated while reading the first sentence of (3), specifically the segment "dark clouds began to gather." This, in effect, is a prediction (it will rain) the reader might make, a forward inference (Graesser et al., 1994). But such an inference has little warrant. Maybe rain would be the next event, and maybe it would not. Adding a predicted event to the current model is at best a probabilistic cognitive move. Certainly the comprehension of the dark clouds in the first sentence allows a readiness to understand "the rain" when it does appear in the next sentence—hence, the N400 to (3) is not more negative than in (2)—but it does not compel a forward inference (McKoon & Ratcliff, 1992). The N400 results of Yang et al. (2007) strongly suggest that the forward inference was not made consistently, and thus readers had to make a bridging inference when they came to the word *rain* in the second sentence.

The conditions under which people make predictive inferences remain somewhat unclear, although it is fair to say that such inferences are less compelling and less often made than inferences that are needed to support coherence (Graesser et al., 1994; McKoon & Ratclif, 1992). Coherence is not necessarily served by prediction because predictions can go wrong and because for a skilled reader, coherence is quickly established by reading words and integrating their meanings into the mental model of the text. Perhaps in highly engaging narrative situations where reading is not involved, such as the movie watching studied by Magliano and Zacks (2011), forward inferences are more common. In reading, despite considerable belief that such inferences are characteristic of good comprehension, there is very little evidence—or none (McKoon & Ratcliff, 1992)—that such inferences are made immediately, allowing their effects to be measured on a single word, as opposed to later, when new text affirms the event.

We see our research as pointing to an important integration process during reading, exemplified (but not restricted to) the paraphrase effect, by which word meanings are integrated when possible with what has already been understood. More skilled comprehenders show this paraphrase effect more robustly than do less skilled comprehenders. We believe this result points to an important conclusion about comprehension skill: It depends in part on local word-to-text integration processes that are less about inferring and more about using word meanings to update a mental model, that is, to understand the meaning of the text.

## Comprehension Skill and Word-to-Text Integration

Why do skilled comprehenders show better word-to-text integration than do less skilled comprehenders? Word-to-text integration is important for maintaining coherence and thus for smoothly moving the reader forward in comprehension. The implicit indicators of integration obtained from ERP measures may indicate that less skilled comprehenders have accumulating difficulty in understanding a text, although we cannot make this conclusion based on our studies. If word-to-text integration is indeed a significant source of comprehension difficulty for less skilled comprehenders, we need to understand why.

We should be wary of concluding that some readers suffer from an integration deficit, as if this explains why they have trouble with comprehension (or at least why they score low on comprehension tests). Instead, we can ask what cognitive processes might be at risk during comprehension and thus cause word-to-text integration difficulties. Perhaps less skilled readers, because they tend to have lower working memory capacity (Just & Carpenter, 1992), do not retain the information from the first sentence well enough to integrate a new word with the prior text memory. Or, perhaps the skilled comprehenders are better at written word identification. Less skilled comprehenders, on average, know fewer words than do skilled comprehenders; for example, there are correlations between .36 and .50 for measures of comprehension and vocabulary in children (after controlling for age; Ouellette, 2006), and .43 correlation between comprehension and vocabulary in Pittsburgh's adult reading database (Nelson, 2010). Thus, perhaps less skilled comprehenders fail to know the meanings of the words on which we take our ERP measures. Or perhaps the case is that although less skilled comprehenders retrieve meanings for the word, their meaning selection processes fail to settle quickly on the meaning most appropriate for the current context.

Another possibility is that the paraphrase effect is not about building a mental model at all, but about lexical associations. For example, the word *cloud* could trigger an association to the word *rain* and thus facilitate the subsequent reading of *rain*. Indeed, it is likely that strongly interlinked lexical networks that allow this kind of association are characteristic of skilled comprehenders (Landi & Perfetti, 2007). There are noncognitive possibilities as well; and these, although usually ignored, are very important: Readers need a reasonably high standard of coherence (van den Broek, Lorch, Linderholm, & Gustafson, 2001; van den Broek, Risden, &

Husebye-Hartman, 1995) to engage the integrative processes we are studying. It is likely that less skilled comprehenders are less engaged in maintaining coherent understanding.

At this point, we cannot narrow down these possibilities very much. Our studies have addressed some of them, however, including whether memory differences are involved, whether written word identification is part of the issue, and to what extent lexical associations are part of the paraphrase effect and the skill differences we see. Adlof and Perfetti (2011), for example, examined the paraphrase effect in a listening ERP study with adults who differed in comprehension but were matched on word identification. The researchers found the same kind of paraphrase effect (a reduced N400 on the critical spoken word) in listening as Yang et al. (2007) found in reading. Comprehension skill differences in the effect appear similar, albeit somewhat less robust than those found in reading. As another example, we are attempting to distinguish whether the paraphrase effect reflects the integration of a word's referential meaning into a mental model or the activation of word associations that affect the integration of a word across a sentence boundary. Learning more about this integration process during actual reading may shed light on the comprehension skill differences in associative and nonassociative meaning processes that have been observed in word-level semantic tasks (Landi & Perfetti, 2007; Nation & Snowling, 1999).

## CONCLUSION

Text comprehension research has focused on the comprehension processes that are distinct from word-reading processes. This emphasis is warranted by the nature of the text comprehension processes and the very meaning of comprehension. Transferring the analysis of text comprehension to the study of text comprehension problems is incomplete, however, unless doing so also takes into account word processes. It is necessary to consider not only word identification but also what a reader knows about words and how this knowledge is used during reading. We have illustrated this general argument with a research program that studies word-to-text integration through the use of ERP measures. The ability to integrate a word currently being read into a model of the text is an essential part of fluent comprehension that allows text understanding without debilitating disruption from comprehension glitches. It appears likely that one source of comprehension problems—not the only one—lies in this word-to-text integration process.

## REFERENCES

Adlof, S.M., & Perfetti, C.A. (2011, July). *Are integrative processes the same in reading and listening?* St. Pete Beach, FL: Society for the Scientific Study of Reading.

American Psychiatric Association. (2012). *Diagnostic and Statistical Manual–Fifth Edition.* DSM-5 Development. Retrieved from http://www.dsm5.org

Anderson, R.C., & Freebody, P. (1981). Vocabulary knowledge. In J. Guthrie (Ed.), *Comprehension and teaching: Research reviews* (pp. 77–117). Newark, DE: International Reading Association.

Baker, L. (1984). Spontaneous versus instructed use of multiple standards for evaluating comprehension: Effects of age, reading proficiency, and type of standard. *Journal of Experimental Child Psychology, 38,* 289–311.

Balass, M., Nelson, J.R., & Perfetti, C.A. (2010). Word learning: An ERP investigation of word experience effects on recognition and word processing. *Contemporary Educational Psychology, 35,* 126–140.

Bishop, D.M., & Snowling, M.J. (2004). Developmental dyslexia and specific language impairment: Same or different? *Psychological Bulletin, 130*(6), 858–886.

Bolger, D.J., Balass, M., Landen, E., & Perfetti, C.A. (2008). Context variation and definitions in learning the meaning of words: An instance-based learning approach. *Discourse Processes, 45,* 122–159.

Brown, C., & Hagoort, P. (1993). The processing nature of the N400: Evidence from masked priming. *Journal of Cognitive Neuroscience, 5*(1), 34–44.

Cain, K. (2010). *Reading development and difficulties: An introduction.* Oxford, England: Wiley-Blackwell.

Catts, H.W. (1991). Early identification of dyslexia: Evidence from a follow-up study of speech language impaired children. *Annals of Dyslexia, 41,* 163–177.

Catts, H.W., Adlof, S.M., & Ellis Weismer, S. (2006). Language deficits of poor comprehenders: A case for the simple view of reading. *Journal of Speech, Language, and Hearing Research, 49,* 278–293.

Catts, H.W., Adlof, S.M., Hogan, T.P., & Ellis Weismer, S. (2005). Are SLI and dyslexia distinct disorders? *Journal of Speech, Language, and Hearing Research, 48,* 1378–1396.

Ericsson, K.A., Krampe, R.T., & Tesch-Romer, C. (1993). The role of deliberate practice in the acquisition of expert performance. *Psychological Review, 100*(3), 363–406.

Garner, R. (1980). Monitoring of understanding: An investigation of good and poor readers' awareness of induced miscomprehension of text. *Journal of Reading Behavior, 12,* 55–63.

Goldman, S.A., & Varma, S. (1995). CAPing the construction-integration model of discourse comprehension. In C.A. Weaver, S. Mannes, & C.R. Fletcher (Eds.), *Discourse comprehension: Essays in honor of Walter Kintsch* (pp. 337–358). Hillsdale, NJ: Erlbaum.

Graesser, A.C., Singer, M., & Trabasso, T. (1994). Constructing inferences during narrative text comprehension. *Psychological Review, 101*(3), 371–395.

Hamm, V.P., & Hasher, L. (1992). Age and the availability of inferences. *Psychology and Aging, 7*(1), 56–64.

Hasher, L., & Zacks, R.T. (1988). Working memory, comprehension, and aging: A review and a new view. In G.H. Bower (Ed.), *The psychology of learning and motivation* (Vol. 22, pp. 193–225). San Diego, CA: Academic Press.

Johnson-Laird, P.N. (1980). Mental models in cognitive science. *Cognitive Science, 4,* 71–115.

Johnson-Laird, P.N. (1981). Comprehension as the construction of mental models. *Philosophical Transactions of the Royal Society of London, Series B, 295*(1077), 353–374.

Johnson-Laird, P.N. (1983). *Mental models.* Cambridge, MA: Harvard University Press.

Just, M., & Carpenter, P.A. (1980). A theory of reading: From eye fixations to comprehension. *Psychological Review, 87,* 329–354.

Just, M.A., & Carpenter, P.A. (1992). A capacity theory of comprehension: Individual differences in working memory. *Psychological Review, 99*(1), 122–149.

Kutas, M., & Federmeier, K.D. (2000). Electrophysiology reveals semantic memory use in language comprehension. *Trends in Cognitive Sciences, 4*(12), 463–470.

Kutas, M., & Hillyard, S.A. (1980). Reading senseless sentences: Brain potentials reflect semantic incongruity, *Science, 207,* 203–205.

Landi, N., & Perfetti, C.A. (2007). An electrophysiological investigation of semantic and phonological processing in skilled and less-skilled comprehenders. *Brain and Language, 102*(1), 30–45.

Lau, E., Almeida, D., Hines, P.C., & Poeppel, D. (2009). A lexical basis for N400 context effects: Evidence from MEG. *Brain & Language, 111,* 161–172.

Locascio, G., Mahone, E.M., Eason, S.H., & Cutting, L.E. (2010). Executive dysfunction among children with reading comprehension deficits. *Journal of Learning Disabilities, 43*(5), 441–454. doi:10.1177/0022219409355476

Magliano, J.P., & Zacks, J.M. (2011). The impact of continuity editing in narrative film on event segmentation. *Cognitive Science, 35,* 1489–1517.

McKoon, G., & Ratcliff, R. (1992). Inference during reading. *Psychological Review, 99*(3), 440–466.

Nagy, W.E., Herman, P.A., & Anderson, R.C. (1985). Learning words from context. *Reading Research Quarterly, 20,* 233–253.

Nation, K., Cocksey, J., Taylor, J.S.H., & Bishop, D.V.M. (2010). A longitudinal investigation of the early reading and language skills in children with poor reading comprehension. *Journal of Child Psychology and Psychiatry, 51*(9), 1031–1039.

Nation, K., & Snowling, M.J. (1997). Assessing reading difficulties: The validity and utility of current measures of reading skill. *British Journal of Educational Psychology, 67,* 359–370.

Nation, K., & Snowling, M.J. (1999). Developmental differences in sensitivity to semantic relations among good and poor comprehenders: Evidence from semantic priming. *Cognition, 70*(1), B1–B13.

Nelson, J. (2010). *Reading skill and components of word knowledge affect eye movements during reading* (Unpublished doctoral dissertation). University of Pittsburgh, Pittsburgh, PA.

Oakhill, J., & Garnham, A. (1988). *Becoming a skilled reader.* New York, NY: Basil Blackwell.

Ouellette, G.P. (2006). What's meaning got to do with it: The role of vocabulary in word reading and reading comprehension. *Journal of Educational Psychology, 98*(3), 554–566.

Perfetti, C.A. (1999). Comprehending written language: A blueprint of the reader. In C. Brown & P. Hagoort (Eds.), *The neurocognition of language* (pp. 167–208). New York, NY: Oxford University Press.

Perfetti, C.A., Wlotko, E.W., & Hart, L.A. (2005). Word learning and individual differences in word learning reflected in event-related potentials. *Journal of Experimental Psychology: Learning, Memory, and Cognition, 31,* 1281–1292.

Perfetti, C.A., Yang, C.-L., & Schmalhofer, F. (2008). Comprehension skill and word-to-text processes. *Applied Cognitive Psychology, 22*(3), 303–318.

Singer, M., & Halldorson, M. (1996). Constructing and validating motive bridging inferences. *Cognitive Psychology, 30,* 1–38.

Stanovich, K.E., & West, A. (1989). Exposure to print and orthographic processing. *Reading Research Quarterly, 24,* 402–433.

Stothard, S.E., & Hulme, C. (1995). A comparison of phonological skills in children with reading comprehension difficulties and children with decoding difficulties. *Journal of Child Psychology and Psychiatry, 36,* 399–408.

Tyler, L.K., & Marslen-Wilson, W.D. (1977). The on-line effects of semantic context on syntactic processing. *Journal of Verbal Learning and Verbal Behavior, 16,* 683–692.

van den Broek, P., Lorch, R.F., Jr., Linderholm, T., & Gustafson, M. (2001). The effects of readers' goals on inference generation and memory for texts. *Memory & Cognition, 29*(8), 1081–1087.

van den Broek, P.W., Risden, K., & Husebye-Hartman, E. (1995). The role of readers' standards for coherence in the generation of inferences during reading. In R.F. Lorch, Jr., & E.J. O'Brien (Eds.), *Sources of coherence in reading* (pp. 353–373). Hillsdale, NJ: Erlbaum.

van Dijk, T.A., & Kintsch, W. (1983). *Strategies of discourse comprehension.* San Diego, CA: Academic Press.

Yang, C.-L., Perfetti, C.A., & Schmalhofer, F. (2005). Less skilled comprehenders ERPs show sluggish word-to-text integration processes. *Written Language & Literacy, 8*(2), 233–257.

Yang, C.-L., Perfetti, C.A., & Schmalhofer, F. (2007). Event-related potential indicators of text integration across sentence boundaries. *Journal of Experimental Psychology: Learning, Memory, and Cognition, 33*(1), 55–89.

Zwaan, R.A., & Radvansky, G.A. (1998). Situation models in language comprehension and memory. *Psychological Bulletin, 123*(2), 162–185.

CHAPTER 4

# How Might Comprehension Deficits Be Explained by the Constraints of Text and Multilevel Discourse Processes?

Art Graesser and Haiying Li

Models of reading routinely assume that there are multiple levels of language, meaning, and discourse that must be proficiently encoded or constructed in order for comprehension to succeed. Lower level *basic reading components* include phonology, morphology, word decoding, and possibly vocabulary (Adams, 1990; Perfetti, 2007; Rayner, Foorman, Perfetti, Pesetsky, & Seidenberg, 2001), although vocabulary is usually included at deeper levels because many words are intimately tied to world knowledge. A proficient reader automatizes the basic reading components after years of reading experiences, so these components are quickly executed and impose small demands on cognitive resources. If the basic reading components are not mastered, there will be consequences on the development of deeper comprehension (Cain, 2010; Compton et al., 2010; Connor et al., 2010; Kendeou, van den Broek, White, & Lynch, 2009; Stanovich, 1986; van den Broek, White, Kendeou, & Carlson, 2009; Vaughn et al., 2008). The higher level *deeper comprehension components* move from words into sentence interpretation, construction of inferences, use of background knowledge, reasoning, and knowledge of discourse structures (Diakidoy, Mouskounti, & Ioannides, 2011; Graesser & McNamara, 2011; Graesser, Singer, & Trabasso, 1994; Kintsch, 1998; McNamara, 2007; Perfetti, 1999). The deeper comprehension components are more time consuming, strategic, and taxing on cognitive resources for the proficient reader. These deeper levels are the focus of this edited volume on dyslexia.

The deeper levels of comprehension have been the most mysterious to reading researchers. The simple view of reading (Hoover & Gough, 1990), for example, does not decompose comprehension with the same zest as lexical decoding. Reading teachers often struggle with comprehension training because of the abstractness of syntax and semantics, the diversity

This research was supported by grants from the National Science Foundation (BCS 0904909, DRK-12-0918409), the Institute of Education Sciences (R305G020018, R305A080589, R305A080594, R305C120001), and the Gates Foundation (Student Achievement Partners). Any opinions, findings, and conclusions or recommendations expressed in this chapter are those of the authors and do not necessarily reflect the views of these funding agencies. We thank Zhiqiang Cai for the Coh-Metrix software development.

of comprehension curricula, the open-ended scope of world knowledge, and cultural constraints on rhetorical structures, among other reasons. The murkiness of comprehension has motivated various research efforts, including the Reading for Understanding initiative (Sabatini & Albro, 2012; Snow, 2002) and centers funded by the U.S. Institute of Education Sciences (e.g., Goldman et al., 2010), as well as the symposium associated with the chapters in this volume. This chapter will, we hope, help demystify the deeper levels of comprehension.

## A MULTILEVEL THEORETICAL FRAMEWORK

Researchers in the interdisciplinary field of discourse processes have been investigating different levels of comprehension for over four decades (Graesser, Gernsbacher, & Goldman, 2003; Kintsch, 1998; Perfetti, 1999). The field has been dominated by psychologists who have conducted laboratory experiments in their investigations of the representations, structures, strategies, and processes at multiple levels of language and discourse. The field has also had a strong presence of other disciplines, notably linguistics and education, so the work of these researchers has a salient presence in the reading comprehension community.

Graesser and McNamara (2011) recently articulated a multilevel theoretical framework that integrates the large body of research on comprehension in discourse processes, and more broadly the cognitive sciences. This framework is compatible with other multilevel frameworks that have attempted to identify and integrate deeper level reading components (Goldman et al., 2010; Kintsch, 1998; Perfetti, 1999; van Dijk & Kintsch, 1983). Graesser and McNamara (2011) identified six primary levels: *words, syntax,* the explicit *textbase,* the referential *situation model* (sometimes called the mental model), the discourse *genre and rhetorical structure* (the type of discourse and its composition), and the *pragmatic communication* level (between speaker and listener, or writer and reader). Words and syntax are self-explanatory and form what is sometimes called the *surface code.* The other levels are briefly described and elaborated in this section.

### Textbase

The textbase consists of the explicit ideas in the text that preserve the meaning but not the surface code of wording and syntax (Kintsch, 1998; van Dijk & Kintsch, 1983). According to Kintsch's theory, idea units consist of *propositions,* which are constituents that contain a predicate (main verb, adjective, connective) and one or more arguments (noun-phrases, embedded propositions). For example, in the sentence "A passenger is allergic to peanuts," the predicate is "allergic" and the arguments are "passenger" and "peanuts." *Co-reference* is an important linguistic method of connecting propositions, clauses, and sentences in the textbase (Halliday & Hasan, 1976). Referential cohesion occurs when a noun, pronoun, or noun-phrase refers to another constituent in the text. For example, in the sentence "If a passenger is allergic to peanuts, such an allergy will prevent the stewardess from serving that snack," the "allergy" in the second clause refers to the state associated with the predicate "allergic" in the first clause. Similarly, "peanuts" and "snack" are linked as bridging coreference. A referential cohesion gap occurs when the words in a sentence or clause do not connect to other sentences in the text. Such cohesion gaps at the textbase level increase reading time and may disrupt comprehension (Haberlandt & Graesser, 1985; McNamara & Kintsch, 1996).

## Situation Model

The situation model refers to the subject matter content that the text is describing. In narrative text, this includes the characters, objects, spatial settings, actions, events, processes, plans, thoughts and emotions of characters, and other details about the story. In informational text, the situation model is the substantive subject matter being described. For example, a text on allergies would include 1) causal networks of the events, processes, and enabling states that explain allergy mechanisms; 2) properties of entities in the biological system; 3) the spatial composition of the entities in the system; and 4) goal-oriented actions of patients and doctors and the family who try to help someone cope with an allergy. To fully comprehend this situation model requires world knowledge about allergies. The model includes inferences that are activated by the explicit text and encoded in the meaning representation (Graesser, Singer, & Trabasso, 1994; Kintsch, 1998; McNamara & Kintsch, 1996; van den Broek et al., 2009; Wiley et al., 2009; Zwaan & Radvansky, 1998). More specifically, Zwaan and Radvansky (1998) proposed five dimensions of the situation model that apply to the thread of deep comprehension: causation, intentionality (goals), time, space, and people. A break in text cohesion occurs when there is a discontinuity on one or more of these situation model dimensions. Such cohesion breaks result in an increase in reading time and generation of inferences (O'Brien, Rizzella, Albrecht, & Halleran, 1998; Rapp, van den Broek, McMaster, Kendeou, & Espin, 2007; Zwaan & Radvansky, 1998). Whenever such discontinuities occur, it is important to have connectives, transitional phrases, adverbs, or other signaling devices that convey to the readers that there is a discontinuity.

## Genre and Rhetorical Structure

Genre refers to the category of text, such as whether the text is narration, exposition, persuasion, or description (Biber, 1988). These major genre categories can be broken down into subcategories within a taxonomy; for example, editorials and religious sermons are different forms of persuasion. Features of language and discourse signal text genre very early in a text. There is evidence that training readers (in grade 5 to high school) to recognize genre and global text structures helps improve their comprehension (Meyer et al., 2010; Williams, Stafford, Lauer, Hall, & Pollini, 2009). In addition to the global genre of the text, a text has a rhetorical composition that provides a more differentiated functional organization of the message. Sections, paragraphs, and sentences have discourse functions that are, in well written texts, coherently linked to the macro-organization of the text.

### Pragmatic Communication

Just as a speaker in a conversation has a purpose in conveying a message to the listener, the writer tries to convey a message to the reader. Every text needs to be carefully analyzed with respect to its communication value. In essence, the central questions are why this article was written and why it is being read. What is the point, theme, moral, or message of the text? Is it useful? Is it engaging? What will the reader learn?

## COH-METRIX: SCALING TEXTS ON MULTIPLE LEVELS

This unique point in history allows us to use computer tools to analyze texts in large text repositories (called *corpora*). There have been landmark advances in computational linguistics (Jurafsky & Martin, 2008), statistical representations of world knowledge (Landauer, McNamara, Dennis, & Kintsch, 2008), corpus analyses (Biber, Conrad, & Reppen, 1998), and discourse processing (Graesser et al., 2003). Traditional approaches to analyzing text complexity have relied on a small number of factors. Specifically, word frequency, word length, and sentence length have been the mainstay of text complexity metrics (the flip side being readability). The traditional approach to scaling texts is to have a single metric of text ease or difficulty, as in the case of Flesch-Kincaid Grade Level or Reading Ease (Klare, 1974–75) and Lexile scores (Stenner, 2006). These metrics of text difficulty are highly correlated according to statistical analyses we have conducted ($r = 0.89$ to 0.94).

Nevertheless, there needs to be a more fine-grained scale for analyzing text characteristics, particularly for the levels articulated in the multilevel theoretical framework. A single dimension of text difficulty does not provide enough information for researchers who want to analyze meaning at different levels, for the assessments that attempt to diagnose particular deficits of a reader, and for instructors who want to assign texts and interventions that target a particular reading deficit of a reader. This motivated the development of Coh-Metrix (Graesser & McNamara, 2011; Graesser, McNamara, Louwerse, & Cai, 2004). Coh-Metrix is a computer application that analyzes texts on most of the levels of the multilevel theoretical framework. The original goals of the Coh-Metrix project were to 1) enhance standard text difficulty measures by providing scores on various cohesion and language characteristics and 2) determine the appropriateness of a text for a reader with a particular profile of cognitive characteristics. Coh-Metrix is available in a public version for free on the web (http://www.cohmetrix.com, http://www.tea.cohmetrix.com).

The original version of Coh-Metrix had nearly a thousand measures, 60 of which were put on the web site for colleagues to use. However, we were encouraged by proponents of the Common Core State Standards (CCSS) to simplify the analysis and converge on a smaller number of factors. Therefore, a principal components analysis (PCA) was performed on 37,520 texts in order to identify central constructs of text complexity (Graesser, McNamara, & Kulikowich, 2011). The PCA resulted in eight dimensions that accounted for 67% of the variance in variations among texts. The top five of these dimensions were incorporated in Coh-Metrix-Text Easability Assessor (TEA). These five dimensions of Coh-Metrix-TEA have also been validated in a comprehensive analysis of texts in the CCSS of the National Governors Association (2010, http://www.corestandards.org), as well as in various high-stakes assessments in the United States (Nelson, Perfetti, Liben, & Liben, 2012). These five major dimensions are listed and defined below.

1. *Narrativity.* Narrative text tells a story, with characters, events, places, and things that are familiar to the reader. Narrative is closely affiliated with everyday oral conversation.
2. *Referential cohesion.* High cohesion texts contain words and ideas that overlap across sentences and the entire text, forming threads that connect the explicit text together for the reader.
3. *Situation model cohesion.* Causal, intentional, and temporal connectives help the reader to form a more coherent and deeper understanding of the text.
4. *Syntactic simplicity.* Sentences with few words and simple, familiar syntactic structures are easier to process and understand than are complex structures. Complex sentences have structurally embedded syntax.
5. *Word concreteness.* Concrete words evoke mental images and richer semantic specifications than abstract words.

Each of the foregoing five dimensions is expressed in terms of ease of comprehension. Text complexity is defined as the opposite of ease, so principal component scores are reversed in measures of text complexity.

The five Coh-Metrix dimensions have been correlated with such unidimensional metrics of text complexity as Flesh-Kincaid, Degrees of Reading Power (DRP), and Lexiles. Using grade level as a yardstick, we have discovered a variety of trends that support the claim that we need to consider multiple levels and resist the temptation to settle for a single dimension of text complexity (Graesser et al., 2011). We have shown that grade level robustly decreases as a function of narrativity and syntactic simplicity and moderately decreases with increasing word concreteness. However, the correlation between grade level and cohesion is extremely small and sometimes not statistically significant. Apparently, cohesion is not on the radar of the standard readability metrics, even though discourse-processing researchers have established that cohesion is an important predictor of reading time and comprehension, as discussed earlier.

Equally illuminating were the trade-offs among the different levels as they correlated with the texts in different age groups and genres. For example, informational texts (nonnarratives) are typically on topics that are or may be unfamiliar to readers. These informational texts tend to have higher referential cohesion and simpler syntax than do the narrative texts, perhaps to compensate for the difficulty of the material. Narrative texts have generally been found more often at early grade levels, whereas informational texts are more often found at later grade levels. Therefore, any analysis of texts at different grade levels needs to take into account the trade-offs among narrativity, cohesion, and syntax. Coh-Metrix is a useful tool to sort out complex interactions among text constraints, test performance at different grade levels, and data reported in laboratory experiments (Eason, Goldberg, Young, Geist, & Cutting, 2012; McNamara, Louwerse, McCarthy, & Graesser, 2010).

## PROCESSING DIFFICULTIES AND INTERACTIONS AMONG LEVELS

Graesser and McNamara (2011) reported some weak evidence that proficient readers have most of their reading time variance taken up with low frequency words, the textbase, and the situation model as opposed to the other levels of the multilevel theoretical framework. The processing of words, syntax, genre, and pragmatic communication is sufficiently automatized, whereas the rare words, textbase, and situation model levels of a text are novel. This generalization explains reading times for college students (Haberlandt & Graesser, 1985), but we are uncertain whether it generalizes to individuals with dyslexia.

An important question arises as to how these levels influence one another during the course of processing. If one level fails, how does it influence other levels? We can explore alternatives that were raised in Graesser and McNamara (2011). Before turning to these, however, it is important to acknowledge the complex interdependencies among levels. Proficient reading requires that both lower-level as well as higher-level skills be highly developed, working both interactively and independently. Skilled reading depends upon the weaving together of several levels, only some of which are automatized. Comprehension components at higher levels require strategy development, whereas basic reading levels require extensive experience and automatization. Tight integration of the multiple and different types of strands or skills is needed as the substrate on which flexible and fluent reading comprehension processes can be based (Scarborough, 2001).

This being said, we can identify some possible interactions among levels that reading researchers might consider in their thinking. There are four principles of processing that might be considered. For convenience of reference we reiterate here the levels of our multilevel framework: 1) components of words, 2) words, 3) syntax, 4) textbase, 5) situation model, 6) genre and rhetorical structure, and 7) pragmatic communication. Assume the processing stream is bottom-up, following the ordering from 1 to 7. This is a crass simplification but, we believe, worthy of deliberation. The four principles follow:

(A) *Process bottom-up until an impasse is reached.* The reader attempts to achieve the deepest, most global level. So the ordering is 1 → 2 → 3 → 4 → 5 → 6 → 7. An impasse at one level prevents higher levels from being processed successfully.

(B) *Intermediate levels demand cognitive resources.* Levels 3 and 4 are most novel and most likely to demand cognitive resources unless there are unusual features of the higher and lower levels.

(C) *Top-down processing of levels can circumvent the need to process lower levels.* Sometimes the reader can assume that lower levels are handled if they trust that the higher, deeper levels are intact. Lower level processing requires resources, so a good strategy is to assume that higher levels trump lower levels.

(D) *Levels can compensate for other levels.* A deficit at one level can be compensated by other levels that inferentially fill in information about the level with the deficit.

Some concrete scenarios illustrate these processing principles.

*Scenario 1.* A child has trouble recognizing letters in the alphabet, so there is an obstacle in lexical decoding at the word-components level (Level 1). The lexical decoding blocks him from understanding any of the text at the word through functional communication levels (2–7). This is compatible with processing principle A, working from the bottom level upward.

*Scenario 2.* Parents take their children to a new Disney movie that they discover has a few adult themes. The children notice the parents laughing at different points in the movie than they do. The children are making it successfully through discourse from words to the situation level (Levels 1–5), but genre and rhetorical structure and functional communication (Levels 6 and 7) are not yet intact. This, too, is compatible with processing principle A, working bottom-up.

*Scenario 3.* An adult reads a health insurance document that has lengthy sentences with embedded clauses, numerous quantifiers (*all, many, rarely*), and many logical operators (*and, or, not, if*). She understands nearly all the words; but because of complex syntax, a dense textbase, and a confusing situation model (i.e., deficits at Levels 3–5), she only vaguely understands what the document explicitly states. However, she signs the contract because she understands its purpose and trusts the people with whom she is working. Thus genre, rhetoric, and communicative function (Levels 6 and 7) circumvent the need to understand Levels 3–5 completely. This is compatible with processing principle C, namely, that top-down processing can efficiently circumvent lower levels of processing.

*Scenario 4.* Laboratory partners in an engineering course read the directions to assemble a new computer. They argue about how to hook up the cables on the dual monitors. They have no problem understanding the words and textbase in the directions (Levels 1–4) and no problem understanding the genre and purpose of the document (Levels 6 and 7), but they do have a deficit at the situation model level (Level 5). This is compatible with processing principle B, namely, that intermediate levels have the most novel information and require more cognitive resources.

*Scenario 5.* A science student asks his roommate to proofread a term paper, but the roommate is a journalism major who knows little about science and complains that there is a problem with logical flow. The science major revises the text by adding connectives (e.g., *because, so, therefore, before*) and other words to improve the cohesion. The revised composition is deemed more comprehensible. In this case, improvements in processing words and the textbase (Levels 2 and 4) compensated for a deficit in the situation model (Level 5). This is compatible with processing principle D, namely, that levels can compensate for other levels .

This chapter has presented our multilevel theoretical framework and discussed how readers can face reading obstacles at any of the levels in this framework. In addition, there can be deficits in the reader (e.g., lack of knowledge or skill), the text (e.g., incoherent text, esoteric irrelevant jargon), or the training (e.g., an emphasis on shallow levels of reading). The severity of an obstacle can range from a minor irregularity that adds cost in processing time to a major impasse that results in a complete breakdown in comprehension. Attempts can be made to compensate for the problem by recruiting information from other levels of discourse, from prior knowledge, from external sources (e.g., other people or technologies), or from strategies.

## REFERENCES

Adams, M. (1990). *Beginning to read: Thinking and learning about print.* Cambridge, MA: MIT Press.

Biber, D. (1988). *Variation across speech and writing.* Cambridge, England: Cambridge University Press.

Biber, D., Conrad, R., & Reppen, P. (1998). *Corpus linguistics: Investigating language structure and use.* Cambridge, England: Cambridge University Press.

Cain, K. (2010). *Reading development and difficulties.* Oxford, England: Wiley-Blackwell.

Common Core State Standards Initiative (CCSS). (2010). *Common Core State Standards for English language arts & literacy in history/social studies, science, and technical subjects.* Washington, DC: CCSSO & National Governors Association. Retrieved from http://www.corestandards.org

Compton, D.L., Fuchs, D., Fuchs, L.S., Bouton, B., Gilbert, J.K., Barquero, L.A., … Crouch, R.C. (2010). Selecting at-risk readers in first grade for early intervention: Eliminating false positives and exploring the promise of a two-stage screening process. *Journal of Educational Psychology, 102,* 327–340.

Connor, C.M., Ponitz, C.C., Philips, B.M., Travis, Q.M., Glasney, S., & Morrison, F.J. (2010). First graders' literacy and self-regulation gains: The effect of individualizing student instruction. *Journal of School Psychology, 48,* 433–455.

Diakidoy, I.N., Mouskounti, T., & Ioannides, C. (2011). Comprehension and learning from refutation and expository texts. *Reading Research Quarterly, 46,* 22–38.

Eason, S.H., Goldberg, L.F., Young, K.M., Geist, M.C., & Cutting, L.E. (2012). Reader–text interactions: How differential text and question types influence cognitive skills needed for reading comprehension. *Journal of Educational Psychology, 105,* 515–528.

Goldman, S.R., Britt, M.A., Brown, M., Greenleaf, C., & Lee, C.D. (2010). *Reading for understanding across grades 6 through 12: Evidence-based argumentation for disciplinary learning* (Grant No. R305F100007). Funded July 2010 by the Institute of Education Sciences, U.S. Department of Education.

Graesser, A.C., Gernsbacher, M.A., & Goldman, S.R. (2003). Introduction to the Handbook of Discourse Processes. In A.C. Graesser, M.A. Gernsbacher, & S.R. Goldman (Eds.), *Handbook of discourse processes* (pp. 1–24). Mahwah, NJ: Erlbaum.

Graesser, A.C., & McNamara, D.S. (2011). Computational analyses of multilevel discourse comprehension. *Topics in Cognitive Science, 3,* 371–398.

Graesser, A.C., McNamara, D.S., & Kulikowich, J. (2011). Coh-Metrix: Providing multilevel analyses of text characteristics. *Educational Researcher, 40,* 223–234.

Graesser, A.C., McNamara, D.S., Louwerse, M.M., & Cai, Z. (2004). Coh-Metrix: Analysis of text on cohesion and language. *Behavioral Research Methods, Instruments, and Computers, 36,* 193–202.

Graesser, A.C., Singer, M., & Trabasso, T. (1994). Constructing inferences during narrative text comprehension. *Psychological Review, 101,* 371–395.

Haberlandt, K.F., & Graesser, A.C. (1985). Component processes in text comprehension and some of their interactions. *Journal of Experimental Psychology: General, 114,* 357–374.

Halliday, M.A.K., & Hasan, R. (1976). *Cohesion in English.* London, England: Longman.

Hoover, W.A., & Gough, P.B. (1990). The simple view of reading. *Reading and Writing: An Interdisciplinary Journal, 2,* 127–160.

Jurafsky, D., & Martin, J. (2008). *Speech and language processing.* Upper Saddle River, NJ: Prentice-Hall.

Kendeou, P., van den Broek, P., White, M.J., & Lynch, J.S. (2009). Predicting reading comprehension in early elementary school: The independent contributions of oral language and decoding skills. *Journal of Educational Psychology, 101,* 765–778.

Kintsch, W. (1998). *Comprehension: A paradigm for cognition.* Cambridge, England: Cambridge University Press.

Klare, G.R. (1974–1975). Assessing readability. *Reading Research Quarterly, 10,* 62–102.

Landauer, T., McNamara, D.S., Dennis, S., & Kintsch, W. (Eds.). (2008). *Handbook of latent semantic analysis.* Mahwah, NJ: Erlbaum.

McNamara, D.S. (Ed.). (2007). *Reading comprehension strategies: Theory, interventions, and technologies.* Mahwah, NJ: Erlbaum.

McNamara, D.S., & Kintsch, W. (1996). Learning from text: Effects of prior knowledge and text coherence. *Discourse Processes, 22,* 247–287.

McNamara, D.S., Louwerse, M.M., McCarthy, P.M., & Graesser, A.C. (2010). Coh-Metrix: Capturing linguistic features of cohesion. *Discourse Processes, 47,* 292–330.

Meyer, B.F., Wijekumar, K., Middlemiss, W., Higley, K., Lei, P., Meier, C., & Spielvogel, J. (2010). Web-based tutoring of the structure strategy with or without elaborated feedback or choice for fifth and seventh grade readers. *Reading Research Quarterly, 45,* 62–92.

Nelson, J., Perfetti, C., Liben, D., & Liben, M. (2012). *Measures of text difficulty: Testing their predictive value for grade levels and student performance.* New York, NY: Student Achievement Partners.

O'Brien, E.J., Rizzella, M.L., Albrecht, J.E., & Halleran, J.G. (1998). Updating a situation model: A memory-based text processing view. *Journal of Experimental Psychology: Learning, Memory, & Cognition, 24,* 1200–1210.

Perfetti, C.A. (1999). Comprehending written language: A blueprint of the reader.

In C. Brown & P. Hagoort (Eds.), *The neurocognition of language* (pp. 167–210). New York, NY: Oxford University Press.

Perfetti, C.A. (2007). Reading ability: Lexical quality to comprehension. *Scientific Studies of Reading, 11,* 357–383.

Rapp, D.N., van den Broek, P., McMaster, K.L., Kendeou, P., & Espin, C.A. (2007). Higher-order comprehension processes in struggling readers: A perspective for research and intervention. *Scientific Studies of Reading, 11,* 289–312.

Rayner, K., Foorman, B., Perfetti, C., Pesetsky, D., & Seidenberg, M. (2001). How psychological science informs the teaching of reading. *Psychological Science in the Public Interest, 2,* 31–74.

Sabatini, J.P., & Albro, L. (2012). (Eds.), *Assessing reading in the 21st century: Aligning and applying advances in the reading and measurement sciences.* Lanham, MD: R&L Education.

Scarborough, H.S. (2001). Connecting early language and literacy to later reading (dis)abilities: Evidence, theory, and practice. In D.K. Dickinson & S.B. Neuman (Eds.), *Handbook of early literacy research* (Vol. 1, pp. 97–110). New York, NY: Guilford Press.

Snow, C. (2002). *Reading for understanding: Toward an R&D program in reading comprehension.* Santa Monica, CA: RAND Corporation.

Stanovich, K.E. (1986). Matthew effects in reading: Some consequences of individual differences in the acquisition of literacy. *Reading Research Quarterly, 21,* 360–406.

Stenner, A.J. (2006, October). *Measuring reading comprehension with the Lexile framework.* Paper presented at the California Comparability Symposium, October 1996. Retrieved January 30, 2006, from http://www.lexile.com/DesktopDefault.aspx?view=re

van den Broek, P., White, M.J., Kendeou, P., & Carlson, S. (2009). Reading between the lines. Developmental and individual differences in cognitive processes in reading comprehension. In R.K. Wagner, C. Schatschneider, & C. Phythian-Sence (Eds.), *Beyond decoding: The behavioral and biological foundations of reading comprehension* (pp. 107–123). New York, NY: Guilford Press.

van Dijk, T.A., & Kintsch, W. (1983). *Strategies of discourse comprehension.* New York, NY: Academic Press.

Vaughn, S., Fletcher, J.M., Francis, D.J., Denton, C.A., Wanzek, J., Wexler, J., Romain, M.A. (2008). Response to intervention with older students with reading difficulties. *Learning and Individual Differences, 18,* 338–345.

Wiley, J., Goldman, S.R., Graesser, A.C., Sanchez, C.A., Ash, I.K., & Hemmerich, J.A. (2009). Source evaluation, comprehension, and learning in Internet science inquiry tasks. *American Educational Research Journal, 27,* 255–265.

Williams, J.P., Stafford, K.B., Lauer, K.D., Hall, K.M., & Pollini, S. (2009). Embedding reading comprehension training in content-area instruction. *Journal of Educational Psychology, 101,* 1–20.

Zwaan, R.A., & Radvansky, G.A. (1998). Situation models in language comprehension and memory. *Psychological Bulletin, 123,* 162–185.

CHAPTER 5

# Sources of Comprehension Problems During Reading

Anne Helder, Paul van den Broek, Linda Van Leijenhorst, and Katinka Beker

The ability to comprehend written material is essential for success in school and everyday life, and it is one of the key abilities that have to be mastered over the course of development. However, many children struggle to learn to read and comprehend texts, and a subgroup of these children will continue to experience difficulties specific to reading comprehension throughout their lives. This chapter outlines possible sources of reading comprehension problems based on recent research findings and theories.

Central to current models of reading comprehension is the notion that successful comprehension involves the process of identification of meaningful connections between text elements, as well as between information in the text and the reader's semantic memory or background knowledge. Through integration of these connections, readers construct a coherent mental representation of a text—the outcome of successful comprehension (Graesser, Singer, & Trabasso, 1994; Kintsch, 1988; van den Broek, 1994). This notion depicts reading comprehension as emerging from the interaction between text and reader characteristics and emphasizes the distinction between the *product* (the coherent mental representation of the text) and the *process* (what happens in the mind of a reader during reading) of reading comprehension. In this chapter we argue that an understanding of the *process* of reading comprehension across development is particularly useful to better understand reading comprehension difficulties and that doing so has the potential to lead to the design of interventions to help children and adults who struggle with texts in everyday life.

Several reader characteristics contribute to the process of constructing a coherent mental representation of a text, and difficulties in the construction of such a mental representation can originate at different levels of processing. A useful distinction is between *basic reading skills,* such as orthographic and phonological processing skills, and *higher-order reading skills,* or such comprehension skills as the ability to make inferences, knowledge of story structure, and cognitive control functions (Oakhill & Cain, 2011; Perfetti, Landi, & Oakhill, 2005). This distinction between basic and higher-order reading skills is also seen in the influential simple view of reading model (Gough & Tunmer, 1986; Hoover & Gough, 1990; Kendeou, Savage, & van den Broek, 2009), which proposes that acquiring reading comprehension abilities requires the development of both types of skills. Recent research on the development of basic and higher-order reading skills shows that each cluster of skills starts developing well before formal reading education begins (Kendeou, White, van den Broek, & Lynch, 2009). The two clusters of reading skills develop relatively independently, coming together when the individual starts to read for comprehension, with each cluster uniquely predicting reading comprehension. Such findings have led to a strong increase in interest in the development of comprehension skills and in the design of possible interventions (e.g., McMaster et al., 2012, in primary and secondary school; van den Broek, Kendeou, Lousberg & Visser, 2011, in preschool years).

There is a considerable body of knowledge on the causes of basic reading skill problems, but systematic investigations of the factors involved in individual and developmental differences in higher-order reading skills are sparse in comparison. In this chapter we describe the higher-order cognitive processes that contribute to text comprehension and discuss sources of individual differences and comprehension difficulties.

## HIGHER-ORDER COGNITIVE FACTORS AND PROCESSES DURING READING

To understand sources of individual and developmental differences in reading comprehension, it is important to recognize that reading comprehension is not a single, unitary skill but, rather, a conglomerate of processes that take place in constantly changing combinations during reading of a text (McNamara & Magliano, 2009). As a reader proceeds through a text, each new input (e.g., sentence) triggers a new set of cognitive processes. Some of these processes are automatic; others are strategic, initiated by the reader to create coherence. The processes may support, compensate, or even interfere with each other. Through these processes background knowledge is activated, earlier portions of the text are reactivated, and text elements become semantically connected to each other and to the reader's prior knowledge. The specific mix of processes changes from cycle to cycle as a function of properties of the new input and of the reader. With each new cycle, the reader's mental representation is expanded, modified, and updated until reading is complete. The final representation captures the reader's understanding of the text as a whole (van den Broek, 2010).

The cognitive factors and processes that determine success and failure constructing a coherent, accurate representation generally fall into three clusters (see Table 5.1; van den Broek & Espin, 2012). First, such general cognitive resources as executive functions, attention processes, and working memory capacity allow readers to interact flexibly with texts, to notice errors in comprehension, and to repair these errors or resolve uncertainties when needed. Second, such comprehension processes as those related to inference making and coherence building allow readers

**Table 5.1.** Three clusters of higher-order cognitive factors and processes that contribute to developmental change and individual differences in reading comprehension

| General cognitive factors and processes |
| --- |
| Executive functions<br>Working memory capacity<br>Background knowledge |
| **Comprehension factors and processes** |
| Coherence building<br>Inference generation<br>Sensitivity to structural centrality<br>Standards of coherence |
| **Text comprehension factors and processes** |
| Cognitive toolbox of reading comprehension strategies<br>Text-related factors<br>  Knowledge of text genre<br>  Knowledge and use of text signals<br>Reading motivation |

to identify connections within the text and between the text and their background knowledge. Third, readers have strategies and knowledge specific to written material. For example, they may use their knowledge of different text structures or genres to guide their comprehension processes. We describe each cluster, emphasizing possible causes for developmental and individual differences in reading comprehension.

## General Cognitive Factors and Processes

Reading comprehension is a complex cognitive ability that involves execution and coordination of a multitude of processes. Moreover, these processes are executed in the context of limited attentional capacities. As a result, cognitive processes that enable cognitive control, such as those described in the framework of executive functions (Miyaki et al., 2000), play an important role in determining success and failure in comprehension. Executive functions include *inhibition, shifting,* and *updating*. Inhibition is the ability to override prepotent responses, shifting is the ability to switch flexibly between different cognitive tasks or mental states, and updating is the process of continuous monitoring and changing the contents of working memory. Each of these executive functions undergoes considerable change with development (Cragg & Nation, 2008; Huizinga, Dolan, & van der Molen, 2006). Executive functions strongly influence comprehension skills in 9–15-year-olds (Sesma, Mahone, Levine, Eason, & Cutting, 2009) and are related to individual differences in reading comprehension skills (Borella, Carretti, & Pelegrina, 2010; Locascio, Mahone, Eason, & Cutting, 2010).

Of these functions, working memory has received the most attention from researchers. Working memory capacity dramatically increases with development, from early childhood (Gathercole, Pickering, Ambridge, & Wearing, 2004; Luna, Garver, Urban, Lazar, & Sweeney, 2004). This increase in working memory capacity is an important factor in the development of executive functions (Demetriou, Christou, Spanoudis, & Platsidou, 2002). Although working memory is a complex construct and is conceptualized in various ways (Baddeley, 2003; Cowan, 2010), it is generally agreed that working memory maintains and manipulates information and keeps it accessible for further processing, enabling working memory to guide behavior.

Working memory capacity correlates positively with reading comprehension skills in adults (Just & Carpenter, 1992) as well as in children (Cain & Oakhill, 2007). When children first learn to read, their working memory capacity and competing demands for it limit the available cognitive resources that can be allocated to higher-order comprehension skills; the demands of processes necessary for basic language processing and reading skills, such as phonological processes and decoding, are high (e.g., Perfetti et al., 2005). Both automatization of these basic skills and an increase in the capacity of working memory with development allow more resources to be devoted to higher-order reading skills. Thus, differences in executive functions and working memory capacity are likely to contribute to developmental and individual differences in reading comprehension. It is worth mentioning that executive function and working memory capacity themselves are complex concepts and depend on various underlying processes that could each have an influence on reading proficiency (e.g., Borella et al., 2010; Carretti, Borella, Cornoldi, & De Beni, 2009).

In addition to working memory and executive functions, the background knowledge that a reader has concerning the topics or issues in the text has a powerful influence on his or her comprehension. As described in detail below, coherence building and inference making crucially depend on automatic and strategic access to one's background knowledge. Consequently, differences in the breadth and depth of this knowledge influence the extent to which a coherent representation can be obtained.

## Comprehension Factors and Processes

Whether received through text or through other media, comprehension of discourse and other complex communications requires the construction of a mental representation in which the various parts of the information are connected to each other and to the individual's background knowledge (e.g., Gernsbacher, Varner, & Faust, 1990; Kendeou, Bohn-Gettler, White, & van den Broek, 2008). To create a coherent mental representation, readers establish semantic relations between different parts of the incoming information. Sometimes these relationships are explicit, but frequently they are only implied and need to be inferred by the reader through activation of relevant portions of the individual's background knowledge (Graesser et al., 1994; Kintsch, 1988; van den Broek, 1994). In addition, the recipient can make inferences that elaborate his or her representation by activating and incorporating background knowledge that is not strictly required for comprehension of the communication per se but that expands on it by adding context and details. The elaborated representation, called the *situation model,* is strengthened and enriched (although not necessarily more accurate; see Kendeou & van den Broek, 2007). Individuals differ not only in their ability to create coherence and to generate the required inferences but also in the extent to which they are able to create a situation model of a particular communication.

Inference generation itself is a complex cognitive ability that involves processes that vary in the mental resources they require and in the degree to which they are under conscious control of the reader. Some inferential processes occur automatically, for example, when spread of activation in a reader's semantic memory network facilitates the generation of inferences (Gerrig & O'Brien, 2005; McKoon & Ratcliff, 1992; Perfetti & Hart, 2002). Other inferential processes are strategic (Graesser et al., 1994). For example, a person may actively search his or her background knowledge to maintain a sufficient level of comprehension. Together, the automatic and strategic processes result in inferences that provide coherence to the reader's mental representation (van den Broek, Rapp, & Kendeou, 2005).

The mental representation can be thought of as a conceptual network, one consisting of nodes and lines that represent individual elements and the inferred relationships between them, respectively (Trabasso, Secco, & van den Broek, 1984; Trabasso, van den Broek, & Suh, 1989). Elements of the communication differ in their contribution to the overall coherence of the mental model; some, for example, have many connections to other elements and are therefore more important to the semantic structure of the text. Ideally, during comprehension an individual allocates attention to the elements and relations that are most relevant to understand the main ideas in the communication (van den Broek, 2010). The degree to which a comprehender is able to identify and process information that is central to the message is captured in the individual's *sensitivity to structural centrality* (van den Broek, Helder, & Van Leijenhorst, 2012). Sensitivity to structural centrality is an important source of individual and developmental differences in comprehension of texts as well as other types of discourse.

Developmental studies on inference generation have revealed that both the quantity and quality of the inferences that children make change with development. Children as young as 4 years of age, before the start of reading education, are already sensitive to the semantic structure of a text that is read to them: Their recall shows a preference for text elements that are central to the semantic structure of the text (Kendeou et al., 2008). With development, sensitivity to structural centrality increases (Lynch et al., 2008), as does the overall number of inferences that are generated during reading (Lynch & van den Broek, 2007). Moreover, generated inferences become more abstract, are more focused on the internal states of a story's protagonist, and span longer distances in the text (Thompson & Myers, 1985; van den Broek, 1997; Williams, 1993).

Likewise, there are individual differences in inferential and coherence-building skills. For example, poorly comprehending children and adults make fewer correct inferences and have a less coherent mental representation than do their proficiently comprehending peers (Long, Seely, & Oppy, 1997; Oakhill, 1982). Consistent with the notion that comprehension consists of multiple subskills, children (and, presumably, adults) may have difficulty building coherence for different reasons. Investigation of the on-line processing by good and poor reading comprehenders at various elementary and secondary grades, using eye tracking and think-aloud methods, show that there are at least two systematic subgroups of poor readers (McMaster et al., 2012; Rapp, van den Broek, McMaster, Kendeou, & Espin, 2007). One subgroup of poor comprehenders consists of *elaborators*, who make the same number of inferences as do good comprehenders but of different quality, for they are more likely to generate inferences that are not related to the central structure of the text. The other subgroup of poor comprehenders consists of *paraphrasers*, who make fewer inferences than do good comprehenders; their think-aloud data revealed that they mostly paraphrase or repeat the text. For both groups, the resulting mental representation was weak compared with that of good comprehenders, as evidenced by poor performance on such offline tasks as recall and question answering. Thus, poor comprehension can be the result of different causes, even within the domain of inference generation. This finding suggests that specific interventions may be designed to benefit different subgroups. Such differential effectiveness of interventions has been observed. Elaborators appear to benefit more from an intervention that promotes causal inferences (by asking causal questions during reading) than from an intervention that is promoting inference generation in general (by asking how a sentence connects to any information that was previously read). In contrast, paraphrasers show the opposite pattern, benefiting most from the general inference-generation intervention (McMaster et al., 2012).

Besides coherence building, inference making, and sensitivity to structural centrality, there are developmental and individual differences in the *standards of coherence* that a comprehender employs. Standards of coherence refer to the degree of coherence a comprehender strives for during the processing of information. Because this notion is investigated mostly in the context of reading comprehension, we will discuss it in that section.

## Text Comprehension Factors and Processes

The preceding section describes general and comprehension-specific cognitive processes that contribute to reading comprehension. These processes form a cognitive "toolbox" a reader can use to aid in the creation of a coherent mental representation of a text. However, there are several processes and skills that are specific to written materials. Individual and age-related differences in these processes and skills contribute to variations in reading comprehension skill as well. One example concerns the ability to effectively apply comprehension strategies that are particular to texts, such as rereading difficult-to-comprehend text segments, interrupting reading to allow for more processing time (e.g., to reflect), looking back to earlier text to comprehend the current sentence, and so on.

Text-specific factors also include a reader's knowledge and use of text properties to modulate his or her processing. For example, text signals and paragraph or section structures are intended to direct attention and processing. Hence, the degree to which a reader recognizes these signals and structures and selects appropriate action determines the quality of his or her comprehension of the text (Lemarié, Lorch, Eyrolle, & Virbel, 2008; Lorch, Lemarié, & Grant, 2011). A second example concerns awareness that different text genres call for different types of reading strategies. For example, narratives usually follow a relatively simple sequence of events and different narratives often have similar elements, such as settings, initiating events, goals, reactions, and outcomes (Mandler & Johnson, 1977; Stein & Glenn, 1979), allowing the reader to use a similar approach across narrative texts. In contrast, expository texts contain more complex relations and come in different formats, and they therefore demand more sophisticated and varied reading strategies (Meyer & Freedle, 1984; Meyer & Ray, 2011). Proficient readers recognize such genre differences and adjust their reading behavior accordingly, whereas poor comprehenders do so less reliably. The challenge in adjusting processing commensurate with the demands of these different genres may also underlie the frequently observed decline in reading comprehension performance around fourth grade (the fourth grade "slump"), the grade in which classroom activities frequently transition from a strong focus on learning to read through narratives to reading to learn through expository texts (e.g., Sweet & Snow, 2003).

As mentioned, reading comprehension involves both automatic and strategic processes. The degree to which a reader engages in strategic processes depends on his or her knowledge of and facility with the strategic processes but also on his or her *standards of coherence,* that is, the degree of coherence the reader aims to attain (Bohn-Gettler, Rapp, van den Broek, Kendeou, & White, 2011; van den Broek, Bohn-Gettler, Kendeou, Carlson, & White, 2011). Standards of coherence can vary within a reader, for example, as a function of the reading situation. Some situations do not require a deep comprehension and allow a reader to adopt low standards ("good-enough" processing; Ferreira, Bailey, & Ferraro, 2002). For instance, standards of coherence are usually higher when a reader reads to study for an exam than when he or she reads a magazine for fun. Variations in standards influence the extent of strategic processing and, hence, the coherence of the resulting memory representation (van den Broek, Lorch, Linderholm, & Gustafson, 2001). Standards of coherence also vary between readers and interact with cognitive resources and general comprehension processes. For example, readers with a high working memory capacity are better at adjusting their standards to the specific reading goal than are readers with low working memory capacity (Linderholm & van den Broek, 2002). Similarly, lower standards of coherence may explain why less skilled comprehenders tend to be less engaged in monitoring their comprehension, often resulting in more superficial text representation (Oakhill, Hartt, & Samols, 2005).

Although strictly speaking not cognitive, a final factor that influences the degree of processing—particularly of strategic processing—is a reader's motivation for reading in general (e.g., Wigfield & Guthrie, 1997).

## DISCUSSION

This chapter provides an overview of higher-order cognitive factors and processes that contribute to text comprehension and of sources of individual differences and comprehension difficulties. The factors and processes roughly fall into three clusters (Table 5.1). Some of the factors (e.g., executive control, working memory, background knowledge) provide the cognitive context in which a reader's comprehension processes take place. These comprehension skills and processes, in turn, vary in the degree to which they are particular to reading: Some skills and processes are common to most if not all comprehension situations. On the one hand, such comprehension processes as coherence building and inference making are relevant to comprehension of just about any type of discourse or communication, although their implementation in the reading context may differ from that in other contexts. On the other hand, comprehension factors and processes such as those triggered by uniquely textual properties (e.g., text signals, paragraph structures) are virtually exclusively limited to the reading context. Thus, although we describe these comprehension skills in two clusters, they in fact overlap and form a continuum. It also is important to note that comprehension skill is not entirely determined by higher-order factors and processes. Differences in such basic skills as decoding and in vocabulary (which may be related to background knowledge) strongly determine the input to the higher-order processes as well as the available attentional resources to execute these processes.

A common thread in the review is that reading comprehension is a multidimensional, multicomponential construct. The various components fluctuate and interact over the course of reading a text; they can compensate for, interfere with, and support each other. One implication is that it is unlikely that specific reading comprehension deficits can be traced to problems in a single process or skill (Cain & Oakhill, 2006). Likewise, a single intervention is unlikely to benefit all—or even a large proportion of—poor comprehenders. Subgroups of struggling comprehenders exist, and these respond differentially to different interventions (McMaster et al., 2012).

In conclusion, a reader's understanding of a text is the net result of a large number of factors and processes, any of which may fail to be optimal. Recent insights regarding these factors and processes contribute tremendously toward understanding developmental and individual differences. Further, these insights will point us toward effective diagnosis and intervention.

## REFERENCES


Baddeley, A. (2003). Working memory and language: An overview. *Journal of Communication Disorders, 36*(3), 189–208.

Bohn-Gettler, C.M., Rapp, D.N., van den Broek, P., Kendeou, P., & White, M.J. (2011). Adults' and children's monitoring of story events in the service of comprehension. *Memory & Cognition, 39*(6), 992–1011.

Borella, E., Carretti, B., & Pelegrina, S. (2010). The specific role of inhibition in reading comprehension in good and poor comprehenders. *Journal of Learning Disabilities, 43*(6), 541–552.

Cain, K., & Oakhill, J. (2006). Profiles of children with specific reading comprehension difficulties. *British Journal of Educational Psychology, 76*(4), 683–696.

Cain, K., & Oakhill, J. (2007). Reading comprehension difficulties: Correlates, causes, and consequences. In K. Cain & J. Oakhill (Eds.), *Children's comprehension problems in oral and written language: A cognitive perspective* (pp. 41–75). New York, NY: Guilford Press.

Carretti, B., Borella, E., Cornoldi, C., & De Beni, R. (2009). Role of working memory in explaining the performance of individuals with specific reading comprehension difficulties: A meta-analysis. *Learning and Individual Differences, 19*(2), 246–251.

Cowan, N. (2010). Multiple concurrent thoughts: The meaning and developmental neuropsychology of working memory. *Developmental Neuropsychology, 35*(5), 447–474.

Cragg, L., & Nation, K. (2008). Go or no go? Developmental improvements in the efficiency of response inhibition in mid-childhood. *Developmental Science, 11*(6), 819–827.

Demetriou, A., Christou, C., Spanoudis, G., & Platsidou, M. (2002). The development of mental processing: Efficiency, working memory, and thinking. *Monographs of the Society for Research in Child Development, 67.*

Ferreira, F., Bailey, K.G.D., & Ferraro, V. (2002). Good-enough representations in language comprehension. *Current Directions in Psychological Science, 11*, 11–15.

Gathercole, S.E., Pickering, S.J., Ambridge, B., & Wearing, H. (2004). The structure of working memory from 4 to 15 years of age. *Developmental Psychology, 40*(2), 177–190.

Gernsbacher, M.A., Varner, K.R., & Faust, M. (1990). Investigating differences in general comprehension skill. *Journal of Experimental Psychology: Learning, Memory, and Cognition, 16*, 430–445.

Gerrig, R.J., & O'Brien, E.J. (2005). The scope of memory-based processing. *Discourse Processes, 39*(2–3), 225–242.

Gough, P.B., & Tunmer, W.E. (1986). Decoding, reading, and reading disability. *Remedial and Special Education, 7*(1), 6–10.

Graesser, A., Singer, M., & Trabasso, T. (1994). Constructing inferences during narrative comprehension. *Psychological Review, 101*, 371–395.

Hoover, W.A., & Gough, P.B. (1990). The simple view of reading. *Reading and Writing, 2*(2), 127–160.

Huizinga, M., Dolan, C.V., & van der Molen, M.W. (2006). Age-related change in executive function: Developmental trends and a latent variable analysis. *Neuropsychologia, 44*(11), 2017–2036.

Just, M.A., & Carpenter, P.A. (1992). A capacity theory of comprehension: Individual-differences in working memory. *Psychological Review, 99*(1), 122–149.

Kendeou, P., Bohn-Gettler, C., White, M.J., & van den Broek, P. (2008). Children's inference generation across different media. *Journal of Research in Reading, 31*(3), 259–272.

Kendeou, P., Savage, R., & van den Broek, P. (2009). Revisiting the simple view of reading. *British Journal of Educational Psychology, 79*(2), 353–370.

Kendeou, P., & van den Broek, P. (2007). The effects of prior knowledge and text structure on comprehension processes during reading of scientific texts. *Memory & Cognition, 35*, 1567–1577.

Kendeou, P., White, M.J., van den Broek, P., & Lynch, J.S. (2009). Predicting reading comprehension in early elementary school: The independent contributions of oral language and decoding skills. *Journal of Educational Psychology, 101*(4), 765–778.

Kintsch, W. (1988). The role of knowledge in discourse comprehension—A construction integration model. *Psychological Review, 95*(2), 163–182.

Lemarié, J., Lorch, R.F., Jr., Eyrolle, H., & Virbel, J. (2008). A text-based and reader-based theory of signaling. *Educational Psychologist, 43*, 27–48.

Linderholm, T., & van den Broek, P. (2002). The effects of reading purpose and working memory capacity on the processing of expository text. *Journal of Educational Psychology, 94*(4), 778–784.

Locascio, G., Mahone, E.M., Eason, S.H., & Cutting, L.E. (2010). Executive dysfunction among children with reading comprehension deficits. *Journal of Learning Disabilities, 43*, 441–454.

Long, D.L., Seely, M.R., & Oppy, B.J. (1997). Individual differences in readers' sentence- and text-level representations. *Journal of Memory and Language, 36*, 129–145.

Lorch, R.F., Jr., Lemarié, J., & Grant, R.A. (2011). Signaling hierarchical and sequential organization in expository text. *Scientific Studies of Reading, 15*, 267–284.

Luna, B., Garver, K.E., Urban, T.A., Lazar, N.A., & Sweeney, J.A. (2004). Maturation of cognitive processes from late childhood to adulthood. *Child Development, 75*(5), 1357–1372.

Lynch, J.S., & van den Broek, P. (2007). Understanding the glue of narrative structure: Children's on- and off-line inferences about characters' goals. *Cognitive Development, 22*(3), 323–340.

Lynch, J.S., van den Broek, P., Kremer, K.E., Kendeou, P., White, M.J., & Lorch, E.P. (2008). The development of narrative comprehension and its relation to other early reading skills. *Reading Psychology, 29*(4), 327–365.

Mandler, J.M., & Johnson, N.S. (1977). Remembrance of things parsed: Story structure and recall. *Cognitive Psychology, 9*, 111–151.

McKoon, G., & Ratcliff, R. (1992). Inference during reading. *Psychological Review, 99*, 440–466.

McMaster, K.L., van den Broek, P., Espin, C.A., White, M.J., Rapp, D.N., Kendeou, P., ... Carlson, S. (2012). Making the right connections: Differential effects of reading intervention for subgroups of comprehenders. *Learning and Individual Differences, 22*(1), 100–111.

McNamara, D.S., & Magliano, J.P. (2009). Towards a comprehensive model of comprehension. In B. Ross (Ed.), *The psychology of learning and motivation.* New York, NY: Elsevier Science.

Meyer, B.J., & Freedle, R.O. (1984). Effects of discourse type on recall. *American Educational Research Journal, 21*(1), 121–143.

Meyer, B.J., & Ray, M.N. (2011). Structure strategy interventions: Increasing reading comprehension of expository text. *International Electronic Journal of Elementary Education, 4*(1), 127–152.

Miyaki, A., Friedman, N.P., Emerson, M.J., Witzki, A.H., Howerter, A., & Wagner, T.D. (2000). The unity and diversity of executive functions and their contributions to complex "frontal lobe" tasks: A latent variable analysis. *Cognitive Psychology, 41*(1), 49–100.

Oakhill, J.V. (1982). Constructive processes in skilled and less skilled comprehenders' memory for sentences. *British Journal of Psychology, 73*, 13–20.

Oakhill, J.V., & Cain, K. (2011). The precursors of reading ability in young readers: Evidence from a four-year longitudinal study. *Scientific Studies of Reading, 16*(2), 91–121.

Oakhill, J.V., Hartt, J., & Samols, D. (2005). Levels of comprehension monitoring and working memory in good and poor comprehenders. *Reading and Writing, 18*(7–9), 657–686.

Perfetti, C.A., & Hart, L. (2002). The lexical quality hypothesis. In L. Verhoeven, C. Elbro, & P. Reitsma (Eds.), *Precursors of functional literacy* (pp. 189–213). Amsterdam, The Netherlands: John Benjamins.

Perfetti, C.A., Landi, N., & Oakhill, J. (2005). The acquisition of reading comprehension skill. In M.J. Snowling & C. Hulme (Eds.), *The science of reading: A handbook* (pp. 227–247). Oxford, England: Blackwell.

Rapp, D.N., van den Broek, P., McMaster, K.L., Kendeou, P., & Espin, C.A. (2007). Higher-order comprehension processes in struggling readers: A perspective for research and intervention. *Scientific Studies of Reading, 11,* 289–312.

Sesma, H.W., Mahone, E.M., Levine, T., Eason, S.H., & Cutting, L.E. (2009). The contribution of executive skills to reading comprehension. *Child Neuropsychology, 15*(3), 232–246.

Stein, N., & Glenn, C. (1979). An analysis of story comprehension in elementary school children. In R.D. Freedle (Ed.), *Advances in discourse processes: New directions in discourse processing* (pp. 53–119). Norwood, NJ: Ablex.

Sweet, A.P., & Snow, C.E. (Eds.). (2003). *Rethinking reading comprehension.* New York, NY: Guilford Press.

Thompson, J.G., & Myers, N.A. (1985). Inferences and recall at ages four and seven. *Child Development, 56,* 1134–1144.

Trabasso, T., Secco, T., & van den Broek, P.W. (1984). Causal cohesion and story coherence. In H. Mandl, N.L. Stein, & T. Trabasso (Eds.), *Learning and comprehension of text* (pp. 83–111). Hillsdale, NJ: Erlbaum.

Trabasso, T., van den Broek, P.W., & Suh, S.Y. (1989). Logical necessity and transitivity of causal relations in stories. *Discourse Processes, 12,* 1–25.

van den Broek, P. (1994). Comprehension and memory of narrative texts: Inferences and coherence. In M.A. Gernsbacher (Ed.), *Handbook of psycholinguistics* (pp. 539–588). New York, NY: Academic Press.

van den Broek, P. (1997). Discovering the cement of the universe: The development of event comprehension from childhood to adulthood. In P. van den Broek, P.W. Bauer, & T. Bourg (Eds.), *Developmental spans in event comprehension and representation* (pp. 321–342). Mahwah, NJ: Erlbaum.

van den Broek, P. (2010). Using texts in science education: Cognitive processes and knowledge representation. *Science, 328*(5977), 453–456.

van den Broek, P., Bohn-Gettler, C., Kendeou, P., Carlson, S., & White, M.J. (2011). When a reader meets a text: The role of standards of coherence in reading comprehension. In M.T. McCrudden, J. Magliano, & G. Schraw (Eds.), *Relevance instructions and goal-focusing in text learning* (pp. 123–140). Greenwich, CT: Information Age.

van den Broek, P.W., & Espin, C.A. (2012). Connecting cognitive theory and assessment: Measuring individual differences in reading comprehension. *School Psychology Review, 41,* 315–325.

van den Broek, P.W., Helder, A., & Van Leijenhorst, L. (2012). Sensitivity to structural centrality: Developmental and individual differences in reading comprehension skills. In M.A. Britt, S.R. Goldman, & J.-F. Rouet (Eds.), *Reading: From words to multiple texts:* New York, NY: Taylor & Francis.

van den Broek, P., Kendeou, P., Lousberg, S., & Visser, G. (2011). Preparing for reading comprehension: Fostering text comprehension skills in preschool and early elementary school children. *International Electronic Journal of Elementary Education, 4,* 259–268.

van den Broek, P., Lorch, R., Linderholm, T., & Gustafson, M. (2001). The effects of readers' goals on inference generation and memory for texts. *Memory & Cognition, 29*(8), 1081–1087.

van den Broek, P., Rapp, D., & Kendeou, P. (2005). Integrating memory-based and constructionist processes in accounts of reading comprehension. *Discourse Processes, 39*(2), 299–316.

Wigfield, A., & Guthrie, J.T. (1997). Relations of children's motivation for reading to the amount and breadth of their reading. *Journal of Educational Psychology, 89,* 420–432.

Williams, J.P. (1993). Comprehension of students with and without learning disabilities: Identification of narrative themes and idiosyncratic text representations. *Journal of Educational Psychology, 85,* 631–641.

CHAPTER 6

# Reading Comprehension Difficulties in Struggling Readers

Kate Cain

Reading is a widespread and varied activity. We read different types of text for different purposes. For example, we read fiction for pleasure and entertainment; we read information (or expository) texts in order to learn new ideas and extend our knowledge; and we read e-mails, text messages, and the contents of social message boards to communicate with family and friends. Clearly, reading plays a central role in our educational, working, recreational, and social lives. Although these various reading scenarios cover a range of task-specific goals, they also include a common aim: Readers seek to understand the content of what they read. The focus of this chapter is comprehension and why some children struggle to understand what they read.

## WHAT IS INVOLVED IN READING COMPREHENSION?

Before we can examine and determine the reasons for reading comprehension failure, we must first identify what is involved in the act of comprehending. Consider the following text:

> Ruby was carrying the glass of juice. She tripped on the step. Her eyes filled with tears. Mum fetched the mop. *"Don't worry, darling,"* said Mum, *"there's no use crying over spilt milk."*

Skilled comprehenders recognize the individual words on the page and readily access their meanings. The strings of words form meaningful sentences, and skilled comprehenders identify the connections between them and integrate their meanings. In the example above, there are cohesive cues that signal some of these links: *she* and *her* and *darling* all refer back to Ruby, the main protagonist. Good memory aids the integration process: Readers need to store the meanings from individual sentences accurately in order to establish the overlap between them. In fiction, such as the foregoing passage, we want to find out what happens and why. What is the motivation for a character's action? Why does Mum fetch the mop? The text does not explicitly state that Ruby spilled some of the juice when she tripped, but that is a reasonable inference to make. In generating such inferences, to make sense of Mum's actions we use general knowledge about the likely consequences of tripping when carrying a glass of juice.

Skilled comprehenders are also sensitive to context and appreciate that Mum is not literally referring to spilt milk; rather, she is using a figurative expression.

These processes do not occur sequentially, but in parallel. Thus, comprehension is a dynamic process. The current situation model informs the recognition of subsequent words, the comprehension of the current sentence, and the interpretation of new events. By engaging in these processes during reading as well as drawing on knowledge that is external to the text (i.e., general knowledge), skilled comprehenders construct a memory-based representation of the text's meaning. This representation is not a verbatim record of the individual words or sentences; rather, it is a coherent and integrated account of the state of affairs described in the text, referred to as a *mental model* or *situation model* (Johnson-Laird, 1983; Kintsch, 1998). For skilled adult comprehenders, the act of comprehension is not cognitively demanding when the text is considerate and readers have sufficient background knowledge of the topic; but for younger and/or struggling readers the task is not so effortless, and comprehension failures can and do occur.

## WHO HAS READING COMPREHENSION DIFFICULTIES?

Reading is a complex cognitive activity: It draws on a range of knowledge bases and skills that must be coordinated to achieve successful understanding, and sufficient memory resources are required to support this. For this reason, skilled reading has been likened to the performance of a symphony orchestra (Anderson, Hiebert, Scott, & Wilkinson, 1985), and there are several potential barriers to successful comprehension.

A useful framework within which to consider the most likely sources of comprehension difficulty is the simple view of reading (Gough & Tunmer, 1986). According to this framework, reading comprehension is the product of two sets of knowledge and skills: those that enable the individual to read the words on the page in order to access their meanings and those that support comprehension of the text. The primary challenge for beginner readers is to learn to decode, but they must also draw on their existing listening comprehension skills to make sense of what they read. For young readers, reading comprehension will be limited by word-reading proficiency: thus they will be able to understand more complex texts if these are read aloud to them. For the mature reader, for whom word reading is effortless and automatic, reading and listening comprehension are strongly related and predictive of each other (Gough, Hoover, & Peterson, 1996).

Proficiency in each component of the simple view of reading lies on a continuum. Furthermore, as illustrated in Figure 6.1, three different types of poor readers exist: children with poor word recognition skills

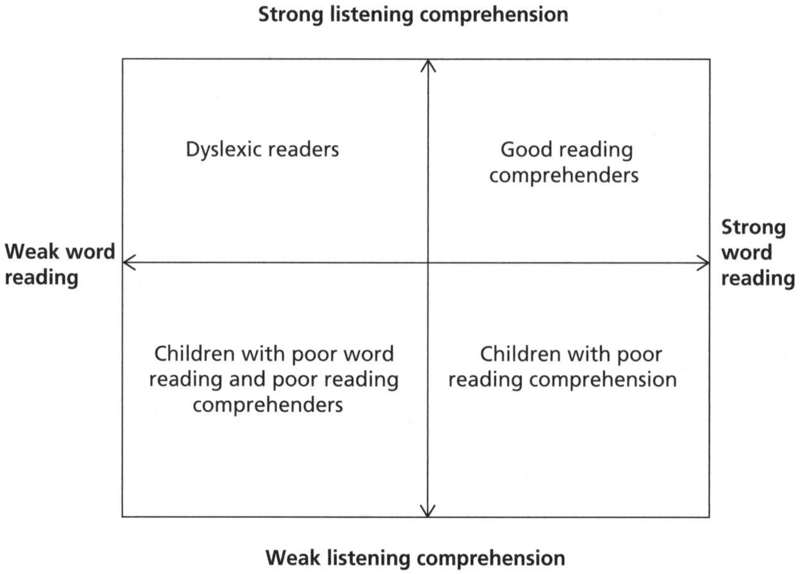


**Figure 6.1.** Different types of readers predicted by the simple view of reading.

(children with dyslexia, poor decoders), who may have relatively intact language comprehension; children with poor reading comprehension in the presence of adequate word recognition skills (poor comprehenders); and children who have poor reading comprehension because they have both poor word recognition and poor language comprehension (poor word readers and poor comprehenders). Readers with dyslexia may have reading comprehension problems when they struggle to decode an adequate number of critical words in a text. This is not always the case, however. Because their oral language skills are intact, some poor decoders probably use these oral skills to compensate for their poor word reading: as a result, they can have reading comprehension scores that exceed their word-reading ability (Catts, Adlof, & Weismer, 2006; Leach, Scarborough, & Rescorla, 2003). However, readers who lack fast and efficient word-decoding skills may be unable to retain sufficient information in memory to enable integration between sentences because their cognitive resources have been directed at word decoding (Perfetti, 1985). Thus, some readers have a secondary deficit in reading comprehension as a result of a primary deficit in decoding. For children with unexpectedly poor reading comprehension relative to their word reading, weak language comprehension is the primary source of reading comprehension difficulties. This chapter will explore how weak language comprehension and limited processing resources can result in poor reading comprehension.

## A CLOSER LOOK AT THE BARRIERS TO SUCCESSFUL COMPREHENSION

The ability to read words is essential for reading comprehension to occur. There is now a fairly consistent literature that has unpacked the word-reading component of the simple view and identified the critical factors that support its development, namely, print awareness, letter-sound knowledge, phonological processes (including phonological awareness and memory), and orthographic knowledge (Ehri, 2005). Researchers are now gaining a detailed picture of the different knowledge, skills, and resources that contribute to the language comprehension component and, therefore, serve as the critical barriers (or pressure points) to comprehension during reading development. These factors include both lower and higher level language skills (Perfetti, 2007).

Such lower level language skills as vocabulary and knowledge of grammar are needed to understand individual words and sentences. Typically, however, the reader's goal is not to understand words and sentences in isolation: rather, the goal is to relate the information between successive sentences and between what is in the text and the reader's own general knowledge in order to construct the situation model of the text's meaning. These processes of integration and inference interact with our ability to monitor our comprehension, for example, by detecting when something just read does not fit with the meaning of a previous part of the text and with our current situation model. In such instances, strategic readers may reread and/or generate an inference to ensure that the situation model is coherent. Skilled comprehenders are also guided by knowledge about text structure, which can provide a framework for processing the relations between different parts of a text and, therefore, for the construction of the situation model. Thus, reading comprehension involves both lower and higher level language skills.

Although some poor comprehenders have difficulties with both lower and higher level language skills, others have intact lower level language but weaknesses at the higher level. For example, Catts and colleagues (2006) found that poor comprehenders identified in grade 8 had poorer receptive vocabulary, grammar, and discourse comprehension than did same-age typical readers, a pattern that indicates widespread oral language comprehension difficulties. In contrast, Cain and Oakhill (2006) identified 7- to 8-year-old poor comprehenders who had age-appropriate receptive vocabulary and grammar skills. These children showed weak performance not only on a standardized measure of reading comprehension but also on experimenter-designed tasks that tap the skills critical to the construction of the situation model: integration and inference, comprehension monitoring, and knowledge and use of (narrative) text structure (see Box 6.1 for examples). Other research groups have also identified poor comprehenders with good receptive vocabulary skills (Stothard & Hulme, 1992). Thus,

**BOX 6.1**

*Extract from a Text to Assess Inference Making*

Jenny was late getting home from school. She was angry because the bus had broken down.

*Note:* Children read or listen to texts containing sentence pairs such as these. They are then asked questions to tap their ability to integrate information within the text and to generate such inferences as "Why was Jenny late home from school?"

*Example of an Inconsistency Detection Task to Assess Comprehension Monitoring*

Gorillas are clever animals that live together in groups in Africa. *Gorillas sleep on the ground on a bed of leaves and they like to eat different types of fruit.* They are shy and gentle and they hardly ever fight with each other. Gorillas have flat noses and a very poor sense of smell but their eyesight is very good. *Gorillas sleep up in trees and they often build a shelter out of leaves above them to keep out the rain.*

*Note:* Children read the text and are required to underline the bits that do not make sense. The two sentences in italics, which contain inconsistent information, are the target information. Here, the sentences are separated by filler text, which increases the working memory load. When these two sentences are adjacent, poor comprehenders are more likely to detect the inconsistency.

*Example of a Story Anagram Task Used to Assess Knowledge of Story Structure*

Once there was a farmer with a horse.
The farmer wanted to get his horse into the barn.
The horse wanted to play in the field so she wouldn't go.
The farmer went into the barn and held out some sugar.
The horse had a sweet tooth and walked into the barn.
The horse felt foolish because she had been tricked.

*Note:* Children are presented with the story as separate sentences in a randomized order and asked to rearrange the sentences into a story that makes sense. Children who have a good sense of story structure are better able to respond with the target sequence, shown above. This text is adapted from Stein and Policastro (1984).

these different patterns of language strength and weakness cannot be dismissed as spurious findings. They point to the complexity readers face when unpacking reading comprehension and how reading comprehension ability develops over time, something that we will return to later.

Cognitive resources that support language processing, such as the working memory system, are important for good reading. Children with poor word reading often have weak short-term memory: they are poorer than same-age typical readers at retaining and recalling strings of verbal stimuli (Shankweiler, Liberman, Mark, Fowler, & Fischer, 1979). Children with good word reading but poor comprehension do not typically have difficulties with short-term retention of information, but they are weak on memory tasks that require both the retention and the manipulation (or processing) of verbal information (Cain, 2006). A consistent finding across the life span is that memory tasks that tap the capacity to store and process information simultaneously are more highly predictive of reading comprehension level than are tasks that assess only storage (Shah & Miyake, 1996). This is because these more complex working memory tasks mimic, in part, the integrative processes involved in constructing the mental representation of a text's meaning. Indeed, when memory resources are stressed because information in a text has to be integrated over several sentences (as illustrated in Box 6.1), children with poor reading comprehension are particularly impaired at making inferences and detecting inconsistencies (Cain, Oakhill, & Lemmon, 2004; Catts et al., 2006; Oakhill, Hartt, & Samols, 2005).

## WHAT CAN READING COMPREHENSION DEVELOPMENT TELL US ABOUT THE SOURCES OF READING COMPREHENSION DIFFICULTIES?

By examining reading comprehension within a developmental context, we can gain insight into the knowledge bases, skills, and resources that not only drive its development but also enable good reading comprehension. In doing so, we gain a more detailed picture of the weaknesses that underlie comprehension failure.

Acquisition of good word-reading skills does not guarantee successful comprehension, as shown by the identification of children with unexpectedly poor reading comprehension in relation to their word-reading level. Similar to research into word-reading development that has sought to identify which skills and knowledge contribute to word reading, recent work has sought to identify the best concurrent (Cain, Oakhill, & Bryant, 2004; Vellutino, Tunmer, Jaccard, & Chen, 2007) and longitudinal predictors (Oakhill & Cain, 2012) of reading comprehension. The following key findings emerge. Specific discourse skills that aid the ability to construct meaning from text—inference and integration, comprehension monitoring, and knowledge and use of text structure—each account for unique variance in concurrent measures of reading comprehension at ages 8, 9, and 11, over and above vocabulary knowledge, word reading, and general verbal ability (Cain, Oakhill, et al., 2004). In addition, working memory makes a separate contribution to reading comprehension performance (Cain, Oakhill, et al., 2004). When we look across time, discourse skills explain reading comprehension development from 8 to 11 years of age, in addition to verbal IQ and vocabulary (Oakhill & Cain, 2012). Thus, the meaning-making skills that are weak in poor comprehenders predict reading comprehension development in unselected samples.

Comprehension of extended discourse develops before literacy instruction begins: Children enjoy sharing storybooks and personal narratives from an early age (Reese & Newcombe, 2007). Thus, it is not surprising to find that oral language skills, including vocabulary, inferencing, and integration, are related to preschoolers' comprehension of spoken text (Florit, Roch, & Levorato, 2011; Lynch et al., 2008) and that these, in turn, are related to later reading comprehension (Kendeou, van den Broek, White, & Lynch, 2009).

Longitudinal studies also reveal the interactive nature of language and literacy development. Oakhill and Cain (2012) found that reading comprehension at 8 years influenced later inferential and comprehension monitoring skills, which, in turn, influenced reading comprehension outcomes. A similar pattern was found between early vocabulary, inferencing, and reading comprehension. Other work has also found reciprocal relationships between comprehension and vocabulary (Verhoeven, van Leeuwe, & Vermeer, 2011). Together, these studies point to the need to consider the dynamics of development when we consider which skills might be associated with reading comprehension and why.

## WHAT DO LONGITUDINAL STUDIES OF POOR COMPREHENDERS TELL US ABOUT THE CAUSES AND CONSEQUENCES OF POOR READING COMPREHENSION?

Research that has tracked the progress of poor comprehenders over time can identify potential earlier predictors of poor reading comprehension and likely consequences of this reading profile. Retrospective studies of poor comprehenders in childhood indicate that oral language comprehension problems are present from an early age. Nation, Cocksey, Taylor, and Bishop (2010) found that poor comprehenders identified at 8 years had weaker vocabulary and sentence comprehension than controls aged 6 and 7 years. A study by Catts and colleagues (2006), which covered a longer period in development, found that 13- to 14-year-old poor comprehenders had vocabulary, grammar, and discourse-level weaknesses evident from kindergarten. Together with the longitudinal work of Kendeou et al. (2009), these studies suggest that oral language comprehension skills are potential preliteracy markers of later reading comprehension difficulties.

More evidence is required before we can draw firm conclusions about whether we need to include just one or all of these skills in any early diagnostic battery because for some children, early language comprehension difficulties resolve themselves; when that occurs, the initial difficulties do not lead to later literacy problems (Bishop & Adams, 1990). In addition, different skills may emerge as the best predictors at different points in development, as has been found for word-reading development (Scarborough, 2005). We should also consider whether particular combinations of factors place children at greater risk of reading comprehension difficulties and/or more general language comprehension weaknesses. For example, the poor comprehenders studied by Catts et al. (2006) and Nation et al. (2010) had weak (though not diagnostically impaired) performance IQ. In contrast, poor comprehenders with age-appropriate nonverbal IQ have been found to have intact receptive vocabulary and grammar (Cain & Oakhill, 2006). Together with the evidence that nonverbal IQ affects the language and literacy outcomes of children with specific language impairment (Bishop & Adams, 1990), this finding points to the need to determine whether nonverbal IQ is simply a general correlate or something more specific, such as an index of learning capacity and wider difficulties. Clearly, future research should consider measures beyond those tapping language and ensure the testing of interactions between different potential causal factors in research models.

Without intervention, poor comprehenders do not become better comprehenders over time; typically, they also have poorer educational outcomes (Cain & Oakhill, 2006). They may also be at risk for *emerging* broader language weaknesses. We know that reading comprehension and inference skills are associated with the ability to derive the meanings of new words from context (Cain, Oakhill, et al., 2004). We also know that across the life span, growth in vocabulary is related to literacy habits, probably because reading affords learning opportunities (Cain & Oakhill, 2011; Stanovich, 1993). Perhaps, then, it is not surprising that prospective longitudinal work reports reduced growth in written and receptive vocabulary knowledge between 8 and 11 years for poor comprehenders (Cain & Oakhill, 2011). A similar pattern has been found for poor comprehenders' morphosyntactic skills (Tong, Deacon, Kirby, Cain, & Parrila, 2011). Again, we may be looking at complex reciprocal relationships: vocabulary and morphosyntax will influence comprehension of discourse, but the quality and level of reading comprehension experiences may influence vocabulary and grammar use and their development, resulting in emergent differences between good and poor comprehenders during middle childhood.

## THE DYNAMICS OF THE READING COMPREHENSION PROCESS

Thus far, we have looked at research that has measured the *product* of reading comprehension; but as described earlier, reading comprehension is a dynamic process that occurs in real time. Thus, the quality of the situation model will be influenced by how readily readers access information from long-term memory, such as vocabulary and background knowledge relevant to the topic of the text, and use cues within a text that signal integration as they are reading.

As discussed earlier, not all poor comprehenders have poor vocabulary knowledge (Cain, Oakhill, et al., 2004; Stothard & Hulme, 1992), but differences in the quality of that knowledge and/or how readily it is accessed might influence the on-line processing of text. This idea sits at the core of the lexical quality hypothesis (Perfetti, 2007), which specifies what it is about word-level knowledge that might limit text comprehension skill. A high-quality lexical representation for a given word is one for which the lexical representation of the form and meaning components is both precise and flexible. The reader who can retrieve the appropriate representation for a written word in a given context will have greater cognitive resources available for other aspects of the meaning-construction process, such as inference (Perfetti, 2007). In relation to this, although adults do not activate the implied instrument *hammer,* on reading the sentence *"He pounded the wooden planks together"* they do activate related features (Harmon-Vukic, Gueraud, Lassonde, & O'Brien, 2009; see also Chapter 15, this volume), which will aid subsequent integration and inference making if required.

We can apply a similar argument to the availability and use of background knowledge, which is critical for generating inferences and making sense of text (Cromley & Azevedo, 2007). Young readers and poorer comprehenders' inference-making skills cannot be explained simply by availability of the necessary background knowledge (Cain, Oakhill, Barnes, & Bryant, 2001); but for young readers, at least, accessibility is important: Facts that are more speedily accessed are more likely to be integrated with information presented in a text to generate necessary inferences (Barnes, Dennis, & Haefele-Kalvaitis, 1996). Together with the work on vocabulary, these studies suggest that we need to look more closely not only at the activation of knowledge but also at how easily and readily young readers incorporate what is relevant into their current situation model. Doing so will help researchers better understand how knowledge availability and accessibility interact to influence the on-line construction of a situation model.

Integration of new information into the situation model is not always strongly guided by word meanings. For example, pronouns such as *he* and *they* carry little meaning other than that the referent is male or a group, respectively; these words take their meaning from their referent. Thus, the reader who readily resolves a pronoun will be able to construct a more fully integrated and accurate situation model. A critical factor in pronoun resolution for poor comprehenders is its proximity to the referent: Distant antecedents are harder to resolve (Megherbi & Ehrlich, 2005; Yuill & Oakhill, 1988). Connectives are another class of cohesive devices that act as processing signals specifying temporal and causal relations between events. Younger children and poorer comprehenders are poor at using these signals in off-line tasks (Cain & Nash, 2011; Cain, Patson, & Andrews, 2005). Researchers are currently exploring how connectives influence poor comprehenders' on-line processing and memory representation of text.

There is clearly a need for more work on the dynamics of text processing in poor comprehenders because studies of the dynamics of comprehension to date paint a complex picture. Children with poor comprehension make eye movements to likely referents as readily as do good comprehenders when processing sentences (Nation, Marshall, & Altmann, 2003), and adult poor comprehenders show appropriate activation of word knowledge (Gernsbacher & Faust, 1991), although see also Perfetti, Stafura, and Adlof (Chapter 3, this volume). These findings suggest that the dynamics of text processing are intact. If so, why do poor comprehenders construct less accurate and coherent situation models than do peers? One explanation is that their ability to select the *appropriate* meanings of words in a given context and to encode integrative relations is weak: Thus, their management of the information stored in working memory and the situation model is impaired. Future research needs to explore the locus of difficulty in young children's on-line language comprehension.

## SUMMARY AND CONCLUSIONS

In this chapter, I have outlined how weaknesses in knowledge, skills, and processing resources can affect children's and adults' comprehension of written text. Because these difficulties are apparent in tasks in which text is spoken aloud, researchers have to look beyond word decoding to understand why, for some individuals, comprehension breaks down. In the search for the cause of reading comprehension difficulties, researchers must be mindful of the complexity of reading comprehension. Given the range of factors that contribute to reading comprehension, investigators will be unlikely to find either a consistent single profile of the poor comprehender or a single cause of comprehension failure. More likely is that several factors interact to influence the range and or severity of associated difficulties, the development of reading comprehension across time, and the on-line construction of a coherent and integrated representation of a text's meaning.

## REFERENCES


Anderson, R.C., Hiebert, E., Scott, J., & Wilkinson, I. (1985). *Becoming a nation of readers: The report of the Commission on Reading.* Urbana, IL: Center for the Study of Reading.

Barnes, M.A., Dennis, M., & Haefele-Kalvaitis, J. (1996). The effects of knowledge availability and knowledge accessibility on coherence and elaborative inferencing in children from six to fifteen years of age. *Journal of Experimental Child Psychology, 61,* 216–241.

Bishop, D.V.M., & Adams, C. (1990). A prospective study of the relationship between specific language impairment, phonological disorders and reading retardation. *Journal of Child Psychology and Psychiatry, 31,* 1027–1050.

Cain, K. (2006). Individual differences in children's memory and reading comprehension: An investigation of semantic and inhibitory deficits. *Memory, 14,* 553–569.

Cain, K., & Nash, H. (2011). The influence of connectives on young readers' processing and comprehension of text. *Journal of Educational Psychology, 103,* 429–441.

Cain, K., & Oakhill, J. (2006). Profiles of children with specific reading comprehension difficulties. *British Journal of Educational Psychology, 76,* 683–696.

Cain, K., & Oakhill, J.V. (2011). Matthew Effects in young readers: Reading comprehension and reading experience aid vocabulary development. *Journal of Learning Disabilities, 44,* 431–443.

Cain, K., Oakhill, J.V., Barnes, M.A., & Bryant, P.E. (2001). Comprehension skill, inference making ability and their relation to knowledge. *Memory and Cognition, 29,* 850–859.

Cain, K., Oakhill, J.V., & Bryant, P.E. (2004). Children's reading comprehension ability: Concurrent prediction by working memory, verbal ability, and component skills. *Journal of Educational Psychology, 96,* 671–681.

Cain, K., Oakhill, J., & Lemmon, K. (2004). Individual differences in the inference of word meanings from context: The influence of reading comprehension, vocabulary knowledge, and memory capacity. *Journal of Educational Psychology, 96,* 671–681.

Cain, K., Patson, N., & Andrews, L. (2005). Age- and ability-related differences in young readers' use of conjunctions. *Journal of Child Language, 32,* 877–892.

Catts, H.W., Adlof, S.M., & Weismer, S.E. (2006). Language deficits in poor comprehenders: A case for the simple view of reading. *Journal of Speech, Language, and Hearing Research, 49*, 278–293.

Cromley, J.G., & Azevedo, R. (2007). Testing and refining the direct and inferential mediation model of reading comprehension. *Journal of Educational Psychology, 99*, 311–325.

Ehri, L.C. (2005). Learning to read words: Theory, findings, and issues. *Scientific Studies of Reading, 9*(2), 167–188.

Florit, E., Roch, M., & Levorato, M.C. (2011). Listening text comprehension of explicit and implicit information in preschoolers: The role of verbal and inferential skills. *Discourse Processes, 48*, 119–138.

Gernsbacher, M.A., & Faust, M. (1991). The mechanism of suppression: A component of general comprehension skill. *Journal of Experimental Psychology: Learning, Memory and Cognition, 17*, 245–262.

Gough, P.B., Hoover, W.A., & Peterson, C.L. (1996). Some observations on a simple view of reading. In C. Cornoldi & J. Oakhill (Eds.), *Reading comprehension difficulties: Processes and interventions* (pp. 1–13). Mahwah, NJ: Erlbaum.

Gough, P.B., & Tunmer, W.E. (1986). Decoding, reading and reading disability. *Remedial and Special Education, 7*, 6–10.

Harmon-Vukic, M., Gueraud, S., Lassonde, K., & O'Brien, E.J. (2009). The activation and instantiation of instrumental inferences. *Discourse Processes, 46*, 467–490.

Johnson-Laird, P.N. (1983). *Mental models: Towards a cognitive science of language, inference, and consciousness.* Cambridge, England: Cambridge University Press.

Kendeou, P., van den Broek, P., White, M., & Lynch, J.S. (2009). Predicting reading comprehension in early elementary school: The independent contributions of oral language and decoding skills. *Journal of Educational Psychology, 101*, 765–778.

Kintsch, W. (1998). *Comprehension: A paradigm for cognition.* New York, NY: Cambridge University Press.

Leach, J.M., Scarborough, H.S., & Rescorla, L. (2003). Late-emerging reading disabilities. *Journal of Educational Psychology, 95*, 211–224.

Lynch, J.S., van den Broek, P., Kremer, K., Kendeou, P., White, M.J., & Lorch, E.P. (2008). The development of narrative comprehension and its relation to other early reading skills. *Reading Psychology, 29*, 327–365.

Megherbi, H., & Ehrlich, M.-F. (2005). Language impairment in less skilled comprehenders: The on-line processing of anaphoric pronouns in a listening situation. *Reading and Writing, 18*(7–9), 715–753.

Nation, K., Cocksey, J., Taylor, J.S.H., & Bishop, D.V.M. (2010). A longitudinal investigation of early reading and language skills in children with poor reading comprehension. *Journal of Child Psychology and Psychiatry, 51*, 1031–1039.

Nation, K., Marshall, C.M., & Altmann, G.T.M. (2003). Investigating individual differences in children's real-time sentence comprehension using language-mediated eye movements. *Journal of Experimental Child Psychology, 86*, 314–329.

Oakhill, J.V., & Cain, K. (2012). The precursors of reading comprehension and word reading in young readers: Evidence from a four-year longitudinal study. *Scientific Studies of Reading, 16*(2), 91–121.

Oakhill, J.V., Hartt, J., & Samols, D. (2005). Levels of comprehension monitoring and working memory in good and poor comprehenders. *Reading and Writing, 18*, 657–713.

Perfetti, C.A. (1985). *Reading ability.* New York, NY: Oxford University Press.

Perfetti, C.A. (2007). Reading ability: Lexical quality to comprehension. *Scientific Studies of Reading, 11*, 357–383.

Reese, E., & Newcombe, R. (2007). Training mothers in elaborative reminiscing enhances children's autobiographical memory and narrative [Article]. *Child Development, 78*, 1153–1170.

Scarborough, H. (2005). Developmental relationships between language and reading: Reconciling a beautiful hypothesis with some ugly facts. In H.W. Catts & A.G. Kamhi (Eds.), *The connections between language and reading disabilities* (pp. 3–24). Mahwah, NJ: Erlbaum.

Shah, P., & Miyake, A. (1996). The separability of working memory resources for spatial thinking and language processing: An individual differences approach. *Journal of Experimental Psychology: General, 125*, 4–27.

Shankweiler, D., Liberman, I.Y., Mark, L.M., Fowler, C.A., & Fischer, F.W. (1979).

The speech code and learning to read. *Journal of Experimental Psychology: Human Learning and Memory, 5,* 521–545.
Stanovich, K.E. (1993). Does reading make you smarter? Literacy and the development of verbal intelligence. In H. Reese (Ed.), *Advances in child development and behavior* (Vol. 24, pp. 133–180). New York, NY: Academic Press.
Stein, N.L., & Policastro, M. (1984). The concept of a story: A comparison between children's and teachers' viewpoints. In H. Mandl, N.L. Stein, & T. Trabasso (Eds.), *Learning and comprehension of text* (pp. 113–155). Hillsdale, NJ: Ablex.
Stothard, S.E., & Hulme, C. (1992). Reading comprehension difficulties in children: The role of language comprehension and working memory skills. *Reading and Writing, 4,* 245–256.
Tong, X., Deacon, S.H., Kirby, J., Cain, K., & Parrila, R. (2011). Morphological awareness: A key to understanding poor reading comprehension in English. *Journal of Educational Psychology, 103,* 523–534.
Vellutino, F.R., Tunmer, W.E., Jaccard, J.J., & Chen, R. (2007). Components of reading ability: Multivariate evidence for a convergent skill model of reading development. *Scientific Studies of Reading, 11,* 3–32.
Verhoeven, L., van Leeuwe, J., & Vermeer, A. (2011). Vocabulary growth and reading development across the elementary years. *Scientific Studies of Reading, 15,* 8–25.
Yuill, N., & Oakhill, J. (1988). Understanding of anaphoric relations in skilled and less skilled comprehenders. *British Journal of Psychology, 79,* 173–186.

# CHAPTER 7
# Oral Language Disorders and Reading Comprehension Problems

Hugh W. Catts

Reading comprehension is among our most complex cognitive abilities. The complexity of this ability has represented a significant challenge for researchers and practitioners who have tried to understand and intervene with problems in reading comprehension. To address this challenge, Gough and Tunmer (1986) proposed the simple view of reading model. This view is not a simplistic view of reading but, rather, one that divides the complexities of reading into two components: word recognition and language or listening comprehension. By making this division, the simple view highlights the importance of language processes in reading comprehension and has led many to consider the relationship between oral and written language development and disorders (e.g., Catts, Adlof, & Ellis Weismer, 2006). In this chapter, I review research that has examined the association between oral language impairments and difficulties in reading comprehension from two perspectives. First, I consider the reading outcomes of children with oral language impairment; and second, I examine the language abilities of children with problems in reading comprehension. I also suggest how the simple view of reading can be used to subgroup readers at different grades. Finally, I provide a brief consideration of the clinical and educational implications of this work.

## ORAL LANGUAGE IMPAIRMENT

The oral language impairment that has been examined most often in relationship to reading disabilities is specific language impairment (SLI; Catts & Kamhi, 2012), which is a disorder involving the delayed and protracted development of spoken language abilities in the absence of difficulties in other areas of development. In defining SLI, deficits in hearing and broader cognitive abilities are typically ruled out. Children with SLI have numerous language and cognitive deficits that could lead to difficulties in learning to read. They are slow to learn words, have limited vocabularies, and have word retrieval problems (Gray, 2004; Kail & Leonard, 1986; Leonard, Miller, & Gerber, 1999; McGregor, 1997). They also have impairments in grammatical understanding and narrative comprehension (Bishop, Bright, James, Bishop, & van der Lely, 2000; Fey, Catts, Proctor-Williams, Tomblin, & Zhang, 2004; van der Lely, 1998). Other deficits include difficulties in phonological awareness (Catts, 1993; Kamhi & Catts, 1986), phonological memory (Dollaghan & Campbell, 1998; Ellis Weismer et al., 2000; Kamhi & Catts, 1986; Kamhi, Catts, Mauer, D., Apel, & Gentry, 1988), and broader deficits in speed of processing and/or working memory (Archibald & Gathercole, 2006; Miller, Kail, Leonard, & Tomblin, 2001).

## Reading Outcomes

Numerous studies have examined the reading comprehension abilities of children with a history of SLI (e.g., Bishop & Adams, 1990; Catts, 1993). The most comprehensive study to date has been the Iowa Longitudinal Study (Catts, Bridges, Little, & Tomblin, 2008; Catts, Fey, Tomblin, & Zhang, 2002). In this study, 226 children with language impairment (LI) and 379 children with typical language were identified in kindergarten and followed through 10th grade. Children with LI were divided into those with nonverbal IQ greater than 85 (SLI, *N* = 123) and those with nonverbal IQ less than 85 (nonspecific language impairment, NLI, *N* = 103). In second, fourth, eighth, and tenth grades, children were administered measures of word recognition and reading comprehension. To assess word reading, we gave the Word Identification and Word Attack subtests from the Woodcock Reading Mastery Tests–Revised (WRMT-R; Woodcock, 1997). To measure reading comprehension, we administered the Passage Comprehension subtest from the WRMT-R, the Gray Oral Reading Test–3 (Wiederholt & Bryant, 1992) and the Diagnostic Assessment Battery–2 (DAB-2; Newcomer, 1990). In eighth and tenth grades, the Qualitative Reading Inventory–2 (Leslie & Caldwell, 1995) was substituted for the DAB-2. The individual measures of word recognition and reading comprehension were converted to *z*-scores and combined to form composite measures for each construct.

Figure 7.1 shows the percentage of children in the SLI, NLI, and typical groups who had a deficit in reading comprehension in each of the various grades. Children were defined as having a deficit in reading comprehension if they scored at least one standard deviation below the mean, which was based on local weighted norms. Results showed that approximately 40% of kindergarten children with SLI and 65% of those with NLI had a subsequent deficit in reading comprehension. These rates were about five or eight times greater, respectively, than that of children with typical language. It should also be noted that whereas some children with a history of SLI or NLI did not meet the definition of having a reading comprehension deficit, few of these children had good reading comprehension. For example, in second grade, only 11% of children with SLI and 3% of those with NLI scored above the mean on the composite score of reading comprehension. Most of the latter children also no longer met the definition for a language impairment.

Many children with SLI and NLI also had a deficit in word recognition. Our results showed that about 30% of children with SLI and 55% of those

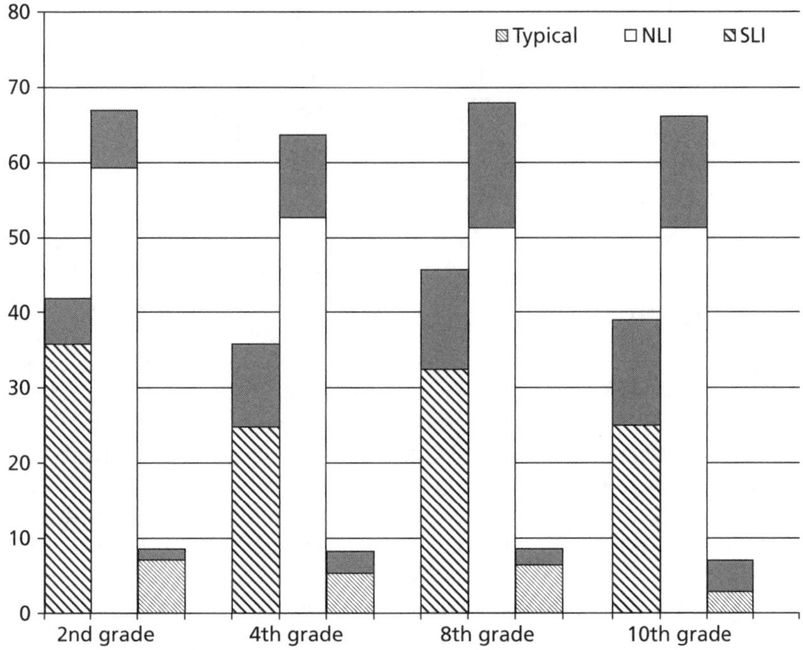


**Figure 7.1.** Percentage of children in the specific language impairment (SLI), nonspecific language impairment (NLI), and typical subgroups who had reading comprehension deficits in second, fourth, eighth, and tenth grades. Shaded portion refers to those individuals with specific comprehension deficits.

with NLI had a deficit in word reading across the school grades. Catts, Adlof, Hogan, and Ellis Weismer (2005) reported that about 20%–25% of children with SLI also met a typical definition for dyslexia. Whereas many children with LI had both word-reading and reading comprehension deficits, a small proportion of children with LI had specific deficits in reading comprehension (i.e., word-reading ability was greater than the 30th percentile). The latter children are sometimes referred to as poor comprehenders and are represented by the darker portion of the bars in Figure 7.1. In general, about one third to one quarter of children with LI were poor comprehenders. As seen in Figure 7.1, the proportion doubled as children moved into the fourth and/or eighth grades. As such, these children could be described as having late-emerging reading disabilities. Presumably these reading problems did not emerge until the demands on language became more prominent in later grades.

## Late-Emerging Reading Disorders

Late-emerging reading disabilities not only are present in children with a history of LI but also occur in the general population (Leach, Scarborough,

& Rescorla, 2003). Recently, my colleagues and I used the Iowa Longitudinal data set to more directly investigate the prevalence and nature of late-emerging poor readers (Catts, Compton, Tomblin, & Bridges, 2012). In this study, we employed latent transition analyses to explore intra-individual change across grades in latent variables representing word reading and reading comprehension (e.g., Bollen & Curran, 2006). We first classified children as good or poor readers on the basis of word-reading or reading comprehension scores at second, fourth, eighth, or tenth grades. Four reading classes were possible at each grade. These were good readers, poor readers with deficits in word reading, poor readers with deficits in comprehension, or poor readers with deficits in both areas. Latent transition analysis was then used to identify children who changed class from one grade to another. With the latent transition model, a total of 512 different latent change classes were possible: 2 classes representing children who moved or stayed in a class from one grade to the next times $4^4$ (4 possible reading classes at each of four grades). Only 26 of the 512 possible classes (5%) were represented in the data, and these classes could further be reduced to 5 general classes. Analyses showed that the largest percentage of children (67.9%) were in a class representing good readers across grades. Another 18.7% of children showed deficits in either word reading or comprehension in second grade and, for the most part, had problems that were persistent across grades. The remaining 13.4% of the children fell into one of three late-emerging poor reader classes. These were late-emerging poor readers with comprehension deficits (7.0%), late-emerging poor readers with word-reading deficits (4.8%), or late-emerging poor readers with deficits in both areas (1.6%). Our results further showed that the vast majority of transitions took place between second and fourth grades, with far fewer occurring between fourth and eighth grades, and a negligible number occurring between eighth and tenth grades. In addition, children changing classes from one grade to the next were not simply those moving from one side of a cut-score to the other but, rather, ones making a sizable change in reading scores (>0.5 *SD* on average). Additional analyses showed that 46% of the late-emerging poor readers had a history of SLI or NLI and the remainder had normal language development. Thus, these results show a strong link between SLI, poor comprehenders, and late-emerging poor readers.

## POOR COMPREHENDERS

The relationship between oral language impairments and reading comprehension problems can also be examined from the perspective of poor comprehenders. As noted above, children referred to as poor comprehenders have adequate word-reading abilities but deficits in reading comprehension. In recent years, researchers have begun to examine the cognitive-linguistic abilities of these children in search of potential causal factors for their comprehension problems. This work has shown that poor comprehenders have deficits in vocabulary and grammar, as well as discourse-level language processing (Cain, Oakhill, Barnes, & Bryant, 2001; Nation, Clarke, Marshall, & Durand, 2004). In the Iowa Longitudinal Study, we also investigated the language abilities of poor comprehenders (Catts et al., 2006). We identified three subgroups of children from our longitudinal sample based on their strengths and weaknesses in word reading and reading comprehension in eighth grade. We chose to use eighth-grade reading scores rather than second- or fourth-grade scores because word-reading and reading comprehension performances were more independent by eighth grade. We identified a subgroup of 57 poor comprehenders who scored below the 25th percentile in reading comprehension and above the 40th percentile in word recognition and a subgroup of 27 poor decoders who scored below the 25th percentile in word reading but above the 40th percentile in reading comprehension. The third subgroup included 98 typical readers who performed between the 40th and 84th percentile in both aspects of reading. Analysis of variance showed that typical readers did not differ significantly from poor comprehenders in word reading and from poor decoders in reading comprehension, but they did differ significantly from these subgroups in their particular deficit areas.

In one set of analyses, we compared reading subgroups on concurrent measures of language abilities. In these and other analyses concerning poor comprehenders, we used weighted scores to reduce the potential bias that might result from our sample having more children with language impairments than a more representative sample. Analyses indicated that poor comprehenders performed significantly less well than did typical readers and poor decoders in receptive vocabulary and significantly less well than did typical readers in grammatical understanding. Whereas the poor comprehenders scored lower in grammatical understanding than did poor decoders, the difference was not significant. The poor comprehenders were also found to have significantly poorer abilities in discourse comprehension and inference making than did typical readers and poor decoders. One area of strength for poor comprehenders was phonological processing. Poor comprehenders performed at a comparable level to typical readers and significantly better than poor decoders in phoneme deletion and nonword repetition.

In a second set of analyses, we looked retrospectively at the earlier language abilities of the three reading subgroups. Measures were available for vocabulary, grammar, discourse, and phonological processing in kindergarten, second grade, and fourth grade. Again, poor comprehenders performed less well than did the children in the other subgroups across grades on measures of vocabulary, grammar, and discourse. However, for the most part, they performed comparably to typical readers and significantly better than did poor decoders on measures of phonological processing. We further compared subgroups in terms of kindergarten diagnosis of language impairments. Results showed that only a small percentage of typical readers (4.4%) and poor decoders (8.5%) met the diagnostic criteria for SLI or NLI in kindergarten. On the other hand, 32% of poor comprehenders had a history of SLI or NLI. Although many poor comprehenders had LI, most had language problems in the subclinical range. Nevertheless, these "hidden deficits," as Nation et al. (2004) referred to them, could work by themselves, or in combination with other factors, to cause problems in reading comprehension. Alternatively, some of the language problems of poor comprehenders may actually be the result of their reading disability. That is, because of their reading problems, poor comprehenders likely gain less vocabulary and acquire less literate language knowledge than do children in other subgroups.

In further analyses, we examined how poor comprehenders and decoders (based on eighth-grade reading) had performed in reading achievement in second and fourth grades. Data showed that subgroup differences in word recognition observed in eighth grade were equally apparent at the earlier grades. However, this was not the case for subgroup differences in reading comprehension. Poor comprehenders identified at eighth grade were less impaired in reading comprehension in the earlier grades and, in fact, performed equal to or better than poor decoders on several of the comprehension measures in these grades. This result is not surprising because measures of reading comprehension in the early school grades are particularly dependent on word recognition skills (Francis, Fletcher, Catts, & Tomblin, 2005). The observation that subgroup differences in reading comprehension in the early grades differ from those in the later grades represents a significant challenge for identifying subgroups based on reading comprehension. That is, children identified as poor comprehenders at one grade may not be identified as poor comprehenders at other grades.

## Classifying Poor Readers Based on the Simple View of Reading Model

The above findings suggest that rather than classifying readers based on reading comprehension (and word recognition), another approach may be necessary to assure more classification stability for poor comprehenders from one grade to the next. One such approach would be to subgroup readers on the basis of the simple view of reading. Recall that the simple view proposes that reading comprehension is the product of word reading and listening comprehension (Gough & Tunmer, 1986). Numerous studies have shown that word recognition and listening comprehension are relatively independent of each other but highly correlated with reading comprehension (Catts, Hogan, & Adlof, 2005; Hoover & Gough, 1990). Furthermore, investigations employing multiple regression analyses have shown that when these components are combined, they account for a large proportion of the variance in reading comprehension (Aaron, Joshi, & Williams, 1999; Catts et al., 2005; de Jong & van der Leij, 2002).

The simple view predicts the occurrence of four subgroups of children who differ in their relative strengths and/or weaknesses in word recognition and listening comprehension. Some children would be expected to have deficits in word recognition but relatively good listening comprehension. This subgroup of children would generally be considered to have dyslexia (Lyon, Shaywitz, & Shaywitz, 2003). A second subgroup is predicted to have poor listening comprehension and relatively good word recognition. Children in this subgroup may be said to have a specific comprehension deficit. (These children would not necessarily qualify as poor comprehenders unless they also had problems in reading comprehension.) A third subgroup is predicted to have problems in both word recognition and listening comprehension. This subgroup might be considered to have a mixed disability (Catts & Kamhi, 2012). A final subgroup, the largest in size, would include children with typical abilities in both word recognition and listening comprehension.

Although children are not subgrouped on the basis of reading comprehension in this system, we would expect to find varying degrees of impairments in reading comprehension across the subgroups. Children with deficits in word recognition and listening comprehension would most likely have problems in reading comprehension, whereas those with typical abilities in these reading components would not be expected to have comprehension problems. Children with dyslexia and a specific comprehension deficit would also be likely to have problems in reading comprehension. However, this need not be the case if these children had strengths in other areas that allowed them to compensate for their deficit area.

To investigate how subgroups differed in reading comprehension, children from the Iowa Longitudinal Study were classified based on the simple view. In this analysis, second-grade word recognition and listening comprehension scores were used. We used second-grade scores to subgroup children because we were interested in classifying children in an early grade and examining how their problems in reading comprehension changed across grades. Children were considered to have a deficit in word recognition or listening comprehension if their performance was more than one standard deviation below the mean in the target ability. A similar criterion was used to identify children with deficits in reading comprehension. Weighted analyses were again used to control for the fact that we had more children in our sample with language impairments than are found in the general population.

A weighted frequency analysis demonstrated that 75.5% of the children were classified in the typical subgroup, 8.2% in the dyslexic group, 10.0% in the specific comprehension subgroup, and 6.3% in the mixed subgroup. Table 7.1 shows that the percentage of children with reading comprehension problems in second grade varied across subgroups. The vast majority of children in the mixed subgroup (83.7%) and a large proportion of children

**Table 7.1.** Percentage of children with comprehension problems in each simple view subgroup in second and eighth grades

| | Dyslexia | Mixed | SCD | Typical |
|---|---|---|---|---|
| Second grade | 58.8 | 83.7 | 24.8 | 3.3 |
| Eighth grade | 26.3 | 64.5 | 40.1 | 6.6 |

*Key:* SCD, specific comprehension deficit.

in the dyslexic subgroup (58.8%) had reading comprehension problems. Only 24.8% of the children in the specific comprehension deficit subgroup and 3.3% in the typical subgroup had problems in reading comprehension. The small percentage of children in the specific comprehension subgroup who had reading comprehension problems is likely a reflection of the relative importance of word recognition, and not listening comprehension, in reading comprehension difficulties at second grade. However, by eighth grade, language factors likely play a more important role. In fact, our results showed that the percentage of children with a specific comprehension deficit in second grade who had reading comprehension problems in eighth grade (40.1%) had nearly doubled from second grade. Again consistent with this view is the fact that far fewer children with dyslexia had problems in reading comprehension in eighth grade (26.3%) as compared to second grade (58.8%).

These data also show that while problems in listening comprehension in second grade were an antecedent to deficits in reading comprehension in eighth grade for many children, a large percentage of poor comprehenders at eighth grade had normal listening comprehension abilities at second grade (i.e., many came from the typical subgroup). Actually, in terms of percentages, more children with reading comprehension deficits in eighth grade were unimpaired (32.7%) rather than impaired (26.8%) in listening comprehension in second grade. Thus, these data indicate that early deficits in listening comprehension (at least severe deficits) cannot account for a large proportion of the problems in reading comprehension in later grades. To more fully understand the causal basis of reading comprehension problems, we will also need to consider factors other than listening comprehension (and word reading).

## IMPLICATIONS FOR IDENTIFICATION AND INTERVENTION

Despite the fact that language problems do not account for all reading comprehension difficulties, there is a clear association between problems in oral language development and poor outcomes in reading comprehension. Such an association highlights the need to identify children with oral language impairments early in development and provide them with appropriate intervention. Children with severe language impairments can often be identified through parent referral or screening by speech-language pathologists. However, to identify children with less severe but potentially significant language problems, it may be necessary to rely on universal screening approaches. Universal screening typically involves administering brief assessments to all school-age children one or more times a year (Jenkins, Hudson, & Johnson, 2007). Unfortunately, most research on universal screening has focused on word reading and associated language problems (e.g., phonological awareness deficits). Studies have not generally examined the full range of oral language abilities that may underlie problems in reading comprehension. In our work, however, we have shown that to identify children at risk for problems in reading comprehension, screening instruments will need to include measures of grammar or narration (Adlof, Catts, & Lee, 2010). Even with these measures included, screening batteries may not be successful in accurately identifying children with comprehension problems, especially those with specific comprehension deficits and/or those who demonstrate late-emerging reading disorders. For example, Catts et al. (2012) found that although late-emerging poor readers often had a profile that included problems in grammar and narration, these problems were generally mild and were shared by at least some children with normal reading achievement.

One potential approach that could improve the accuracy of language screening is dynamic assessment. In dynamic assessment, children are provided feedback during testing in order to differentiate those who have "true" language deficits from those who do not. Most reading-related dynamic assessments have been directed toward word-reading skills or related language abilities (Bridges & Catts, 2011; Fuchs, Compton, Fuchs, Bouton, & Caffrey, 2011). However, several groups of investigators have developed dynamic assessments of narrative comprehension that may be predictive of reading comprehension problems (Elleman, Compton, Fuchs, Fuchs, & Bouton, 2012; Pena et al., 2006), but more work is necessary to fully understand the potential of this approach.

Once identified, children at risk for reading comprehension problems should receive intervention directed at their language deficits. Unfortunately, only limited research is available at this point to guide practitioners in choosing specific language interventions and protocols that can significantly reduce problems in reading comprehension. In most cases, language intervention outcomes have been assessed in terms of the impact on oral language comprehension, and relatively little is known about the effect of this intervention on reading comprehension. There is, however, an emerging body of work with some direct implications. For example, Nelson and Stage (2007) showed that a contextually based multiple-meaning vocabulary intervention improved both vocabulary and reading comprehension in elementary school children. In a somewhat related study, Zipke, Ehri, and Cairns (2009) reported that instruction on metalinguistic awareness of semantic ambiguity had a positive impact on reading comprehension. Beyond vocabulary, Williams, Stafford, Lauer, Hall, and Pollini (2009) have shown that an intervention that included instruction of expository text structure (compare-contrast) and clue words significantly influenced oral and written language outcomes. Finally, Garner and Bochna (2004) have provided similar support for the effectiveness of teaching narrative text structure on reading comprehension. Whereas these studies offer preliminary support for language intervention, it is unclear at this point what the intensity, frequency, and duration of this intervention must be to significantly reduce problems in reading comprehension. Additional research on language-based intervention will be necessary to address these issues.

## REFERENCES


Aaron, P.G., Joshi, M., & Williams, K.A. (1999). Not all reading disabilities are alike. *Journal of Learning Disabilities, 32,* 120–137.

Archibald, L.M.D., & Gathercole, S. (2006). The complexities of complex memory span: Storage and processing deficits in specific language impairment. *Journal of Memory & Language, 57,* 177–194.

Bishop, D.V.M., & Adams, C. (1990). A prospective study of the relationship between specific language impairment, phonological disorders and reading retardation. *Journal of Child Psychology and Psychiatry, 31,* 1027–1050.

Bishop, D.V.M., Bright, P., James, C., Bishop, S.J., & van der Lely, H.K.J. (2000). Grammatical SLI: A distinct subtype of developmental language impairment. *Applied Psycholinguistics, 21,* 159–181.

Bollen, K.A., & Curran, P.J. (2006). *Latent curve models: A structural equation perspective.* Hoboken, NJ: Wiley.

Bridges, M., & Catts, H.W. (2011). The use of dynamic assessment of phonological awareness for the early identification of reading disabilities in kindergarten children. *Journal of Learning Disabilities, 44,* 330–338.

Cain, K., Oakhill, J.V., Barnes, M.A., & Bryant, P.E. (2001). Comprehension skill, inference making ability and their relation to knowledge. *Memory and Cognition, 29,* 850–859.

Catts, H.W. (1993). The relationship between speech-language impairments and reading disabilities. *Journal of Speech and Hearing Research, 36,* 948–958.

Catts, H.W., Adlof, S.M., & Ellis Weismer, S. (2006). Language deficits in poor comprehenders: A case for the simple view of reading. *Journal of Speech, Language, and Hearing Research, 49,* 278–293.

Catts, H.W., Adlof, S., Hogan, T.P., & Ellis Weismer, S. (2005). Are specific language impairments and dyslexia distinct disorders? *Journal of Speech, Language, and Hearing Research, 48,* 1378–1396.

Catts, H., Bridges, M., Little, T., & Tomblin, J. (2008). Reading achievement growth in children with language impairments. *Journal of Speech, Language, and Hearing Research, 51,* 1569–1579.

Catts, H.W., Compton, D., Tomblin, J.B., & Bridges, M. (2012). Prevalence and nature of late-emerging poor readers. *Journal of Educational Psychology, 104*(1), 166–181.

Catts, H.W., Fey, M.E., Tomblin, J.B., & Zhang, X. (2002). A longitudinal investigation of reading outcomes in children with language impairments. *Journal of Speech, Language, and Hearing Research, 45,* 1142–1157.

Catts, H., Hogan, T., & Adlof, S. (2005). Developmental changes in reading and reading disabilities. In H. Catts & A. Kamhi, A. (Eds.), *Connections between language and reading disabilities* (pp. 25–40). Mahwah, NJ: Erlbaum.

Catts, H.W., & Kamhi, A.G. (Eds.). (2012). *Language and reading disabilities.* Boston, MA: Pearson Education.

de Jong, P.F., & van der Leij, A. (2002). Effects of phonological abilities and linguistic comprehension on the development of reading. *Scientific Studies of Reading, 6*(1), 51–77.

Dollaghan, C., & Campbell, T. (1998). Nonword repetition and child language impairment. *Journal of Speech, Language, and Hearing Research, 41,* 1136–1146.

Elleman, A.M., Compton, D., Fuchs, D., Fuchs, L., & Bouton, B. (2012). Exploring dynamic assessment as a means of identifying children at risk for developing comprehension difficulties. *Journal of Learning Disabilities, 44*, 348–357.

Ellis Weismer, S., Tomblin, J.B., Zhang, X., Buckwalter, P., Chynoweth, J.G., & Jones, M. (2000). Nonword repetition performance in school-age children with and without language impairment. *Journal of Speech, Language, and Hearing Research, 43*, 865–878.

Fey, M.E., Catts, H.W., Proctor-Williams, K., Tomblin, J.B., & Zhang, X. (2004). Oral and written story composition skills of children with language impairment. *Journal of Speech, Language, and Hearing Research, 47*, 1301–1318.

Francis, D.J., Fletcher, J.M., Catts, H.W., & Tomblin, J.B. (2005). Dimensions affecting the assessment of reading comprehension. In S.G. Paris & S.A. Stahl (Eds.), *Children's reading comprehension and assessment* (pp. 369–394). Mahwah, NJ: Erlbaum.

Fuchs, D., Compton, D., Fuchs, L., Bouton, B., & Caffrey, E. (2011). The construct and predictive validity of a dynamic assessment of young children learning to read: Implications for RTI frameworks. *Journal of Learning Disabilities, 44*, 339–347.

Garner, J.K., & Bochna, C.R. (2004). Transfer of a listening comprehension strategy to independent reading in first grade students. *Early Childhood Education Journal, 32*, 69–74.

Gough, P.B., & Tunmer, W.E. (1986). Decoding, reading, and reading disability. *Remedial and Special Education, 7*, 6–10.

Gray, S. (2004). Word learning by preschoolers with specific language impairment. *Journal of Speech, Language, and Hearing Research, 47*, 1117–1132.

Hoover, W.A., & Gough, P.B. (1990). The simple view of reading. *Reading and Writing: An Interdisciplinary Journal, 2*, 127–160.

Jenkins, J., Hudson, R.F., & Johnson, E.S. (2007). Screening for service delivery in an RTI framework: Candidate measures. *School Psychology Review, 36*(4), 582–601.

Kail, R., & Leonard, L.B. (1986). *Word-finding abilities in language-impaired children* (ASHA Monograph No. 25). Rockville, MD: American Speech-Language-Hearing Association.

Kamhi, A., & Catts, H. (1986). Toward an understanding of developmental language and reading disorders. *Journal of Speech and Hearing Disorders, 51*, 337–347.

Kamhi, A., Catts, H., Mauer, D., Apel, K., & Gentry, B. (1988). Phonological and spatial processing abilities in language- and reading-impaired children. *Journal of Speech and Hearing Disorders, 53*, 316–327.

Leach, J.M., Scarborough, H.S., & Rescorla, L. (2003). Late-emerging reading disabilities. *Journal of Educational Psychology, 95*(2), 211–224.

Leonard, L.B., Miller, C., & Gerber, E. (1999). Grammatical morphology and the lexicon in children with specific language impairment. *Journal of Speech, Language, and Hearing Research, 42*, 678–689.

Leslie, L., & Caldwell, J. (1995). *Qualitative Reading Inventory–II*. New York, NY: HarperCollins.

Lyon, G.R., Shaywitz, S.E., & Shaywitz, B.A. (2003). A definition of dyslexia. *Annals of Dyslexia, 53*, 1–4.

McGregor, K.K. (1997). The nature of word-finding errors of preschoolers with and without word-finding deficits. *Journal of Speech, Language, and Hearing Research, 40*, 1232–1244.

Miller, C.A., Kail, R., Leonard, L.B., & Tomblin, J.B. (2001). Speed of processing in children with specific language impairment. *Journal of Speech, Language, and Hearing Research, 44*, 416–433.

Nation, K., Clarke, P., Marshall, C.M., & Durand, M. (2004). Hidden language impairments in children: Parallels between poor reading comprehension and specific language impairment. *Journal of Speech, Language, and Hearing Research, 47*, 199–211.

Nelson, J.R., & Stage, S.A. (2007). Fostering the development of vocabulary knowledge and reading comprehension through contextually-based multiple meaning vocabulary instruction. *Education and Treatment of Children, 30*, 1–22.

Newcomer, P. (1990). *Diagnostic Achievement Battery, Second Edition*. Austin, TX: Pro-Ed.

Pena, E.D., Gillam, R.G., Malek, M., Ruiz-Felter, R., Resendiz, M., Fiestas, C., & Sabel, T. (2006). Dynamic assessment of school-age children's narrative ability. *Journal of Speech, Language, and Hearing Research, 49*, 1037–1057.

Wiederholt, J., & Bryant, B. (1992). *Gray Oral Reading Test, Third Edition*. Austin, TX: Pro-Ed.

Williams, J.P., Stafford, K.B., Lauer, K.D., Hall, K.M., & Pollini, S. (2009). Embedding reading comprehension training in content-area instruction. *Journal of Educational Psychology, 101*(1), 1–20.

Woodcock, R.W. (1997). *Woodcock Reading Mastery Tests–Revised/Normative Update.* Circle Pines, MN: American Guidance Service.

Zipke, M., Ehri, L., & Cairns, H. (2009). Using semantic ambiguity instruction to improve third graders' metalinguistic awareness and reading comprehension: An experimental study. *Reading Research Quarterly, 44*(3), 300–321.

CHAPTER 8

# Is Reading the Same as Viewing?

## An Exploration of the Similarities and Differences Between Processing Text- and Visually Based Narratives

Joseph P. Magliano, Lester C. Loschky, James A. Clinton, and Adam M. Larson

The title of this chapter explores to what extent there are shared cognitive systems that support the processing of narratives across print and visual media. An initially obvious answer to the question is no, given that viewing images and reading texts involve different cognitive and brain systems during encoding. In fact, we contend that there are aspects of how narratives are conveyed across media that may lead to differences in encoding that are less obvious. On the other hand, if we assume that mental models provide the basis of comprehension across modalities of experiences (McNamara & Magliano, 2009), surely there are shared cognitive systems that lead to the construction of these mental models (Gernsbacher, 1990; Gernsbacher, Varner, & Faust, 1990; Magliano, Radvansky, & Copeland, 2007).

Consider the shot sequence from the James Bond movie *Moonraker* (Broccoli & Gilbert, 1979), shown in Figure 8.1, which constitutes about 15 seconds of film. Just prior to this sequence, we find Bond on an airplane filled with enemy agents who want to kill him. Bond throws one of the bad guys (who has a parachute) out of the plane and then subsequently gets pushed out of the plane himself (without a parachute). Most viewers of this sequence infer that Bond has the goal to steal the parachute and will be successful in doing so at the start of Shot 6, when Bond starts his dive (Magliano, Dijkstra, & Zwaan, 1996). Upon review of the shot sequence in Figure 8.1, one can see that the sequence is carefully constructed to constrain the possible interpretation of the narrative events. More important, it illustrates some conventions in filmmaking that may not have correlates in text; but at the same time, the sequence also illustrates that there must be overlapping processes between film and text.

Consider Shots 1 and 2, which are extreme, high-angle, long shots of two figures in the air and heading toward the earth. These shots establish the nature of a complication or problem for Bond to solve, specifically that he is falling through the air without a parachute. Shot 2 also introduces a potential solution to that problem, namely, the parachute possessed by the bad guy. Although processing the events conveyed in these camera shots may be different in many ways from processing analogous sentences in a text-based version of the narrative, in doing so viewers need to engage in mapping processes across the images that are also central to text

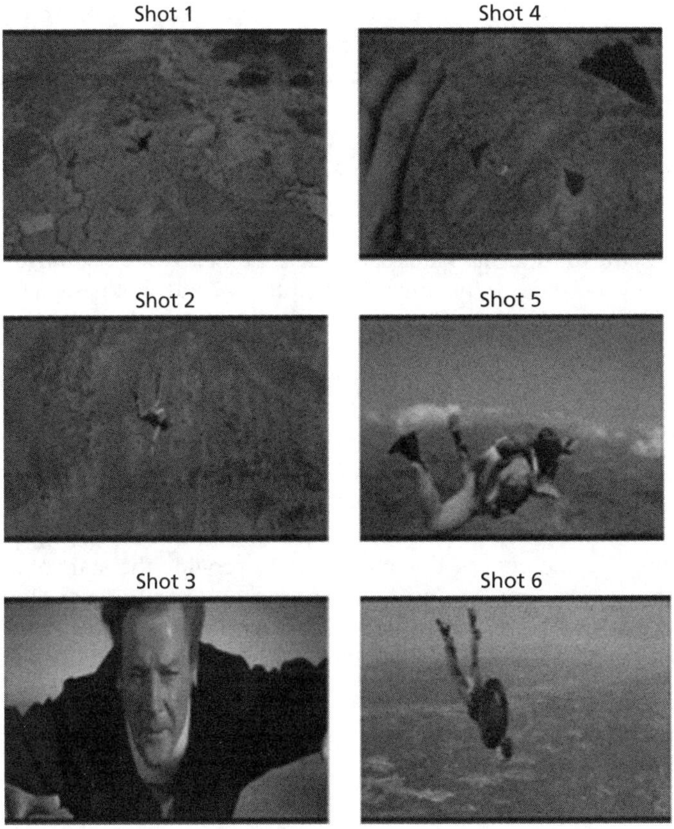


**Figure 8.1.** Shot summary of a scene from *Moonraker*.

comprehension (McNamara & Magliano, 2009). For example, viewers must establish that the figures in Shots 1 and 2 are the previously seen Bond and the bad guy, respectively, and reinstate knowledge of which of these entities has or does not have a parachute. These mapping processes are akin to the kinds of bridging inferences we know that readers generate (e.g., anaphoric reference; see Graesser, Singer, & Trabasso, 1994, for an extensive review).

Another issue to consider is that understanding the internal states of characters (goals, beliefs, emotions) is an important part of narrative comprehension (e.g., Graesser, Singer, & Trabasso, 1994). However, text and film may differ in the extent to which internal states can readily be conveyed. Authors can rely on a variety of narrative conventions to provide explicit information regarding the internal states of characters (e.g., free indirect speech, omniscient narration). However, filmmakers usually rely on dialogue to explicitly convey internal states of characters. Other techniques, such as voice-over, can be used to explicitly convey internal states of characters, but these are rarely used and not well received by critics. That said, there are filmmaking conventions for conveying internal states that build upon editing and actors' facial expressions, body postures, and actions to help the viewer infer the internal states of a protagonist. For example, Shots 3 and 4 illustrate one important convention, namely, a point-of-view shot sequence. This is a shot sequence that shows a close-up of a character's face, followed by eye-line match shots (i.e., a camera shot from the implied location of the characters' eyes). This shot sequence is critical for conveying the internal states of characters (Bordwell & Thompson, 2003) but will always require the inference that the second shot is seen from the viewpoint of the character shown in the first shot. Based on that inference, in the case of the example in Figure 8.1, viewers must further infer that Bond is cognizant of the bad guy with the parachute, arguably a necessary condition for his generating the goal of stealing the parachute.

As this example illustrates, to be able to give a detailed answer to the question of whether reading and viewing narratives are the same requires a detailed systematic investigation. We contend that such an investigation is critical for directing empirical studies in order to answer the question meaningfully. The goal of this chapter is to provide the start of such an investigation. We structure our discussion around features of the media, the psychological processes involved in processing and comprehending narratives across media, and research comparing processing across media.

## FEATURES OF THE MEDIA

Any discussion regarding the similarities and differences in the cognitive processes that support narrative comprehension across media should start with a discussion of the nature of the media. Such an exploration can yield hypotheses suggesting where and when there will be divergences and convergences between media, which can then lead to future empirical studies. To this end, we have identified four dimensions that warrant consideration across the media of texts, graphic narratives, and films, which are shown in Table 8.1. These dimensions are by no means exhaustive; rather, they reflect the dimensions that we feel warrant consideration, given the goals of this chapter.

One fundamental issue to consider is the *minimal production unit of meaning*, the smallest unit that needs to be processed to understand what is happening "now" in the narrative, namely, the salient events that make up the narrative plot. With narrative text, an obvious production unit of meaning is the sentence. It is easily recognized (in English) by starting with a capital letter and ending with specific punctuation (e.g., a period). Similarly, in such graphic narratives as comics, an obvious minimal production unit of meaning is the panel, which is also easily recognized by typically being bounded by a box. Finally, in film, a comparable minimal production unit of meaning is the shot, which is easily recognized by a change in camera

**Table 8.1.** Considerations regarding the media

| Dimension | Text | Graphic narrative | Film |
|---|---|---|---|
| Unit of meaning | Sentence | Panel | Shot |
| Multimodality | Text | Text and pictures | Dialog, sounds, images |
| Presentation control | Self-paced | Self-paced | Generally not self-paced |
| Plot structure | Goal episodes | Goal episodes | Goal episodes |

angle and/or an editing boundary (e.g., a fade-out or dissolve). Each of these minimal production units is widely recognized by producers and consumers of these respective media.

Nevertheless, there are certain problems with each of these minimal meaningful units from the standpoint of psychological processes that support comprehension. With text, a single sentence can include multiple clauses, each of which contains a subject and predicate (i.e., a verb phrase). Verbs in these clauses are particularly important in conveying the events that are being conveyed in a narrative (e.g., walking, stopping, and seeing; Zwaan, Langston, & Graesser, 1995). Much research has shown that as readers reach the end of each clause in a text, they update their representation to incorporate that information into the mental model that they are constructing (Gernsbacher, 1990). Thus, from a psycholinguistic standpoint, clauses seem more reasonable as a minimal unit of meaning than a sentence. Alternatively, one could also argue that the individual word is an even more minimal meaningful unit. Eye-movement studies have shown that readers fixate most words in a text sequentially (Rayner, 1998), and ease of word recognition is an important predictor of children's reading development (Rayner, Foorman, Perfetti, Pesetsky, & Seidenberg, 2001).

In the case of graphic narratives, the panel is also a somewhat problematic minimal meaningful unit. A given panel generally contains multiple objects (animate or inanimate) and one or more actions, either of which could be argued to be more appropriate minimal meaningful units. For example, in Figure 8.2 (*The Fantom of the Fair*, Gustavson, 1939), we see a man (the fantom) and a woman, each of which must be recognized, as well as their respective actions (flying, calling), in order to comprehend the event(s) in the panel. Such objects are rather comparable to concrete nouns in text processing, and their actions are comparable to verbs. Similarly, in film, a given shot usually contains multiple objects engaged in one or more actions. Thus, again, objects and their actions could be argued to be more appropriate minimal meaningful units. Furthermore, a given camera shot in film can convey several events, or several shots can be used to convey a single event.

Finally, both graphic narratives and films usually contain language. Consider a panel excerpt from Gustavson's 1939 graphic story *The Fantom of the Fair* (see Figure 8.2). The Fantom has just rescued a circus high-diver, Jane, and he is now flying away from her. Viewers have to integrate the

**Figure 8.2.** Example panel from *Fantom of the Fair*.

dialogue with the images to understand what is happening now in the narrative moment. The same is true in film, where integration of both visual and linguistic processing is necessary for comprehension. Thus, one can ask whether the sentence (or clause, or word) should also be a minimal meaningful unit in graphic narratives and film.

The next dimension that warrants discussion is the extent to which the narrative is a multimedia experience. Texts obviously are not, whereas graphic narratives and film are. Multimedia experiences can be complex to process because the comprehender has to integrate linguistic and perceptual information, which can place a higher cognitive load on the comprehender (Mayer, 2009). We suspect that graphic narratives are the most complex and resource demanding because they require text reading and pictorial comprehension. Consider again Figure 8.2 from *The Fantom of the Fair* (Gustavson, 1939). The dialog and image contain both convergent and divergent semantic content. An interesting empirical question is the extent to which the semantic overlap between these two sources of information affects comprehension.

It is also important to understand that there are differences in the extent to which comprehenders can control the pacing of processing the narrative. With text and graphic narratives, comprehenders can control the pace at which they read and view. This allows comprehenders to pause, look back, reevaluate, and repair any comprehension problems. On the other hand, when viewing a film there is generally no control over the pacing. If comprehension problems arise, the viewer very often cannot or does not view that part of the film again. The exception is if the viewer has the ability to rewind. Whereas this option is available to individuals watching a film on their own viewing device, films are often watched in theaters or other social settings in which rewinding is either not an option or is not generally taken advantage of to repair comprehension problems.

Although the dimensions discussed thus far vary to one degree or another across the modalities, we contend that the final dimension, plot structure, does not. We argue that all narratives are structured around hierarchical goal episodes regardless of media (Trabasso, van den Broek, & Suh, 1989). Based on this assumption, we further assume that there will be commonalities in the mental models constructed by readers and viewers of comparable narratives. We will discuss empirical evidence supporting this claim in the context of the psychological processes involved in processing the different forms of media. One point that we do want to emphasize now, however, is that the different forms of media have different *affordances* in terms of which aspects of the goal episodes can be made explicit. As discussed above, films do not afford ways of explicitly conveying the internal states of characters (outside of dialogue or voice-over narration); thus viewers must instead infer them from the facial expressions, gestures, and actions of the actors. Conversely, this information can be stated explicitly in a text if an author chooses to do so. Given the importance of inferring and tracking goals of characters, one would think that this may make processing complex goals and internal states of characters more complex for narrative films more than for texts. However, basic emotions are readily inferred by facial expressions, and this inferencing skill is learned at an early age (McClure, 2000). Moreover, viewers appear to regularly monitor the goal states of characters when viewing a film (Magliano, Taylor, & Kim, 2005). The extent to which viewers can infer internal state of characters in film (i.e., the kinds of internal states and their complexity) and how they do so warrant further investigation.

## FRONT-END AND BACK-END PROCESSES ACROSS MEDIA

We make a broad distinction between what we call front-end and back-end processing of narrative media (Loschky, Magliano, & Larson, 2012). Front-end processes are those involved in extracting information from the visual stream, which lead to the computation of the event model that represents the "now" moment in a narrative. Table 8.2 shows a list of processes that compose front-end processing across the three media considered here. These processes cluster into those processes involved in processing language and those involved in scene perception. It is beyond the scope of this chapter to present a detailed discussion of each of these processes, however. Given that most readers of this volume will be more familiar with the language-based processes than with those that are film based, we do not describe them here. Nonetheless, a brief description of the processes involved in scene perception is warranted.

When constructing a representation of the "now" moment in a scene, front-end processes begin by extracting visual information during each

**Table 8.2.** Considerations regarding front-end and back-end processes

| | Text | Graphic narrative | Film |
|---|---|---|---|
| **Front-end** | | | |
| ***Processes*** | | | |
| Orthographic | X | X | |
| Phonological | X | X | X |
| Lexical–syntactic | X | X | X |
| Semantics | X | X | X |
| Gist processing | | X | X |
| Object processing | | X | X |
| Motion processing | | (X) | X |
| ***Product*** | | | |
| Event model | X | X | X |
| **Back-end** | | | |
| ***Processes*** | | | |
| Event segmentation | X | X | X |
| Inferences | X | X | X |
| Structure building | X | X | X |
| ***Products*** | | | |
| Text base | X | X | ? |
| Situation model | X | X | X |

*Note:* (X) denotes that this process may be present.

eye fixation. In scene perception, eye fixations last, on average, a third of a second, after which the eyes move to fixate a new object or location (Rayner, 1998). During the first 150 ms of the first fixation, front-end processes extract global semantic meaning from the scene, called scene gist (Fei-Fei, Iyer, Koch, & Perona, 2007). For example, the viewer will rapidly understand whether a scene is "natural" or "man made," a "beach" or a "forest" (Loschky & Larson, 2010) and whether it has positive or negative emotional valence (Maljkovic & Martini, 2005). Likewise, the scene gist will also include global information about key objects in the scene, such as whether there are people or animals (Fei-Fei et al., 2007) and some idea of what action is being performed (Larson, Hendry, & Loschky, 2012). This scene gist representation will guide the eyes to fixate other objects to gather more detailed information (Eckstein, Drescher, & Shimozaki, 2006) and form the foundation of the event model. The event model will be further developed by the back-end processes in order to comprehend the dynamic structure of the visual narrative.

One obvious observation that can be derived from Table 8.2 is that there is some shared overlap in processes, but this is most evident for the two forms of visually based narratives. Obviously, reading and scene perception involve some different cognitive and brain systems associated with encoding linguistic versus scenic input. However, there is a growing body of evidence for the perspective that language understanding is "grounded," meaning that the brain systems that are involved in perceiving and moving through the world support the processing of language (e.g.,

Zwaan, 2004). It is beyond the scope of this chapter to discuss this literature; rather, we will focus on the shared overlap in language processing across the three media.

The primary difference between the linguistic demands of reading (whether it be in the context of texts or graphic narratives) and film is that graphemic processing is minimal in film because most of the language is presented aurally. As such, there are fewer reading demands on the cognitive system during front-end processing of film. Indeed, preliterate children begin to develop narrative comprehension skills by viewing purely visually based narratives (Trabasso & Nickels, 1992). However, a large body of evidence shows that oral language skills are important for narrative comprehension, as reflected in the Simple View of Reading model (Gough & Tunmer, 1986). This evidence raises an interesting empirical question as to whether these skills account for variance in individual differences in comprehending film.

Another interesting case is comprehending graphic narratives. As we have discussed, this multimedia experience involves both reading and visual processing skills. It makes sense that the visual images could serve as a scaffold for processing the language, but as mentioned above, this is completely contingent on the semantic overlap between the texts and the images. In the panel of examples in Figure 8.2, the text is in the form of dialogue between the characters and conveys additional information not contained in the image (e.g., the fantom has other pressing business), and thus elaborates upon the image and explains why the fantom is leaving Jane.

A critically important difference between graphic narratives and film is that film contains motion, but graphic narratives do not. This leads to greater *attentional synchrony,* in which different viewers look at the same things at the same time when viewing a film as opposed to when viewing a sequence of related still images (e.g., in a graphic narrative; Dorr, Martinetz, Gegenfurtner, & Barth, 2010).[1] Nevertheless, other research has shown that still images that imply motion, which is ubiquitous in comics, lead to greater activation of motion-processing brain regions (e.g., area MT) than do still images that do not imply motion (Osaka, Matsuyoshi, Ikeda, & Osaka, 2010). Thus, even graphic narratives with static images seem to involve some degree of motion processing. To our knowledge there is scant research comparing processing of graphic narratives versus film. However, there is a substantial literature on multimedia learning that could guide systematic study of these media.

We identified three back-end processes that lead to a mental model (i.e., the product of back-end processes). This mental model contains two products, the textbase, which corresponds to the explicitly experienced

[1] This difference in attentional synchrony is also likely related to the fact that in normal film viewing, the filmmaker sets the viewing pace, whereas with comics the viewer or reader controls the pace, likely producing less attentional synchrony.

content, and the situation model, which includes the inferences that are generated in order to coherently connect that content to world knowledge (e.g., Kintsch, 1998). The mental model is generally believed to be structured around a hierarchically organized sequence of goal episodes (e.g., Trabasso et al., 1989). There is good evidence that viewers of graphic narratives and film produce situation models, for they clearly draw inferences that require integrating information from what they saw and their prior knowledge (e.g., Magliano et al., 1996). However, we know of no clear evidence indicating whether film viewers form a language-like propositional representation of what they saw, which we could call a textbase.

The first of the back-end processes is *event segmentation,* which involves understanding the boundaries between story episodes (e.g., Kurby & Zacks, 2008). As will be discussed below, viewers and readers segment narratives based on changes in such story dimensions as space, time, causality, and the goal episode (e.g., Magliano, Kopp, McNerney, Radvansky, & Zacks, 2012). The next process involves *inferencing,* which primarily involves establishing relationships between explicitly experienced story elements and drawing upon relevant background knowledge (McNamara & Magliano, 2009). Finally, both event segmentation and inferencing are in the service of *structure building,* which constitutes several processes involved in building mental models (laying the foundation, mapping, shifting to new mental structures, inference generation; Gernsbacher, 1990).

## PSYCHOLOGICAL RESEARCH COMPARING COMPREHENSION ACROSS MEDIA

A number of scholars who study discourse comprehension have argued that models of discourse comprehension can be viewed as general models that extend to other media and even naturalistic events (Gernsbacher, 1990; Kintsch, 1998; Magliano et al., 2007). However, there are very few empirical investigations of that claim, in particular when controlling for content (e.g., Baggett, 1979; Magliano et al., in press). There have been a number of studies that have assessed the extent to which comprehension skills and proficiencies share variance (e.g., Gernsbacher et al., 1990; Kendeou, Bohn-Gettler, White, & van den Broek, 2008; Pezdek, Lehrer, and Simon, 1984). In this section, we discuss both of these lines of research.

Baggett (1979) conducted a seminal study assessing whether mental models for text-based and visually based narratives were similar. Across several experiments, college student participants were asked to identify the goal episodes that composed the film *The Red Balloon* (Lamorisse, 1956). However, they either read a text-based version of the story, viewed the film-based version of it, or looked at still picture frames from it. Participants identified the same goal episodes regardless of the medium. In addition, in one experiment they were asked to recall the narratives; the content of the recall protocols was remarkably similar in content and structure. This study provided fairly convincing evidence that back-end processes are surprisingly similar regardless of the modality of the experience.

A more recent study was conducted by Magliano, Kopp, McNerney, Radvansky, and Zacks (2012). The researchers had participants (college students or older adults) view a popular series of children's picture stories that contained only images and no language or read a version for which the researchers wrote text that captured the major events depicted. Participants identified when they perceived boundaries between the events that made up the stories. The researchers found remarkable convergences in the event boundary judgments within and across the two media, albeit convergence was greater within a medium than across the two.

Next consider research that has explored the extent to which comprehension is similar or different across media (i.e., text and film), which has produced conflicting evidence. For example, Pezdek, Lehrer, and Simon (1984) found that there was minimal shared variance in comprehension skill across media. They had children (8–11 years old) listen to (oral text), read (graphic narratives combining language and images), or view (TV) different versions of the same story. The researchers assessed comprehension in a variety of ways but found no significant overall difference between television comprehension and reading comprehension scores. However, they found that comprehension scores across the media were not significantly correlated, suggesting that comprehension proficiencies were not similar, at least for children at this age. On the other hand, Kendeou, Bohn-Gettler, White, and van den Broek (2008) had children (6–8 year olds) listen to, read, or view narratives and assessed comprehension proficiencies. A notable difference from the Pezdek et al. (1984) study was that the children's inferencing skills across the media were consistently, albeit moderately, correlated—demonstrating a stronger convergence across back-end processes than found in the earlier study. The divergence of these two studies clearly indicates that this issue warrants further investigation. Nevertheless, across the five studies considered here (Baggett, 1979; Gernsbacher et al., 1990; Kendeou et al., 2008; Magliano et al., in press; Pezdek et al., 1984), there is converging evidence for both shared processes and proficiencies in narrative comprehension across textual and visual media.

## CONCLUDING REMARKS AND PROMISING FUTURE DIRECTIONS

This chapter was necessarily a general overview of an area of theoretical and empirical explorations that shows great promise. We believe that our distinction between front-end and back-end processes provides a heuristic for future research and deeper reflection that has validity in reading, vision, and comprehension sciences. We conclude this chapter by identifying what we believe to be some interesting future research directions. One caveat is that each research suggestion warrants greater discussion than is afforded here.

One critical line of research that warrants further exploration is the extent to which comprehension processes are functionally similar across media. We provided a framework for this exploration with the introduction of the distinction between front- and back-end processes. Although we have argued that back-end processes likely share larger overlap across media than do front-end processes, it is important to recognize that such front-end processes as eye movements and fixations are heavily guided by back-end processes, such as what one is trying to comprehend at that moment. For example, consistent with results from reading (Anderson & Pichert, 1978), viewers of pictures of home interiors looked at different objects for different amounts of time depending on whether they took the perspective of a home buyer or a burglar, which in turn influenced their memory (Kaakinen, Hyönä, & Viljanen, 2011). Further research on the effects of back-end processes on front-end processes across media is greatly needed.

As a second issue, there is growing evidence that both linguistic and grounded systems (i.e., perceptual and embodied symbols) support comprehension processes (e.g., Fincher-Kiefer, 2001). However, still an open question is the extent to which these different types of representations are involved while perceiving and comprehending narratives presented in different media (e.g., text, graphic novel, or movie). Specifically, are the roles of linguistic and grounded symbols in the representation of linguistic and visually based narratives similar or different?

A final issue that warrants exploration pertains to the topic of this volume. Specifically, what factors affect individual differences in comprehension ability across different media? Do the same factors that predict individual differences in the comprehension of texts also account for individual differences in visually based narratives? The research discussed in this chapter indicates that the answer to this question is currently equivocal. Similarly, do individuals who have disorders known to negatively affect language comprehension, such as dyslexia or autism spectrum disorder, similarly experience troubles comprehending visually based narratives? If not, can visually based narratives be used in the context of interventions as a scaffold to promote language comprehension skills of such individuals?

Although the foregoing list of possibilities is by no means exhaustive, we believe it points to a rich future for research in comprehension across media. By conducting this research, we will gain better insights into the nature of comprehension and the cognitive and brain systems that support it.

## REFERENCES

Anderson, R.C., & Pichert, J.W. (1978). Recall of previously unrecallable information following a shift in perspective. *Journal of Verbal Learning and Verbal Behavior, 17*(1), 1–12. doi:10.1016/s0022-5371(78)90485-1

Baggett, P. (1979). Structurally equivalent stories in movie and text and the effect of the medium on recall. *Journal of Verbal Learning & Verbal Behavior, 18*(3), 333–356.

Bordwell, D., & Thompson, K. (2003). *Film art: An introduction*. New York, NY: McGraw-Hill.

Broccoli, A.R.P., & Gilbert, L.D. (Writers). (1979). *Moonraker* [Film]. Available from CBS/Fox Video, Industrial Park Drive, Farmington Hills, MI 48024.

Dorr, M., Martinetz, T., Gegenfurtner, K.R., & Barth, E. (2010). Variability of eye movements when viewing dynamic natural scenes. *Journal of Vision, 10*(10), 1–17.

Eckstein, M.P., Drescher, B.A., & Shimozaki, S.S. (2006). Attentional cues in real scenes, saccadic targeting, and Bayesian priors. *Psychological Science, 17*(11), 973–980.

Fei-Fei, L., Iyer, A., Koch, C., & Perona, P. (2007). What do we perceive in a glance of a real-world scene? *Journal of Vision, 7*(1), 1–29.

Fincher-Kiefer, R. (2001). Perceptual components of situation models. *Memory & Cognition, 29*, 336–343.

Gernsbacher, M.A. (1990). *Language comprehension as structure building* (Vol. 11). Hillsdale, NJ: Erlbaum.

Gernsbacher, M.A., Varner, K.R., & Faust, M.E. (1990). Investigating differences in general comprehension skill. *Journal of Experimental Psychology: Learning, Memory, and Cognition, 16*(3), 430–445.

Gough, P., & Tunmer, W. (1986). Decoding, reading, and reading disability. *Remedial and Special Education, 7*, 6–10.

Graesser, A.C., Singer, M., & Trabasso, T. (1994). Constructing inferences during narrative text comprehension. *Psychological Review, 101*, 371–395.

Gustavson, P. [Artist]. (1939). *The fantom of the fair* [Public domain comic strip]. Available from http://goldenagecomics.co.uk

Kaakinen, J.K., Hyönä, J., & Viljanen, M. (2011). Influence of a psychological perspective on scene viewing and memory for scenes. *Quarterly Journal of Experimental Psychology, 64*(7), 1372–1387. doi:10.1080/17470218.2010.548872

Kendeou, P., Bohn-Gettler, C., White, M.J., & van den Broek, P. (2008). Children's inference generation across different media. *Journal of Research in Reading, 31*(3), 259–272. doi:10.1111/j.1467-9817.2008.00370.x

Kintsch, W. (1998). Comprehension: A paradigm for cognition. New York, NY: Cambridge University Press.

Kurby, C.A., & Zacks, J.M. (2008). Segmentation in the perception and memory of events. *Trends in Cognitive Sciences, 12*, 72–79.

Lamorisse, A. (Writer). (1956). *The red balloon* [Film]. Paris, France: Films Montsouris.

Larson, A.M., Hendry, J., & Loschky, L.C. (2012, May). *Scene gist meets event perception: The Time course of scene gist and event recognition*. Poster presented at the 12th annual meeting of the Vision Sciences Society, Naples, FL.

Loschky, L.C., & Larson, A.M. (2010). The natural/man-made distinction is made prior to basic-level distinctions in scene gist processing. *Visual Cognition, 18*(4), 513–536.

Loschky, L.C., Magliano, J.P., & Larson, A.M. (2012). The need for an integrated theory of film perception and comprehension. Paper presented at the Workshop on Intelligent Cinematography and Editing 2012 workshop, Raleigh, NC.

Magliano, J.P., Dijkstra, K., & Zwaan, R. (1996). Generating predictive inferences while viewing a movie. *Discourse Processes, 22*, 199–224.

Magliano, J.P., Kopp, K., McNerney, M.W., Radvansky, G.A., & Zacks, J.M. ( 2012). Aging and perceived event structure as a function of modality. *Aging, Neuropsychology, and Cognition, 19*, 264–282.

Magliano, J.P., Radvansky, G.A., & Copeland, D.E. (2007). Beyond language comprehension: Situation models as a form or autobiographical memory. In F. Schmalhofer & C. Perfetti (Eds.), *Higher level language processes in the brain: Inference and comprehension processes* (pp. 379–391). Mahwah, NJ: Erlbaum.

Magliano, J.P., Taylor, H.A., & Kim, H.J. (2005). When goals collide: Monitoring the goals of multiple characters. *Memory & Cognition, 33*, 1357–1367.

Maljkovic, V., & Martini, P. (2005). Short-term memory for scenes with affective content. *Journal of Vision, 5*(3), 215–229.

Mayer, R.E. (2009). *Multimedia learning* (2nd ed.). New York, NY: Cambridge University Press.

McClure, E.B. (2000). A meta-analytic review of sex differences in facial expression processing and their development in infants, children, and adolescents. *Psychological Bulletin, 126*(3), 424–453.

McNamara, D.S., & Magliano, J.P. (2009). Towards a comprehensive model of comprehension. In B. Ross (Ed.), *The psychology of learning and motivation* (Vol. 51, pp. 297–384). New York, NY: Elsevier Science.

Osaka, N., Matsuyoshi, D., Ikeda, T., & Osaka, M. (2010). Implied motion because of instability in Hokusai Manga activates the human motion-sensitive extrastriate visual cortex: An fMRI study of the impact of visual art. *NeuroReport: For Rapid Communication of Neuroscience Research, 21*(4), 264–267. doi:10.1097/WNR.0b013e328335b371

Pezdek, K., Lehrer, A., & Simon, S. (1984). The relationship between reading and cognitive processing of television and radio. *Child Development, 55*, 2072–2082.

Rayner, K. (1998). Eye movements in reading and information processing: 20 years of research. *Psychological Bulletin, 124*(3), 372–422.

Rayner, K., Foorman, B.R., Perfetti, C.A., Pesetsky, D., & Seidenberg, M.S. (2001). How psychological science informs the teaching of reading. *Psychological Science in the Public Interest, 2*(2), 31–74.

Trabasso, T., & Nickels, M. (1992). The development of goal plans of action in the narration of picture stories. *Discourse Processes, 15*, 249–275.

Trabasso, T., van den Broek, P., & Suh, S. (1989). Logical necessity and transitivity of causal relations in stories. *Discourse Processes, 12*, 1–25.

Zwaan, R.A. (2004). The immersed experiencer: Toward an embodied theory of language comprehension. In B.H. Ross (Ed.), *The psychology of learning and motivation* (pp. 35–62). New York, NY: Academic Press.

Zwaan, R.A., Langston, M.C., & Graesser, A.C. (1995). The construction of situation models in narrative comprehension: An event-indexing model. *Psychological Science, 6*, 292–297.

INTEGRATIVE SUMMARY 1

# What Goes Wrong When Reading Comprehension Fails?

Peggy McCardle

Reading comprehension, the goal of reading, requires a complex orchestration of abilities that come together to enable learning of new information from text. The chapters in this section tease apart those various abilities to try to determine what goes wrong at what points in the developmental process of learning to read—a key step in the design of successful interventions. How do the various levels of processing interact and influence one another? What is the role of word-level processes, and how do these interact with syntactic complexity? How does a reader begin to use these processes in relation to experiential knowledge to begin to draw inferences, to build a coherent mental model that allows him or her to understand and interpret what is read? What is the role of working memory, and how does that change over time? What about other components of executive function and cognitive control? How do some processes become automatized, and which ones really remain under conscious control; does the distinction between the two change developmentally, and if so, how? How does exposure to visual media as well as oral language influence the ability to fully comprehend written language and contribute to the development of a reader's ability to fully understand and interpret what is read? The authors in this section tackle several of these key challenges, approaching the development and integration of these processes from bottom-up, top-down, or some central point to try to determine when, why, and how these various processes might fail.

Perfetti, Stafura, and Adlof (Chapter 3) begin the discussion of reading comprehension and the points at which it might begin to break down by pointing out that we often skip an aspect of word-level reading that is crucial to understanding—namely, word-to-text integration. Their basic premises are that to learn words, the student must learn both word form and meaning; and that to comprehend text, students must not only understand words but be able to integrate them into the situation model they are mentally building as they read. Perfetti, Stafura, and Adlof make a clear case that this ability to integrate the information carried by words into the situation model is a key "pressure point" (although only one of several) where comprehension might fail; any view of reading comprehension that ignores word-to-text integration, they assert, is incomplete. This point is well taken by the other authors in this section.

Graesser and Li (Chapter 4) discuss the multiple levels of language and discourse that theories of reading and text comprehension encompass—words and their components, syntax, the textbase (explicit ideas in text), the referential situation model, and genre and rhetorical structure—and argue for better examination of the complexity of text, including all these levels, as a window into both better understanding how deeper levels of comprehension work and how best to recognize and remediate problems. Using Coh-Metrix, a computerized tool for text complexity analysis (Graesser, McNamara, Louwerse, & Cai, 2004), as a model, Graesser and Li describe how its levels lead to four principles of top-down, bottom-up, and cross-level processing that delineate linkages among these levels. These levels are useful as we apply a developmental lens to reading comprehension and emphasize the major thread in this section—namely, that comprehension can look very different in the same individual at different points in learning and development and can break down at many different points within any of these many levels.

Helder, van den Broek, Van Leijenhorst, and Beker (Chapter 5) envision the complexity of comprehension processes not in terms of levels but as an interconnected cluster of cognitive factors—general cognitive resources (executive function components including working memory), inferencing, and reading comprehension strategies—that change developmentally over time and differ across individuals. Working memory is important to basic reading skills, and as these basic skills are automatized, together with developmental increases in working memory capacity and other executive function components (e.g., flexibility in task switching, updating the contents of working memory), greater resources become available for the higher order processing needed for comprehension.

Inferencing, Helder et al. explain, involves both automatic (activation of the semantic memory network based on existing vocabulary) and consciously controlled strategic processes such as searching background knowledge to maintain an adequate level of comprehension as the reader progresses through the text. Others (including Perfetti et al., Chapter 3, this volume) have noted these same processes; how one integrates automatic processes with those under conscious control has yet to be fully delineated, although Perfetti et al.'s logically laid out approach holds promise.

In typically developing readers, these inferencing processes provide coherence to the reader's mental representation; that is, a la Helder et al., they enable the reader to construct a conceptual network across text elements. How well a reader can identify information as central to the text, or what van den Broek, Helder, and Van Leijenhorst (2012) refer to as sensitivity to structural centrality, is cited as a potential source of variation across development and individuals. In several studies using eye movement and behavioral think-aloud procedures, they identified two subgroups of poor comprehenders: elaborators, who differed in quality but not quantity of inferences compared to successful readers;

and paraphrasers, who made fewer and slightly less elaborate inferences than did successful readers, despite an equally elaborate mental model, but who produced inferences that were less centrally related to the text. An interesting exercise would be to apply Graesser and Li's principles to some of Helder et al.'s elaborators and paraphrasers, or to examine the paraphrasers in terms of Perfetti et al.'s sense of paraphrase at the word level to determine which pressure points are weakening or breaking down in these struggling readers.

Cain (Chapter 6) too invokes the need to examine the complexity of reading comprehension through a developmental lens. Based on the simple view of reading (Gough & Tunmer, 1986), which has as its axes word reading and listening comprehension, she divides reading and reading difficulties into a 2 × 2 table of high versus low reading comprehension and high versus low word reading (decoding) as a starting point for considering how to best recognize early predictors for each quadrant.

Similar to Perfetti et al., Cain examines comprehension in terms of its dependence on lower level language skills—vocabulary and knowledge of grammar—that are mastered in service of the higher level ability to integrate information and make inferences to construct a situation model. Cain sees text structure as a guiding framework for constructing the situation model, although she does not enlarge on this interesting assertion (which may be interesting to consider in light of Magliano, Loschky, Clinton, and Larson's thoughts [Chapter 8] about narrative structure in text and visual media). In her discussion, Cain distinguishes between simple short-term memory requirements versus more complex working memory tasks that require both retention and manipulation of verbal information in order to integrate and construct the situation model. When this working memory system is stressed, poor comprehenders show particular difficulty with inferencing and the detection of inconsistencies in text. Cain cites work that she feels demonstrates that the "meaning-making skills," that is, integration, inferencing, comprehension monitoring, and knowledge and use of text structure, predict reading comprehension. Looking retrospectively at the early language abilities of comprehenders, she cites oral language comprehension problems in poor comprehenders. Although more research is needed, Cain offers language comprehension ability as a potentially strong predictor of later reading comprehension, with varying patterns of strengths and weaknesses within this.

When Cain sorts her readers into the four cells of her 2 × 2 simple view table (Chapter 6, Figure 6.1), telling us that good word readers who are poor comprehenders are good on short-term memory but weaker on retaining and integrating information, for example, one wishes that to know how they would perform on Perfetti et al.'s tasks, in which they examine ERP N400s as readers encounter words in text that either require inferencing or do not, to tease out whether this pressure point might coincide with some of the patterns Cain observes. And at what point might such information become sufficiently explanatory that it can be used to inform intervention approaches? Because language changes rapidly during development, however, Cain reminds us of Scarborough's caution (2005) that we may see different predictors at different points in the same child's development. Cain also clearly acknowledges that combinations of factors may contribute to severity of risk; examining what those might be and how they might interact to impair or constrain reading abilities should be a priority.

As do all the authors in this section, Cain emphasizes the dynamic nature of the reading comprehension process. The quality of vocabulary knowledge and whether a child has rapid on-line access to that knowledge may differentially affect reading comprehension, but simply having a good vocabulary may not rule out the possibility that vocabulary may contribute to poor comprehension (Perfetti, 2007; see also Perfetti et al., Chapter 3, this volume). In addition, Cain argues, the availability of background knowledge for making inferences and constructing a situation model may constrain comprehension ability, so not only whether a reader has information that can be activated but how easily and readily what is relevant can be selected from that information and incorporated should be examined; Helder et al. and Graesser and Li also make this point, albeit from different perspectives. Poor readers may have impaired ability to select contextually appropriate meanings or to encode integrative relations between words or sentences, so management of stored information rather than the existence of and access to that information may be a limiting factor. Thus the authors agree that no single cause or profile will emerge as the key to comprehension failure.

Catts (Chapter 7) approaches reading comprehension problems by examining children with oral language impairments, drawing heavily from the comprehensive Iowa Longitudinal Study (e.g., Catts, Bridges, Little, & Tomblin, 2008; Catts, Fey, Tomblin, & Zhang, 2002). Of those children showing either specific or nonspecific language impairment in kindergarten, most demonstrated subsequent weak or deficient reading comprehension abilities, many with concomitant word-level reading problems. In this study, in the children with language impairment Catts and colleagues also noted that the proportion showing comprehension problems doubled from fourth to eighth grade; many appeared to have late-emerging reading disabilities (LERD). However, LERD is not specific to children with language impairment but also occurs in the general population (Catts, Compton, Tomblin, & Bridges, 2012; Leach, Scarborough, & Rescorla, 2003). Taking another cut at the Iowa data, Catts notes that nearly half of the individuals they identified from the total dataset as LERD (46%) had a history of language impairment.

In general, Catts and colleagues (Catts, Bridges, Little, & Tomblin, 2008; Catts, Compton, Tomblin, & Bridges, 2012; Catts, Fey, Tomblin, & Zhang, 2002) have shown that poor comprehenders not only have difficulty with higher level (discourse-level) language processing but also have deficits in vocabulary and grammar. Based on eighth-grade reading scores, they identified three subgroups of poor readers: relatively poor reading comprehension but relatively intact word recognition, poor decoders with relatively intact reading comprehension, and individuals who were poor in both decoding and comprehension. On receptive vocabulary and grammatical understanding, the poor comprehenders performed less well than did typical readers, better than poor decoders, but had unimpaired phonological processing; they also had poorer discourse comprehension and inferencing abilities than had the other groups. Examining their earlier performance, Catts et al. (2008, 2012) found that although only some (32%) of the eighth-grade poor comprehenders had had a kindergarten diagnosis of language impairment, most had had subclinical language problems that could have caused or contributed to their reading comprehension difficulties (although in Chapter 7, this volume, Catts acknowledges that these language issues could also have resulted from their reading disability).

Catts attempts to instantiate the 2 × 2 table from the simple view of reading with children from the Iowa Longitudinal Study; the correspondence between those individuals who fit the quadrants based on poor listening comprehension (the simple view) are not identical to those who have reading comprehension difficulties. Whereas Cain's simple view table seems to equate listening and reading comprehension, Catts's data indicate that these categories are neither static nor truly categorical. The dynamic nature of reading comprehension development is borne out whether we are talking about typical developmental changes over time or atypical development of reading abilities; both change over time and will therefore require careful assessment and examination and care in predicting abilities and planning, implementing, and tailoring interventions for reading comprehension difficulties.

Magliano, Loschky, Clinton, and Larson (Chapter 8) take what initially seems to be a very different approach to comprehension, examining the similarities between viewing a sequence of events and reading a narrative, specifically whether there are shared cognitive systems that engage in the construction of the mental or situation model. He shows these comparisons in tabular form and argues convincingly based on both his own work and other extant research that evidence points to shared processes and proficiencies for both written text and visual media. He offers what he refers to as front-end processes (those needed to extract initial information to build an event model, the basics) and back-end processes (those more complex process such as inferencing, used to build a situation model) as a heuristic within which to consider these media when studying comprehension. He challenges researchers to examine the extent to which front-end processes influence back-end processes, how this influence might differ across media, and how comprehension in one medium might be used to enhance or intervene with comprehension in another, for example, using aspects of or factors involved in comprehending visual narratives to design or contribute to reading interventions. Although the parallels with reading and the bottom-up and top-down views seem clear, there are challenges to comparing text to visual media, which Magliano et al. acknowledge. Nonetheless, doing so challenges researchers to think in new ways about our theories of what affects reading comprehension and where it might break down, as well as how we might be innovative about approaches to remediation for those who struggle with print.

What is required of developing readers is a highly complex orchestration of word-level reading and higher level cognitive processes. What is required of researchers is no less complex: Their role is to determine how the developing reader accomplishes this orchestration and to write the musical score for how it happens and thus to be able to predict where problems might occur, how and when to intervene to prevent as many of those problems as possible, and how and when to best minimize the unpreventable problems. Viewing their task through a developmental lens, researchers examine reading comprehension as a moving target that acknowledges that although individual differences are important and can make the data messy, the concomitant changes with development that can augment or alter the rate of progression resulting from instruction or intervention or both take the complexity of studying reading comprehension to an even greater level. Yet, each of these chapters also clearly shows us that although they do not always agree on the details, these researchers seem to have the same big picture and are pursuing it in ways that demonstrate that we can and eventually will understand reading comprehension and its failure. We know it has no single point of breakdown, but it would be naïve to think that anything so complex would have a simple explanation of its breakdown. More clearly understanding what the points of possible breakdown are will make the task of preventing failure and remediating the struggles more doable and more likely to succeed. This research—basic but with clear application—continues to show great promise even beyond the current gains it gives us.

## REFERENCES

Catts, H., Bridges, M., Little, T., & Tomblin, J. (2008). Reading achievement growth in children with language impairments. *Journal of Speech, Language, and Hearing Research, 51,* 1569–1579.

Catts, H.W., Compton, D., Tomblin, J.B., & Bridges, M. (2012). Prevalence and nature of late-emerging poor readers. *Journal of Educational Psychology, 104*(1), 166–181.

Catts, H.W., Fey, M.E., Tomblin, J.B., & Zhang, X. (2002). A longitudinal investigation of reading outcomes in children with language impairments. *Journal of Speech, Language, and Hearing Research, 45,* 1142–1157.

Gough, P.B., & Tunmer, W.E. (1986). Decoding, reading, and reading disability. *Remedial and Special Education, 7,* 6–10.

Graesser, A., McNamara, D.S., Louwerse, M., & Cai, Z. (2004). Coh-Metrix: Analysis of text on cohesion and language. *Behavioral Research Methods, Instruments, and Computers, 36,* 193–202.

Leach, J.M., Scarborough, H.S., & Rescorla, L. (2003). Late-emerging reading disabilities. *Journal of Educational Psychology, 95*(2), 211–224.

Perfetti, C.A. (2007). Reading ability: Lexical quality to comprehension. *Scientific Studies of Reading, 11,* 357–383.

Scarborough, H.S. (2005). Developmental relationships between language and reading: Reconciling a beautiful hypotheses with some ugly facts. In H.W. Catts & A.G. Kamhi (Eds.), *The connections between language and reading disabilities* (pp. 3–24). Mahwah, NJ: Erlbaum.

van den Broek, P.W., Helder, A., & Van Leijenhorst, L. (2012). Sensitivity to structural centrality: Developmental and individual differences in reading comprehension skills. In M.A. Britt, S.R. Goldman, & J.-F. Rouet (Eds.), *Reading: From words to multiple texts.* New York, NY: Routledge.

SECTION III

# How Can Assessment and Statistical and Computational Modeling Help Us Understand Reading Comprehension?

CHAPTER 9

# Rationale for a New Generation of Reading Comprehension Assessments

John P. Sabatini and Tenaha O'Reilly

Existing reading assessments have increasingly been criticized by researchers, educators, and policy makers, especially regarding their coverage, utility, and authenticity (e.g., Magliano, Millis, Ozuru, & McNamara, 2007; Pellegrino, Chudowsky, & Glaser, 2001; Rupp, Ferne, & Choi, 2006). Specifically, there are the following concerns about current assessments: They are poorly aligned with contemporary theoretical constructs and empirical findings pertaining to reading processes and development, are insufficiently sensitive for detecting changes in the kinds of skills that are targeted by interventions, use mainly multiple-choice formats that emphasize strategic reasoning rather than understanding of the text, provide little diagnostic information for guiding instruction, and measure comprehension using tasks and texts that do not represent the full range of the purposeful literacy activities of 21st-century reading.

In view of the foregoing criticisms, it is clear that new reading assessments are needed and desired by educators and researchers. These new assessments should draw upon the lessons that have been learned over the past several decades from prior experiences in the classroom and the laboratory. Our aim is to integrate and extend strengths of past approaches in an innovative way yet adhere to rigorous design principles that will ensure feasible implementation, good construct coverage, and strong psychometric properties. The instruments' validity and educational utility will also be enhanced if the new assessments are based on contemporary theory and research on reading, learning, and instruction.

The research reported here was supported by the Institute of Education Sciences, U.S. Department of Education, through Grant R305F100005 to the Educational Testing Service as part of the Reading for Understanding Research Initiative. The opinions expressed are those of the authors and do not represent views of the Institute, the U.S. Department of Education, or the Educational Testing Service. We wish to give special thanks to Jennifer Lentini for her help in preparing this chapter. We would also like to thank Laura Halderman and Gary Feng for their helpful comments and editorial support.

## A CONCEPTUAL FRAMEWORK FOR ASSESSING READING FOR UNDERSTANDING

The conceptual framework for the design of reading comprehension assessments we propose is a distillation of ideas and evidence drawn from and integrated over several long-standing theories (Sabatini, Albro, & O'Reilly, 2012; Sabatini, O'Reilly, & Albro, 2012). At its foundation are six principles, which are consistent with most contemporary models of reading development and reading disabilities. Associated with each principle are key design implications for assessments. These serve as a guide for the development of 21st-century reading assessments and an accompanying research agenda that can test the validity and utility of particular constructs; design approaches to operationalize them; and develop procedures for implementing, scoring, and communicating results.

There is no extant theory for which empirical support has been collected across the life span to test a unified model that integrates all facets of reading. Collectively, however, research and theories have been proposed and tested on a smaller scale in numerous studies. The empirical work is at present developmentally uneven (i.e., it is stronger on componential theories of reading in the K–3 range, stronger on mental representation models of understanding at the upper grades), and there remain healthy debates about which specific theories and models best fit the data. Nonetheless, there is sufficient agreement among theories to identify some basic principles in common, and there is ample empirical support for those principles. This framework represents our best synthesis of reading research as it relates to assessment constructs and design.

### Principle 1

Print skills and linguistic comprehension are each necessary components of reading proficiency, though neither individually is sufficient to ensure proficiency. This principle captures the essence of the simple view (Gough & Tunmer, 1986; Hoover & Gough, 1990), in which reading comprehension is seen as the product of two necessary but nonsufficient abilities: word recognition and linguistic comprehension. In the 20 years since its introduction, this model has been well supported in numerous studies (e.g., most recently, Adlof, Catts, & Little, 2006; Johnston & Kirby, 2006; Vellutino, Tunmer, & Jaccard, 2007). There is also extensive evidence for the validity and utility of word-reading and text comprehension measures for younger students and for older readers who lack mastery of basic print and language skills (e.g., Deno, Fuchs, Marston, & Shin, 2001; Perfetti, Landi, & Oakhill, 2005; Sabatini, 2002; Sabatini, Sawaki, Shore, & Scarborough, 2010).

Inefficient print processing (at both the word level and the text level) can also detract from reading proficiency, particularly as texts and tasks become longer and more complex. Across development, print-processing skills gradually become more efficient, fluent, and automatized, allowing most cognitive resources to be applied to higher order processes that are necessary for comprehension. With regard to understanding, when basic processes (e.g., decoding, word recognition) are not automatized, they require conscious effort and draw the reader's attention away from higher level comprehension processes (Cain, Oakhill, & Bryant, 2004; LaBerge & Samuels, 1974; Perfetti, 1985). Indeed, it is well demonstrated that reading proficiency correlates well with the fluency of word and text reading (Daane, Campbell, Grigg, Goodman, & Oranje, 2005; Wayman, Wallace, Wiley, Ticha, & Espin, 2007).

Furthermore, unsuccessful reading comprehension can arise from word recognition limitations in young students and in struggling older readers; assessing comprehension proficiency solely in the print modality may underestimate the competence of these students. As shown in differential boost studies (e.g., Cahalan-Laitusis, Cook, Cline, King, & Sabatini, 2008; Fletcher, Denton, & Francis, 2005), these students can often demonstrate stronger comprehension skills when provided accommodations for their weak print skills.

Compelling evidence is not available to identify the subskills that are necessary and useful to measure for summative purposes. For instance, there are many reliable and valid instruments for assessing phonological decoding, word recognition, word-reading efficiency, and text-reading fluency. However, it is not clear which of these subconstructs (at what grade or proficiency levels) adds value in assessment. Furthermore, the "linguistic comprehension" construct is rather vaguely defined in the literature and has been operationalized in various ways in research (e.g., Hagtvet, 2003; Keenan, Betjemann, & Olson, 2008), but this construct consistently demonstrates strong predictive power at most ages (Aouad & Savage, 2009; Catts, Adlof, & Weismer, 2006; Catts, Hogan, & Fey, 2003).

**Design Implications** Reading comprehension difficulties can arise from weaknesses in either print processing or oral language comprehension. In the lower grades, both skills should be measured directly. For nonproficient readers in higher grades, continuing the direct assessment of components can add value to summative assessment claims and interpretations.

## Principle 2

Both breadth and depth of vocabulary knowledge are essential for understanding. As readers mature, their vocabulary knowledge typically keeps pace with increases in world knowledge and increases largely by inferring the meanings of unfamiliar words from context. Vocabulary knowledge is important for reading comprehension, and strong correlations ($r$ = .6–.7) between them are typically observed (Anderson & Freebody, 1981; Daneman, 1988; Hirsch, 2003). This association is evident from the start of schooling and strengthens thereafter (Stanovich, West, & Harrison,

1995). Understanding of a written text is likely to be thwarted if the readers inaccurately recognize the meanings of just 5%–10% or more of the words in that text (Nagy & Scott, 2000). The reader's depth as well as breadth of word knowledge is important because many words have multiple meanings or idiomatic usages (Ouellet, 2006).

Given its strong link with comprehension, vocabulary is often measured in reading assessments. Many tests employ multiple-choice items to evaluate knowledge of synonyms and definitions, and vocabulary items can also be embedded in continuous text passages to examine contextual effects (e.g., Sheehan, Kostin, & Persky, 2006). Oral language measures of receptive and expressive vocabulary may include picture naming, picture matching, definitions, and synonym production, among others. Although there is evidence linking reading skills to the use of morphological structure to infer word meaning (Carlisle & Stone, 2003; Kieffer & Lesaux, 2007), assessment of morphology is rarely integrated into reading assessment.

**Design Implications** It is important to determine what drives weaknesses in vocabulary: lack of supporting knowledge and vocabulary in specific domains, inability to make context-based inferences about new words, or limited general vocabulary. Hence, comprehension assessments must measure lexical knowledge both within context and out of context.

## Principle 3

Readers construct mental models of text meaning at multiple levels, from literal to gist to complex situation models. These models reflect and depend on the reader's aims and prior knowledge. Contemporary views of reading comprehension emphasize the importance of differing levels or depths of understanding. To exemplify this principle, we rely on the construction integration model (Kintsch, 1988, 1998), which posits three levels of understanding that vary in their stability and depth. The *surface* level is a verbatim representation of the literal words, phrases, and structures of the text. It is typically retained only briefly, during which time the reader analyzes semantic and syntactic relationships to build the *textbase* representation or "gist" of the text. At this level, verbatim retention is lost, but critical meaning is represented abstractly as the key propositions and relationships that can be inferred among them.

The intended meaning of a text cannot always be understood from the textbase because important pertinent information may be left out (Beck, McKeown, & Gromoll, 1989). The reader must infer meaning based on prior knowledge, resulting in a deeper and more robust level of representation, the situation model (McNamara & Kintsch, 1996). Construction of a situation model allows a reader to learn new information from text by integrating unfamiliar terms and ideas with familiar schemas and knowledge.

A useful assessment should, therefore, indicate how well a student can construct different levels of understanding. It is also valuable to assess the extent to which doing so is constrained by limited background knowledge and different reading goals, tasks, and instructions.

**Design Implications** Because depth of comprehension varies between and within individuals, assessments should distinguish the literal surface code, textbase, and complex mental schemas (situation models) for texts varying in topic familiarity.

## Principle 4

Reading is ordinarily a purposeful activity, aimed at attaining a coherent understanding of a text that is sufficient for the reader's goal. Successful readers monitor and self-regulate their comprehension, enabling the repair of mental models as needed. Strategies provide a vehicle for driving deeper levels of processing. One's purpose for reading can influence what is attended to, how it is analyzed, what "standard of coherence" (desired level of comprehension) is adopted, and thus how deeply text is comprehended (van den Broek, Risden, & Husebye-Hartman, 1995). When readers adopt a low standard of coherence, they tolerate gaps in understanding; whereas when readers adopt a high standard of coherence, they must expend additional effort to deepen and embellish understanding to ensure that information is integrated into a coherent situation model and to monitor and repair breaks in understanding.

When a higher standard of coherence or deeper level of processing is demanded, the reader may call upon reading strategies as a vehicle for how to construct and organize more robust models of the text. A *reading comprehension strategy* is "a cognitive or behavioral action that is enacted under particular contextual conditions, with the goal of improving some aspect of comprehension" (Graesser, 2007, p. 6). Such strategies include question asking (e.g., King, 2007), self-explanation (e.g., McNamara, O'Reilly, Rowe, Boonthum, & Levinstein, 2007), summarization (e.g., Yu, 2003), and use of graphic organizers and tools for making text structure explicit (e.g., Meyer & Wijekumar, 2007). Although a reader's goals are often self-selected, they can be influenced by the nature of the task and text. By varying the texts and instructions during assessment, goals conducive to high versus low standards of coherence can be set and performance differences can be evaluated, providing key information for understanding the nature of comprehension difficulties for guiding instruction.

**Design Implications** More valid inferences about reading will be obtained by specifying goals for reading activities during assessment because able readers will evaluate the adequacy of their mental models in relation to those goals and will reconstruct the models accordingly.

## Principle 5

Skilled reading includes proficiency in evaluating and synthesizing information across multiple texts and text types. This requirement is magnified by the increasing prevalence of digital literacy activities. Reading skills will increasingly be deployed in evolving digital environments, and a hybrid of print and digital skills will be essential to proficiency. Even in elementary school, students are expected to consult multiple sources when engaging in literacy activities involving the Internet. However, search engines retrieve enormous numbers of documents on many topics. If a report on "the rainforest" is assigned, for example, hits will likely include a Wikipedia web page, numerous blogs, the Rainforest Café site, government policy statements, and so forth, which vary in content, media (pictures, videos), genre (narrative, argument), and intention (entertain, persuade).

To acquire a deep understanding of multiple documents, the reader must also construct a *documents model* (Perfetti, Rouet, & Britt, 1999) that integrates the information from multiple *document nodes.* A documents model requires a skilled reader to 1) encode source information, 2) evaluate relevance and trustworthiness, and 3) determine which propositional content from the documents should be emphasized in the documents model or product (e.g., report, poster).

The relatively recent advent and widespread societal use of the Internet has expanded the skill set for literacy; 21st-century readers must be facile in navigating and utilizing e-print environments (Partnership for 21st Century Skills, 2008). Today's proficient reader must be able to deploy skills of searching, retrieving, understanding, locating, evaluating, interpreting, and integrating documents in digital contexts as well as in print. Compared to print, digital environments are likely to provide novel affordances for deploying literacy skills, including using e-mail, blogging, text messaging, using search engines, and navigating web sites (Coiro, 2009). These activities do not have exact parallels in the print world, and the easily accessed information is largely unfiltered for quality and credibility and imposes a heavy burden on the reader to understand, evaluate, and interpret the information appropriately and wisely.

**Design Implications** Assessing the understanding of just one text at a time does not cover the full construct. Evaluation of document models constructed from multiple sources can be used to examine students' evaluation, integration, and synthesis of information. New assessments should be designed to be appropriate for evaluating skills in print and digital environments.

## Principle 6

Growth in reading proficiency consists of incremental expansion of knowledge and skills for the understanding of increasingly complex texts and task demands. Growth is driven primarily by the quality and quantity of instruction, experience, and practice, resulting in substantial variability within and between grade levels, schools, and socioeconomic strata. In our discussion of guiding principles, we have noted that there are developmental shifts in the relative importance of each principle in accounting for proficiency differences in reading, and consequently there are implications for assessment. In our view, these developmental changes are gradual and incremental. Although differences in reading performance between students in 1st versus 4th grade, or 6th versus 12th grade, can look qualitatively dissimilar, there is no firm evidence for discrete stages; instead, dramatic improvements over the longer term result from relatively small continuous increments in the mastery and automaticity of acquired print skills (Principle 1), in the breadth and depth of oral language knowledge and skills (Principles 1, 2), and in the variety and complexity of texts and tasks (Principles 3, 4, 5).

The rate of growth of these aspects of reading for understanding can differ in ways that will guide the design of the proposed assessments. Notably, as grade increases, 1) less emphasis will be placed on examining children's acquisition of print skills and 2) more emphasis will be placed on assessing the construction of mental models for differing text types, reading aims, and multiple media sources. Nonetheless, for certain older readers, it might also be useful to measure basic skills.

**Design Implications** Assessments should include tasks and reading materials along a developmental continuum of increasing proficiency in all aspects of reading that yield valuable information about achievement differences and sources of difficulty in reading comprehension.

## DESCRIPTION OF A NEW ASSESSMENT SYSTEM OF READING FOR UNDERSTANDING

Building on the foregoing conceptual foundation, we have been designing a new theoretically based, developmentally sensitive assessment system that consists of two main parts: 1) a set of integrated comprehension tasks, in which students read for understanding to attain a defined aim; and 2) a set of supplementary tests of component skills to use with nonproficient readers in order to provide information to identify or rule out potential bases for comprehension difficulties.

The logic of this approach is that global, integrated reading texts and task performances afford multiple cues (e.g., inferential, knowledge) that an individual can exploit to bootstrap performance to compensate for weak individual component subskills (O'Reilly & McNamara, 2007; Walczyk, Marsiglia, Johns, & Bryan, 2004). For proficient readers, the availability of multiple, overlapping sources of information reduces the complexity of processing. For the nonproficient reader, the wealth of sources may actually enable performance at an artificially high level that is not sustainable as the student encounters more complex texts and tasks in subsequent years. Thus, given their utility for predicting potential risk for a decline in achievement, separate tests of component skills are warranted because weaknesses in those areas could be masked in an integrated assessment.

## A GLOBAL, INTEGRATED SUMMATIVE ASSESSMENT OF READING FOR UNDERSTANDING

We envision a global, integrated summative assessment (GISA) of reading comprehension that parallels the kinds of activities that students typically engage in. These activities begin with a specific purpose or goal and proceed with actions that achieve that goal. The actions include searching for relevant information, evaluating the information's quality and pertinence, synthesizing and integrating it with other information, and producing a product that satisfies the goal. As such, reading for understanding usually is not a passive activity that involves answering comprehension questions on a collection of unrelated passages but rather a focused and more complex process of constructing meaning from text(s) in order to meet task goals.

We recognize the challenges and pitfalls of previous performance assessments that relied on a small set of complex tasks and that yielded limited information per individual (weakening reliability and discrimination). In contrast, we envision maintaining a large percentage of discrete, objectively scored items, with a smaller mix of constructed-response items. We have had success in models stemming from other reading comprehension projects to build upon (Bennett, 2011; Deane, Sabatini, & O'Reilly, 2011; O'Reilly & Sheehan, 2009; Sheehan & O'Reilly, 2011).

The GISA will examine the student's 1) proficiencies in constructing different levels of representations (textbase, situation, multiple source; Kintsch, 1998), 2) familiarity with text structure and genre differences (Goldman & Rakestraw, 2000), 3) deployment of executive or metacognitive processes (Schraw, 2000), and 4) application of strategies for attaining a literacy goal (McCrudden & Schraw, 2007). The goal is to broaden the coverage of the assessment while maintaining standardized testing conditions and adequate measurement.

## COMPONENT SKILLS ASSESSMENTS

For assessments to more appropriately cover the full reading construct range, we hypothesize that measurement of component skills for nonproficient readers is justified and will provide more useful information to guide instructional decision making than relying solely on integrated measures. Separate component skill subsections of a summative assessment targeted at less proficient readers can solve the problem and provide more specific information on strengths and weaknesses underlying nonproficient reading. However, component skills do not, on their own, sum up to reading proficiency. That is, one could hypothetically be proficient in each subskill and still fail to adequately integrate them.

## CONCLUSIONS AND IMPLICATIONS

Reading or reading comprehension have always been and will always be social constructs. Writing systems change, languages evolve, technologies advance, cultures and societies shift, and the social value and meaning of literacy follow along. We cannot define or legislate what reading comprehension is, but we can observe and describe it in the historical moment, then use the tools of science to understand and interpret it, and then, we hope, help individuals and groups to better acquire and use this valuable social technology of learning, communication, personal growth, and societal participation (Venezky, 1990). The rationale and assessment system we have described tries to capture key aspects of literacy in this historical moment. It tries to be as explicit as current research permits, in parsing the construct into elements or principles that we anticipate may interact with individual differences among learners.

The complexities of one's language, one's writing system, and the social context of literacy practices and uses will interact with individual differences, resulting in relative advantages or disadvantages for individuals as they learn to read and become literate. Being more explicit about the elements of the construct will, we hope, improve the value and utility of resulting assessment scores in informing researchers how best to help individuals with differences to demonstrate what they can do and what they struggle with en route to their acquiring proficiency.

## REFERENCES


Adlof, S.M., Catts, H.W., & Little, T.D. (2006). Should the simple view of reading include a fluency component? *Reading and Writing, 19,* 933–958.

Anderson, R.C., & Freebody, P. (1981). Vocabulary knowledge. In J.T. Guthrie (Ed.), *Comprehension and teaching* (pp. 77–117). Newark, DE: International Reading Association.

Aouad, J., & Savage, R. (2009). The component structure of preliteracy skills: Further evidence for the simple view of reading. *Canadian Journal of School Psychology, 24,* 183–200.

Beck, I.L., McKeown, M.G., & Gromoll, E.W. (1989). Learning from social studies texts. *Cognition & Instruction, 6,* 99–158.

Bennett, R.E. (2011). *CBAL: Results from piloting innovative K–12 assessments* (ETS Research Report No. RR-11-23). Princeton, NJ: Educational Testing Service.

Cahalan-Laitusis, C., Cook, LL., Cline, F., King, T., & Sabatini, J. (2008). *Examining the impact of audio presentation on tests of reading comprehension* (ETS Research Report No. RR-08-23). Princeton, NJ: Educational Testing Service.

Cain, K., Oakhill, J., & Bryant, P. (2004). Children's reading comprehension ability: Concurrent prediction by working memory, verbal ability, and component skills. *Journal of Educational Psychology, 96,* 31–42.

Carlisle, J.F., & Stone, C.A. (2003). The effects of morphological structure on children's reading of derived words. In E. Assink & D. Santa (Eds.), *Reading complex words: Cross-language studies* (pp. 27–52). New York, NY: Kluwer Academic.

Catts, H., Adlof, S., & Weismer, S. (2006). Language deficits in poor comprehenders: A case for the simple view of reading. *Journal of Speech, Language & Hearing Research, 49,* 278–293.

Catts, H.W., Hogan, T.P., & Fey, M.E. (2003). Subgrouping poor readers on the basis of individual differences in reading-related abilities. *Journal of Learning Disabilities, 36,* 151–164.

Coiro, J. (2009). Rethinking reading assessment in a digital age: How is reading comprehension different and where do we turn now? *Educational Leadership, 66,* 59–63.

Daane, M.C., Campbell, J.R., Grigg, W.S., Goodman, M.J., & Oranje, A. (2005). *Fourth-grade students reading aloud: NAEP 2002 special study of oral reading* (NCES No. 2006-469). Washington, DC: National Center for Education Statistics, Institute of Education Sciences, U.S. Department of Education.

Daneman, M. (1988). Word knowledge and reading skill. In M. Daneman, G.E. Mackinnon, & T.G. Waller (Eds.), *Reading research: Advances in theory and practice* (Vol. 6, pp. 145–175). San Diego, CA: Academic Press.

Deane, P., Sabatini, J., & O'Reilly, T. (2011). *English language arts literacy framework.* Princeton, NJ: Educational Testing Service.

Deno, S.L., Fuchs, L.S., Marston, D., & Shin, J. (2001). Using curriculum-based measurements to establish growth standards for students with learning disabilities. *School Psychology Review, 30,* 507–524.

Fletcher, J.M., Denton, C., & Francis, D.J. (2005). Validity of alternative approaches for the identification of learning disabilities: Operationalizing unexpected underachievement. *Journal of Learning Disabilities, 38,* 545–552.

Goldman, S.R., & Rakestraw, J.A. (2000). Structural aspects of constructing meaning from text. In M.L. Kamil, P.B. Mosenthal, P.D. Pearson, & R. Barr (Eds.), *Handbook of reading research* (Vol. 2, pp. 311–335). Mahwah, NJ: Erlbaum.

Gough, P.B., & Tunmer, W.E. (1986). Decoding, reading, and reading disability. *Remedial and Special Education, 7,* 6–10.

Graesser, A.C. (2007). Theories of text comprehension: The importance of reading strategies to theoretical foundations of reading comprehension. In D.S. McNamara (Ed.), *Reading comprehension strategies: Theories, interventions, and technologies* (pp. 3–26). Mahwah, NJ: Erlbaum.

Hagtvet, B.E. (2003). Listening comprehension and reading comprehension in poor decoders: Evidence for the importance of syntactic and semantic skills as well as phonological skills. *Reading & Writing, 16,* 505–539.

Hirsch, E.D. (2003). Reading comprehension requires knowledge of words and the world. *American Educator, 27,* 10–31.

Hoover, W.A., & Gough, P.B. (1990). The simple view of reading. *Reading and Writing: An Interdisciplinary Journal, 2,* 127–160.

Johnston, T.C., & Kirby, J.R. (2006). The contribution of naming speed to the simple view of reading. *Reading and Writing, 19,* 339–361.

Keenan, J.M., Betjemann, R.S., & Olson, R.K. (2008). Reading comprehension tests vary in the skills they assess: Differential dependence on decoding and oral comprehension. *Scientific Studies of Reading, 12,* 281–300.

Kieffer, M.J., & Lesaux, N.K. (2007). Breaking down words to build meaning: Morphology, vocabulary, and reading comprehension in the urban classroom. *Reading Teacher, 61,* 134–144.

King, A. (2007). Beyond literal comprehension: A strategy to promote deep understanding of text. In D.S. McNamara (Ed.), *Reading comprehension strategies: Theory, interventions, and technologies* (pp. 267–290). Mahwah, NJ: Erlbaum.

Kintsch, W. (1988). The role of knowledge in discourse comprehension: A construction–integration model. *Psychological Review, 95,* 163–182.

Kintsch, W. (1998). *Comprehension: A paradigm for cognition.* Cambridge, England: Cambridge University Press.

LaBerge, D., & Samuels, S.J. (1974). Toward a theory of automatic information processing in reading. *Cognitive Psychology, 6,* 293–323.

Magliano, J.P., Millis, K.K., Ozuru, Y., & McNamara, D.S. (2007). A multidimensional framework to evaluate reading assessment tools. In D.S. McNamara (Ed.), *Reading comprehension strategies: Theory, interventions, and technologies* (pp. 107–136). Mahwah, NJ: Erlbaum.

McCrudden, M.T., & Schraw, G. (2007). Relevance and goal-focusing in text processing. *Educational Psychology Review, 19,* 113–139.

McNamara, D.S., & Kintsch, W. (1996). Learning from text: Effects of prior knowledge and text coherence. *Discourse Processes, 22,* 247–288.

McNamara, D.S., O'Reilly, T., Rowe, M., Boonthum, C., & Levinstein, I. (2007). iSTART: A web-based tutor that teaches self-explanation and metacognitive reading strategies. In D.S. McNamara (Ed.), *Reading comprehension strategies: Theory, interventions, and technologies* (pp. 397–420). Mahwah, NJ: Erlbaum.

Meyer, B., & Wijekumar, K. (2007). A web based tutoring system for the structure strategy: Theoretical background, design, and findings. In D.S. McNamara (Ed.), *Reading comprehension strategies: Theory, interventions, and technologies* (pp. 347–374). Mahwah, NJ: Erlbaum.

Nagy, W., & Scott, J. (2000). Vocabulary process. In M. Kamil, P.B. Mosenthal, P.D. Pearson, & R. Barr (Eds.), *Handbook of reading research* (Vol. 3, pp. 269–284). Mahwah, NJ: Erlbaum.

O'Reilly, T., & McNamara, D.S. (2007). The impact of science knowledge, reading skill, and reading strategy knowledge on more traditional "high stakes" measures of high school students' science achievement. *American Educational Research Journal, 44,* 161–196.

O'Reilly, T., & Sheehan, K.M. (2009). *Cognitively based assessment of, for, and as learning: A framework for assessing reading competency* (ETS Research Report No. RR-09-26). Princeton, NJ: Educational Testing Service.

Ouellet, G.P. (2006). What's meaning got to do with it: The role of vocabulary in word reading and reading comprehension. *Journal of Educational Psychology, 98,* 554–566.

Partnership for 21st Century Skills. (2008). *21st century skills and English map.* Retrieved from http://www.p21.org/storage/documents/21st_century_skills_english_map.pdf

Pellegrino, J.W., Chudowsky, N., & Glaser, R. (2001). *Knowing what students know: The science and design of educational assessment.* Washington, DC: National Academy Press.

Perfetti, C.A. (1985). *Reading ability.* New York, NY: Oxford University Press.

Perfetti, C.A., Landi, N., & Oakhill, J. (2005). The acquisition of reading comprehension skill. In M.J. Snowling & C. Hulme (Eds.), *The science of reading: A handbook* (pp. 227–247). Oxford, England: Blackwell.

Perfetti, C.A., Rouet, J., & Britt, M.A. (1999). Toward a theory of document representation. In H. van Oostendorp & S.R. Goldman (Eds.), *The construction of mental representations during reading* (pp. 99–122). Mahwah, NJ: Erlbaum.

Rupp, A., Ferne, T., & Choi, H. (2006). How assessing reading comprehension with multiple-choice questions shapes the construct: A cognitive processing perspective. *Language Testing, 23,* 441–474.

Sabatini, J.P. (2002). Efficiency in word reading of adults: Ability group comparisons. *Scientific Studies of Reading, 6,* 267–298.

Sabatini, J., Albro, E., & O'Reilly, T. (2012). *Measuring up: Advances in how we assess reading ability.* Lanham, MD: Rowman & Littlefield Education.

Sabatini, J., O'Reilly, T., & Albro, E. (2012). *Reaching an understanding: Innovations in how we view reading assessment.* Lanham, MD: Rowman & Littlefield Education.

Sabatini, J., Sawaki, Y., Shore, J., & Scarborough, H. (2010). Relationships among reading skills of low-literate adults. *Journal of Learning Disabilities, 43,* 122–138.

Schraw, G. (2000). Assessing metacognition: Implications of the Buros symposium. In G. Schraw & J.C. Impara (Eds.), *Issues in the measurement of metacognition* (pp. 297–321). Lincoln, NE: Buros Institute of Mental Measurements.

Sheehan, K.M., Kostin, I., & Persky, H. (2006, April). *Predicting item difficulty as a function of inferential processing requirements: An examination of the reading skills underlying performance on the NAEP grade 8 reading assessment.* Paper presented at the Annual Meeting of the National Council on Measurement in Education, San Francisco, CA.

Sheehan, K.M., & O'Reilly, T. (2011). *The CBAL reading assessment: An approach for balancing measurement and learning goals* (ETS Research Report No. RR-11-21). Princeton, NJ: Educational Testing Service.

Stanovich, K.E., West, R.F., & Harrison, M.R. (1995). Knowledge growth and maintenance across the life span: The role of print exposure. *Developmental Psychology, 31,* 811–826.

van den Broek, P., Risden, K., & Husebye-Hartman, E. (1995). The role of the reader's standards of coherence in the generation of inference during reading. In R.F. Lorch, Jr. & E.J. O'Brian (Eds.), *Sources of coherence in text comprehension* (pp. 353–373). Mahwah, NJ: Erlbaum.

Vellutino, F., Tunmer, W., & Jaccard, J. (2007). Components of reading ability: Multivariate evidence for a convergent skills model of reading development. *Scientific Studies of Reading, 11,* 3–32.

Venezky, R.L. (1990). Definitions of literacy. In R.L. Venezky, D.A. Wagner, & B.S. Ciliberti (Eds.), *Toward defining literacy* (pp. 2–16). Newark, DE: International Reading Association.

Walczyk, J.J., Marsiglia, C.S., Johns, A.K., & Bryan, K.S. (2004). Children's compensations for poorly automated reading skills. *Discourse Processes, 37,* 47–66.

Wayman, M.M., Wallace, T., Wiley, H.I., Ticha, R., & Espin, C.A. (2007). Literature synthesis on curriculum-based measurement in reading. *Journal of Special Education, 41,* 85–120.

Yu, G. (2003). Reading for summarization as reading comprehension test method: Promises and problems. *Language Testing Update, 32,* 44–47.

CHAPTER 10

# The Development of Eye-Movement Control and Reading Skill

Erik D. Reichle

Recent refinements of eye-tracking technology have made it possible to examine how children's eye-movement behavior changes as they become skilled adult readers (for a review, see Blythe & Joseph, 2011). This development provides a tremendous opportunity to learn more about the development of reading skill; eye tracking has arguably taught us more about what transpires in the mind of a reader than has any other methodology (Rayner, 1998, 2009). Apart from the fact that eye movements provide an unobtrusive way to measure the time course of cognitive processing in an on-line, ecologically valid manner, the recent development of computational models of eye-movement control provides rigorous theoretical frameworks for thinking about how the perceptual, cognitive, and oculomotor systems that support skilled reading give rise to the patterns of eye movements that are observed during reading (Reichle, Rayner, & Pollatsek, 2003). These advances have recently resulted in attempts to understand the changes that occur as beginning readers (i.e., 7–8-year-old children who are capable of reading simple sentences and correctly answering comprehension questions about the meaning of those sentences) become skilled adult readers (Reichle et al., 2012) and as skilled readers become elderly readers (Kliegl, Grabner, Rolfs, & Engbert, 2004; Rayner, Reichle, Stoud, Williams, & Pollatsek, 2006). These efforts have provided important new hypotheses about the life-span trajectory of reading skill development, and it is this topic that will be the focus of the remainder of this chapter. More specifically, this chapter has four main goals: 1) to briefly review what is known about the eye-movements of skilled adult readers, 2) to review what is known about how the eye movements of this group differ from those of both beginning readers and elderly readers, 3) to describe a computational framework that is sufficient to account for these findings, and 4) to suggest a framework for thinking about age-related differences in reading skill.

## EYE MOVEMENTS DURING READING

Contrary to what most people subjectively experience, the eyes of skilled adult readers do not move continuously or smoothly across the printed page but instead make rapid ballistic movements (called *saccades*) that move the eyes to viewing locations (called *fixations*) where the eyes remain relatively stationary (for reviews, see Rayner, 1998, 2009). In alphabetic languages like English, 70%–80% of saccades move the eyes forward to the next word; the remaining saccades move the eyes to a new viewing location within the same word (resulting in a *refixation*), a word farther to the right of the next word (resulting in the next word being *skipped*), or to a previously viewed word to the left of the fixated word (resulting in an interword *regression*). Although saccades can be almost any length, most are shorter than 15 character spaces, with the mean being about 7–9 character spaces. Because useful visual information is not extracted from the page during saccades, the information that is needed to identify printed words is obtained during fixations, which are typically 200–250 ms in duration but can be considerably shorter or longer. The rate at which useful visual information can be extracted is also limited by two important factors: limitations in visual acuity and the manner in which attention (which is necessary to lexical processing) can be allocated.

Rayner and Morrison (1981) demonstrated the importance of limited visual acuity in an experiment wherein subjects identified printed words that were displayed at various eccentricities from the center of vision. (An eye-tracker was used to ensure that subjects did not move their eyes to identify words that were displayed in peripheral vision.) The main finding was that subjects' response accuracies decreased and their response latencies increased as words were displayed farther from the center of vision. This result is not unanticipated, given the known physiology of the eye; the photoreceptors that are necessary to perceive fine detail (e.g., letter features) are concentrated in the central 2° of the visual field, in the *fovea,* but decrease precipitously outside this region.

The important role of attention was most convincingly demonstrated by McConkie and Rayner (1975, 1976) using *gaze-contingent paradigms,* in which what a subject views on a computer monitor at any point in time is contingent upon where that subject is looking. For example, in the *moving-window paradigm,* the text outside a moving "window" that is centered on a subject's fixation is manipulated in some manner (e.g., replaced with random letters) to determine how this manipulation affects the *perceptual span,* or spatial extent over which useful visual information is extracted during reading. It is somewhat surprising that the results of many such studies (for reviews, see Rayner, 1998, 2009) indicate that the perceptual span is remarkably limited, allowing information about word boundaries to be extracted up to 15 character spaces to the right of fixation, but allowing information about individual letters to be extracted only up to 7–8 characters to the right of fixation. Although one might wonder whether this limitation reflects attention per se rather than the limitations of visual acuity that were discussed earlier, an experiment involving English-Hebrew bilinguals provides compelling evidence that the perceptual span reflects attention and not limitations in visual acuity: When these subjects read English, their perceptual span extended asymmetrically to the *right* of fixation; but when they read Hebrew (which is read from right to left), their perceptual span extended asymmetrically to the *left* of the fixation (Pollatsek, Bolozky, Well, & Rayner, 1981).

The rate of information extraction is, of course, also influenced by the processing difficulty associated with the text that is being read, with these influences being both global and local. At the global level, overall reading rate decreases as text difficulty increases (Rayner, 1998, 2009). At the local level, the number and duration of individual fixations are both affected by a variety of variables that are related to lexical and linguistic processing difficulty. For example, words that are infrequent in the language are the recipients of more, longer fixations than are words that occur frequently (Schilling, Rayner, & Chumbley, 1998). Similarly, words that are predictable from their preceding sentence context are fixated for less time than are unpredictable words (Rayner, Ashby, Pollatsek, & Reichle, 2004). The basic fact that fixation durations are sensitive to these types of local processing difficulties is one of the primary reasons that eye tracking has been so useful for understanding language processing; eye movements have been productively used to study a wide variety of topics related to lexical, sentence, and discourse processing (Rayner, 1998, 2009).

Of course, this discussion of eye movements in reading has so far focused almost exclusively on the perceptual and cognitive variables that influence readers' eye movements. Eye movements during reading are also influenced by the operating characteristics of the oculomotor system itself. For example, contrary to subjective experiences, eye movements are not executed instantaneously but are instead programmed in two successive stages, each of which takes some amount of time to complete. These facts were demonstrated by Becker and Jürgens (1979) using a *double-step paradigm* in which subjects were instructed to simply move their eyes as quickly as possible from a centrally displayed fixation cross to a dot that would appear at various locations. On some proportion of the trials, the dot would briefly appear but then instantaneously move to a second location. The key findings from this study were as follows: First, subjects required 125–175 ms to program and then initiate their eye movements. Second, if the time interval between the onset of the first and second dot was short enough, subjects moved their eyes directly to the second dot location, indicating that the initial saccadic program had been canceled; otherwise, subjects made a very brief fixation on the first location followed by a rapid saccade to the second. Based on these findings, Becker and Jürgens concluded that eye movements are completed in two stages: an early, *labile stage* that requires 100–125 ms to complete and that can be canceled by the initiation of a second saccade (e.g., to the second dot location), followed by a second, *nonlabile stage* that requires 25–50 ms to complete and that causes saccade execution to be obligatory.

The actual movement of the eyes is also not instantaneous but instead increases in duration with length; so in the context of reading, most saccades are 20–40 ms in duration. The saccades are also subject to two types of motor error, random and systematic (McConkie et al., 1991). The random error causes the fixations to deviate from their intended targets in a Gaussian manner, so fixation landing-site distributions are approximately normal with missing tails that reflect instances where the eye either under- or overshoots the intended targets. The systematic error likewise causes fixations to deviate from their intended targets; so in English, at least, saccades shorter than about seven character spaces tend to go past their targets and saccades longer than about seven character spaces tend to fall short of their targets. Thus, whereas the random error reflects the inherent variability associated with the oculomotor system in making eye movements, the systematic error reflects some type of task-specific tuning of the oculomotor system to prefer saccades of a particular length.

Given what is known about how visual, cognitive, and oculomotor constraints affect readers' eye movements, the challenge has been to develop computational models that specify exactly how these different factors produce the patterns of eye movements that are observed during reading. The third section of this chapter will focus exclusively on one of these models, E-Z Reader (Reichle, Pollatsek, Fisher, & Rayner, 1998; Reichle, Warren, & McConnell, 2009; for a review, see Reichle, 2011), because of its conceptual transparency and because it has been used as a theoretical framework for thinking about how age-related differences in reading ability influence readers' eye movements (Rayner et al., 2006; Reichle et al., 2012). Before doing this, however, it is first necessary to briefly review what is known about these age-related differences in eye movements.

## AGE-RELATED DIFFERENCES IN READERS' EYE MOVEMENTS

A number of studies have shown that the eye movements of beginning readers, or children who have developed enough lexical-processing proficiency to read simple sentences, differ in fundamental ways from those of skilled adult readers (Blythe & Joseph, 2011). For example, relative to adult readers, children tend to make more frequent, longer fixations, with shorter saccades and more of those saccades being regressions back to earlier parts of the text. These differences contribute to the fact that, with all else being equal, children are slower readers than adults. In addition, children have smaller perceptual spans (Rayner, 1986); for example, whereas skilled adult readers respectively extract letter identities from up to 8 character spaces to the right of fixation and word boundaries from up to 15 character spaces to the right of fixation, children extract each of these respective types of information from only 5 and 11 characters to the right of fixation (Häikiö, Bertram, Hyönä, & Niemi, 2009).

To explain this basic pattern of differences, a number of eye-movement experiments have documented the extent to which various lexical and linguistic variables influence children's versus adults' eye movements. For example, both children and adults seem to be similarly affected by word length, being more apt to fixate long than short words and guiding their eyes toward the centers of words (Vitu, McConkie, Kerr, & O'Regan, 2001). Both groups are also more likely to refixate long than short words, although the children seem to be more likely to refixate, especially following an initial fixation near the end of a word (Joseph, Liversedge, Blythe, White, & Rayner, 2009). These results suggest that saccade targeting and execution are similar between adults and children and that both groups make similar decisions about *where* to move their eyes during reading. But similarity is less true of the decisions about *when* to move the eyes. For example, studies have shown that the effects of word frequency are more pronounced with children than adults (Blythe, Liversedge, Joseph, White, & Rayner, 2009). And although children detect semantic anomalies (e.g., "Robert used a radio to play the horrible mouse") in a manner similar to adults, adults rapidly detect such violations on the anomalous words themselves, whereas children are slower, detecting such violations after the anomalous words (Joseph et al., 2008).

With the attainment of adult reading levels, individuals appear to have stable reading skills, although recent evidence suggests that reading skill again changes with advanced age. For example, two studies comparing college-age versus elderly readers found that, relative to the former group, elderly readers tended to make longer fixations and tended to skip words more often, but they were also more likely to make regressions to the skipped words (Kliegl et al., 2004; Rayner et al., 2006). It is therefore necessary to explain these findings to have a full account of reading skill and its development; the next section of this chapter is intended to provide such an account.

## AN ACCOUNT OF AGE-RELATED DIFFERENCES

As indicated earlier, one theoretical framework that has already proven useful for thinking about age-related differences in readers' eye movements is the E-Z Reader model (Reichle, 2011). This model consists of a small number of equations and parameters that specify the time required to complete various perceptual, cognitive, and motoric processes that are involved in reading. Because the length of this chapter prohibits a detailed discussion of the model and its assumptions, and because prior simulation results have demonstrated that varying the parameters associated with lexical and postlexical processing is sufficient to account for observed developmental changes in readers' eye movements (see Reichle et al., 2012), the following model description will focus on those model components that are most relevant to development.

Figure 10.1 is a schematic diagram of the model. As the figure shows, the model consists of several components that determine the metrics of saccadic programming and execution, as well as the time course of lexical and postlexical processing and how this processing influences saccadic programming. The three core model assumptions are that 1) attention, which is necessary to identify printed words, is allocated in a strictly serial manner to only one word at a time; 2) the completion of an early stage of lexical processing, called the *familiarity check,* on $word_n$ initiates saccadic programming to move the eyes to $word_{n+1}$; and 3) the completion of *lexical access* of $word_n$ causes attention to shift to $word_{n+1}$.

The times (in milliseconds) required to complete the familiarity check and lexical access during any given simulation are random deviates that are sampled from gamma distributions (see Figure 10.1, inset) having means determined by Equations 10.1 and 10.2, respectively. As the equations specify, the mean maximum times required to complete these processes for a given word are determined by a free parameter $\alpha_1$ (= 104) that is attenuated by a word's log frequency of occurrence in printed text and within-sentence predictability (i.e., the mean proportion of time that the word can be guessed from its preceding sentence context), as modulated by the parameters $\alpha_2$ (= 3.5) and $\alpha_3$ (= 39), respectively. As Equation 10.2 shows, the mean time required to complete lexical access is some fixed proportion $\Delta$ (= 0.34) of the time required to complete the familiarity check.

$$\text{Familiarity check (ms)} = \alpha_1 - \alpha_2 \ln(\text{frequency}) - \alpha_3 \text{ predictability} \quad \text{(Equation 10.1)}$$

$$\text{Lexical access (ms)} = \Delta\,[\alpha_1 - \alpha_2 \ln(\text{frequency}) - \alpha_3 \text{ predictability}] \quad \text{(Equation 10.2)}$$

Finally, each identified word is processed during a stage of postlexical integration that, on average, requires *I* (= 25) ms to complete. In most

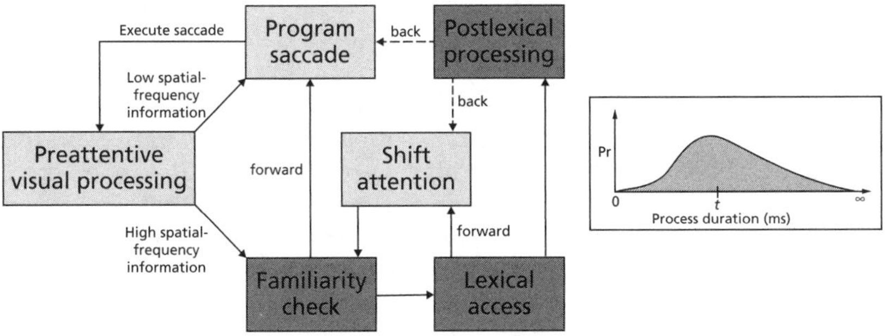


**Figure 10.1.** A schematic diagram of the E-Z Reader model of eye movements in reading. The inset shows a gamma distribution; the times required to complete each of the model's component processes (in milliseconds) are random deviates that are sampled from such distributions.

instances, integration proceeds without difficulty, but if word$_n$ has not been integrated before word$_{n+1}$ has been identified, or if integration fails (with probability $p_F = 0.01$), then the eyes and attention are directed back to the source of integration difficulty, often resulting in an interword regression. It is important to note that the values of each of the aforementioned parameters were selected to allow the model to simulate various eye-movement measures obtained from skilled adult readers (Schilling et al., 1998). For that reason, the model's default parameters are theoretical constructs that specify what happens with adult readers; also for that reason, it is possible to make inferences about what is happening with beginning readers by adjusting the values of the parameters to simulate children's data.

Reichle et al. (2012) completed such simulations and found that simply increasing the value of $\alpha_1$ (e.g., from 104 ms to 185 ms) to simulate a reduced rate of lexical processing in children was sufficient to account for all but one of the basic differences that have been observed between the eye movements of adults and those of children; the one exception was the finding that children are slower at detecting semantic anomalies (Joseph et al., 2008). To explain this last finding, it was also necessary to increase the value of $I$ (e.g., from 25 ms to 100 ms) to simulate a reduced rate of postlexical integration in children. Based on these results, Reichle et al. concluded that their simulations are consistent with the hypothesis that increasing linguistic proficiency mainly explains why children's eye movements come to resemble those of skilled adult readers. (Simulations conducted to test whether adjustments of the parameters that control the rate and accuracy of saccadic programming and execution indicated that such adjustments were not sufficient to explain children's eye movements during reading, thus providing evidence against the hypothesis that increasing oculomotor skill is the primary difference between children and adults.)

This *linguistic-proficiency hypothesis* is also consistent with simulations that were completed to examine the reason why the eye movements of elderly adult readers differ from those of college-level readers (Rayner et al., 2006). To explain the finding that elderly readers typically make longer fixations, it was necessary only to increase the value of $\alpha_1$ to simulate the decreased rate of lexical processing that results from the general cognitive slowing that occurs with age. Similarly, to explain the finding that elderly readers skip words more often but are also more likely to make regressions to those words, it was necessary only to increase the value of $\alpha_3$ to simulate the elderly readers' increased reliance upon word predictability to constrain their identities from context and to assume that some fraction of those words are "guessed" incorrectly, resulting in interword regressions. That these simple parameter adjustments were sufficient to account for the observed differences between the eye movements of college-age readers and those of elderly readers again lends support to the linguistic-proficiency hypothesis, suggesting that, across a reader's life span, the main determinant of reading skill is the speed and accuracy of identifying printed words to build linguistic representations of text. The final section of this chapter will explore a few of the theoretical implications of this hypothesis.

## CONCLUSIONS

The developmental account of readers' eye movements that emerges from the preceding discussion and the simulation results using the E-Z Reader model (Reichle et al., 2012) suggests that three basic components of reading determine reading skill: 1) basic oculomotor control (e.g., tuning of the oculomotor system); 2) proficient lexical processing; and 3) proficient (postlexical) linguistic processing. To facilitate the discussion of how these components might contribute to the development of reading skill and explain between-individual differences in this capacity, it is first necessary to discuss the possible developmental trajectory of these components. Figure 10.2 attempts to schematically depict this trajectory.

As Figure 10.2 shows, the ability to control one's eyes as necessary to read efficiently presumably develops very early in life because the capacity to rapidly and accurately move one's eyes to the location of an unidentified word is presumably co-opted from an even more basic skill—namely, the capacity to rapidly and accurately move one's eyes to the location of an unidentified object. As such, eye-movement behaviors that are observed in reading (e.g., directing the eyes toward the centers of words) presumably emerge rapidly in response to perceptual (e.g., visual acuity) and oculomotor (e.g., saccadic error) constraints and the task demands of reading (e.g., identify words rapidly, in their correct order; see Reichle & Laurent, 2006).

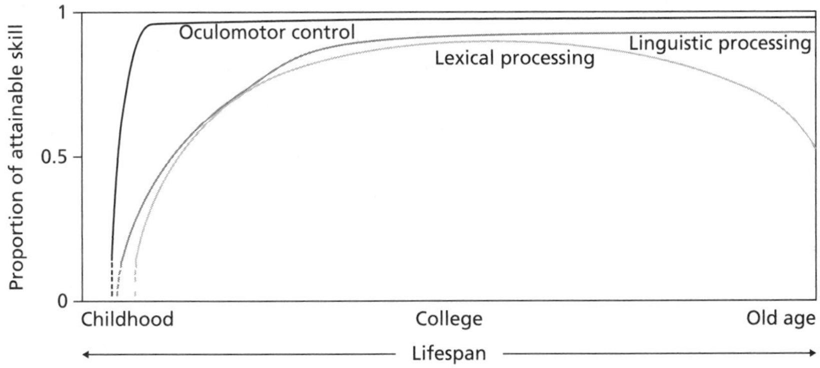


**Figure 10.2.** The development of oculomotor control, lexical processing, and linguistic processing across a reader's life span (*x*-axis not drawn to scale) to some proportion of a theoretically maximum attainable skill level (*y*-axis also not drawn to scale).

In stark contrast to basic oculomotor control, the capacity to identify printed words requires extensive practice to become rapid and accurate. As a result, this skill probably continues to develop late into childhood, perhaps even continuing into adulthood where college-age students continue to learn new (mostly technical) vocabulary. It is important to note that reading skill continues to increase as this basic skill becomes increasingly proficient; that is, as the previously reported simulations suggest, as the rate of lexical processing continues to increase, the reader becomes increasingly proficient at extracting information from the printed page, thereby increasing his or her overall reading rate and producing the pattern of eye movements indicative of skilled adult readers.

As Figure 10.2 also shows, however, at some much later point in life the capacity to rapidly and accurately identify printed words actually begins to decline. This decline in lexical-processing efficiency probably reflects a general slowing in cognitive processing as a result of advancing age. This decline might be partially compensated for, however, by an increasing reliance upon linguistic and/or pragmatic knowledge to help process text. As Figure 10.2 shows, higher-level language proficiency continues to improve with age, thereby providing a means that some (skilled) elderly readers might exploit to offset the decreased rate of lexical processing that results from age.

If this general sketch of reading skill is approximately accurate, then it suggests that, at any point in the life span of a reader, his or her reading skill will reflect some balance in the three underlying component skills, although the preponderance of the variance is presumably accounted for by proficiency in lexical and linguistic processing. As Figure 10.2 also shows, however, considerable uncertainty remains concerning the earliest stages of reading skill development and how children learn to coordinate their eye movements to support lexical and linguistic processing.

In the next few years, this area of residual ignorance will benefit from new empirical research and the application of computational models to better understand how the perceptual, cognitive, and oculomotor processes intrinsic to reading change as a child becomes a skilled reader (e.g., see Reichle, forthcoming). Such models will provide theoretical frameworks for understanding the full complexity of reading and its development, as well as how suboptimal performance of one or more of its component processes and/or their lack of coordination might result in poor reading comprehension (e.g., dyslexia). The capacity to accurately simulate good versus poor readers might also make the models invaluable tools for evaluating the efficacy of different remediation programs; for example, such a reading model might be used to rapidly predict the degree to which a particular training program will improve the performance of a struggling reader. This type of application of models will therefore provide a new level of rigor to the understanding and treatment of reading disorders.

## REFERENCES


Becker, W., & Jürgens, R. (1979). An analysis of the saccadic system by means of double step stimuli. *Vision Research, 19*, 967–983.

Blythe, H.I., & Joseph, H.S.S.L. (2011). Children's eye movements during reading. In S.P. Liversedge, I.D. Gilchrist, & S. Everling (Eds.), *Oxford handbook on eye movements* (pp. 643–662). Oxford, England: Oxford University Press.

Blythe, H.I., Liversedge, S.P., Joseph, H.S.S.L., White, S.J., & Rayner, K. (2009). Visual information capture during fixations in reading for children and adults. *Vision Research, 49*, 1583–1591.

Häikiö, T., Bertram, R., Hyönä, J., & Niemi, P. (2009). Development of the letter identity span in reading: Evidence from the eye movement moving window paradigm. *Journal of Experimental Child Psychology, 102*, 167–181.

Joseph, H.S.S.L., Liversedge, S.P., Blythe, H.I., White, S.J., Gathercole, S.E., & Rayner, K. (2008). Children's and adults' processing of anomaly and implausibility during reading: Evidence from eye movements. *Quarterly Journal of Experimental Psychology, 61*, 708–723.

Joseph, H.S.S.L., Liversedge, S.P., Blythe, H.I., White, S.J., & Rayner, K. (2009). Word length and landing position effects during reading in children and adults. *Vision Research, 49*, 2078–2086.

Kliegl, R., Grabner, E., Rolfs, M., & Engbert, R. (2004). Length, frequency, and predictability effects of word on eye movements in reading. *European Journal of Cognitive Psychology, 16*, 262–284.

McConkie, G.W., & Rayner, K. (1975). The span of effective stimulus during a fixation in reading. *Perception & Psychophysics, 17*, 578–586.

McConkie, G.W., Zola, D., Grimes, J., Kerr, P.W., Bryant, N.R., & Wolff, P.M. (1991). Children's eye movements during reading. In J.F. Stein (Ed.), *Vision and visual dyslexics* (pp. 251–262). London, England: MacMillan.

Pollatsek, A., Bolozky, S., Well, A.D., & Rayner, K. (1981). Asymmetries in the perceptual span for Israeli readers. *Brain and Language, 14*, 174–180.

Rayner, K. (1986). Eye movements and the perceptual span in beginning and skilled readers. *Journal of Experimental Child Psychology, 41*, 211–236.

Rayner, K. (1998). Eye movements in reading and information processing: 20 years of research. *Psychological Bulletin, 124*, 372–422.

Rayner, K. (2009). The Thirty-Fifth Sir Frederick Bartlett Lecture: Eye movements and attention during reading, scene perception, and visual search. *Quarterly Journal of Experimental Psychology, 62*, 1457–1506.

Rayner, K., Ashby, J., Pollatsek, A., & Reichle, E.D. (2004). The effects of frequency and predictability on eye fixations in reading: Implications for the E-Z Reader model. *Journal of Experimental Psychology: Human Perception and Performance, 30*, 720–732.

Rayner, K., & McConkie, G.W. (1976). What guides a reader's eye movements? *Vision Research, 16*, 829–837.

Rayner, K., Reichle, E.D., Stroud, M.J., Williams, C.C., & Pollatsek, A. (2006). The effects of word frequency, word predictability, and font difficulty on the eye movements of young and elderly readers. *Psychology and Aging, 21*, 448–465.

Rayner, K. & Morrison, R.E. (1981). Eye movements and identifying words in parafoveal vision. *Bulletin of the Psychonomic Society, 17*, 135–138.

Reichle, E.D. (2011). Serial attention models of reading. In S.P. Liversedge, I.D. Gilchrist, & S. Everling (Eds.), *Oxford handbook on eye movements* (pp. 767–786). Oxford, England: Oxford University Press.

Reichle, E.D. (forthcoming). *Computational models of reading*. Oxford University Press.

Reichle, E.D., & Laurent, P.A. (2006). Using reinforcement learning to understand the emergence of "intelligent" eye-movement behavior during reading. *Psychological Review, 113*, 390–408.

Reichle, E.D., Liversedge, S.P., Dreighe, D., Blythe, H.I., Joseph, H.S.S.L., White, S.J., & Rayner, K. (2012). Using E-Z Reader to examine the concurrent development of eye-movement control and reading skill. *Developmental Review, 33*(2), 110–149.

Reichle, E.D., Pollatsek, A., Fisher, D.L., & Rayner, K. (1998). Toward a model of eye movement control in reading. *Psychological Review, 105*, 125–157.

Reichle, E.D., Rayner, K., & Pollatsek, A. (2003). The E-Z Reader model of eye movement control in reading: Comparisons to other models. *Behavioral and Brain Sciences, 26,* 445–476.

Reichle, E.D., Warren, T., & McConnell, K. (2009). Using E-Z Reader to model the effects of higher-level language processing on eye movements during reading. *Psychonomic Bulletin & Review, 16,* 1–21.

Schilling, H.E.H., Rayner, K., & Chumbley, J.I. (1998). Comparing naming, lexical decision, and eye fixation times: Word frequency effects and individual differences. *Memory & Cognition, 26,* 1270–1281.

Vitu, F., McConkie, G.W., Kerr, P., & O'Regan, J.K. (2001). Fixation location effects on fixation durations during reading: An inverted optimal viewing position effect. *Vision Research, 41,* 3513–3533.

CHAPTER 11

# Taking Models and Neuroimaging to Task

## What Do We Know About How People Actually Read?

Jason D. Zevin and Jianfeng Yang

Research on reading and dyslexia has focused to a great extent on single-word recognition. In part this has been because word recognition is easy to operationalize: A single word is presented, and behavioral or neural responses to that word can be measured in isolation. Computational models of reading have focused almost entirely on single-word reading (e.g., Coltheart, Rastle, Perry, Langdon, & Ziegler, 2001; Harm & Seidenberg, 1999, 2004; Seidenberg & McClelland, 1989; but see Reichle, Chapter 10, this volume); as such, they have provided a rich, mechanistic account of the processes involved in mapping from spelling to sound and spelling to meaning and have shown how these processes can develop atypically in the presence of more general perceptual or linguistic deficits. Neuroimaging studies, too, have focused at the single-word level (e.g., Petersen, Fox, Posner, Mintun, & Raichle, 1988; Pugh et al., 1996; Schlaggar et al., 2002), providing a robust and highly replicable map of the neural network engaged during reading, along with insights about how this network develops in typical as well as struggling readers.

Computational modeling and neuroimaging have thus proven to be extremely powerful ways of developing a mechanistic understanding of reading and dyslexia, and part of this power derives from the use of such standard laboratory tasks as word naming and lexical decision that can be carefully controlled at the single-word level. At the same time, the use of artificial tasks with single words reflects the need for some form of low dimensional output in behavioral studies, where the only available measurements are accuracy and response time. Data from computational models and neuroimaging, in contrast, have the potential to be much richer than this. Here, we discuss the challenges that emerge when disentangling basic functions of the reading system from behavioral and neural patterns that are shaped by artificial task demands, how these have shaped the field, and how they might change if we incorporate measures of reading in more naturalistic contexts.

The authors wish to thank The Dyslexia Foundation and the organizers of the 2012 meeting in Tallinn, Estonia, for the opportunity to present this work. This work was supported by Grants NIH R01 HD06579 and R01 HD067364 (J.Z.) and by NSF of China Grant 31171077 (J.Y.).

In the behavioral literature, it is clear that task demands interact with basic reading processes to create a wide variety of context and task effects. Debates about the mechanisms behind these interactions have focused on whether task demands can introduce a bias to process stimuli at different levels of description (Monsell, Patterson, Graham, Hughes, & Milroy, 1992; Zevin & Balota, 2000), whether mixing lists of stimuli that vary in difficulty merely introduces a shift in time criterion (Lupker, Brown, & Colombo, 1997; Taylor & Lupker, 2001), or whether the time dynamics of the task are best simulated by changing a general parameter governing how rapidly activation accumulates throughout the reading system. In extreme cases, we can ask participants to make responses that conflict with their usual output (Balota, Law, & Zevin, 2000). Such experiments likely tell us something interesting about the typical functions of the reading system, but their consequences for models of how it functions under more usual circumstances can be complicated to work out.

Determining the consequences of these experiments for models is challenging because it requires introducing a layer of assumptions about how the task is accomplished that can be fine-tuned to the experimental environment, creating a nearly infinite set of free parameters. The types of simulation models that have focused on understanding the relationship between typical development and dyslexia (Harm & Seidenberg, 1999, 2004) have largely focused on how skilled reading emerges from learning the mappings among spelling, meaning, and sound. As such, they can provide a mechanistic description of the emergence of representations that support reading. Insofar as a task such as single-word naming reflects the speed and accuracy with which a phonological representation is computed, it is fairly natural to simulate this task in such a model. Attempting to directly address the results of experiments that involve priming, lexical decision, or other artificially introduced laboratory conditions, on the other hand, requires introducing a large number of assumptions about task performance that have little to do with the reading system itself. For example, it has long been recognized that the lexical decision task (LDT)—a task in which participants view lists of real words and such word-like strings as *GLORP* and must classify each stimulus as either a real word or a nonword—includes both word recognition processes and general decision processes (Balota & Chumbley, 1984). Modeling results from this task, then, requires assumptions about what parts of the reading system the decision process has access to, what decision rules are applied and how they should be parameterized, and whether they might be influenced by lexical properties (e.g., familiarity) in a way that distorts the impact those properties have within the reading system itself.

Similarly, in neuroimaging studies, although there appears to be a relatively stable network of regions engaged during a wide range of reading tasks (these involve basic features of this network, among them its connectivity), the stimulus selectivity of individual regions interacts strongly with task. Task parameters can also interact with the properties of writing systems in ways that create difficulties for cross-language comparisons. There is always the possibility that differences between writing systems are driven more by the distinct affordances and constraints of different languages and scripts for stimulus generation and task design than by basic differences between the two languages in terms of the processes they engage during normal reading.

Thus, interpreting either modeling results or brain-imaging data is always complicated by task. For instance, to say that a specific model simulates consistency effects makes little sense without some qualifications. Consistency effects are most readily simulated by looking at how a model converts spelling to sound because the effects are most readily observed in naming tasks (as opposed to lexical decision or semantic tasks where the consistency effects are small or nonexistent; Andrews, 1982). Similarly, results from imaging studies are often interpreted to mean that a particular area is sensitive to a specific stimulus property (e.g., the visual word form area is sensitive to word-likeness), when this sensitivity is actually highly dependent on the particular task and stimulus parameters (e.g., Wang, Yang, Shu, & Zevin, 2011; Yang, Wang, Shu, & Zevin, 2012).

As a result, although both modeling and neuroimaging provide increasingly sophisticated accounts of the mechanisms and representations that underlie typical and disordered reading development, the relationship between these two approaches remains tenuous. This uncertain relationship motivates our exploring how specific tasks or types of tasks can interact with the functional organization of the reading system. We think this discussion strongly motivates approaches in which brain activity is studied under more naturalistic conditions, which enables us to ask questions about the degree to which our understanding of the reading system is distorted by the tasks we have used to study it and to discuss some very promising recent work that points a way forward.

## TASK EFFECTS AND COMPUTATIONAL MODELS

Task effects complicate the interpretation of computational models. Computational models that seek to explain the development and use of reading skill in terms of learned associations among spelling, sound, and meaning (Harm & Seidenberg, 2004; Seidenberg & McClelland, 1989, inter alia) model the reading system without directly addressing the specific tasks used to study reading in human subjects. It is relatively natural for such models to capture response latency in terms of the summed squared error (or settling time) of activation in the phonological layer, and this technique has been used to simulate the results of many behavioral studies using naming.

At the same time, there are a number of processes associated with naming that seem to be squarely outside the model and have some impact on naming times. The simplest of these processes is the acoustical differences between sounds at the beginnings of words, which differ in their likelihood of triggering a voice key and therefore explain a large amount of variance in human naming response times (Spieler & Balota, 1997). The controversy over whether this feature of words can interact with effects that are core to the model's explanatory adequacy has never really been settled (Kawamoto, Kello, Jones, & Bame, 1998; Kawamoto & Kello, 1999; Rastle & Coltheart, 1999).

Improvements of the phonological representations in such models so that they have a more realistic representation of the dynamics of speech production are, in fact, a goal of current models and would help address part of this issue. There is, however, a deeper problem, which is that human subjects are extremely flexible in their ability to control the dynamics of their performance. It is not clear how to account for, or even include, this level of flexibility in the predominant computational models of word reading.

If the goal of modeling word recognition were to account for the results of as many word recognition studies as possible, then individuals' flexibility in controlling performance would be a fatal flaw. But the radical artificiality of laboratory tasks is critical when one has only response time and accuracy as dependent variables. We want to know, for example, whether, when, and how homophones activate each other's meanings during reading. In human subjects, this activation requires priming with a variety of interstimulus intervals and masking conditions. Interpreting the data involves dealing with a large number of assumptions about how a wide range of experimental parameters are related to performance and determining whether differing results across studies are from differences that are core to the reading system or not.

In a computational model, it is actually quite straightforward to present the word *rows* on the input and observe the evolution, over time, of the activity for semantic features comprising the representation of the word *rose* (Harm & Seidenberg, 2004). The difficulty arises in relating this to the behavioral data. What level of semantic activation corresponds to a yes response in the semantic categorization task? What is the effect of masking on the flow of information among orthographic, phonological, and semantic representations? Thus, the simulation and experiment have complementary problems. In the experiment, we know what the behavioral outputs were, but not what dynamics of processing in the reading system led to these outputs. In the model, we have all the information we could possibly want about the dynamics of processing, but no a priori motivation for any number of possible assumptions required to turn these into low-dimensional response properties (i.e., accuracy and response latency).

A clear example of this problem arises when we consider how various models have addressed the results of experiments using the LDT. Lexical decision is perhaps the most widely used task in studies of word recognition and has a history stretching back to Meyer and Schvaneveldt (1971). Performance in the LDT is clearly influenced by a large number of factors that largely influence the decision stage rather than word recognition processes (e.g., Balota & Yap, 2006). For example, the composition of the items used to elicit "no" responses can dramatically affect overall response time and even enhance various stimulus effects. This is obvious if we consider two hypothetical experiments, one in which the nonwords are constructed of low-probability sequences of letters such as *QJZXVW,* and another in which they share many features of real words, such as *THEAR.* This difference in task difficulty clearly bears little relationship to anything that typically happens in our brains when we read. Indeed, when reading for meaning, we are relatively insensitive to misspellings, more so when what the misspellings produce is relatively wordlike (Andrews, 1982).

Even in a model that is geared toward simulating data from such studies (e.g., the dual-route cascaded model, or DRC; Coltheart et al., 2001), a number of ancillary assumptions must be introduced in order to address the LDT. In fact, the simulations of the LDT by Coltheart et al. (2001) require three decision-specific parameters: an activation threshold for individual words, another activation threshold for the sum of activity over the whole lexicon, and a deadline parameter (by which if neither threshold is met, the model issues a "no" response). The premise is that we consider two different sources of information about a stimulus in deciding whether it is a word or not: 1) whether we identify it as a particular word or 2) whether it is wordlike enough to elicit partial activation over many real words. This premise is well motivated enough, but there is no real way to motivate the specific values of the parameters used to implement it (0.69, 10, and 42). Further, these thresholds and deadlines change dynamically over the course of each trial based on activation patterns within the model; for example, the threshold for activation over the whole lexicon is reduced from 10 to 1.98 if specific conditions hold after 20 cycles of processing.

Beyond the decision parameters themselves, Coltheart et al. (2001) also changed a parameter in the model that governs the inhibitory connections between words in the lexicon. This actually has the effect of making the LDT harder by making it easier for activity across the lexicon to reach critical levels for nonwords. One final assumption required to link the model's performance to human LDT data is that the decision process and motor programming for yes/no responses takes substantially longer than motor planning for the naming task. This is the only way to explain why response latencies in the model's LDT simulations are about half as long as latencies in naming, whereas in human data, LDT responses are typically much slower than naming. Elsewhere we have pointed out that some of these parameter manipulations raise questions about the generality of the DRC (Seidenberg, Zevin, Sibley, Woollams, & Plaut, 2013); but even a more sympathetic evaluation of these simulations would have to include the consideration that a large number of task-specific choices had to be made in order to conduct them and that many of these are difficult to motivate on theoretical grounds, at least in their details.

Similarly, simulations using an implementation of the "triangle" model require assumptions about how the LDT is performed that are not properly part of the model of reading but are instead a set of task assumptions (Plaut, 1997). These simulations include an assumption about how decisions are made (i.e., that a stochastic decision process is in place, that faster decisions are made when the sampled parameter is closer to a critical value) and, critically, about what parameter of the model to sample in order to implement this decision process. Plaut (1997) selected "stress"—a measure based on the information theoretic notion of entropy—across units that make up the model's distributed semantic representation.

The selection of the stress measure is well motivated, on the view that real words will generate relatively sharp and specific responses in a distributed semantic network, whereas nonwords will generate relatively "fuzzy" activity because of their similarity to many words and lack of any learned meaning. It is not difficult, however, to imagine a number of other possible measures, or combinations of measures, that might just as well have been taken into account. Indeed, later work by Harm and Seidenberg (2004) identified conditions under which an additional spelling-check procedure was required.

Thus, addressing a task in which there is a decision component that is so clearly outside the domain of the process being modeled necessarily creates a situation in which the modeler must make arbitrary choices about how to simulate the decision and what information to assume the decision is based on. These decisions can, of course, affect how well the model fits the target data, creating difficulties for model evaluation.

It may be that such tasks as lexical decision are simply a poor test of such models because the requirement to derive a low-dimensional response (i.e., a yes/no answer) creates a need for assumptions that are difficult to motivate by much beyond practical considerations (i.e., what works for the data under consideration). Instead, because of their architecture and activation dynamics, such models are more appropriate for capturing general facts about the mappings that emerge from learning to read and about the division of labor between semantic and phonological processing in skilled reading.

## TASK EFFECTS IN fMRI

An analogous issue arises in the functional neuroimaging literature. In this case, the dependent variables available to us are much richer than those found in behavioral data. We can explore where, and to some extent when, brain activity is sensitive to different stimulus properties; we can use tests that tap reading-related skills only indirectly (e.g., Booth et al.,

2004; Desroches et al., 2010; Pugh et al., 1996) in order to compare activity in the reading network between groups that cannot be matched on reading skill. Neuroimaging also offers the promise of being able to measure activity in the reading system when written words (and even a wide range of control nonword stimuli) are presented without an overt reading task (Vinckier et al., 2007). In contrast to behavioral studies, in which the reading system must be channeled toward some output measurable in terms of response latency and accuracy, the neuroimaging data in principle allows us to observe operating characteristics of the system that are oblique to the specific tasks themselves.

Task manipulations can, of course, be used to ask questions about the organization of the reading system. For example, employing a range of task demands, Bitan et al. (2005) examined effective connectivity in a network of regions associated with reading and found distinct patterns of connectivity for a spelling task (focusing attention on orthographic information) compared to a rhyming task (focusing attention on phonological information). In particular, connectivity with the left inferior frontal gyrus was strongly modulated by task. In children (Bitan et al., 2006), this modulation was much weaker, suggesting a greater role for top-down processing in adults. These and related studies (e.g., Booth et al., 2006; Pugh et al., 1996) provide important information about the organization of the reading system, but they also suggest there is not really a fixed functional architecture of the reading system. Instead, the network of regions engaged by reading can be reconfigured on the fly according to task demands.

Further, differences in task difficulty over development, or between typically developing and struggling readers, can introduce problems of interpretation into such studies because of differences in task difficulty for the different groups. One common technique is to create equivalent performance by calibrating the demands of the task until the adults and children are performing at a similar level of accuracy and/or reaction time. This can most readily be done by post hoc performance matching, using subgroup analyses based on overt performance measures (i.e., reaction time and accuracy). This approach permits not only analyses of age effects on sets of participants matched for performance but also analyses of performance-driven effects in groups matched for age (e.g., Church, Petersen & Schlaggar, 2010; Schlaggar et al., 2002).

An alternative is to develop tasks whose demands are oblique to the stimulus properties of interest, similar to the control task described earlier (a task in which participants monitor for low-level orthographic properties of the stimuli; Binder, Medler, Westbury, Liebenthal, & Buchanan, 2006). The premise behind these studies is that many of the processes of interest in the reading system are essentially automatic, so they can be elicited by passive presentation of text, particularly in skilled readers. The task serves mostly to reassure the researcher that the participant is alert and responding throughout the study.

These studies aim to characterize the "best stimulus" parameters for different regions in the reading network, doing so in the spirit of classical neurophysiological studies of the receptive field properties of complex cells in primary visual cortex (Hubel & Wiesel, 1962). For example, Vinckier et al. (2007) used a rapid serial visual presentation design in which stimuli ranged from least wordlike (pseudofont, strings of low-frequency letters) to pronounceable pseudowords, and finally to real words. Stimulus presentation was blocked by type so that 20 stimuli of the same type were presented at a rate of one every 300 ms. The participants' task was to detect a row of hash marks inserted pseudorandomly into half of the blocks. The results were consistent with a hierarchical organization of ventral temporal cortex, with the greatest selectivity for words observed in an anterior region often referred to as the visual word form area.

These studies generally support the view that the reading system, and in particular the visual word form areas, is exquisitely tuned to particular stimulus features that determine the relatively abstract notion of word-likeness. This is a remarkable example of how perceptual systems may be tuned up by experience. At the same time, it is clear that the stimulus selectivity of regions throughout the reading system is task dependent in curious ways. For example, using a one-back task, in which the primary behavioral demands involve only visual working memory—here, participants are shown a series of stimuli and must respond when a stimulus is repeated from one trial to the next—it is possible to observe patterns of stimulus selectivity throughout the reading system that are related to the orthographic, phonological, and semantic properties of the stimuli (Yang et al., 2011). It is interesting to note that stimulus selectivity under these task conditions is very different from what has been reported for such other, ostensibly oblique tasks as symbol detection (Vinckier et al., 2007; Yang et al., 2012). That is, when task demands emphasize visual working memory, stimulus selectivity throughout much of the reading network tends to reflect the relative difficulty of remembering the prior stimulus from trial to trial, and this is inversely related to word-likeness.

In contrast, when task demands involve distinguishing words from nonwords, in a lexical decision paradigm (Yang et al., 2012), responses throughout the reading network track with task difficulty. In the same study, we looked for task-by-stimulus interactions by comparing activity in the LDT to activity in a symbol detection task. Perhaps because of important differences in the timing and response demands of our version of this task relative to the original Vinckier et al. (2007) study on which it was based, we observed yet another pattern of response under the symbol detection task: Responses throughout the reading system were essentially flat, that is, showing no effect of stimulus class.

The complexities of task-by-stimulus interactions are further multiplied when we try to match tasks across languages in order to understand differences between the functional architecture for reading across writing systems. In Chinese, we can create stimuli with some very interesting properties that give word-likeness manipulations a different character than is possible in alphabetic orthographies. For example, we can create nonwords that are perfectly well formed orthographically but contain no cues to their pronunciation; or we can create items that have some orthographic cues to meaning, but none about their pronunciation. These conditions can be created because of the somewhat unique properties of the Chinese writing system. One question that emerges when considering differences between writing systems with respect to the patterns of brain activity observed across studies is whether these differences actually reflect differences that are present under more ecologically valid conditions or are artifacts of the experimental design. That is, the different writing systems afford different possibilities with respect to stimulus manipulations that experimenters can create; they also afford different strategies for readers given tasks that are, by design, oblique to the normal functioning of the reading system. What if these factors are the driving force behind differences between readers of different writing systems observed in many fMRI studies (Bolger, Perfetti, & Schneider, 2005; Tan et al., 2005)?

One way to approach this question directly is to examine brain activity under more naturalistic conditions, such as reading connected text for meaning. Yarkoni, Speer, Balota, McAvoy, and Zacks (2008) did just this. By taking advantage of natural variability in stimulus features over time (e.g., some stretches of text contained relatively dense concentrations of shorter or longer words, or words that occur more frequently in the language, as opposed to words that occur less frequently), they were able to study the effects of a set of variables that are known to affect the reading network in different ways. Somewhat reassuringly, the results largely replicated findings from prior research using more artificial paradigms.

In our own preliminary data from an experiment with connected text in both English and Chinese (Yang, Wang, Shu, Mencl, & Zevin, 2013), there is a striking similarity between the reading networks observed in the two languages. This is in stark contrast to differences typically observed in artificial tasks (Tan et al., 2000, 2001). Whether this is because of mappings from written to spoken forms or because of higher-level comprehension processes that are common to spoken and written forms of the language is an important question for future research. Thus, in order to truly understand what is happening in the reading system, even at the word level, researchers must create conditions in which higher order comprehension processes are necessarily engaged. Researchers must do so because these are the conditions under which people ordinarily read, and in fact there is no way to understand how the artificial tasks designed to tap word-level processing may distort our view of the system without actually looking at how it typically functions.

## CONCLUSIONS

Thus far, computational modeling and functional neuroimaging have largely focused on tasks that were initially developed in order to produce low-dimensional data, that is, response time and accuracy. There is a rich literature demonstrating that such tasks reflect the flexible deployment of both basic reading skills and general cognitive processes (e.g., decision making, working memory) in response to behavioral goals. This flexibility creates serious problems of interpretation that are often swept aside when considering how reading is modeled or when evaluating neuroimaging studies of reading.

Computational models, especially those that have had the greatest success in addressing issues of typical development and developmental dyslexia, have the potential to reveal mechanisms in a much richer, multidimensional way than by generating proxies for response time and percentage of correct responses. Novel techniques that permit the analysis of brain activity during naturalistic processing of text may provide more appropriate target data for such models. Thus far, results from such experiments are surprisingly well aligned with data from more artificial studies, which is an encouraging outcome because it sets the stage for future research. In particular, it will be important to understand how the discourse processes that naturally come on-line when people read for meaning interact with word-level processes that have been so intensively studied. This line of inquiry will be an important early step in understanding the brain basis of persistent deficits in reading comprehension and how these deficits relate to other forms of reading disability.

## REFERENCES


Andrews, S. (1982). Phonological recoding: Is the regularity effect consistent? *Memory and Cognition, 10*, 565–575.

Balota, D.A., & Chumbley, J.I. (1984). Are lexical decisions a good measure of lexical access? The role of word frequency in the neglected decision stage. *Journal of Experimental Psychology: Human Perception and Performance, 10*, 340–357.

Balota, D.A., Law, M.B., & Zevin, J.D. (2000). The attentional control of lexical processing pathways: Reversing the word frequency effect. *Memory & Cognition, 28*, 1081–1089.

Balota, D.A., & Yap, M.J. (2006). Attentional control and flexible lexical processing: Explorations of the magic moment of word recognition. In S. Andrews (Ed.), *From inkmarks to ideas: Current issues in lexical processing* (pp. 229–258). New York, NY: Psychology Press.

Binder, J.R., Medler, D.A., Westbury, C.F., Liebenthal, E., & Buchanan, L. (2006). Tuning of the human left fusiform gyrus to sublexical orthographic structure. *Neuroimage, 33*(2), 739–748.

Bitan, T., Booth, J.R., Choy, J., Burman, D.D., Gitelman, D.R., & Mesulam, M.M. (2005). Shifts of effective connectivity within a language network during rhyming and spelling. *Journal of Neuroscience, 25*, 5397–5403.

Bitan, T., Burman, D.D., Lu, D., Cone, N.E., Gitelman, D.R., Mesulam, M.M., & Booth, J.R. (2006). Weaker top-down modulation from the left inferior frontal gyrus in children. *Neuroimage, 33*, 991–998.

Bolger, D.J., Perfetti, C.A., & Schneider, W. (2005). Cross-cultural effect on the brain revisited: Universal structures plus writing system variation. *Human Brain Mapping, 25*(1), 92–104.

Booth, J.R., Burman, D.D., Meyer, J.R., Gitelman, D.R., Parrish, T.B., & Mesulam, M.M. (2004). Development of brain mechanisms for processing orthographic and phonological representations. *Journal of Cognitive Neuroscience, 16,* 1234–1249.

Booth, J.R., Lu, D., Burman, D.D., Chou, T.-L., Jin, Z., Peng, D.-L.,... Liu, L. (2006). Specialization of phonological and semantic processing in Chinese word reading. *Brain Research, 1071,* 197–207.

Church, J.A., Petersen, S.E., & Schlaggar, B.L. (2010). The "Task B problem" and other considerations in developmental functional neuroimaging. *Human Brain Mapping, 31*(6), 852–862.

Coltheart, M., Rastle, K., Perry, C., Langdon, R., & Ziegler, J. (2001). DRC: A dual route cascaded model of visual word recognition and reading aloud. *Psychological Review, 108*(1), 204–256.

Desroches, A., Cone, N., Bolger, D., Bitan, T., Burman, D., & Booth, J. (2010). Children with reading difficulties show differences in brain regions associated with orthographic processing during spoken language processing. *Brain Research, 1356,* 73–84.

Harm, M.W., & Seidenberg, M.S. (1999). Phonology, reading, and dyslexia: Insights from connectionist models. *Psychological Review, 163,* 491–528.

Harm, M.W., & Seidenberg, M.S. (2004). Computing the meanings of words in reading: Cooperative division of labor between visual and phonological processes. *Psychological Review, 111*(3), 662–720.

Hubel, D.H., & Wiesel, T.N. (1962). Receptive fields, binocular interaction and functional architecture in the cat's visual cortex. *Journal of Physiology, 160,* 106–154.

Kawamoto, A.H., & Kello, C.T. (1999). Parallel processing and initial phoneme criterion in naming words: Evidence from frequency effects on onset and rime durations. *Journal of Experimental Psychology: Learning, Memory and Cognition, 25*(2), 362–381.

Kawamoto, A.H., Kello, C.T., Jones, R.J., & Bame, K. (1998). Initial phoneme versus whole word criterion to initiate pronunciation: Evidence based on response latency and initial phoneme duration. *Journal of Experimental Psychology: Learning, Memory, and Cognition, 24,* 862–885.

Lupker, S.J., Brown, P., & Colombo, L. (1997). Strategic control in a naming task: Changing routes or changing deadlines? *Journal of Experimental Psychology: Learning, Memory, and Cognition, 23*(3), 570–590.

Meyer, D.E., & Schvaneveldt, R.W. (1971). Facilitation in recognizing pairs of words: Evidence of a dependence between retrieval operations. *Journal of Experimental Psychology, 90*(2), 227–234.

Monsell, S., Patterson, K.E., Graham, A., Hughes, C.H., & Milroy, R. (1992). Lexical and sublexical translation of spelling to sound: Strategic anticipation of lexical status. *Journal of Experimental Psychology: Learning, Memory, and Cognition, 18,* 452–467.

Petersen, S.E., Fox, P.T., Posner, M.I., Mintun, M., & Raichle, M.E. (1988). Positron emission tomographic studies of the cortical anatomy of single-word processing. *Nature, 331*(6157), 585–589.

Plaut, D.C. (1997). Structure and function in the lexical system: Insights from distributed models of word reading and lexical decision. *Language and Cognitive Processes, 12,* 765–805.

Pugh, K.R., Shaywitz, B.A., Shaywitz, S.E., Constable, R.T., Skudlarski, P., Fulbright, R.K.,... Gore, J.C. (1996). Cerebral organization of component processes in reading. *Brain, 119*(Pt. 4), 1221–1238.

Rastle, K., & Coltheart, M. (1999). Serial and strategic effects in reading aloud. *Journal of Experimental Psychology: Human Perception and Performance, 25,* 482–503.

Schlaggar, B.L., Brown, T.T., Lugar, H.M., Visscher, K.M., Miezin, F.M., & Petersen, S.E. (2002). Functional neuroanatomical differences between adults and school-age children in the processing of single words. *Science, 296*(5572), 1476–1479.

Seidenberg, M.S., & McClelland, J.L. (1989). A distributed, developmental model of word recognition and naming. *Psychological Review, 96,* 523–568.

Seidenberg, M.S., Zevin, J.D., Sibley, D.E., Woollams, A.W., & Plaut, D.C. (2013). What are computational models for? A critical analysis of dual-route models of reading. Manuscript in preparation.

Spieler, D.H., & Balota, D.A. (1997). Connectionist models of word naming: An examination of item level performance. *Psychological Science, 8,* 411–416.

Tan, L.H., Laird, A.R., Li, K., & Fox, P.T. (2005). Neuroanatomical correlates of phonological processing of Chinese characters and alphabetic words: A meta-analysis. *Human Brain Mapping, 25*(1), 83–91.

Tan, L.H., Liu, H.-L., Perfetti, C.A., Spinks, J.A., Fox, P.T., & Gao, J.-H. (2001). The neural system underlying Chinese logograph reading. *NeuroImage, 13,* 836–846.

Tan, L.H., Spinks, J.A., Gao, J.-H., Liu, H.-L., Perfetti, C.A., Xiong, J., ... Fox, P.T. (2000). Brain activation in the processing of Chinese characters and words: A functional MRI study. *Human Brain Mapping, 10,* 16–27.

Taylor, T.E., & Lupker, S.J. (2001). Sequential effects in naming: A time-criterion account. *Journal of Experimental Psychology: Learning, Memory and Cognition, 27,* 117–138.

Vinckier, F., Dehaene, S., Jobert, A., Dubus, J.P., Sigman, M., & Cohen, L. (2007). Hierarchical coding of letter strings in the ventral stream: Dissecting the inner organization of the visual word-form system. *Neuron, 55,* 143–156.

Wang, X., Yang, J., Shu, H., & Zevin, J.D. (2011). Left fusiform BOLD responses are inversely related to word-likeness in a one-back task. *NeuroImage, 55*(3), 1346–1356.

Yang, J., Wang, X., Shu, H., & Zevin, J.D. (2012). Task by stimulus interactions in brain responses during Chinese character processing. *NeuroImage, 60*(2), 979–990.

Yarkoni, T., Speer, N., Balota, D., McAvoy, M., & Zacks, J. (2008). Pictures of a thousand words: Investigating the neural mechanisms of reading with extremely rapid event-related fMRI. *NeuroImage, 42,* 973–987.

Zevin, J.D., & Balota, D.A. (2000). Priming and attentional control of lexical and sublexical pathways during naming. *Journal of Experimental Psychology: Learning, Memory, and Cognition, 26*(1), 121–135.

CHAPTER 12

# What Can Be Learned About the Reading Comprehension of Poor Readers Through the Use of Advanced Statistical Modeling Techniques?

Donald L. Compton, Amanda C. Miller,
Jennifer K. Gilbert, and Laura M. Steacy

The comprehension of written material requires the seamless orchestration of a complex set of skills by the reader that vary as a function of text and purpose. In an attempt to capture the multifaceted nature of reading comprehension, the RAND Reading Study Group defined reading comprehension as "the process of simultaneously extracting and constructing meaning through interaction and involvement with written language" (Snow, 2002, p. 11). The words *extracting* and *constructing* were used to emphasize both the importance and the insufficiency of the text as a determinant of reading comprehension. In addition to proposing a working definition of reading comprehension, the RAND group put forward a heuristic for thinking about reading comprehension that consists of three elements: the *reader,* the *text,* and the *activity,* all embedded within the larger sociocultural context of reading (see Figure 12.1). In the heuristic, the reader brings to the task a set of capacities, abilities, knowledge, and experiences; the text is broadly conceived to include any printed or electronic text; and the activity includes a complex set of actions influenced by the purposes, processes, and consequences associated with the act of reading. At the center of the heuristic is the intersection of reader, text, and activity, illustrating how these elements interact to characterize skilled reading comprehension. Whereas previous work has examined the separate contributions of reader, text, and to a lesser extent activity to reading comprehension, for methodological reasons much less is known about interactions between reader and text. The purpose of this chapter is to demonstrate a relatively new analytic technique that allows examination of individual differences in

This research was supported in part by Grants R324G060036 and R305A100034 from the U.S. Department of Education, Institute of Education Sciences, and Core Grant HD15052 from the *Eunice Kennedy Shriver* National Institute of Child Health and Human Development to Vanderbilt University. Statements do not reflect the position or policy of these agencies, and no official endorsement by them should be inferred.

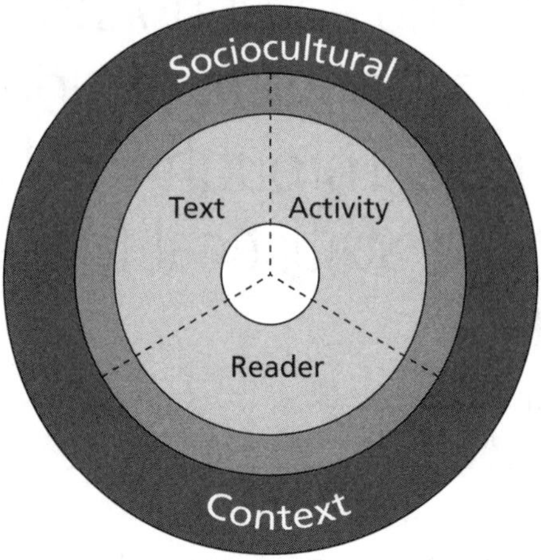


**Figure 12.1.** RAND Reading Study Group heuristic for thinking about reading comprehension.

reading comprehension skill related to the reader, the text, and the reader-by-text interaction within a single model.

From the standpoint of the reader, individual differences on a host of skills and abilities have been linked to reading comprehension variance across development, including cognitive capacities, motivation, and various types of knowledge and experiences (see Cain & Oakhill, 2009; Perfetti, Landi, & Oakhill, 2005; Snow, 2002). In addition, studies have explored differences between reader groups (e.g., good versus poor comprehenders) in an attempt to identify important differences in component skills that help to explain group performance on reading comprehension measures (Cain & Oakhill, 2006; Catts, Compton, Tomblin, & Bridges, 2012; Nation, Cocksey, Taylor, & Bishop, 2010). In terms of the text, difficulty can vary as a function of the vocabulary load, coherence, linguistic structure, discourse style, and genre. When too many of these factors are not matched to a reader's knowledge and experience, the text may be too easy or too difficult for optimal comprehension to occur (see van den Broek, Boh-Gettler, Panayiota, Carlson, & White, 2011). For instance, McNamara, Kintsch, Songer, and Kintsch (1996) investigated the role of text coherence in the comprehension of science texts by examining interactions among local and global text coherence, readers' background knowledge, and levels of understanding. Results indicated that readers who know little about the domain of the text benefit from a coherent text, whereas high-knowledge readers benefit from a minimally coherent text.

Studies like that of McNamara et al. (1996) examining the interrelationship between reader and text have the potential to further our understanding of the processes underlying reading comprehension and inform practices that promote reading comprehension skills in poor readers (see Rapp, van den Broek, McMaster, Kendeou, & Espin, 2007). However, for researchers interested in exploring the relationship between reader and text, it was mostly necessary to run separate models aggregating to the level of text (losing the ability to examine reader-level variance) or aggregating to the level of the reader (losing the ability to examine text-level variance), thereby eliminating the ability to examine important reader, text, and reader-by-text interactions in the same model. A host of new statistical modeling techniques is now available to partition variance in reading comprehension skill that do not require aggregating at the level of person or text. These techniques allow us to delve deeper into the interrelationship between these elements related to reading comprehension.

In this chapter we highlight one of these techniques, item response random effects modeling, which allows us to explain variability in reading comprehension by simultaneously partitioning variance across reader, passage, and question characteristics along with interactions between reader, passage, and question features. Because the focus of this chapter is on children with comprehension difficulties, we explore reading group as a reader characteristic by classifying children into latent classes representing two subtypes: children who are typically developing (TD) and children with reading disability (RD). These subtypes are based on two different grouping techniques: 1) latent transition analysis (LTA), which is based on the simple view of reading (Gough & Tunmer, 1986) and is used to identify groups of children who are TD, children with early identified RD (ERD), and children with late-emerging RD (LERD); and 2) latent profile analysis (LPA), which uses variables related to reading comprehension to identify classes of high, medium, and low potential readers based on language and knowledge profiles. This subtyping allowed us to explore the effects of question and passage features on RD groups, with groups derived from different theoretical perspectives and empirical procedures.

In the next sections we briefly describe the procedures for identifying latent classes of readers using LTA and LPA, followed by an overview of item response random effects modeling. Models for this chapter are based on a subsample of a larger longitudinal study, following children in grades 1–5 (Compton, Fuchs, & Fuchs, 2006, 2010), comprising 119 fifth-grade children assessed on the Qualitative Reading Inventory (QRI-3; Leslie & Caldwell, 2001), along with measures of general knowledge (Academic Knowledge subtest of Woodcock-Johnson–Third Edition [WJ-III]; Woodcock, McGrew, & Mather, 2001), passage oral reading fluency (Fuchs & Fuchs, 1999), and vocabulary knowledge (Peabody Picture Vocabulary Test; Dunn & Dunn, 2007). Because our primary interest was to explore the relationship between reader and text in children with reading comprehension problems, we removed the data for children with primary word-reading problems from the study.

## IDENTIFICATION OF LATE-EMERGING READING DIFFICULTIES

Some children demonstrate adequate reading achievement in early school grades but fall significantly behind their peers in later grades. These children are often referred to as having LERD. Many children who exhibit LERD develop serious reading comprehension difficulties in the absence of word-reading problems. This class of children is often referred to as exhibiting "specific comprehension disability" and represents approximately 7% of the population of school-age children (Catts et al., 2012). For the study, LTA was used to model changes in reading classification (good versus poor reader) across grades. Here, we focus on the movement of children across RD and TD categories defined by the latent variables; an arbitrary cut score of the 25th percentile was used to designate TD from RD on each of the latent indicators of word reading and reading comprehension. In addition, LTA was used to classify children into classes of ERD, LERD, or TD across time. Partial independence of reading comprehension and word recognition skill allows for the possibility of three major RD classes: 1) reading comprehension problems only (-C); 2) word-reading problems only (-W); and 3) both reading comprehension and word-reading problems (-CW). Based on our model results, we classified children into seven distinctive classes across time: ERD-W, ERD-C, ERD-CW, LERD-W, LERD-C, LERD-CW, and TD. However, for this study we analyze only children with RD who had primary reading comprehension deficits and therefore limit our analyses to the following groups: TD ($n$ = 64), ERD-C ($n$ = 18), and LERD-C ($n$ = 37).

## LATENT PROFILES WITHIN THE SUBTYPE OF LATE-EMERGING READING DIFFICULTIES

Using the same 119 fifth-grade children, we formed classes of children using LPA based on language and knowledge variables irrespective of TD, ERD-C, or LERD-C class designation. The LPA technique is used for classifying individuals into mutually exclusive groups such that individuals within groups have similar values on a set of variables. In LPA, membership in a latent class is probabilistic rather than deterministic and provides probabilities for each person's membership in each class. In our case, the word *profile* refers to a set of scores from within a test battery consisting of language and knowledge measures (i.e., vocabulary, suffix choice, morphological relatedness, syntactic processing, general knowledge, listening comprehension, inference making, semantic fluency) administered in fifth grade. Using LPA, we identified three meaningful subtypes that differ in terms of language and knowledge functioning: High ($n$ = 27), medium ($n$ = 49), and low ($n$ = 43). The overlap between subtypes based on LTA and LPA is displayed in Table 12.1. Overall, LPA identified three subtypes with different constellations of skills that only partially overlapped with the theoretical groups identified using LTA. We might expect that across

**Table 12.1.** Overlap between latent class subtypes using latent transition and latent profile analyses

| | | LTA subtypes | | | |
|---|---|---|---|---|---|
| | | ERD-C | LERD-C | TD | Total |
| LPA subtypes | Low | 15 | 20 | 8 | 43 |
| | Medium | 3 | 14 | 32 | 49 |
| | High | 0 | 3 | 24 | 27 |
| | Total | 18 | 37 | 64 | |

*Key:* LTA, latent transition analysis; LPA, latent profile analysis.

these grouping techniques, significant and differential patterns of subtype-by-text interactions might exist.

## READER, PASSAGE, AND QUESTION CHARACTERISTICS

Using item response random effects modeling, it is possible to simultaneously explain variability in comprehension with person (previously referred to as the reader), passage, and question characteristics (De Boeck & Wilson, 2004; Van den Noortgate, De Boeck, & Meulders, 2003). This modeling approach not only provides the opportunity to explore research questions related to multiple sources of variance, including person-by-item covariates, but also provides less biased estimates and fewer standard errors than evident in traditional by-person, by-question, or by-passage regression models (Baayen, Davidson, & Bates, 2008). Figure 12.2 illustrates the data structure for our study: Item responses are cross-classified by person and question, and questions are nested within passages. The equation for our proposed unconditional model, one with no predictors, is as follows: $\text{Logit}(\pi_{ijk}) = \beta_0 + u_{1i} + u_{2j} + u_{3k}$, where $\beta_0$ is the average logit for the probability of a correct answer across all people, questions, and passages, $u_{1i}$ is the random effect for persons, $u_{2j}$ is the random effect for questions or items, and $u_{3k}$ is the random effect for passages. Because variance in this model is partitioned among persons, questions, and passages, predictors related to each can be assessed.

Data from the QRI-3, along with measures of general knowledge, oral reading fluency, and vocabulary knowledge, were used in the analyses. Our dependent variable was item responses from the comprehension questions on the QRI-3. The QRI-3 consists of four passages at the fifth-grade level, two of which were read by the students and two of which were read to the students by the test administrator. Prior to students' reading or hearing each passage, their knowledge of the passage topic was assessed. Comprehension of each passage was assessed with six associated questions. Three of the questions ask about information that was stated literally in the text, whereas the other three questions ask about information that is implied in the text and requires inference. Students were required to provide oral answers to the comprehension questions; scores of correct (1)

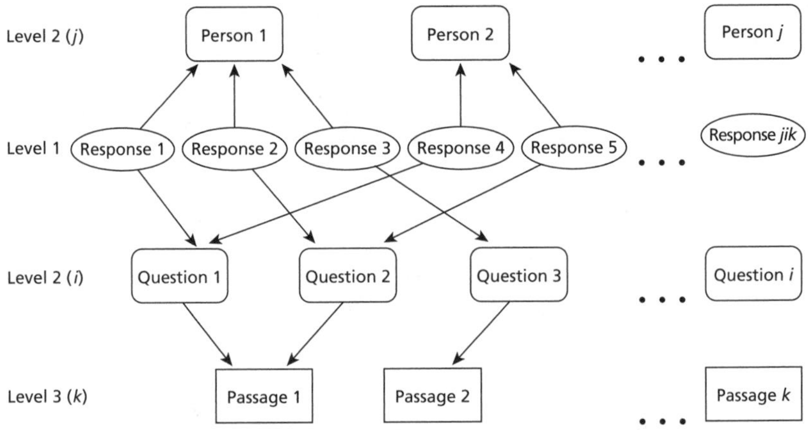


**Figure 12.2.** Cross-classified data structure for the item response random-effects modeling (with item responses cross-classified by persons and questions, and questions nested within passages).

and incorrect (0) were assigned according to the rubric found in the testing manual (interrater reliability exceeded .93). Our research question regarding whether variability in comprehension can be explained by person, question, and passage characteristics was addressed by adding the following predictors to the previously mentioned unconditional model: general knowledge, passage-reading fluency, and vocabulary knowledge for persons. In addition, question type (literal or inferential) and modality (listening or reading) were coded as covariates and included in the model. For Question Type, we coded 1 for literal questions, 0 for inferential questions; for Modality, we coded 1 for passages that were read to the student and 0 for passages that they read themselves. We also added passage-specific topic background knowledge (BK) to the model; if students were unable to provide accurate information about the passage topic, they received a score of 0 for that passage; if they were able to provide some or full accurate information, they received a score of 1. With passage-specific BK included in the model, person, question, and passage effects were adjusted for whether the student knew something about the topic of the passage.

## RESULTS

Initial results for the item response random effects models are in Table 12.2. The left column contains results from the unconditional model. It shows that the average logit for giving a correct response across questions, passages, and persons was –0.473, which corresponds to a probability of .38. Variability around the mean probability of response existed among questions, passages, and persons. The plausible value range (expressed as the

**Table 12.2.** Results of item response random effects models

| | Unconditional model | | | | Conditional model | | | |
|---|---|---|---|---|---|---|---|---|
| | Estimate | *SE* | *z* | *p* | Estimate | *SE* | *z* | *p* |
| *Fixed effects* | | | | | | | | |
| Grand-mean | | | | | | | | |
| Intercept, $\gamma_{00}$ | −0.473 | 0.550 | −0.861 | .389 | −0.702 | 0.514 | −1.367 | .172 |
| Passage BK, $\gamma_{10}$ | | | | | 0.531 | 0.222 | 2.392 | .017 |
| Person effects | | | | | | | | |
| General knowledge, $\gamma_{40}$ | | | | | 0.070 | 0.050 | 1.402 | .161 |
| Reading fluency, $\gamma_{50}$ | | | | | 0.005 | 0.004 | 1.250 | .211 |
| Vocabulary, $\gamma_{60}$ | | | | | 0.020 | 0.009 | 2.195 | .028 |
| Question | | | | | | | | |
| Literal, $\gamma_{70}$ | | | | | 1.565 | 0.547 | 2.863 | .004 |
| Passage | | | | | | | | |
| Listen, $\gamma_{80}$ | | | | | −1.676 | 0.568 | −2.951 | .003 |
| | *Variance* | *SD* | | | *Variance* | *SD* | | |
| *Random effects* | | | | | | | | |
| Person | 0.763 | 0.874 | | | 0.349 | 0.591 | | |
| Question | 2.697 | 1.642 | | | 1.643 | 1.282 | | |
| Passage | 0.682 | 0.826 | | | 0.000 | 0.000 | | |

95% plausible value range; see Raudenbush & Bryk, 2002) of a correct response for questions was .02 to .94, for passages was .11 to .76, and for persons was .11 to .78. This variability warrants explanation using covariates associated with each portion of variance, which was our intent in the conditional model.

The conditional model included person covariates (general knowledge, reading fluency, vocabulary knowledge), a passage covariate (listening versus reading mode of access), and a question type covariate (literal versus inferential). In addition, passage-specific BK, a type of passage-by-person covariate, was added. Results in the right column of Table 12.2 reveal a significant positive effect of passage-specific BK (0.531, $z$ = 2.39, $p$ = .017), controlling for the effects of other covariates in the model. The effect of passage-specific knowledge was significant even after controlling for person-level general knowledge. The only person covariate that was significantly associated with item responses was vocabulary knowledge (0.02, $z$ = 2.20, $p$ = .028). This means that after controlling for passage-specific BK and the other effects in the model, higher vocabulary knowledge was associated with a higher logit (and, in turn, probability) of a correct response. Question type and mode of text access were also influential. Controlling for other effects in the model, questions about information that was stated literally in the text were easier to answer than questions about information that required an inference to be made (1.57, $z$ = 2.86, $p$ = .004). Finally, controlling for other effects, correct responses from passages that were read to the students were less likely than from passages that the students read themselves (–1.68, $z = -2.95$, $p = .003$).

We then added dummy variables representing subtype membership (based on LTA and LPA procedures) to the previous conditional model, including person covariates (general knowledge, reading fluency, vocabulary knowledge), a passage covariate (listening versus reading mode of access), and a question type covariate (literal versus inferential). Dummy variables were formed using the LERD-C group as the reference group in the LTA-based analysis and the Medium group in the LPA-based analysis. In this coding system, the TD/High variable compares TD versus LERD-C groups for LTA-base subtypes, and High versus Medium groups for the LPA-based subtypes; whereas the ERD/Low variable compares ERD-C versus LERD-C groups for LTA-based subtypes, and Low versus Medium for LPA-based subtypes. Incorporation of subtype variables into the model allows for person-by-passage knowledge, person-by-passage mode, and person-by-question type interactions.

Table 12.3 presents results of adding subgroup as a person effect allowing subgroup to interact with passage-specific background knowledge as a person-by-passage interaction effect. The first column represents reader subtype comparisons based on the LTA analysis, and the second column reader subtype comparisons based on the LPA analysis, permitting a side-by-side comparison. In terms of person effects, substantial differences emerged across latent class identification methods (LTA versus LPA), with no difference in the average logit for providing a correct response across TD versus LERD-C groups (0.22, $z = 0.94$) and ERD-C versus LERD groups (–0.38, $z = -1.28$, $p = .20$), but with significant differences between High and Medium subtypes (1.46, $z = 5.54$) and Low and Medium subtypes (–0.59, $z = -2.60$, $p = .01$). In terms of person-by-passage interactions, across both latent class identification methods, no significant interaction emerged between reader group passage-specific BK. Results indicate that although there are differences in person effects across latent class identification methods, these differences did not lead to significant person-by-passage effects as reflected by passage-specific BK interactions. However, there was a significant interaction between passage-specific BK and mode of access to text for both classification models. The nature of this interaction is that there was relatively little effect of passage-specific BK when students read passages to themselves but a positive effect of passage-specific BK when listening to passages.

Our final model used the subtype variables, derived from LTA and LPA, to explore possible person-by-question and person-by-mode-of-access interactions (see Table 12.4). There were no significant interactions between reader subtype and question type (literal versus inferential) for either method of identifying latent classes. There was, however, a significant interaction between subtype (High versus Low) and mode of access to text (listen versus read). This interaction is presented in Figure 12.3. As displayed

**Table 12.3.** Results of conditional model with background knowledge interactions

| | LTA | | LPA | |
|---|---|---|---|---|
| | Est. (SE) | *z* | Est. (SE) | *z* |
| *Fixed effects* | | | | |
| Person-by-passage effects | | | | |
| Intercept, $\gamma_{00}$ | 0.61 (0.60) | 1.02 | 0.30 (0.54) | 0.56 |
| BK, $\gamma_{10}$ | 0.27 (0.30) | 0.90 | 0.10 (0.29) | 0.35 |
| TD/high_BK, $\gamma_{11}$ | −0.24 (0.24) | −1.03 | −0.56 (0.29) | −1.95 |
| ERD/low_BK, $\gamma_{12}$ | −0.57 (0.33) | −1.71 | 0.09 (0.24) | 0.37 |
| Listen_BK, $\gamma_{13}$ | 0.69 (0.33) | 2.13 | 0.67 (0.32) | 2.11 |
| Person effects | | | | |
| TD/high, $\gamma_{20}$ | 0.22 (0.23) | 0.94 | 1.46 (0.26) | 5.54 |
| ERD/low, $\gamma_{30}$ | −0.38 (0.30) | −1.28 | −0.59 (0.23) | −2.60 |
| General knowledge, $\gamma_{40}$ | 0.08 (0.03) | 2.73 | 0.03 (0.02) | 1.31 |
| Reading fluency, $\gamma_{50}$ | 0.01 (0.00) | 1.86 | 0.00 (0.00) | 1.59 |
| Vocabulary, $\gamma_{60}$ | 0.02 (0.01) | 3.43 | 0.01 (0.01) | 1.10 |
| Question effects | | | | |
| Literal, $\gamma_{70}$ | 1.49 (0.56) | 2.68 | 1.49 (0.55) | 2.73 |
| Passage effects | | | | |
| Listen, $\gamma_{80}$ | −2.23 (0.61) | −3.66 | −2.20 (0.60) | −3.69 |
| | *Variance* | *SD* | *Variance* | *SD* |
| *Random effects* | | | | |
| Person (intercept), $\tau_{u10}$ | 0.30 | 0.55 | 0.15 | 0.39 |
| Person (BK), $\tau_{u11}$ | 0.06 | 0.24 | 0.07 | 0.26 |
| Question (intercept), $\tau_{u20}$ | 1.78 | 1.33 | 1.70 | 1.31 |
| Passage (intercept), $\tau_{u30}$ | 0.00 | 0.00 | 0.00 | 0.00 |
| Passage (BK), $\tau_{u31}$ | 0.00 | 0.00 | 0.00 | 0.00 |

*Key:* BK, passage-specific background knowledge; LTA, latent transition analysis; LPA, latent profile analysis; TD/high, dummy variable comparing typical reader group versus late-emerging reading disability group for LTA and high versus medium for the LPA; ERD/low, dummy variable comparing early versus late-emerging reading disability groups for LTA and low versus medium for LPA.

in the figure, the difference between the high and medium subtypes is larger when students are asked to listen to the passage rather than read the passage; this was especially true when the mode of access to text was listening. By exploring interactions of this type, we are forced to think about why subtypes might vary as a function of passage characteristic, question type, and mode of access.

## CONCLUSIONS

Item response random effects modeling makes it possible to simultaneously explain variability in comprehension with person, passage, and question characteristics. This modeling approach not only provides the opportunity to explore research questions related to multiple sources of variance, including person-by-item covariates, but also provides less

**Table 12.4.** Results of conditional model with reader status interactions

| | LTA | | LPA | |
|---|---|---|---|---|
| | Est. (SE) | *z* | Est. (SE) | *z* |
| *Fixed effects* | | | | |
| Person-by-passage effects | | | | |
| Intercept, $\gamma_{00}$ | −0.02 (0.59) | −0.03 | 0.03 (0.50) | 0.05 |
| BK, $\gamma_{10}$ | 0.45 (0.21) | 2.19 | 0.40 (0.16) | 2.48 |
| TD/high&_listen, $\gamma_{81}$ | 0.13 (0.23) | 0.56 | 0.66 (0.27) | 2.48 |
| ERD/low&_listen, $\gamma_{82}$ | 0.34 (0.33) | 1.05 | −0.08 (0.24) | −0.35 |
| Person effects | | | | |
| TD/high, $\gamma_{20}$ | 0.11 (0.25) | 0.46 | 0.74 (0.27) | 2.74 |
| ERD/low, $\gamma_{30}$ | 0.08 (0.32) | 0.25 | −0.38 (0.24) | −1.57 |
| General knowledge, $\gamma_{40}$ | 0.08 (0.03) | 2.74 | 0.03 (0.03) | 1.36 |
| Reading fluency, $\gamma_{50}$ | 0.01 (0.00) | 1.79 | 0.00 (0.00) | 1.53 |
| Vocabulary, $\gamma_{60}$ | 0.02 (0.01) | 3.44 | 0.01 (0.01) | 1.24 |
| Question effects | | | | |
| Literal, $\gamma_{70}$ | 1.60 (0.58) | 2.76 | 1.55 (0.56) | 2.78 |
| Person-by-question effects | | | | |
| TD/high&_literal, $\gamma_{71}$ | −0.19 (0.23) | −0.83 | 0.01 (0.26) | 0.05 |
| ERD/low&_literal, $\gamma_{72}$ | −0.03 (0.32) | −0.11 | −0.17 (0.23) | −0.74 |
| Passage effects | | | | |
| Listen, $\gamma_{80}$ | −2.03 (0.60) | −3.37 | −1.92 (0.57) | −3.36 |
| | *Variance* | *SD* | *Variance* | *SD* |
| *Random effects* | | | | |
| Person (intercept), $\tau_{u10}$ | 0.31 | 0.55 | 0.16 | 0.40 |
| Person (BK), $\tau_{u11}$ | 0.07 | 0.26 | 0.07 | 0.27 |
| Question (intercept), $\tau_{u20}$ | 1.79 | 1.34 | 1.70 | 1.30 |
| Passage (intercept), $\tau_{u30}$ | 0.00 | 0.00 | 0.00 | 0.00 |
| Passage (BK), $\tau_{u31}$ | 0.04 | 0.21 | 0.00 | 0.00 |

*Key:* BK, passage-specific background knowledge; LTA, latent transition analysis; LPA, latent profile analysis; TD/high, dummy variable comparing typical reader group versus late-emerging reading disability group for LTA and high versus medium for the LPA; ERD/low, dummy variable comparing early versus late-emerging reading disability groups for LTA and low versus medium for LPA.

biased estimates and fewer standard errors than do traditional by-person, by-question, or by-passage regression models. Our hope is that these models will motivate researchers to explore important questions regarding person and text characteristics that affect reading comprehension. Our models suggest that having some knowledge about a passage's topic is positively associated with the likelihood of correctly answering questions about that passage, which we take to mean comprehension of the passage. When controlling for passage-specific BK, general knowledge ability was not related to the likelihood of correctly answering comprehension questions, nor was reading fluency. Vocabulary knowledge, however, remained significantly associated with correct responses. We also conclude, not surprisingly, that regardless of passage-specific BK, questions about information that is

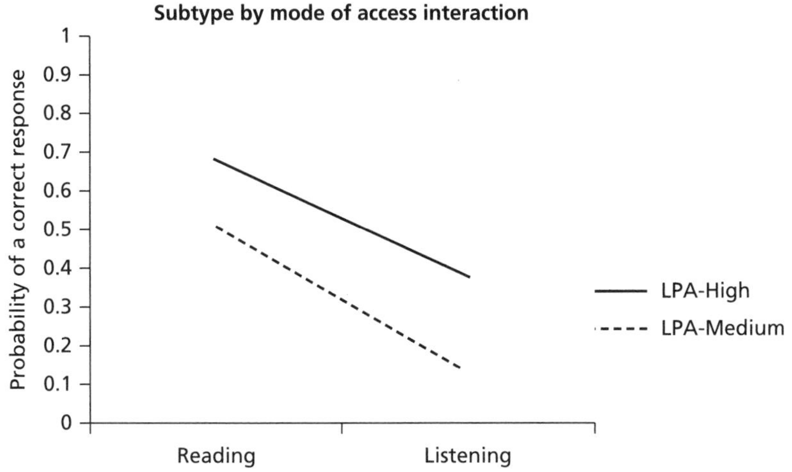


**Figure 12.3.** The interaction between reader subtype and mode of text access. *Key:* LPA, latent profile analysis.

stated literally in the text are easier to answer than are questions about implied information. Finally, the likelihood of answering comprehension questions was higher when the questions were associated with passages that students read to themselves rather than passages that were read to them. What this could mean for instruction is that students may be better able to comprehend what they read rather than what they hear, even when considering reading skill, general knowledge, vocabulary knowledge, and passage-specific BK.

We further pushed the models to explore the effects of reader subtype, subtype-by-passage-specific BK, subtype-by-passage interactions (mode of text access), and subtype-by-question type interactions. We found significant differences in the main effect of subtype based on the procedure used to identify latent classes, reminding us that subtyping populations of poor readers must be done carefully with an eye toward theory. The LPA subtypes based on language and knowledge variables resulted in classes that differed significantly in the ability to correctly answer comprehension items, whereas the LTA subtypes derived from the simple view of reading across time did not. Interactions between subtype and passage and between subtype and question type were rare in our data (the only detected significant interaction was between passage-specific BK and mode of access to text); however, we were extremely underpowered to detect these interactions. For instance, several of the subtype-by-person-specific BK interactions approached significance.

Our hope is that this demonstration will encourage others who are interested in exploring person-by-text interaction to adopt item response random effects models. We have tried to illustrate the flexibility of these models and the potential for them to help flush out complicated relationships between reading comprehension performance as a function of reader and text characteristics. These data are not without limitations. First, four passages are too few to draw reliable conclusions about passage variability. Second, there existed a confound in our data whereby passages that students read to themselves were also the passage that they knew most about in terms of background information. Although the model statistically controls for the relations among independent variables, in reality, separating mode of text access and passage-specific BK is extrapolating beyond our sample data. Still, despite these limitations, we believe we have accomplished our goal of demonstrating the utility of item response random effects models in modeling and understanding comprehension.

## REFERENCES

Baayen, R.H., Davidson, D.J., & Bates, D.M. (2008). Mixed-effects modeling with crossed random effects for subjects and items. *Journal of Memory and Language, 59*, 390–412.

Cain, K., & Oakhill, J. (2006). Profiles of children with specific reading comprehension difficulties. *British Journal of Educational Psychology, 76*(4), 683–696.

Cain, K., & Oakhill, J. (2009). Reading comprehension development from 8 to 14 years: The contribution of component skills and processes. In R.K. Wagner, C. Schatschneider, & C. Phythian-Sence (Eds.), *Beyond decoding: The behavioral and biological foundations of reading comprehension* (pp. 143–175). New York, NY: Guilford Press.

Catts, H.W., Compton, D., Tomblin, J.B., & Bridges, M.S. (2012). Prevalence and nature of late-emerging poor readers. *Journal of Educational Psychology, 104*(1), 166–181.

Compton, D.L., Fuchs, D., & Fuchs, L.S. (2006). *Response-to-intervention as an approach to preventing and identifying learning disabilities in reading* (Grant No. R324G060036). Funded by the Institute for Education Sciences.

Compton, D.L., Fuchs, D., & Fuchs, L.S. (2010). *Predictors and subtypes of reading disabilities: Implications for instruction of "late-emergers"* (Grant No. R305A100034). Funded by the Institute for Education Sciences.

De Boeck, P., & Wilson, M. (2004). A framework for item response models. In P. De Boeck & M. Wilson (Eds.), *Explanatory Item Response Models: A generalized linear and nonlinear approach* (pp. 3–42). New York, NY: Springer.

Dunn, L.M., & Dunn, D.M. (2007). *Peabody Picture Vocabulary Test–4*. San Antonio, TX: Pearson.

Fuchs, L.S., & Fuchs, D. (1999). Monitoring student progress toward the development of reading competence: A review of three forms of classroom-based assessment. *School Psychology Review, 28*, 659–671.

Gough, P., & Tunmer, W. (1986). Decoding, reading, and reading disability. *Remedial and Special Education, 7*, 6–10.

Leslie, L., & Caldwell, J. (2001). *Qualitative Reading Inventory–3 (QRI-3)*. New York, NY: Longman.

McNamara, D.S., Kintsch, E., Songer, N.B., & Kintsch, W. (1996). Are good texts always better? Interactions of text coherence, background knowledge, and levels of understanding in learning from text. *Cognition and Instruction, 14*, 1–43.

Nation, K., Cocksey, J., Taylor, J.S.H., & Bishop, D.V.M. (2010). A longitudinal investigation of early reading and language skills in children with poor reading comprehension. *Journal of Child Psychology and Psychiatry, 51*(9), 1031–1039.

Perfetti, C.A., Landi, N., & Oakhill, J. (2005). The acquisition of reading comprehension skill. In M.J. Snowling & C. Hulme (Eds.), *The science of reading: A handbook* (pp. 227–247). Malden, MA: Blackwell.

Rapp, D.N., van den Broek, P., McMaster, K.L., Kendeou, P., & Espin, C.A. (2007). Higher-order comprehension processes in struggling readers: A perspective for research and intervention. *Scientific Studies of Reading, 11,* 289–312.

Raudenbush, S.W., & Bryk, A.S. (2002). *Hierarchical linear models: Applications and data analysis methods* (2nd ed.). Thousand Oaks, CA: Sage.

Snow, C.E. (2002). *Reading for understanding: Toward a research and development program in reading comprehension by the RAND Reading Study Group* (Grant No. MR-1465-OERI, ISBN: 0-8330-3105-8). RAND: Santa Monica, CA.

van den Broek, P., Boh-Gettler, C.M., Panayiota, K., Carlson, S., & White, M.J. (2011). When a reader meets a text: The role of standards of coherence in reading comprehension. In T. McCrudden, J.P. Magliano, & G. Schraw (Eds.), *Text relevance and learning from text* (pp. 123–139). Charlotte, NC: Information Age.

van den Noortgate, W., De Boeck, P., & Meulders, M. (2003). Cross-classification multilevel logistic models in psychometrics. *Journal of Educational and Behavioral Statistics, 28,* 369–386.

Woodcock, R.W., McGrew, K.S., & Mather, N. (2001). *Woodcock-Johnson III.* Itasca, IL: Riverside.

INTEGRATIVE SUMMARY 2

# Understanding Limitations of the Past to Facilitate Future Advances in Reading Comprehension Research

Brett Miller

Reading comprehension continues to be one of the most challenging components of reading to study and to remediate effectively. This section focuses on assessment and statistical and computational modeling of reading comprehension with explicit goals of facilitating our understanding and study of reading comprehension. These chapters directly and indirectly reflect on some of the challenges that continue to face the research community. They reflect science from a range of fields, but uniformly press for improvements and innovations that should move us forward toward the goal of enhancing outcomes for all readers.

In the first chapter in this section, Sabatini and O'Reilly present their conceptual framework for the design of reading comprehension (RC) assessments. The authors argue for the need for a conceptually or theoretically driven and motivated assessment framework and corresponding tool that captures the evolving understanding of reading and, specifically, RC. By this, they mean that the conceptual model is not only grounded in current research conceptualizations of reading and learning but is developed with an eye toward enhancing educational utility where the tool would be utilized. In making this case, Sabatini and O'Reilly express their sensitivity to the continually evolving ideas of what constitutes literacy spurred on by the digital age.

The authors present six design principles generated by synthesizing across research findings from the field. These principles include sensitivity to the importance of word recognition and comprehension (e.g., Gough & Tunmer, 1986; Hoover & Gough, 1990); breadth and depth of vocabulary knowledge; development of mental models of the text at multiple levels (e.g., Kintsch, 1988); utilization of strategies to facilitate cogent understanding of text; comprehension across multiple documents and sources; and an explanation of growth in reading proficiency as occurring through incremental gains in reading-related skills and background knowledge supportive of reading—this growth is spurred by readers' experiential factors and therefore, not surprisingly, one should expect individual differences in performance. Together these principles form the framework for a developmentally sensitive measurement of RC skills where the nature of the construct of RC might evolve, in relative emphasis (e.g., word-level factors being a primary driver for beginning readers), across the life span. At this point, the framework is a concept proof; but with the continued development of their global, integrated summative assessment (GISA) of reading for understanding (i.e., RC), we will see both the benefits and current limitations of this approach. In the end, the drive to conceptually specify an empirically justifiable construct definition or model and align an assessment model with this definition, particularly for a construct as complex as RC, is admirable and likely to bear fruit in the coming years.

The chapter by Reichle demonstrates the potential of computational modeling of eye movements to enhance our understanding of the development of reading and RC skills. Reichle begins by providing a cogent description of some of the key findings from eye-movement research on reading (for a review, see Rayner, 1998, 2009). This research community has made significant strides in enhancing our understanding of reading but has historically focused more extensively on studying skilled adult readers. Within the context of this volume and its focus on readers who struggle or have a reading disability, it becomes clear that this focus is changing; more recent efforts have been underway to include a greater focus on individual differences in readers (e.g., deaf, older, developing) and on exploring developmental hypotheses about these learners (however, see Rayner, 1986, for an early exception). Reichle's modeling effort is a powerful example of how a motivated computational account can help constrain possible interpretations of developmental differences in behavioral patterns (i.e., eye-movement patterns while reading).

Reichle uses the framework of the E-Z Reader model (e.g., Reichle, 2011; Reichle, Pollatsek, Fisher, & Rayner, 1998) to simulate age-related differences in reading skills. For example, children tend to have longer fixation durations, fewer skipped words, and more frequent regressions to previously encountered text than do skilled adult readers; although older adult readers show some similarities to children's eye-movement patterns during reading (e.g., show longer fixation durations and more frequent regressions), older adults demonstrate a different skipping pattern than do children and skip words more frequently than do skilled adult readers (typically studies of younger adult populations; e.g., Kleigl et al., 2004; Rayner, Reichle, Stroud, Williams, & Pollatsek, 2006). Reichle focuses on the specific aspects of the E-Z Reader model critical to simulating this pattern of eye movements; this model is designed to account for eye-movement patterns of reading with relatively few, but sometimes strong, theoretical assumptions (e.g., attention is allocated serially one word at a time). For instance, to demonstrate the difference in eye-movement patterns between children and younger adults, Reichle and colleagues were able to adjust two model parameters corresponding to slower lexical processing and reduced rate of postlexical integration in children—both reasonable and defensible assumptions. The ability to generate theoretically motivated explanations, but more critically predictions of a reader's performance, will be increasingly valuable as this research community continues to expand the breadth of eye-movement research to include a broader population of readers and developing readers, thereby placing further demands on grounded and well-specified models of eye-movement behavior in this domain. Also, there remains a need to integrate eye-movement models of this type with computational models of such lower level phenomena as visual word recognition (e.g., Grainger, 2003; Zevin & Yang, Chapter 11, this volume), which, though underspecified in current eye-movement models of reading, form an integral part of most model predictions.

The chapter by Zevin and Yang focuses on the implications and constraints that experimental tasks place on computational models of reading (and others) as well as on the construction of tasks and interpretation of neuroimaging data. The authors highlight that a large percentage of work on reading, including reading disabilities research, has focused on isolated, single-word reading. The reasons for this focus are fairly apparent, including, for example, enhanced experimental control, relative simplicity of research designs, and widespread availability of methods for testing. When one moves attention to computational models of reading, the focus on single-word reading becomes even more acute (for examples of exceptions, though, see Engbert, Longtin, & Kliegl, 2002; Reichle, Chapter 10, this volume; Reichle et al., 1998). Zevin and Yang argue that the use of more artificial tasks in this domain is because of the "low dimensional output" from behavioral studies of this type; they mean, simply, that we generally have only accuracy and response times as outcomes, despite the potential of computational models to deal with richer data structures than this. This type of data structure from experiments can put computational modelers in a difficult position if they want to account for the breadth of visual word recognition findings. These researchers have to make difficult decisions about the underlying assumptions that are necessary to account for the observed behavioral data; for instance, they must determine how much task performance relates to the reading system and how the task is completed. As Zevin and Yang point out, these assumptions may not be well grounded and can lead to the creation of a very large range of possible free parameters for a model. Similar challenges exist for the neuroimaging community. Zevin and Yang highlight the interpretative risks of stimulus and task selection in neuroimaging experiments. Specifically, they highlight two salient challenges: 1) the response selectivity of individual regions of interest can interact with the task and 2) parameters of chosen tasks can interact with properties of the writing system.

Together, these challenges and choices raise the question, How do research design choices relate to more ecologically valid conditions? Zevin and Yang argue for the consideration of novel, more naturalistic tasks and designs that would allow for greater ecological validity and a richer dimensional output than is available in tasks that focus solely on accuracy and response time. This transition to greater inclusion of more naturalistic tasks would serve as an important complement and counterpoint to help interpret the relevance and applicability of more artificial tasks to the underlying activities that they try to tap, in this case reading.

The final chapter in this section, by Compton, Miller, Gilbert, and Steacy, focuses on exploring the versatility of a newer analytic technique that can help researchers disentangle and examine the role of a reader's reading comprehension skill, the text being read, and the interaction of reader and text within the same statistical model. This class of models allows researchers to simultaneously partition the variance for each level and resolve the pragmatic need in other statistical approaches of collapsing or aggregating at a particular level of analysis in order to accommodate the model structure. The authors highlight the potential of such an approach by utilizing an extant data set; consistent with the focus of the meeting and this volume, they examine readers who are typically developing and those individuals with reading disabilities as a subtype reader characteristic in their model. This approach allowed the authors to demonstrate that one could simultaneously look at the role of passage and question characteristics and multiple classes of reading disability (i.e., typically developing, early emerging, comprehension difficulties, late-emerging comprehension difficulties). In addition to this flexibility, the authors highlight that this statistical approach also generates less biased estimates and fewer standard errors than do other regression models that require one to collapse a level as described above. The critical contribution of this chapter is less about the specific analysis conducted as a demonstration and more in the analysis's demonstration of the power of this approach and the flexibility that it could provide to the educational and learning disabilities research community writ large.

On the surface, this set of chapters seems fairly disparate and loosely tied; however, these chapters all try to articulate a path forward for the field to overcome some of the challenges or limitations with current and previous research methods and approaches. These chapters as a unit argue for conceptually and theoretically motivated approaches to examining reading comprehension, whether through assessment, computational modeling, or other experimental approaches to the questions. They also argue for capturing the complexity of the phenomenon under study, RC in this case; this could be done through either modeling higher dimensional data using more efficient and less biased analytic approaches or more efficiently and effectively assessing the construct(s) at hand. In short, my hope is that when you read through this section, you leave with an invigorated sense of how to move forward and with a need to step out of comfort zones (with appropriate support of collaborators as necessary) to tackle some of the more challenging aspects of our job as researchers and to push research on reading comprehension forward.

## REFERENCES


Engbert, R., Longtin, A., & Kliegl, R. (2002). A dynamic model of saccade generation in reading based upon spatially distributed lexical processing. *Vision Research, 42*(5), 621–636.

Gough, P.B., & Tunmer, W.E. (1986). Decoding, reading, and reading disability. *Remedial and Special Education, 7,* 6–10.

Grainger, J. (2003). Moving eyes and reading words: How can a computational model combine the two? In J. Hyona, R. Radach, & H. Deubel (Eds.), *In the mind's eye: Cognitive and applied aspects of eye movement research* (pp. 457–470). Amsterdam, The Netherlands: North Holland.

Hoover, W.A., & Gough, P.B. (1990). The simple view of reading. *Reading and Writing: An Interdisciplinary Journal, 2,* 127–160.

Kintsch, W. (1988). The role of knowledge in discourse comprehension: A construction–integration model. *Psychological Review, 95,* 163–182.

Kliegl, R., Gabner, E., Rolfs, M., & Engbert, R. (2004). Length, frequency, and predictability effects of words on eye movements in reading. *European Journal of Cognitive Psychology, 16,* 262–284.

Rayner, K. (1986). Eye movements and the perceptual span in beginning and skilled readers. *Journal of Experimental Child Psychology, 41,* 211–236.

Rayner, K. (1998). Eye movements in reading and information processing: 20 years of research. *Psychological Bulletin, 124,* 372–422.

Rayner, K. (2009). The Thirty Fifth Sir Frederick Bartlett Lecture: Eye movements and attention during reading, scene perception, and visual search. *Quarterly Journal of Experimental Psychology, 62,* 1457–1506.

Rayner, K., Reichle, E.D., Stroud, M.J., Williams, C.C., & Pollatsek, A. (2006). The effects of word frequency, word predictability, and font difficulty on the eye movements of young and elderly readers. *Psychology and Aging, 21,* 448–465.

Reichle, E. (2011). Serial attention models of reading. In S.P. Liversedge, I.D. Gilchrist, & S. Everling (Eds.), *Oxford handbook on eye movements* (pp. 767–786). Oxford, England: Oxford University Press.

Reichle, E.D., Pollatsek, A., Fisher, D.L., & Rayner, K. (1998). Toward a model of eye movement control in reading. *Psychological Review, 105,* 125–157.

SECTION IV

# The Neurobiology and Genetics of Reading and Reading Comprehension

CHAPTER 13

# From Words to Text

## Neurobiology and Behavioral Bases of Reading Comprehension

Laurie E. Cutting, Sabrina L. Benedict, Allison Broadwater, Scott S. Burns, and Qiuyun Fan

Research has established that there are multiple critical components associated with reading comprehension, including but not limited to decoding/word recognition, linguistic proficiency (Gough & Tunmer, 1986; Hoover & Gough, 1990; Lyon, 1995; Torgesen, 2000), working memory (Brookshire, Levin, Song, & Zhang, 2004; Willcutt et al., 2001; Willcutt, Sonuga-Barke, Nigg, & Sergeant, 2008), background knowledge (Best, Floyd, & McNamara, 2008), and higher level thinking skills, such as those commonly labeled as within the rubric of executive function (Cutting, Materek, Cole, Levine, & Mahone, 2009). It has been demonstrated that readers who lack proficiency in one or more of these areas are at risk for (or have) poor reading comprehension (Lyon, 1995; Perfetti & Hogaboam, 1975; Perfetti, Marron, & Foltz, 1996; Shankweiler, 1999; Torgesen, 2000; Wolf & Katzir-Cohen, 2001). Dyslexia, which is characterized by poor word-level processing, is one of the most well-researched types of reading difficulty and is in some ways more transparent than other types of reading difficulties: Without being able to decode, it is difficult to be able to comprehend text.

Given the multitude of candidate component processes for reading comprehension, it is not surprising that many different models of reading comprehension have been proposed (see Cutting & Scarborough, 2012; Gough & Tunmer, 1986; Hoover & Gough, 1990; Kintsch, 1998; Perfetti, 2007; van den Broek, 2010). Some models have been more focused on the cognitive profile of readers (Gough & Tunmer, 1986; Hoover & Gough, 1990), whereas others have highlighted critical aspects of reading comprehension external to the reader, such as the type of text and the purpose of reading (Perkins-Gough, 2002). The tradition of a focus on the reader in the developmental and disability literature largely evolved from research on dyslexia, which by definition is intrinsic to the individual (biological in nature) and clearly is a processing issue within the reader (difficulty with decoding words) that is impeding text comprehension. Nevertheless, as the developmental literature seeks to understand where and how reading beyond the word level may break down, the layers of complexity increase. In particular, in understanding the many areas of potential struggle in comprehension, there is a need for understanding the cognitive profile of the reader and the text, as well as the interaction between the two (see Figure 13.1). Our program

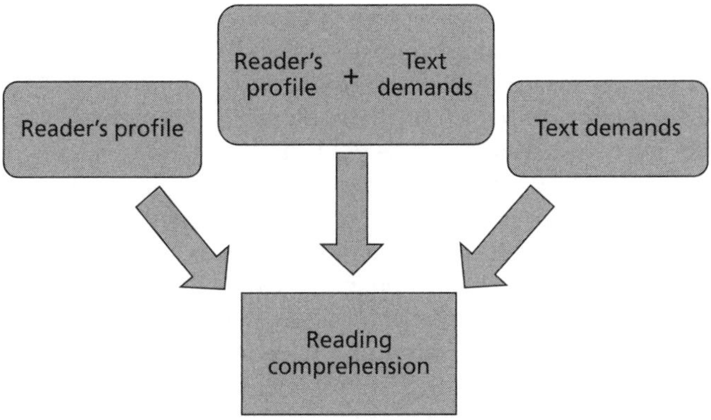


**Figure 13.1.** Reader and text components of reading comprehension.

of research has been focusing on this very issue—namely, understanding the cognitive and neurobiological profiles of children with varying reading comprehension abilities and how various text types interact with these profiles.

In this chapter, we will review the approach we have taken to arrive at ultimately trying to understand this interaction of cognitive/neurobiological profile and text type. We review research findings specifically related to 1) the reader's cognitive and neurobiological profile, 2) related text characteristics, and 3) the interaction between the two.

## READER PROFILE

Early in our research, we focused primarily on the reader's cognitive and neurobiological profile. For this approach, we compared readers with different profiles in order to learn specifically about reading comprehension separate from word reading or decoding; we also examined readers' cognitive and neurobiological profiles on a continuum. In several studies, we compared typically developing readers to readers with dyslexia and to those with specific reading comprehension deficits (S-RCD). Readers with S-RCD have adequate word-level decoding skills but poor reading comprehension, thus showing a specific deficit in reading comprehension. Individuals with S-RCD have been shown to have difficulties or weaknesses in a variety of areas, including vocabulary development and semantics (Cain & Oakhill, 2011; Nation, Snowling, & Clarke, 2007; Ricketts, Bishop, & Nation, 2008), oral language (Cain, 2006; Catts, Adlof, & Weismer, 2006), inference (Cain, 2006; Cain & Towse, 2008), and morphology (Tong, Deacon, Kirby, Cain, & Parrila, 2011). Individuals with S-RCD are also reported to have had fewer outside school literacy experiences than typically developing readers have had (Cain & Oakhill, 2011; Torppa et al., 2007).

Executive function has also been reported to be an area of weakness in S-RCD, specifically working memory (Cain & Oakhill, 2006; Yuill, Oakhill, & Parkin, 1989) and planning and organization (Cutting et al., 2009; Locascio, Mahone, Eason, & Cutting, 2010). Two of our studies specifically focused on the role of executive function in S-RCD. Findings from these two studies revealed that children with S-RCD, ages 9 through 14, showed prominent weaknesses in strategic planning and organization even after controlling for presence of attention-deficit/hyperactivity disorder (often associated with poor executive functioning) and phonological processing. In both studies, children with S-RCD performed poorly on strategic planning (Loscascio et al., 2010). This was seen particularly on the Delis–Kaplan Executive Function System (D-KEFS) Tower subtest, measuring spatial planning, rule learning, and the ability to adequately learn and follow instructions: Even though both groups, those with dyslexia and those with S-RCD, had high rule violations, the individuals with S-RCD showed a higher frequency of planning errors. Such poor strategic planning may negatively affect readers' ability to navigate and organize a text in a manner lending itself to comprehension.

More recent neurobiological findings (Cutting et al., 2013) have further revealed interesting findings with regard to children with S-RCD. As expected, those with dyslexia showed the typically reported areas of abnormality (underactivation of left occipito-temporal region and supramarginal gyrus) as compared both to children with S-RCD and to typically developing readers. Although readers with S-RCD showed intact response to word stimuli in regions typically associated with fast and efficient word processing (left occipito-temporal region), not all areas were intact, with abnormalities for processing low-frequency words linked to hippocampal regions. The anomalous areas are not regions typically associated with dyslexia but are instead areas more often associated with declarative memory, suggesting different neural mechanisms for dyslexia versus S-RCD. Understanding more about these differences may reveal more about the nature of reading comprehension and where the breakdowns can occur.

In addition to the characteristics of reading comprehension processes and specific characteristics of S-RCD readers, examination of reading comprehension on a continuum offers insights about various skills that are important for reading comprehension. For example, numerous studies have tested the so-called simple view of reading and show that word-level skills combined with oral language skills do indeed offer a close approximation of reading comprehension. One component of simple view findings that is less often discussed is the shared variance between word-level and oral comprehension measures. For example, Cutting and Scarborough (2006) found between 33% and 51% of the variance was overlapping between word-level and language comprehension. This same shared variance is seen neurobiologically in recent work from our

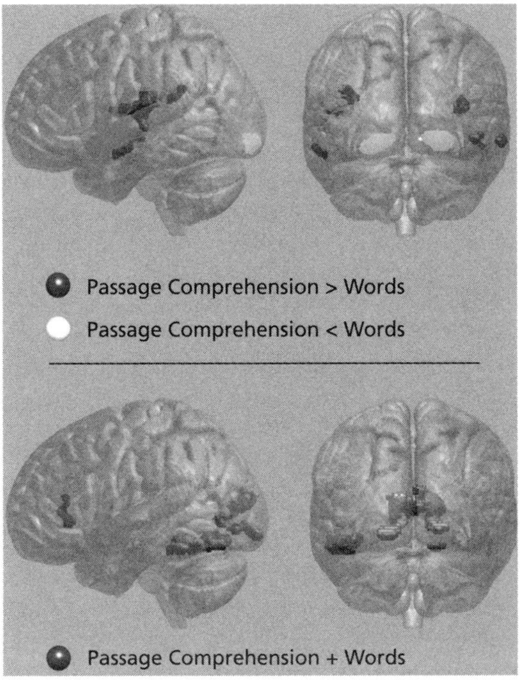


**Figure 13.2.** Brain regions activated in fMRI passage and word-level reading tasks. The difference between passage- versus word-level reading activation is shown in the upper panel: In dark are brain regions where activation was higher when reading passages than when reading words, which includes bilateral insula, superior-, middle-, and transverse-temporal gyri, left pre- and postcentral gyri, and right putamen. Bright areas represent regions where word-level activation was higher than when reading passages and includes bilateral fusiform gyri and occipital gyri. The lower panel shows the areas commonly activated in both passage- and word-level reading, which included bilateral inferior occipital and fusiform gyri, as well as left superior-, middle-, and inferior-temporal gyri and left inferior frontal gyrus.

laboratory examining the neurobiological correlates of word, phrase, and passage comprehension in children. As expected (and consistent with the broader literature), preliminary fMRI data from 15 children with varying reading abilities suggests that passage reading versus word-level reading draws upon different areas of the brain, as well as upon common areas (see Figure 13.2). Consistent with behavioral findings, there was some unique variance and a large amount of shared variance. A focus on this shared variance may in fact reveal clues to why struggle occurs; for example, typically all the overlapping variance in reading is attributed to word-level difficulties, but in fact this variance captures the contributions of both word-level reading and language. Understanding the source of this overlapping variance early in reading development may provide clues to downstream difficulties, as well as to the so-called elusory recovery phenomenon (Scarborough, 2001).

## TEXT TYPE

Understanding the neurobiological profile of S-RCD, and the neurobiological correlates of reading comprehension in general, however, is limited without also considering the type of text an individual is required to read. Variation based on text type seems reasonable; for instance, reading a fictional story places different demands on a reader than reading a scientific article, demands that may substantially affect the reader's comprehension of the text. A narrative is likely to follow a predictable story structure and plot and requires some basic world knowledge. Expository text information, in contrast, can be more difficult because it tends to be less predictable and requires the reader to have prior knowledge of content vocabulary and background knowledge. Other text factors that can significantly affect comprehension include the length of the text and the vocabulary ratio of both known-to-unknown words and concrete-to-abstract words.

When we embarked on studying reading comprehension, the immediate challenge of measuring reading comprehension in order to define good versus poor comprehension ultimately led us to focus on text types. Unlike word-level instruments, reading comprehension measures vary widely in terms of whom they might identify as being a good or poor reader (Cutting & Scarborough, 2012). This problematic state of affairs led us to examine which cognitive skills contributed to various measures of reading comprehension.

Our first investigation (Cutting & Scarborough, 2006) was focused on examining the contribution of word-level and oral language skills to various reading comprehension measures, essentially expanding the well-known simple view of reading (Gough & Tumner, 1986), which states that reading comprehension is the product of decoding and listening comprehension. In Cutting and Scarborough (2006), three reading comprehension measures were compared: the Gates-MacGinitie (MacGinitie, MacGinitie, Maria, & Dreyer, 2000), the Wechsler Individual Achievement Test (WIAT; Wechsler, 1992), and the Gray Oral Reading Test–Third Edition (GORT-3; Wiederholt & Bryant, 1992). Results varied across reading comprehension measures in terms of percentage variance accounted for by oral language (9% for both the WIAT and GORT-3, and 15% for the Gates-MacGinitie) versus word recognition (12% for the WIAT, 8% for the GORT-3, and 6% for the Gates-MacGinitie). Cutting and Scarborough (2006) also examined the differences between sentence versus lexical contributions within oral language. For the Gates-MacGinitie, there was significant unique variance accounted for by sentences (1.8%) and vocabulary (4.5%). The WIAT had a significant unique contribution only from sentences (3.4%), whereas the GORT-3 had a significant unique contribution only from vocabulary (5.3%). Across all measures, however, there was substantial overlapping variance between oral language and word recognition (33%–51%), more than the unique variance of decoding and oral language together.

A subsequent investigation focused more purely on actual text type (Eason, Goldberg, Young, Geist, & Cutting, 2012). Eason and colleagues examined the proportion of variance that different text types accounted for in reading by exploring reader and text interactions of narrative, expository, and functional texts and questions. Findings indicated that whereas word-level and oral language skills were significant predictors across all text types, the contribution of higher order cognitive skills, including the ability to make inferences and to plan and organize information (executive function), contributed differentially to different text types. In particular, comprehension of more complex text (expository) placed greater demands on these executive function measures, whereas narrative passages did not. It is of interest that this was the case even though Coh-Metrix measures (Graesser, McNamara, & Kulikowich, 2011) on these passages indicated that many of the indices of text were actually easier for expository versus narrative text.

Findings from Cutting and Scarborough (2006) and Eason et al. (2012) led us to the conclusion that in order to understand the cognitive and neurobiological correlates of reading comprehension failure, it was critical for us to consider differential demands of text type and how the demands interacted with a reader's cognitive-neurobiological profile. Studies are underway to dig deeper into this approach to reading comprehension through experimental passage manipulations (Street, Davis, Benedict, Harris, & Cutting, 2011). Briefly, we have developed passages that have been manipulated on various dimensions (decoding, vocabulary, syntax, cohesion) in order to examine interactions with readers' cognitive and neurobiological profiles. By manipulations, we mean that we alter approximately 10% of the text to be more difficult on one targeted variable (e.g., decoding) while keeping the other variables constant (cohesion, vocabulary, syntax). In order to accomplish this, we first created 12 equivalent (baseline) passages, after which we manipulated a certain number of the passages on specific dimensions. Readers' background knowledge was also measured. Equivalency was established and manipulations were done using quantifiable metrics (Graesser et al., 2011); passages were then tested on adult skilled readers by using words per minute (WPM) as a proxy for comprehension. The initial adult findings (Street et al., 2011) were that individuals read the baseline passages with a higher WPM (faster) on average than for the manipulated passages, providing evidence that manipulated passages do indeed slow readers down, suggesting that they are more difficult. These same patterns are also seen in more recent preliminary data in children (see Table 13.1).

## READER–TEXT INTERACTIONS: PRELIMINARY NEUROBIOLOGICAL DATA

Findings regarding our ultimate goal of examining reader–text interactions, including neurobiologically, are confirmatory of the behavioral

**Table 13.1.** Words-per-minute passage manipulations results in children

| Passage type | Mean reading rate (seconds) | SD |
|---|---|---|
| Baseline | 155.41 | 25.08 |
| Vocabulary manipulation | 150.35[a] | 27.1 |
| Decoding manipulation | 144.50[a] | 29.74 |
| Syntax manipulation | 149.75[b] | 27.78 |
| Cohesion manipulation | 157.01 | 32.29 |

[a]Baseline > vocabulary and decoding ($p < .05$).
[b]Baseline > syntax ($p = .08$).

literature but also have implications that extend beyond those captured by behavioral findings. For example, preliminary neuroimaging findings suggest that passages with either decoding or vocabulary manipulations both recruit brain regions to a greater extent than baseline passages, often in overlapping areas; however, only the decoding manipulation shows additional areas of recruitment (left middle and superior temporal gyri) separate from vocabulary. After controlling for background knowledge, findings show that there is no significant activation for baseline passages or passages in which vocabulary is manipulated; however, significant activation for the decoding-manipulated passages remains. These findings are largely consistent with what one would hypothesize from the behavioral literature: Vocabulary and background knowledge are highly overlapping, whereas decoding skill is more independent. More refined examination of reader profiles and interactions with text manipulations are underway, but these initial findings support and extend what is known from behavioral research and therefore hold promise for elucidating more about reading comprehension.

## CONCLUSION

Our research program combined with the broader literature base has brought us to several conclusions, which we propose as helpful future directions for reading comprehension research. First, reading comprehension clearly places demands on the reader above and beyond the word level; however, the separation between word level and comprehension is not as distinct as is currently conceptualized. Our research suggests that it may be particularly fruitful to focus on the overlapping variance of word reading and comprehension, rather than just on the unique variance of each. As in the simple view model, in which reading comprehension is a product of word-level decoding and listening comprehension (Hoover & Gough, 1990), the emphasis on how word-reading and comprehension skills work together may enable us to delve into the origin and meaning of comprehension more deeply. Here, the consideration of the lexical quality hypothesis (see Perfetti, Stafura, & Adlof, Chapter 3, this volume) may be particularly fruitful for examining this overlapping variance. The lexical quality hypothesis emphasizes the quality of word representation on a number of levels, including semantic, thus linking word-level processes and reading comprehension. A second conclusion is that we feel, not surprisingly, that as the reading field delves deeper into comprehension, there will be an increasing need to further examine the interaction of text and reader. Particularly at the neurobiological level, it will be pertinent to examine how different stimuli modulate neural activation and connectivity.

Finally, although the field of dyslexia has generally focused more on functional (task-based) neuroimaging, task-*independent* imaging may offer important insights into reading comprehension because it allows for a greater separation between stimuli characteristics (e.g., text type) and basic neurobiological characteristics. A task-independent approach will be particularly important as we launch into investigations that focus on linking gene–brain–behavior relationships. Such an approach to understanding reading comprehension will likely result in many iterations of determining the boundaries of reading comprehension, ultimately offering a more precise and parsimonious neurobiological model of proficient reading comprehension.

## REFERENCES


Best, R.M., Floyd, R.G., & McNamara, D.S. (2008). Differential competencies contributing to children's comprehension of narrative and expository texts. *Reading Psychology, 29,* 137–164.

Brookshire, B., Levin, H.S., Song, J., & Zhang, L. (2004). Components of executive function in typically developing and head-injured children. *Developmental Neuropsychology, 25,* 61–83.

Cain, K. (2006). Individual differences in children's memory and reading comprehension: An investigation of semantic and inhibitory deficits. *Memory, 14*(5), 553–569.

Cain, K., & Oakhill, J. (2006). Profiles of children with specific reading comprehension difficulties. *British Journal of Educational Psychology, 76*(4), 683–696.

Cain, K., & Oakhill, J. (2011). Matthew effects in young readers: Reading comprehension and reading experience aid vocabulary development. *Journal of Learning Disabilities, 44*(5), 431–443.

Cain, K., & Towse, A.S. (2008). To get hold of the wrong end of the stick: Reasons for poor idiom understanding in children with reading comprehension difficulties. *Journal of Speech, Language, and Hearing Research, 51,* 1538–1549.

Catts, H.W., Adlof, S.M., & Weismer, S.E. (2006). Language deficits in poor comprehenders: A case for the simple view of reading. *Journal of Speech, Language, and Hearing Research, 49,* 278–293.

Cutting, L.E., Clements-Stephens, A., Pugh, K.R., Burns, S., Cao, A., Pekar, J., Davis, N., & Rimrodt, S.L. (2013). Not all reading disabilities are dyslexia: Distinct neurobiology of specific comprehension deficits. *Brain Connectivity 3*(2), 199–211.

Cutting, L.E., Materek, A., Cole, C.A.S., Levine, T.M., & Mahone, E.M. (2009). Effects of fluency, oral language, and executive function on reading comprehension performance. *Annals of Dyslexia, 59,* 34–54.

Cutting, L.E., & Scarborough, H.S. (2012). Multiple bases for comprehension difficulties. In J. Sabatini & E. Albro (Eds). *Assessing reading in the 21st century: Aligning and applying advances in the reading and measurement sciences.* Lanham, MD: Rowman & Littlefield.

Cutting, L.E., & Scarborough, H.S. (2006). Prediction of reading comprehension: Relative contributions of word recognition, language proficiency, and other cognitive skills can depend on how comprehension is measured. *Scientific Studies of Reading, 10*(3), 277–299.

Eason, S.H., Goldberg, L.F., Young, K.M., Geist, M.C., Cutting, L.E. (2012). Reader-text interactions: How differential text and question types influence cognitive skills needed for reading comprehension. *Journal of Educational Psychology, 104*, 515–528.

Gough, P.B., & Tunmer, W.E. (1986). Decoding, reading, and reading disability. *Remedial and Special Education, 7*(1), 6–10.

Graesser, A.C., McNamara, D.S., & Kulikowich, J.M. (2011). Coh-Metrix: Providing multilevel analyses of text characteristics. *Educational Researcher, 40*(5), 223–234.

Hoover, W.A., & Gough, P.B. (1990). The simple view of reading. *Reading and Writing, 2*(2), 127–160.

Kintsch, W. (1998). *Comprehension: A paradigm for cognition*. New York, NY: Cambridge University Press.

Loscascio, G.L., Mahone, E.M., Eason, S.H., & Cutting, L.E. (2010). Executive dysfunction among children with reading comprehension deficits. *Journal of Learning Disabilities, 43*(5), 441–454.

Lyon, G.R. (1995). Toward a definition of dyslexia. *Annals of Dyslexia, 45*(1), 1–27.

MacGinitie, W.H., MacGinitie, R.K., Maria, K., & Dreyer, L.G. (2000). *Gates-MacGinitie Reading Tests* (4th ed.). Itasca, IL: Riverside.

Nation, K., Snowling, M.J., & Clarke, P. (2007). Dissecting the relationship between language skills and learning to read: Semantic and phonological contributions to new vocabulary learning in children with poor reading comprehension. *International Journal of Speech-Language Pathology, 9*(2), 131–139.

Perfetti, C.A. (2007). Reading ability: Lexical quality to comprehension. *Scientific Studies of Reading, 11*, 357–383.

Perfetti, C.A., & Hogaboam, T. (1975). Relationship between single word decoding and reading comprehension skill. *Journal of Educational Psychology, 67*, 461–469.

Perfetti, C.A., Marron, M.A., & Foltz, P.W. (1996). Sources of comprehension failure: Theoretical perspectives and case studies. In C. Cornoldi & J. Oakhill (Eds.), *Reading comprehension difficulties: Processes and intervention* (pp. 137–166). Mahwah, NJ: Erlbaum.

Perkins-Gough, D. (2002). RAND report on reading comprehension. *Educational Leadership, 60*(3), 92.

Ricketts, J., Bishop, D.V.M., & Nation, K. (2008). Investigating orthographic and semantic aspects of word learning in poor comprehenders. *Journal of Research in Reading, 31*, 117–135.

Shankweiler, D. (1999). Words to meanings. *Scientific Studies of Reading, 3*, 113–127.

Street, J.S., Davis, N., Benedict, S.L., Harris, H., & Cutting, L.E. (2011, July). *Reader–text interactions and oral reading fluency*. Poster Session presented at the meeting of Scientific Studies of Reading, St. Pete Beach, FL.

Tong, X., Deacon, S.H., Kirby, J.R., Cain, K., & Parrila, R. (2011). Morphological awareness: A key to understanding poor reading comprehension in English. *Journal of Educational Psychology, 103*(3), 523–534.

Torgesen, J.K. (2000). The prevention of reading difficulties. *Journal of School Psychology, 40*(1), 7–26.

Torppa, M., Tolvanen, A., Poikkeus, A.M., Eklund, K., Lerkkanen, M.K., Leskinen, E., & Lyytinen, H. (2007). Reading development subtypes and their early characteristics. *Annals of Dyslexia, 57*(1), 3–32.

van den Broek, P. (2010). Using texts in science education: Cognitive processes and knowledge representation. *Science, 328*(5977), 453–456.

Wechsler, D.L. (1992). *Wechsler Individual Achievement Test*. San Antonio, TX: Psychological Corporation.

Wiederholt, L., & Bryant, B. (1992). *Examiner's manual: Gray Oral Reading Test–3*. Austin, TX: Pro-Ed.

Willcutt, E.G., Pennington, B.F., Boada, R., Ogline, J.S., Tunick, R.A., Chhabildas, N.A., & Olson, R.K. (2001). A comparison of the cognitive deficits in reading disability and attention-deficit/hyperactivity disorder. *Journal of Abnormal Child Psychology, 110*(1), 157–172.

Willcutt, E.G., Sonuga-Barke, E.J., Nigg, J.T., & Sergeant, J.A. (2008). Recent developments in neuropsychological models of childhood psychiatric disorders. In T. Banaschewski & L.A. Rohde (Eds.), *Biological child psychiatry: Recent trends and developments* (pp. 195–226). Basel, Switzerland: Karger.

Wolf, M., & Katzir-Cohen, T. (2001). Reading fluency and its intervention. *Scientific Studies of Reading, 5,* 211–238.

Yuill, N., Oakhill, J., & Parkin, A. (1989). Working memory, comprehension ability and the resolution of text anomaly. *British Journal of Psychology, 80,* 351–361.

CHAPTER 14

# Neuroimaging Studies of Reading Disabilities

## Toward Brain-based Learning Models

Kenneth R. Pugh, Stephen J. Frost, Nicole Landi,
Jonathan L. Preston, W. Einar Mencl, and Jay G. Rueckl

Reading disability (RD) has been defined as a brain-based difficulty in acquiring fluent reading skills (Lyon, Shaywitz, & Shaywitz, 2003) that affects significant numbers of children (5%–20%, depending on criteria applied) and has been associated with negative socioemotional and academic outcomes (Stanovich, 1986; Shaywitz et al., 1999). A major deficit in the vast majority of children presenting with RD is difficulty in operating on the phonological structures of language (Ball & Blachman, 1991). Deficits in phonological processing (especially in the metacognitive understanding of the componential nature of spoken words, that is, phonological awareness) impede the development of high-quality lexical representations of written words, which depend upon integration of orthographic (O), phonological (P), and semantic (S) information (Harm & Seidenberg, 1999; Perfetti & Hart, 2001) and support fluent and automatic word identification. A failure to develop high-quality lexical representations for printed words will also impede the development of adequate connected-text reading fluency, and this bottleneck will limit reading comprehension (Shankweiler et al., 2008).

At the level of brain systems, neuroimaging studies have consistently found that, relative to typically developing (TD) readers, RD readers show evidence of both structural and functional anomalies in left-hemisphere (LH) cortical and subcortical networks that, with literacy instruction, come to comprise a distributed circuitry for O, P, and S processing in reading (Pugh, et al., 2010). Moreover, recent studies have shown that many of these anomalies can be detected even at early stages of literacy learning (Pugh et al., 2013) or, in some cases, prior to literacy acquisition (Raschle, Chang, & Gaab, 2011; Yamada et al., 2011). Although brain and behavior correlational data point to an important association between atypical brain development and well-documented phonological deficits in RD, there are at present no well-established causal brain-based accounts of this condition. A crucial next step, then, in our understanding of RD will be to generate neurocognitive models that specify underlying mechanisms and to test relevant developmental predictions about specific brain structure function patterns that compose reading development in RD (Pugh & McCardle, 2009).

Toward this goal, we have recently focused on two new research questions that we feel will be important for extending our understanding of the causes of the condition. Recent findings from our lab have shown that poor readers exhibit anomalies in functional activation patterns of both cortical and subcortical regions that have been linked more generally to skill acquisition. This finding, combined with findings from other labs suggesting procedural learning deficits in RD (Howard, Howard, Japiske, & Eden, 2006; Stoodley, Harrison & Stein, 2006), has led us to ask whether domain general learning and consolidation problems, along with more well-studied phonological processing deficits, contribute to the severe reading problems associated with RD and, if so, by which brain pathways. The second question asks if and how phonological (and later reading) problems relate to earlier problems in the basic machinery for speaking and listening, given recent information on cognition and language. Cognitive research has shown that spoken language development can play a substantial role in school-age oral and written language performance and that young children at risk for RD may demonstrate subtle deficits in speech perception and production (Scarborough, 2001).

In this chapter we propose a developmental account regarding specific cortical and subcortical anomalies in relation to both learning problems and speech and language problems in RD. We begin first with an overview of some key findings in neurocognitive comparisons of TD and RD learners.

## THE READING CIRCUITRY IN ALPHABETIC ORTHOGRAPHIES

Based on extensive studies from our lab, as well as from many others in the field, some years ago we developed an initial neurobiological model of skilled and impaired *word identification* (decoding) that at the cortical level involves a largely LH distributed circuit with temporoparietal (TP), occipitotemporal (OT), and inferior frontal (IFG) components (Pugh et al., 2010). In typically developing children, there is good evidence that with experience the occipitotemporal component takes on a special role in representing word forms (Booth & Burman, 2001; Church, Coalson, Lugar, Petersen, & Schlaggar, 2008; Shaywitz et al., 2002), and this skill-correlated region has been labeled the visual word form area (VWFA; Dehaene & Cohen, 2011).

Since this initial model, numerous neuroimaging studies have shown marked functional differences, relative to readers who are typically developing (TD), in both children and adults with RD with regard to activity generated in the LH neurocircuits during reading (Pugh et al., 2010). Readers with RD have shown reduced activation and reduced functional connectivity across LH posterior TP and OT networks. At the structural level, both grey matter volumetric and white matter tract anomalies have also been associated with RD in these same LH networks (Klingberg et al.,

2000; Niogi & McCandliss, 2006). Recent research focused on processing connected text in RD reports similar patterns (anomalous activation across key LH circuits) as have been reported in studies of single-word reading (Meyler, Keller, Cherkassy, Gabrieli, & Just, 2008; also see Cutting et al., Chapter 13, this volume, for discussion). All this provides a brain-based description (or neurophenotype) for RD but not an explanation of how and why these brain differences arise during development, nor how they may relate to candidate genes associated with brain development that have recently been proposed (see Grigorenko, Chapter 17, this volume, for discussion).

## SUBCORTICAL NETWORKS AND LEARNING

In recent years, it has become increasingly clear that one deficiency of the initial model and the studies outlined above is the failure to consider how reading circuits come on-line in beginning readers and whether brain pathways that support initial learning to read are at least partially distinct from those that will come to support word identification once the skill has been learned. Moreover, any consideration of learning demands increased focus on the potentially important influences of subcortical networks and their interactions with distributed language, visual, and attentional cortical networks that have been linked to skill acquisition in general (Crosson, 1999; Graybiel, 2005). In terms of structure, histological studies have also suggested subcortical anomalies in RD, showing abnormal cellular organization of the thalamus (see Galaburda, LoTurco, Ramus, Fitch, & Rosen, 2006). More recently, we and others have implicated the basal ganglia (particularly the caudate nucleus and putamen in the striatum) in discriminating skilled from less-skilled learners (McNorgan, Alvarez, Bhullar, Gayda, & Booth, 2011; Preston et al., 2010), and fronto-striatal anomalies have been reported in specific language impairment (SLI) and attention-deficit/hyperactivity disorder (ADHD), conditions that are highly comorbid with RD (see Ullman & Pierpont, 2005).

Two recent reports from a longitudinal study of children ages 7–9 in our lab are relevant. The first (Preston et al., 2010) reported activation anomalies in putamen and caudate nucleus, thalamus, and cerebellum in poor readers with a history of late onset of talking. Participants were asked to engage in an fMRI task involving spoken and written word processing. These late talkers also performed reliably worse than on-time talkers on measures of reading-related skills, replicating previous behavioral findings that implicate late talking as a risk factor for RD (Lyytinen et al., 2004).

The second (Pugh et al., 2013) focused on a large subset of beginning readers (mean age of 7 years) from the longitudinal cohort, with widely varied scores on multiple reading-related predictor tasks (phonological awareness, pseudo-word decoding, and rapid auditory processing) ranging from RD to superior. We reasoned that along with the LH cortical regions implicated in studies of older children or adults with RD (who have either learned or not learned to read well), for children engaged in the business of learning to read, the learning circuitry would be more extensive and would include important contributions from subcortical networks. Consistent with this expectation, using principal component analyses to identify a general skill factor from the three highly correlated tasks, brain–behavior analyses revealed strong positive correlations between variation on this skill measure and brain responses in previously identified LH TP, OT, and IFG networks, as well as in visual cortex, cortical attentional networks, including RH inferior parietal lobule IPL and bilateral precuneus, and the thalamus (centered in LH pulvinar).

The pulvinar finding is noteworthy for two reasons. First, pulvinar nuclei are known to play a critical role in visual selective attention, and particularly in modulation of attention to relevant features in the presence of visual distractors (Serences & Yantis, 2006), and pulvinar is functionally interconnected with the visual area ranging from primary visual cortex to those ventral visual regions implicated in expert visual pattern recognition (especially fusiform cortex, including the VWFA implicated in expert word recognition). We speculate that, given the pattern of connectivity with ventral visual areas as well as additional connectivity from more dorsal aspects of pulvinar with distributed temporoparietal and frontal language networks, the pulvinar might play a key role in learning to read by focusing visual attention on linguistically relevant orthographic patterns. Further, via its connections to ventral visual networks, the pulvinar might play a key role in training the developing VWFA to support fluent decoding. Second, the developmental importance of this subcortical region was reinforced by a recent follow-up, which revealed that activation patterns of this region at age 7 (the point at which we first examined these participants) accounted for unique variance in reading outcomes 2 years later in these children, above and beyond behavioral predictors such as phonological awareness. Such findings, in general, motivate increased attention to how cortical and subcortical networks work together in early learning and ultimately help to shape the LH cortico-cortico circuits (OT, TP, IFG) that will come to support skilled word identification. A major role for subcortical networks in reading acquisition should not be terribly surprising, given the importance of cortical-basal ganglia–thalamus–cortical loops to brain-based accounts of skill learning in general (Graybiel, 2005). However, as noted, most current reading models, including our own, have not focused sufficiently on this (but see McNorgan et al., 2011, for a recent example of a learning account incorporating the basal ganglia). However, the recent findings on subcortical anomalies in RD suggest the need to modify models accordingly, and future research aimed at exploring the implications of basal ganglia and thalamus for both learning and processing will be important. We next consider more generally the current literature on learning problems in RD.

## LEARNING AND CONSOLIDATION IMPAIRMENTS IN READING DISABILITY

Printed-word learning depends not only on efficient on-line O, P, and S binding, but also on processes that allow consolidation of new representations into permanent lexical memory. Reading disability is, by definition, a learning disability, yet relatively little research has focused specifically on learning and memory. With regard to learning and consolidation problems in language-learning tasks, recent studies have shown RD differences in novel vocabulary learning (Perfetti, Wlotoko, & Hart, 2005) and instability of spelling knowledge over sessions (Dietrich & Brady, 2001). It is interesting to note that some recent findings suggest strongly that the learning deficits exhibited by RD individuals may not be specific to language materials; deficits have been reported on tasks tapping procedural learning for both language and nonlanguage stimuli (Howard et al., 2006; Szmalec, Duyck, Vandierendonk, Babera Mata, & Page, 2009). For example, Howard and colleagues (2006) observed abnormalities in individuals with dyslexia on implicit pattern–learning tasks that do not involve verbal stimuli, suggesting procedural learning impairment that is not entirely language specific. Given the documented cortical and subcortical anomalies affecting frontostriatal pathways implicated in procedural learning, discussed earlier, perhaps it is unsurprising that this would be the case.

With regard to potential consolidation deficits in RD, a frequent clinical observation is that RD learners will tend to gain reading-relevant knowledge in a training session but appear to forget it "overnight." A recent fMRI study from our lab presented a rather provocative set of findings along these lines—namely, that RD learners may have problems in modifying neural circuits for lexical memory to create stable long-term representations (Pugh et al., 2008). We examined TD and RD differences in behavioral and brain responses to middle- and high-frequency printed words repeated multiple times while participants performed a simple animacy judgment (living versus nonliving) during fMRI scanning. We found that as tokens were repeated (six times within an imaging run), both TD and RD readers got faster and more accurate, a very similar behavioral benefit of local learning with repetition. But the brain activation patterns in the reading circuitry were strikingly different. Readers with TD, who have a stable neurocircuitry for print, showed a pattern of reduced activation for repeated items, and this result was observed across all components of the LH reading circuit and both cortical and subcortical loci (thalamus). By contrast, readers with RD went from low activation in all of these regions on the first few exposures to a robust activation signal for items by the end of the repetitions (a disordinal interaction for Group X Repetition across the reading circuitry). This "turning on" of circuits suggests latent functionality in these LH systems in RD, in which these learners with a "noisy" system require a local boost in the form of multiple stimulus exposures to reveal coherent signal. This noisy system not only impedes processing efficiency in general but also appears to limit learning and memory consolidation. Indeed, the fact the it takes local repetition to generate activation for a given set of highly familiar words (which it is reasonable to assume have been read many hundreds of times by these adolescent learners with RD) points to a general failure to make a transition from short-term neural patterning to more permanent and stable lexical representations for learned materials. Crosson (1999) has argued from lesion data that nuclei in the thalamus (implicated in this study) play an important role in modulating cortical activation (essentially ramping up or damping down cortical networks associated with phonological and/or semantic information) that is key to efficient language processing.

In summary, we argue that processing efficiency and repetition learning depend on known cortical and subcortical pathways implicated in skill learning and that noise in this system appears to affect the creation of stable representations at the level of brain systems. Thus the study of memory is a crucial next step in RD research, and we next consider the possible differential contributions of memory systems in learning and learning disabilities.

Memory theorists distinguish between declarative and procedural memory systems and their neural substrates (Squire, 2004). Whereas the medial temporal lobe (MTL) is thought to play a key role in declarative memory, other neural pathways, particularly those cortical–striatal–thalamic circuits discussed earlier, have been associated with procedural memory (Graybiel, 2005; Squire, 2004; Ullman & Pierpont, 2005). An extensive body of work has demonstrated that MTL plays key roles in both coding and offline consolidation of declarative memories, via resonance with distributed neocortical circuits (Squire, 2004). Although the MTL is implicated in word learning and consolidation, at present there is no direct evidence that we are aware of that demonstrates MTL anomalies in RD. The role played by MTL remains an open question, and we are currently focused on carefully examining MTL-mediated consolidation, as discussed below.

Whatever the role of MTL, and of declarative memory systems in RD learning problems, there is growing evidence to support the idea that learning and consolidation involve interactive contributions from both declarative and procedural memory systems more generally (cf. Brown & Robertson, 2007). As noted, RD deficits in procedural learning (Howard et al., 2006) and in the cortical and subcortical pathways implicated in procedural learning (McNorgan et al., 2011; Preston et al., 2010; Pugh et al., 2013) have been reported. Thus, though consolidation problems could stem from anomalies in the neural substrates for either memory system (or both), there is a paucity of data at present on precisely how procedural or declarative memory systems contribute to learning and consolidation deficits in RD.

In order to further explore all these questions and to better understand cortical and subcortical contributions to language (as well as nonlanguage) learning and consolidation, we are currently engaged in a National Institutes of Health (NIH)–funded project examining all this. We ask how noisy or unstable brain systems affect on-line learning rates and offline consolidation (both overnight and longer term) in RD for language and nonlanguage tasks. In this project we take measures of the structural and functional integrity of key brain pathways associated with language processing and with procedural and declarative memory in general, and we use these measures as predictors of learning rate versus offline consolidation performance on word-learning tasks, on the one hand, and on nonlinguistic tasks known to rely differentially on procedural or declarative memory, on the other. In short, the general goal of this new investigation is to address a major gap in current understanding by developing brain-based causal models of learning and memory impairments in RD.

## ORIGINS OF READING DISABILITY IN EARLY SPEECH-MOTOR DEVELOPMENT

Recognition that RD anomalies are seen in cortical and subcortical networks implicated in speech perception and production (Pugh et al., 2013) has implications for how we begin to think about the early etiology of RD and its potential connections to the brain specialization for spoken language (Shankweiler et al., 2008).

A long-standing question of whether problems in phonological awareness (and subsequent orthographic learning) are traceable to atypical organization of the machinery for speech perception and production remains a highly debated topic in RD research (Scarborough, 2001). Indeed, a recent study of older TD and RD cohorts failed to find evidence of overt speech perception deficits in RD, and this result led the authors to hypothesize deficits, not in the sensorimotor apparatus for speech but, rather, in the cognitive systems that operate upon phonological representations (Ramus & Szenkovits, 2008). However, although overt differences in production are not always observed in older RD learners, there is a good deal of evidence that encourages a developmental speech-motor account in RD. At the behavioral level of analysis, subtle but measurable speech production and perception problems have been reported in younger learners with RD or at elevated risk for RD, especially under conditions that tax perception or production systems (Elbro, Borstrøm, & Petersen, 1998; Ziegler, Pech-Georgel, George, & Lorenzi, 2009).

As noted above, at the neurobiological level of analysis, early histological studies (Galaburda et al., 2006) and, more recently, structural (volumetric and DTI) studies (Klingberg et al., 2000; Niogi & McCandliss, 2006) have reported anomalies in the micro and macro organization of those LH cortical and subcortical systems associated with speech-motor processing. In another recent report from our investigation of emergent readers (Frost et al., 2009), correlations were found between individual differences in phonemic awareness (PA) ability and print-related activation in the LH superior temporal gyrus, an area specialized for speech. This speech area was coherently activated by print only for children with higher PA, not children with low metaphonological ability; by contrast, activation for speech was nearly identical for both low and high PA learners. From all this we have put forward a new hypothesis.

Motivated by all these data showing neurobiological anomalies in cortical and subcortical speech-motor and sensorimotor systems, we have argued that a mildly compromised speech-motor system could well support "normal range" communicative skills in older learners (in low-noise though usually not in high-noise contexts) while nonetheless failing to adequately underpin the rather extensive reorganization of phonological representations that learning to read demands (Frost et al., 2009). To elaborate, an early and important challenge to brain reorganization comes about as children begin to develop phonologically analytic skills, a critical precondition for learning to read; essentially this entails a modification of phonological representations in order to make them available for cognitive analysis. A second and even more profound challenge to brain plasticity and reorganization occurs when the child modifies phonological representations in order to make them content addressable via orthographic representations, and here we see RD anomalies (see Frost et al., 2009).

Current theory suggests that phonological reorganization and plasticity of speech cortex depend in large measure on the integrity of speech-motor feed-forward and feedback mechanisms (Guenther, Ghosh, & Tourville, 2006), and again these overlap with sites implicated in RD. Accordingly, we hypothesize that these perception–production interactions are suboptimal in children at elevated risk for RD and that these deficits underlie the failure to show age-appropriate reorganization of phonological representations in speech cortex, which in turn will place severe limitations on learning to automate decoding for print. Thus, on this hypothesis, the earliest markers of risk for RD are likely to be found with neurobiological and cognitive indices of the quality of sensorimotor organization for speech.

We are currently testing this hypothesis in a new NIH-supported longitudinal study using integrated neuroimaging and cognitive testing to track speech-motor organization and reading in children who are developing typically and those who are developing atypically from preschool through learning to read. In the new study we also include a cross-language comparative study. An adequate neurobiological theory should account for language-specific and language-invariant patterns associated with typical and atypical development (Paulesu et al., 2001). We need to understand whether neurocognitive trajectories of children with varied risk profiles are similar or dissimilar when acquiring writing systems that contrast in their orthographic to phonological transparency (we examine here Spanish, English, and Chinese). It has been argued (Tan, Spinks, Eden, Perfetti, & Siok, 2005) that the relative importance of fine-grained knowledge of the structure of speech, such as phonemic awareness, differs between alphabetic and nonalphabetic orthographies in discriminating good from poor readers (with a diminished influence in the latter). By implication, this could be taken to suggest differential speech-motor involvement in reading development (Tan et al., 2005). However, there is also considerable evidence for cross-language similarity (Paulesu et al., 2001) in patterns that discriminate typically from atypically developing children, and this encourages a universalist perspective. Indeed, a universalist perspective such as the one we have adopted for many years in our laboratory suggests that despite the possibility of variable contributions of specific phonological skills to reading, learning to read ultimately depends on the quality of the sensorimotor systems that support speech and allow brain reorganization for reading. By examining bidirectional relationships between speech and reading development in highly contrastive orthographies, we will address an important theoretical question.

In summary, there is behavioral evidence of impoverished phonological representations and suboptimal speech-gestural control in children at elevated risk for RD, as well as evidence of neurobiological anomalies in cortical and subcortical pathways associated with perception, production, and feedback in these children (Galaburda et al., 2006). The theory we have outlined provides testable hypotheses concerning links between phonological (and later reading) deficits and earlier problems in speech perception, production, and perception-production interactions. In general, we predict that age-appropriate brain reorganization for phonological and orthographic learning will be especially problematic for high-risk children. We expect measures of brain function to reveal atypical neurobiological organization for speech in high-risk children and diminished structural and functional connectivity between IFG, TP, and subcortical systems. Moreover, we expect that performance on behavioral measures of the quality of the speech perception–production interface will reveal early deviations in children who are developing atypically.

## CONCLUSIONS: TOWARD AN INTEGRATED ACCOUNT OF LEARNING, CONSOLIDATION, AND SPEECH-MOTOR DEVELOPMENT IN READING DISABILITY

In conclusion, in this chapter we have briefly traced a modified brain-based model of anomalies in RD that extends earlier work from our team (Pugh et al., 2000). The new models, motivated by a growing body of evidence implicating cortical-subcortical pathways in RD, considers how subcortical anomalies in both the basal ganglia and the thalamus affect learning to read. We hypothesize (and are currently testing in two new NIH-funded studies) that problems in the cortical-subcortical pathways now implicated in RD not only will affect phonological processing skills needed to create high-quality lexical representations (Perfetti & Hart, 2001) but also more generally will impact learning and consolidation essential for developing fluent reading expertise. Moreover, the focus on this extended set of networks also suggests a possible mechanism that might help us to link early deficits in sensorimotor development for speech perception and production to later limitations on plasticity and reorganization of speech cortex that negatively affect reading acquisition. Critical experiments testing this account are currently the focus of some of our projects. All this research is broadly aimed at developing causal brain-based models of reading disability in which we use both on-line learning and longer-term longitudinal measurements to test directionality of key brain–behavior relationships. While this work is presently focused on the skills of word identification in reading, extensions to the study of comprehension (and comprehension disorders) will be crucially important going forward.

## REFERENCES

Ball, E.W., & Blachman, B.A. (1991). Does phoneme awareness training in kindergarten make a difference in early word recognition and developmental spelling? *Reading Research Quarterly, 26,* 49–66.

Booth., J.R., & Burman, D.D. (2001). Development and disorders of neurocognitive systems for oral language and reading. *Learning Disabilities Quarterly, 24,* 205–215.

Brown, R.M., & Robertson, E.M. (2007). Off-line processing: Reciprocal interactions between declarative and procedural memories. *Journal of Neuroscience, 27,* 10468–10475.

Church, J.A., Coalson, R.S., Lugar, H.M., Petersen, S.E., & Schlaggar, B.L. (2008). A developmental fMRI study of reading reveals changes in phonological and visual mechanisms over age. *Cerebral Cortex, 18,* 2054–2065.

Crosson, B. (1999). Subcortical mechanisms in language: Lexical–semantic mechanisms and the thalamus. *Brain and Cognition, 40,* 414–438.

Dehaene, S., & Cohen, L. (2011). The unique role of the visual word form area in reading. *Trends in Cognitive Sciences, 15*(6), 254–262.

Dietrich, J.A., & Brady, S.A. (2001). Phonological representations of adult poor readers: An investigation of specificity and stability. *Applied Psycholinguistics, 22,* 383–418.

Elbro, C., Borstrøm, I., & Petersen, D.K. (1998). Predicting dyslexia from kindergarten: The importance of distinctness of phonological representations of lexical items. *Reading Research Quarterly, 33*(1), 36–60.

Frost, S., Landi, N., Mencl, W.E., Sandak, R., Fullbright, R.K., Tejada, E.T., Della Porta, G., ... Pugh, K.R. (2009). Phonological awareness predicts cortical activation patterns for print and speech. *Annals of Dyslexia, 59,* 78–97.

Galaburda, A.M., LoTurco, J., Ramus, F., Fitch, R.H., & Rosen, G.D. (2006). From genes to behavior in developmental dyslexia. *Nature Neuroscience, 9*(10), 1213–1217.

Graybiel, A.M. (2005). The basal ganglia: Learning new tricks and loving it. *Current Opinion in Neurobiology, 15,* 638–644.

Guenther, F.H., Ghosh, S.S., & Tourville, J.A. (2006). Neural modeling and imaging of the cortical interactions underlying syllable production. *Brain and Language, 96,* 280–301.

Harm, M.W., & Seidenberg, M.S. (1999). Computing the meanings of words in reading: Cooperative division of labor between visual and phonological processes. *Psychological Review, 106,* 491–528.

Howard, J.H., Jr., Howard, D.V., Japikse, K.C., & Eden, G.F. (2006). Dyslexics are impaired on implicit higher-order sequence learning, but not on implicit spatial context learning. *Neuropsychologia, 44*(7), 1131–1144.

Klingberg, T., Hedehus, M., Temple, E., Salz, T., Gabrieli, J.D.E., Moseley, M.E., & Poldrack, R.A. (2000). Microstructure of temporo-parietal white matter as a basis for reading ability: Evidence from diffusion tensor magnetic resonance imaging. *Neuron, 25*(2), 493–500.

Lyon, G., Shaywitz, S., & Shaywitz, B. (2003). A definition of dyslexia. *Annals of Dyslexia, 53,* 1–14.

Lyytinen, H., Aro, M., Eklund, K., Erskine, J., Guttorm, T., Laakso, M.L., ... Torppa, M. (2004). The development of children at familial risk for dyslexia: Birth to school age. *Annals of Dyslexia, 54*(2), 184–220.

McNorgan, C., Alvarez, A., Bhullar, A., Gayda, J., & Booth, J. (2011). Prediction of reading skill several years later depends on age and brain region: Implications for developmental models of reading. *Journal of Neuroscience, 31,* 9641–9648.

Meyler, A., Keller, T.A., Cherkassy, V.L., Gabrieli, J.E.D., & Just, M.A. (2008). Modifying the brain activation of poor readers during sentence comprehension with extended remedial instruction: A longitudinal study of neuroplasticity. *Neuropsychologia, 46,* 2580–2592.

Niogi, S.N., & McCandliss, B.D. (2006), Left lateralized white matter microstructure accounts for individual differences in reading ability and disability. *Neuropsychologia, 44,* 2178–2188.

Paulesu, E., Démonet, J.-F., Fazio, F., McCrory, E., Chanoine, V., Brunswick, N., ... Frith, U. (2001). Dyslexia: Cultural diversity and biological unity. *Science, 291*(5511), 2165–2167.

Perfetti, C.A., & Hart, L. (2001). The lexical basis of comprehension skill. In D. Gorfein (Ed.), *The consequences of meaning selection* (pp. 67–86). Washington, DC: American Psychological Association.

Perfetti, C.A., Wlotoko, E.W., & Hart, L.A. (2005). Word learning and individual differences in word learning reflected in event-related potentials. *Journal of Experimental Psychology: Learning, Memory, and Cognition, 31*(6), 1281–1292.

Preston, J.L., Frost, S., Mencl, W.E., Fulbright, R.K., Landi, N., Grigorenko, E., ... Pugh, K.R. (2010). Early and late talkers: School-age language, literacy and neurolinguistic differences. *Brain, 133*(Pt 8), 2185–2195.

Pugh, K.R., Frost, S.F., Sandak, R., Landi, N., Moore, D., ... Mencl, W.E. (2010). Mapping the word reading circuitry in skilled and disabled readers. In P.L. Cornelissen, P.C. Hansen, M.L. Kringelback, & K.R. Pugh (Eds.), *The neural basis of reading* (pp. 281–305). Oxford, England: Oxford University Press.

Pugh K.R., Frost, S.J., Sandak, R., Landi, N., Rueckl, J.G., Constable, R.T., ... Mencl, W.E. (2008). Effects of stimulus difficulty and repetition on printed word identification: An fMRI comparison of nonimpaired and reading-disabled adolescent cohorts. *Journal of Cognitive Neuroscience, 20*(7), 1146–1160.

Pugh, K.R., Landi, N., Preston, J.L., Mencl, W.E., Austin, A., Sibley, D, ... Frost, S.J. (in press). The relationship between phonological and auditory processing and brain organization in beginning readers. *Brain and Language, 125,* 173–183.

Pugh, K., & McCardle, P. (Eds.). (2009). *Helping children learn to read: Current issues and new directions in the integration of cognition, neurobiology and genetics of reading and dyslexia research and practice.* New York, NY: Taylor & Francis.

Pugh, K.R., Mencl, W.E., Shaywitz, B.A., Shaywitz, S.E., Fulbright, R.K., Constable, R.T., ... Gore, J.C. (2000). The angular gyrus in developmental dyslexia: Task-specific differences in functional connectivity within posterior cortex. *Psychological Science, 11,* 51–56.

Ramus, F., & Szenkovits, G. (2008). What phonological deficit? *Quarterly Journal of Experimental Psychology, 61*(1), 129–141.

Raschle, N.M., Chang, M., & Gaab, N. (2011). Structural brain alterations associated with dyslexia predate reading onset. *Neuroimage, 57*(3), 742–749.

Scarborough, H.S. (2001). Connecting early language and literacy to later reading (dis)abilities: Evidence, theory, and practice. In S. Neuman & D. Dickinson (Eds.), *Handbook for research in early literacy* (pp. 97–110). New York, NY: Guilford Press.

Serences, J.T., & Yantis, S. (2006). Selective visual attention and perceptual coherence *Trends in Cognitive Sciences, 10*(1), 38–45.

Shankweiler, D., Mencl, W.E., Braze, D., Tabor, W., Pugh, K.R., & Fulbright, R.K.

(2008). Reading differences and brain: Cortical integration of speech and print in sentence processing varies with reader skill. *Developmental Neuropsychology, 33*(6), 745–775.

Shaywitz, B.A., Shaywitz, S.E., Pugh, K.R., Mencl, W.E., Fulbright, R.K., Skudlarski, P., ... Gore, J.C. (2002). Disruption of posterior brain systems for reading in children with developmental dyslexia. *Biological Psychiatry, 52,* 101–110.

Shaywitz, S.E., Fletcher, J.M., Holahan, J.M., Shneider, A.E., Marchione, K.E., Stuebing, K.K., ... Shaywitz, B.A. (1999). Persistence of dyslexia: The Connecticut Longitudinal Study at adolescence. *Pediatrics, 104,* 1351–1359.

Squire, L.R. (2004). Memory systems of the brain: A brief history and current perspective. *Neurobiology of Learning and Memory, 82,* 171–177.

Stanovich, K.E. (1986). Matthew effects in reading: Some consequences of individual differences in the acquisition of literacy. *Reading Research Quarterly, 21*(4), 360–407.

Stoodley, C.J., Harrison, E.P., & Stein, J.F. (2006). Implicit motor learning deficits in dyslexic adults. *Neuropsychologia, 44*(5), 795–798.

Szmalec, A., Duyck, W., Vandierendonk, A., Babera Mata, A., & Page, M. (2009). The Hebb repetition effect as a laboratory analogue of novel word learning. *Quarterly Journal of Experimental Psychology, 62,* 435–443.

Tan, L.H., Spinks, J.A., Eden, G., Perfetti, C.A., & Siok, W.T. (2005). Reading depends on writing, in Chinese. *Proceedings of the National Academies of Science of the United States of America, 102,* 8781–9785.

Ullman, M.T., & Pierpont, E.I. (2005). Specific language impairment is not specific to language: The procedural deficit hypothesis. *Cortex, 41,* 399–433.

Yamada, Y., Stevens, C., Dow, M., Harn, B.A., Chard, D.J., & Neville, H.J. (2011). Emergence of the neural network for reading in five-year-old beginning readers of different levels of pre-literacy abilities: An fMRI study. *NeuroImage, 57*(3), 704–713.

Ziegler, J.C., Pech-Georgel, C., George, F., & Lorenzi, C. (2009). Speech-perception-in-noise deficits in dyslexia. *Developmental Science, 12,* 732–745.

CHAPTER 15

# The Proactive Comprehender

## What Event-Related Potentials Tell Us About the Dynamics of Reading Comprehension

Gina R. Kuperberg

*Several years ago Danny had a scary experience when he went climbing on Mount Whitney. The scene that he witnessed made him quite afraid of venturing up there again. But his mom knew that it was important that Danny overcome his fear, and she wanted him to experience the mountain's beauty and wonder. For months she nagged Danny to join her on the climb. Eventually he agreed, and they bought themselves some safe climbing gear. Nonetheless, about halfway up the mountain, Danny got a fright as he slipped on a piece of rock. At that moment he truly regretted that his mom had persuaded him to come. However, his mom gave Danny a hug and encouraged him to keep going, knowing what awaited them at the top. Finally, they rounded the last bend and were awed by the magnificent…*

Imagine that for his English homework, an 11-year-old boy needs to read this passage for a comprehension test at school the next day. He knows that he has little time and he is reading quickly. It is a challenge: Some of the sentences are complex and some are ambiguous. He is also becoming increasingly distracted as his mom calls him down for dinner. Fortunately, our 11-year-old has some experience with the ideas expressed in the paragraph. He has watched TV shows and read books about mountain climbing; he can understand what it is like to feel scared, and he certainly knows how persuasive moms can be!

In this chapter, I will discuss evidence suggesting that if he can mobilize all this stored knowledge rapidly enough, he should be able to make sense of this text quickly, efficiently, deeply, and flexibly. I will focus mainly on studies that have used event-related potentials (ERPs)—a direct measure of on-line brain activity—to track the neurocognitive mechanisms engaged as the meaning of a text unfolds, word-by-word. I will discuss studies suggesting that we continually draw upon our stored knowledge of events and event structures to predict upcoming information in advance of accessing or combinatorially integrating incoming words.[1] In Part 1,

Thank you to Tufts University for a Sabbatical Leave and Senior Faculty Research Fellowship, which gave me the time to write this review. The discussed experiments that were carried out in my lab were supported by Grant NIMH (R01 MH071635) to Gina Kuperberg.

[1]Throughout this chapter, I use the term *prediction* in the broad Bayesian sense of a prior—an assessment of the probability of accessing information, at a particular representational level, ahead of encountering all the linguistic information required to activate,

I will discuss evidence that this stored event knowledge can be used to preactivate semantic features of upcoming words, thereby facilitating access to their meaning as they are encountered. In Part 2, I will argue that we begin to predictively map, or *link,* activated semantic features on to specific semantic–thematic roles and sometimes on to specific word forms, again ahead of bottom-up linguistic input. If, however, an incoming word disconfirms these event or lexical predictions, the resulting prediction errors will lead to additional costs in neural processing. In Part 3, I will discuss the advantages of this proactive predictive system. Finally, in Part 4, I will speculate how this system might break down, leading to impairments in comprehension.

## PREDICTING EVENTS: FACILITATING ACCESS TO THE SEMANTIC FEATURES OF INCOMING WORDS

The idea that we draw upon our stored real-world knowledge to facilitate the processing of upcoming material is central to most memory-based models of discourse comprehension (e.g., Myers & O'Brien, 1998). What ERP studies tell us is that we can access and use this knowledge extremely quickly. As we make our way through a sentence, paragraph, or novel, whatever discourse-level representation we happen to have constructed at any given time will feed back to memory, preactivating relevant semantic representations that can facilitate access to the semantic features of an incoming word within only a few hundred milliseconds of its onset. This semantic facilitation can be indexed by a reduction in the amplitude of the N400, an ERP component starting from about 300 ms and peaking at approximately 400 ms after word onset (Kutas & Federmeier, 2011).

Studies of the N400 show that we are able to draw upon multiple types of stored conceptual knowledge to preactivate or predict upcoming material.[2] This type of knowledge has traditionally been conceptualized as being stored in networks that encode semantic relationships between individual concepts along multiple associative, categorical, and featural dimensions, henceforth referred to as *semantic relatedness networks.* In this

---

retrieve, or compute this representation. I do not assume that predictive processing is necessarily a conscious, intentional, or active process (although it obviously can be in some situations). By "combinatorial integration" I mean a full, incremental analysis in which all available information, including the semantic and thematic structure of a verb, is used to map the semantic features of arguments on to their semantic-thematic roles, thereby coming up with a full propositional representation of an event or state.

[2]Predictions at a single level of representation (e.g., semantic features) can be conceptualized as occurring through a "resonance" with the context (e.g., Myers & O'Brien, 1998), preactivating material stored within the lexicon and within long-term memory, and leading to "expectations" (Van Petten & Luka, 2012) about upcoming information at the same level of representation. This type of prediction or preactivation of stored material can be distinguished from the predictive linking or mapping between different levels of representation that I discuss in Part 2.

chapter, however, I will argue that we do more than simply activate semantic relationships between "bags of words" to predict upcoming semantic information. Rather, I suggest that we draw upon more structured stored representations of whole events and states. These include our knowledge of the semantic features that are necessary,[3] and most likely (McRae, Ferretti, & Amyote, 1997), to be associated with a particular semantic–thematic role in an individual event or state. It also includes the necessary and likely temporal, spatial, and causal relationships that link multiple events and states together to form sequences of events, sometimes known as scripts, frames, or narrative schemas (Fillmore, 2006; Schank & Abelson, 1977). I will refer to these types of stored representations collectively as *event knowledge.*

Evidence that we use semantic relatedness networks during discourse comprehension comes from studies showing a smaller N400 (facilitated semantic processing) to incoming words that are semantically related in some way to the context (its individual words or its general message) despite being semantically incongruous (e.g., Federmeier & Kutas, 1999; Metusalem et al., 2012; Paczynski & Kuperberg, 2012). For example, in a recent experiment, participants read texts similar to the mountain-climbing scenario above. Sometimes the final word was fully congruous with the context (e.g., *view*), sometimes it was incongruous but nonetheless related to its general theme (e.g., *boots,* which is related to the theme of mountain climbing), and sometimes it was both incongruous and unrelated to the general theme (e.g., *scissors*). The N400 was smaller to words like *boots* than *scissors* (Metusalem et al., 2012; Paczynski & Kuperberg, 2012). These findings suggest that the reader's general discourse-level representation of the context fed back to long-term memory to preactivate a relatedness network encoding concepts associated with the general theme of mountain climbing (e.g., <boots>, <view>, <backpack>[4]). When *boots* was encountered, access to its meaning was facilitated.

A preactivation of general relatedness networks, however, cannot explain all the facilitatory effects of real-world knowledge. For example, Metusalem et al. (2012) reported that although the N400 was attenuated to *boots,* it was attenuated even more to the fully congruous word *view* even though both *boots* and *view* are equally associated with the general theme of mountain climbing.[5] To further preactivate (or predict) the semantic

[3]Here, I refer to the coarse-grained semantic features that constitute a verb's selection restriction. These selection restrictions were originally thought to be encoded within the lexicon, but, following Jackendoff (2002), I conceptualize them as being stored as part of real-world conceptual knowledge.

[4]Throughout this chapter, I will use the symbols < and > around words when I am referring to their semantic features, italics if I am referring to a word's full lexical representation (a representation in which semantic features are linked to a word form).

[5]This was quantified with latent semantic analysis (LSA, available at http://lsa.colorado.edu), which captures knowledge about multiple types of semantic relationships between words and concepts but is relatively insensitive to word order, syntax, or propositional meaning.

features of <view> over those of <boots>, the reader needed to have activated representations of the specific events that led up to the viewing event. This can occur only in rich, "event-constraining" contexts.

By definition, an event constraining context will activate not only the semantic *features* of the participants involved in an event but also their semantic–thematic *roles* (agent, patient, experiencer, stimulus, etc.).[6] For example, in our mountain-climbing scenario, the context of the final sentence tells us not only to expect a set of semantic features associated with the general schema of "mountain climbing" but also to expect a word that will play a likely role of Stimulus in the viewing event that will *cause* Danny and his mother (who take on the role of Experiencers) to feel a state of awe. Most event-constraining contexts will also be lexically constraining (with lexical constraint or predictability usually operationalized through cloze probability measures), leading to preactivations (predictions) for a particular word form, for example, the phonological representation of *view* (DeLong, Urbach, & Kutas, 2005).[7] Having predicted the semantic features, the semantic role, and the form of the upcoming word, we begin to link or map these representations on to one another ahead of bottom-up input. As I will argue in Part 2, if the subsequent input disconfirms these predicted links, we will incur costs. It is important to note, however, that the N400 itself seems to be relatively insensitive to these costs. It cares only about whether an incoming word's semantic features match the semantic features activated by the context.

Although most event-constraining contexts are also lexically constraining, this is not necessarily or always the case: It is possible for a context to constrain for an event or event structure but not for a specific word. For example, consider the context of *Every morning at breakfast the eggs would....* Even though it is not obvious what specific word comes next, we are likely to predict the event, "people eating eggs," and are therefore likely to activate the semantic features of <eat>. If the next word encountered is *eat,* the N400 will therefore be strongly attenuated (Kuperberg, Sitnikova, Caplan, & Holcomb, 2003), even though we have not predicted either its lexical form and even though subsequent combinatorial integration of *eat* yields an event representation that mismatches our event prediction (leading to later costs, as discussed in Part 2).

---

[6]I use the term *semantic–thematic roles,* rather than *thematic roles,* to emphasize that the configurations of participants in an event's conceptual structure are being described. Semantic–thematic roles interface with syntactic structure, but they are not synonymous or reducible to theta roles, which are used to describe the number and type of noun phrases that are syntactically required by a particular verb.

[7]In contexts that are both event and lexically constraining, the divergence of the waveform evoked by predicted (versus nonpredicted) words can start before 300 ms. Indeed, in such constraining contexts, the N400 effect itself can sometimes appear to diverge before 300 ms. This early divergence of the N400 might actually reflect modulation of the N250 ERP component, resulting from a preactivation or prediction of that word's phonological form.

It is also important to recognize that we do not just use our stored knowledge about specific familiar events to generate predictions about the semantic features associated with individual words. We also use our knowledge about more general event structures to predict the semantic features of such whole semantic categories as animacy. For example, we can use the selection restrictions of verbs to predict the animacy features of upcoming arguments (Paczynski & Kuperberg, 2011; see also Paczynski & Kuperberg, 2012), and we can also generate predictions about the animacy features of arguments based simply on the order in which they are encountered in the linguistic input (Paczynski & Kuperberg, 2011). So long as an incoming word's animacy matches these predictions, the N400 will be attenuated to some degree even if the context is short and not lexically constraining.

In sum, there is evidence that we store events and event structures in memory at multiple grains of semantic representation, from coarse (agent <animate>; action; patient <inanimate>) to more specific and finer grained (Experiencer <people>; state <awe>; stimulus <view>). Furthermore, during word-by-word language comprehension, we can activate this information to preactivate information about an upcoming word's semantic features, semantic–thematic role, and even its specific word form. The amplitude of the N400 itself, however, is primarily sensitive to whether the semantic features activated by the context match or mismatch those of the incoming word. If these features are preactivated ahead of the upcoming word, it will be easier to retrieve that word's meaning when it is actually encountered.

## THE COSTS OF PREDICTION: INFLUENCE ON COMBINATORIAL INTEGRATION

The picture of language comprehension that I have painted thus far is a rosy one: We store vast amounts of knowledge about events and states in our memories, and so long as the context allows, we can activate all this knowledge and use it to preactivate the semantic features to facilitate semantic access, as reflected by an attenuation of the N400. In addition, I have argued that we can also use stored event knowledge to predict the semantic role that an upcoming word will play in an upcoming event, and, in some cases, we can also predict its lexical form. Once again, if the incoming word matches these event and lexical predictions, we will have had a head start in all stages of linguistic analysis.

Of course, this scenario is somewhat ridiculous. If the input always matched our predictions, there would be no point in comprehension at all. The distinguishing feature of language is that combinations of words can be put together in infinite ways to convey events and sequences of events that are completely novel, and so we will obviously encounter information that is not already stored. And when this happens, if we have predictively mapped the wrong semantic features onto the wrong word form (predicted the wrong lexical item) and/or on to the wrong semantic–thematic role (predicted the wrong event or event structure), we will incur costs when these predictions are violated—the costs of a prediction error.[8] In this section, I will present evidence that these costs manifest on both positive- and negative-going ERP components, which extend past the N400 time window. This evidence comes from several lines of ERP research.

## Lexical Prediction Errors: Anterior Positivities

The first line of research has focused on the effects of introducing unexpected but fully plausible words in contexts that constrain strongly for events and for specific words, for example, following our event-constraining mountain-climbing scenario, encountering the sentence *Finally, they rounded the last bend and were awed by the magnificent* ***tree***. As discussed in Part 1, unpredicted words like *tree* will produce a larger N400 than predicted words like *view*. An N400, however, is not the only effect produced. Unexpected words also evoke a larger positive-going waveform than predicted words (see Van Petten & Luka, 2012, for a review). This positivity effect has an anterior or anterior-central scalp distribution and can begin within the N400 time window (Delong, Urbach, Groppe, & Kutas, 2011),[9] although it often continues past this window. It is important to note that unlike the N400, which is large to unpredicted words in the absence of a constraining context, the anterior positivity is *not* seen to unpredicted words in nonconstraining contexts (Federmeier, Wlotko, De Ochoa-Dewald, & Kutas, 2007). Also in contrast to the N400, the anterior positivity effect is not modulated by the match between the semantic features of the incoming word and the semantic features activated by the context: It is produced by words whose features are either semantically related or unrelated to the context (Thornhill & Van Petten, 2012). Together, these findings suggest that the anterior positivity effect does not simply reflect a mismatch between the semantic features of an incoming word and the semantic features activated by the context. Rather, it reflects costs that are incurred when the input disconfirms a predicted link between a set of semantic features and a particular word form; that is, it reflects the costs of a lexico-semantic prediction error.[10]

---

[8]I distinguish predictions of *links* or mappings between different levels of representation from the types of preactivation of stored material at a single level of representation, discussed in Part 1. The former implies a commitment to a distinct working memory space (see Jackendoff, 2002 for discussion) and will therefore lead to costs if they are disconfirmed by an analysis of the input and working memory needs to be updated.

[9]Because of this temporal and spatial overlap with the N400, this positivity is sometimes quite difficult to detect at the scalp surface. For example, a large N400 at central sites can obscure a small positivity at central sites. Similarly, a large positivity at central sites can obscure a small N400 at central sites.

[10]Consistent with this idea, a positivity effect is also seen to pseudohomophones (versus correctly spelled words) of semantically expected words in semantically constraining contexts. In this situation, too, the input disconfirms links between a predicted set of semantic features and a specific word form: in this case, its orthographic form (Vissers, Chwilla, & Kolk, 2006).

The precise nature of these costs remains unclear. One possibility, however, is that they reflect prolonged efforts to combinatorially integrate the incoming word into its context. On this account, having predicted a link between a particular set of semantic features (<view>) and a particular word form (*view*), the comprehender begins to map this lexico-semantic prediction onto the emerging syntactic structure; this in turn interferes with, or competes with, attempts to combinatorially integrate the unpredicted word (*sky*) once it is encountered. The unpredicted word (*tree*) will be successfully integrated: It is, after all, fully plausible; the semantic–thematic role it plays in the viewing event (the plausible stimulus of *awe*) was correctly predicted. However, because of competition from the predicted word, more processing resources are required to combinatorially integrate it into its context.

## Event Prediction Errors: Posterior Positivities (the P600) and Anterior Negativities

A second line of ERP studies has examined the effects of introducing *implausible* words in contexts that constrain for events or event structures but not for individual words (reviewed by Kuperberg, 2007). Examples of such sentences include the following: *Every morning at breakfast the eggs would* ***eat****…* (Kuperberg et al, 2003); *Every morning at breakfast the eggs would* ***plant****…* (Kuperberg, Kreher, Sitnikova, Caplan, & Holcomb, 2007); *At the homestead the farmer penalized the* ***meadow****…* (Paczynski & Kuperberg, 2011); *The pianist played his music while the bass was strummed by the* ***drum****…*, and *The pianist played his music while the bass was strummed by the* ***coffin****…* (Paczynski & Kuperberg, 2012). In all these cases, the implausible word (**underlined** in the examples above) produced a positivity effect, sometimes with and sometimes without an N400 effect. This positivity effect has a more posterior scalp distribution than the anterior positivity described earlier and is known as the "semantic P600."[11]

The semantic P600 effect peaks at parietal electrode sites. It starts at around 500 ms after word onset, although it can begin earlier within the N400 time window, or later than 500 ms, and it often continues for several hundred milliseconds. Analogous to the anterior positivity described earlier, and again unlike the N400, the semantic P600 does not seem to be produced in nonconstraining contexts, not even when these words are implausible. Again, similar to the anterior positivity effect, but unlike the N400, the semantic P600 effect is not modulated by the match between the semantic features of the incoming word and semantic features that are

[11]This is a descriptive term used to distinguish it from the P600 that has been traditionally associated with *syntactic* anomalies and ambiguities. However, as pointed out by Van Petten and Luka (2012), evidence for posteriorly distributed positivity effects to semantically implausible (versus plausible) words in semantically constraining contexts has existed for many years.

activated by the context; it can be produced both by words whose semantic features are related and those that are unrelated to the context. For example, following the context *Every morning at breakfast, the eggs would…*, a semantic P600 effect is produced to verbs like *eat* (Kuperberg et al., 2003), as well as to verbs like *plant* (Kuperberg et al., 2007; see also Paczynski & Kuperberg, 2012).[12]

I suggest that the semantic P600 reflects costs that are incurred when full combinatorial integration of the incoming word disconfirms our predictions of specific links between particular semantic features and a particular semantic–thematic role. For example, when we read the context *Every morning at breakfast the eggs would…*, our anticipation of an eating event leads us to predictively link the semantic features of <eggs> with the semantic–thematic role of theme. Similarly, the context *At the homestead the farmer penalized the…* leads us to predict an experiencer that is <animate>, whereas the context *At the church the baptism was performed by the…* leads us to predict an agent that is <animate>. In all these cases, analysis of the input disconfirms the event structures we have predicted. The semantic P600 appears to reflect costs incurred as a result of detecting this event prediction error.

This account can also explain why a P600 effect is produced by words that are *syntactically* ill-formed (Hagoort, Brown, & Groothusen, 1993) or dispreferred in syntactically ambiguous structures (Osterhout & Holcomb, 1992)—the situations where the P600 was first described. Here too the comprehender is likely to detect conflict between the event structure that he predicted and the anomalous event structure that is produced as he attempts to combinatorially integrate the incoming word into its context. Consistent with this idea is the finding that the syntactic P600 is larger when its preceding context is event constraining than nonconstraining (discussed by Kuperberg, 2007).

Finally, a third line of ERP studies suggests that violations of predicted events or event structures can, in some cases, trigger a late anteriorly distributed negativity effect. For example, Baggio, Lambalgen, and Hagoort (2008) reported a sustained negativity on the word *paper* (vs. *desk*) in sentences such as *The girl was writing a letter when her friend spilled coffee on the paper.* Here, the event structure that was predicted (the *completion* of letter writing) is disconfirmed by the "spilling event," requiring some revision of the predicted event structure. We have also observed sustained anterior negativity effects in association with iterative aspectual coercion (e.g., *For several minutes, the cat* ***pounced…***; Paczynski, Jackendoff & Kuperberg, under review), in which a punctive event, *pounced*, must be interpreted

[12]As discussed in Part 1, the N400 produced by words whose features match features that are activated by their context will be small, regardless of whether their semantic–thematic role has been correctly predicted. This can lead to seemingly paradoxical pattern of a large P600 effect and no N400 effect to clear semantic violations (Kuperberg et al., 2003; reviewed by Kuperberg, 2007).

as occurring multiple times, as well as in association with light verb constructions (e.g. *Julius gives a kiss to Anne;* Wittenberg, Paczynski, Wiese, Jackendoff & Kuperberg, under review), in which disconfirmation of the comprehender's prediction of a canonical event structure may trigger some event restructuring ("argument sharing"), as discussed further below. What distinguishes all these situations from the highly implausible or anomalous structures that produce the P600 effect, is that it is possible to revise the anticipated event structure to come up with a plausible representation of meaning. The anterior negativity effect may reflect working memory costs associated with this event restructuring or "frame shifting" (see also Coulson, 2001; Wlotko & Federmeier, 2012). In contrast, the P600 seems to be triggered when attempts to combinatorially integrate the incoming word fail altogether and the comprehender *detects* the event prediction error. As discussed in Part 3, the P600 itself may reflect reanalysis or subsequent discourse-level analysis of the input.

## A Predictive Comprehension System

In sum, ERP studies tell us that we are proactive comprehenders. We use our stored knowledge about events and states to generate predictions at multiple levels of representation. Moreover, we begin to map or link these predicted representations on to one another ahead of the actual input. If our predictions of the semantic features of upcoming words are correct, semantic access to these words is facilitated, as reflected by an attenuation of the N400. If, however, our predictions of the links between these semantic features and specific semantic–thematic roles and/or specific word forms are disconfirmed by the input, we will incur costs, which manifest on a set of later positive-going or anteriorly distributed negative-going ERP components.

As already noted, the most obvious benefit of a predictive language-processing architecture is comprehension efficiency. If we have predicted correctly, then every step of accessing and integrating an incoming word into its context should be easier than if we had not predicted at all. But what about when we predict incorrectly? Are the risks of incurring additional costs in processing—the prediction errors discussed in Part 2—worth the benefits?

In this section, I argue not only that our prediction errors are worth the benefits of more efficient comprehension but also that they themselves are a crucial component of our language-processing system. They can save us from costly garden paths in ambiguous and complex sentences and may also trigger event restructuring mechanisms that help us make sense of the input. I will also argue that the P600 functions to save us from interpretation errors in noisy environments and allows us to recover meaning from sentences that at first seem to make no sense. Finally, I will suggest that prediction errors, and their associated costs, may also offer a mechanism by which we can flexibly adjust our comprehension strategies in rapid response to our linguistic and nonlinguistic environment. To illustrate each of these points, let us return to our 11-year-old boy hurrying to read his homework passage before dinner.

## Avoiding Garden Paths in Ambiguous and Complex Sentences

Our reader is about to encounter the syntactically ambiguous sentence *Danny regretted his mom had persuaded him to join her.* As he reads the first phrase, *Danny regretted his,* he activates his event knowledge about the necessary and likely semantic features of the thing that Danny might regret in this situation (necessary features: something <nonanimate>; most likely features: his <decision>), and he predictively links these semantic features to the theme role and the direct object slot in the emerging syntactic tree structure.[13] This means that when he encounters the word *mom* (an animate entity), he is easily able to attach it to the alternative available syntactic slot, such that it correctly becomes the subject of the embedded sentence complement (see Garnsey, Pearlmutter, Myers, & Lotocky, 1997). This may lead to some processing costs, but these costs are not as severe as those that he would have incurred had he waited for the direct object (*mom*), assigned it as a Theme along a transitive grid, assessed it as being highly implausible, and then used this information to reassign it as the subject of the embedded sentence complement. They are also not as severe as the costs he would have incurred if he waited until *had* to disambiguate the syntactic structure. In effect, by drawing upon his knowledge about events (in this case, the selection restrictions of the verb *regret* and a default expectation that an inanimate argument will be encountered after an animate argument), our proactive reader has avoided a full garden path.[14]

Similarly, upon encountering the syntactically complex but nonambiguous object-relative sentence *The scene that he witnessed made him quite afraid of venturing up there again,* our reader's initial bias to expect

[13]Note that the verb *regretted* occurs roughly equally often with inanimate direct objects and animate subject complements. I therefore suggest that the bias toward predicting an inanimate direct object is based on the default expectancy for an inanimate entity as the second argument in an event. This general expectancy for an animate entity to be encountered first (a more prominent position) and an inanimate entity to be encountered second (a less prominent position) in the linguistic input likely stems from our knowledge that in a prototypical event, a more prominent animate agent does something to a less prominent inanimate theme. However, these types of prediction do not appear to depend on the thematic structure of the verb itself: They are based on a direct link between the animacy hierarchy and linear order of syntactic constituents, as discussed above (and see Paczynski & Kuperberg, 2011).

[14]In this sense, the predictive framework outlined here differs from constraint-based models of language processing (e.g., MacDonald, Pearlmutter, & Seidenberg, 1994), in which real-world knowledge is believed to influence syntactic parsing through assessments of "plausibility" as or after thematic roles are assigned.

an animate subject Agent is immediately disconfirmed by the inanimate word *scene* followed by *that*. This may lead to some costs as he revises his prediction by linking *scene* to the potential role of theme and attaching it to the object position of the relative clause—a prediction that is subsequently confirmed by the verb *witness*. These costs, however, are not nearly as severe as those that he would have incurred in parsing the challenging object-relative sentence if he had made no predictions (Traxler, Williams, Blozis, & Morris, 2005).

## Frame Shifting in Semantically Complex Structures

Now imagine that our reader is about to encounter the phrase *mom gave Danny a hug*. He is likely to predict a default canonical event structure in which the verb assigns the subject of the sentence the semantic–thematic role of Agent. However, in this sentence—a light verb construction—the verb *gave* conveys little information, and it is *hug* that describes the main event. Our reader therefore needs to restructure the input to make sense of the event: he must use both *gave* and *hug* to assign *mom* the role of agent (a process known as "argument sharing") (Wittenberg, Paczynski, Wiese, Jackendoff, & Kuperberg, manuscript under review).

Just as in the cases of syntactic ambiguity and complexity described above, the comprehender's initial event predictions were incorrect, but he was able to revise them to recover meaning. He may well have encountered some costs along the way (manifested as anterior negativity or positivity effects), but at least he avoided full combinatorial failure and garden paths. What is perhaps less obvious is why we would risk predicting when there are many situations in which there are no alternative ways to restructure a sentence. Specifically, why it is worth the risk of a prediction error when this might lead directly to a failure to combinatorially integrate the incoming word into its context, manifested by the semantic P600? These are the cases I turn to next.

## Avoiding Interpretation Errors in Noisy Environments

Envisage our reader at the final sentence of the text, right at the instant before he encounters the final word, *view*. His increasingly irate mom calls him one last time for dinner, and just as he is decoding the word *view*, he hears her yell, "Now!" As a result, he mistakenly interprets *view* as *vow* and ends up processing the final sentence as *They looked around them and were awed by the magnificent vow....* There is nothing inherently ill-formed about being awed by a vow. It is certainly implausible in relation to its discourse context, but it is not a syntactic violation. Fortunately, however, even before he has seen the word *view*, our reader has used his event knowledge to predict its semantic features, its word form, and its semantic–thematic role in the event, and he has begun to map these representations on to one another. When he mistakenly interprets the final word of the sentence as *vow*, therefore, the resulting prediction error, and all the additional analysis that it triggers, ensures that he devotes the necessary resources to interpret the input accurately.

In another situation, the error may be in the input itself. For example, if there was a typo and the text did actually say *vow* instead of *view*, additional analysis would confirm that the input was, in fact, highly implausible. Here, however, the similarity in orthography between the predicted and encountered word may lead our reader to suspect a typo and to interpret the input according to his initial prediction.

What both these situations illustrate is that when inputs are noisy, our predictions can serve us well by triggering us to look more carefully at what we have just read, rather than simply move on (Levy, 2011; van de Meerendonk, Kolk, Chwilla, & Vissers, 2009). This is necessary in the real world when what we hear and read is often incomplete, impoverished, or inaccurate. It would be hugely inefficient to devote additional processing resources to analyzing and reanalyzing the input for every time an incoming word is assessed as being implausible, once integrated into its content. It therefore makes most sense to conserve these resources for when we are most likely to be wrong, that is, when we have predicted an alternative event. Our prediction errors therefore serve a vital function in protecting us from interpretative errors.

## Updating the Situation Model Through Additional Discourse-Level Analysis

Now imagine that instead of ending with the expected word, *view*, the mountain-climbing passage ends unexpectedly and the final sentence reads, *Finally, they rounded the last bend and were awed by the magnificent **dragon***. Just as described earlier, our reader will compute an implausible event (encountering a magnificent dragon) when he predicted a much more likely alternative (encountering a magnificent view). And once again, he will invest additional resources to further analyze the input, manifest as positivity effects. This time, however, the additional analysis will confirm that he was correct on his first reading, that there was no error in the input, and that Danny and his mom were, indeed, awed by a dragon upon reaching the top of the mountain. This additional analysis, however, has not been in vain. It has entailed a reevaluation of the viewing event in relation to its entire discourse context, leading our reader to update his situation model. He now knows that in Danny's world, it is actually plausible to encounter a dragon at the top of a mountain.

This example illustrates a more general point: We often encounter information that at first seems to make little sense and that conflicts with our predictions, but where a reevaluation of the context can allow us to recover some meaning. This type of additional analysis can enable us to make sense of novel events in which participants play unexpected semantic–thematic roles in a given action (Sitnikova, Holcomb, Kiyonaga, & Kuperberg, 2008), to reassign roles to referents in a discourse context (van Berkum, Koornneef, Otten, & Nieuwland, 2007), to comprehend jokes (Coulson, 2001), and to understand metaphorical language (e.g., De Grauwe, Swain, Holcomb, Ditman, & Kuperberg, 2010). All these situations are quite different from one another; but notably, they are all associated with robust P600 effects.

## Error-Based Learning and Adaptation

I have argued that the additional analysis associated with prediction errors can help us avoid garden paths and misinterpretations; it will, in addition, allow us to update our situation model when we encounter implausible, unexpected events. All this additional analysis, however, would be somewhat counterproductive if we failed to learn from our mistakes and continued to predict incorrectly. Suppose, for example, our 11-year-old repeatedly encountered typos in his assigned text. We would hope that by the fifth typo, he would not be investing valuable processing resources in reevaluating the input at the expense of comprehending the passage. We would also hope that having understood that in Danny's world it is plausible to encounter a dragon, our reader will not invest as many processing resources when, the next day at school, he learns about Danny's encounter with a goblin. In both situations, what we want him to do is to use his prediction errors to learn from the linguistic input and come to expect the unexpected.

We have actually known that the P600 is closely linked to our ability to "expect the unexpected" since the late 1990s, when Coulson, King, and Kutas (1998) showed that P600 amplitude was sensitive to the proportion of syntactic anomalies in the experimental environment. At the time this was interpreted as evidence against the P600 being particularly relevant to syntactic (or indeed language) processing. It is only quite recently that predictive error–based learning has been recognized as playing an important role in adult comprehension (e.g., Jaeger & Snider, in press), although it has for some time been discussed in the developmental literature (e.g., Chang, Dell, & Bock, 2006). Here, I would like to suggest that predictive error–based learning is closely linked to the anterior and P600 posterior positivity effects discussed in this chapter and plays an important role in allowing us to adapt our processing strategies in response to changing environmental demands, as well as to continually update our real-world and linguistic knowledge on the basis of what we hear and read.

Some evidence for this idea comes from a recent study in which people listened to language spoken with a foreign accent. They failed to produce a P600 effect at all in response to clear syntactic violations. This suggests that we are quickly able to adjust our expectations about the likelihood of encountering a syntactic anomaly based on speaker identity (Hanulikova, van Alphen, van Goch, & Weber, 2012). In another study, we recently showed that the amplitude of the P600 produced by syntactic violations was smaller when readers had just encountered another syntactic violation in the preceding sentence (Kuperberg, Lau, & Clegg, 2011). This finding suggests that predictive error–based learning may be extremely rapid and can be used to modulate processing in a highly dynamic fashion (cf. Botvinick, Braver, Barch, Carter, & Cohen, 2001).

## IMPLICATIONS FOR POOR COMPREHENSION

It should be clear from this review that readers who can quickly mobilize their real-world knowledge to predict upcoming information—words and events—will be good comprehenders. If readers are correct in their predictions, they will have a head start in all phases of accessing and combinatorially integrating incoming words into their context and interpreting the resulting propositions. If the input is ambiguous or complex, their predictions may allow readers to avoid costly garden paths and flexibly restructure events to make sense of the input. If readers incorrectly decode the input, encounter a typo, or come across a genuine surprise, any predictions they have made ahead of time will have still served them well: By triggering additional analysis, predictions protect readers from misinterpretation, help them interpret novel events, and lead them to adjust their processing strategy in preparation for what lies ahead.

All this, however, hinges on being able to preactivate relevant event knowledge very quickly, prior to encountering the next word. Doing so is not always so simple because it relies on a tight interaction between long-term memory and combinatorial mechanisms of language processing. There are therefore many reasons why, by failing to access this information, comprehension may break down. For example, we may not store relevant event or state knowledge in the first place; combinatorial processing may be too slow to build a partial propositional representation of the linguistic input in time to feed back to semantic memory and activate relevant event knowledge before the next word appears; or the interactions between the combinatorial- and memory-based mechanisms may themselves be slow or inefficient.

Regardless of the underlying cause, the consequences of a reader failing to mobilize event knowledge to predict in this fashion will be the same. Semantic access will be slower and less efficient. He or she will be led down garden paths in ambiguous or complex sentences. He or she will be more prone to error in noisy environments. He or she may fail to make sense of and encode novel, unexpected information. Finally, he or she will fail to flexibly adjust processing strategy in response to the demands of his or her environment.

On a more optimistic note, the very flexibility of the language-processing system provides several points of entry to intervene and improve comprehension, regardless of the underlying causes. The trick is to activate specific event or state knowledge in time to guide parsing. Doing so may entail slowing down the pace of reading. It may require triggering the activation of event or state knowledge through other modalities. And/or it may involve explicit tasks and instructions that encourage predictive strategies. The final approach may be particularly fruitful, given experimental evidence that task instructions can shift the threshold at which additional analysis is initiated, as reflected by the P600 (see Kuperberg, 2007, for discussion).

## CONCLUSIONS

In conclusion, ERP studies tell us that we can mobilize our stored real-world event knowledge amazingly quickly to facilitate access to the meaning of incoming words. I have also suggested that we go still further by mapping our predictions at multiple levels of representation, on to one another, ahead of integrating the input. This strategy helps us parse ambiguous and complex sentences, allows us to allocate our processing resources rationally in noisy environments, helps us make sense of novel information, and ensures that we flexibly adjust our comprehension strategies in response to ever-changing task and environmental demands. Finally, I hope to have shown how a detailed understanding of the neurocognitive mechanisms engaged in word-by-word language processing can potentially directly translate to inform the development of targeted strategies to improve reading comprehension.

## REFERENCES


Baggio, G., van Lambalgen, M., & Hagoort, P. (2008). Computing and recomputing discourse models: An ERP study. *Journal of Memory and Language, 59*(1), 36–53.

Botvinick, M.M., Braver, T.S., Barch, D.M., Carter, C.S., & Cohen, J.D. (2001). Conflict monitoring and cognitive control. *Psychological Review, 108*(3), 624–652.

Chang, F., Dell, G.S., & Bock, K. (2006). Becoming syntactic. *Psychological Review, 113*(2), 234–272.

Coulson, S. (2001). *Semantic leaps: Frame-shifting and conceptual blending in meaning construction.* Cambridge, England: Cambridge University Press.

Coulson, S., King, J., & Kutas, M. (1998). Expect the unexpected: Event-related brain responses to morphosyntactic violations. *Language and Cognitive Processes, 13,* 21–58.

De Grauwe, S., Swain, A., Holcomb, P.J., Ditman, T., & Kuperberg, G.R. (2010.) Electrophysiological insights into the processing of nominal metaphors. *Neuropsychologia, 48*(7), 1965–1984.

Delong, K.A., Urbach, T.P., Groppe, D.M., & Kutas, M. (2011). Overlapping dual ERP responses to low cloze probability sentence continuations. *Psychophysiology, 48*(9), 1203–1207.

DeLong, K.A., Urbach, T.P., & Kutas, M. (2005). Probabilistic word pre-activation during language comprehension inferred from electrical brain activity. *Nature Neuroscience, 8*(8), 1117–1121.

Federmeier, K.D., & Kutas, M. (1999). A rose by any other name: Long-term memory structure and sentence processing. *Journal of Memory and Language, 41,* 469–495.

Federmeier, K.D., Wlotko, E.W., De Ochoa-Dewald, E., & Kutas, M. (2007). Multiple effects of sentential constraint on word processing. *Brain Research, 1146,* 75–84.

Fillmore, C.J. (2006). Frame semantics. *Cognitive Linguistics: Basic Readings, 34,* 373–400.

Garnsey, S.M., Pearlmutter, N.J., Myers, E., & Lotocky, M.A. (1997). The contributions of verb bias and plausibility to the comprehension of temporarily ambiguous sentences. *Journal of Memory and Language, 37*(1), 58–93.

Hanulikova, A., van Alphen, P.M., van Goch, M.M., & Weber, A. (2012). When one person's mistake is another's standard usage: the effect of foreign accent on syntactic processing. *Journal of Cognitive Neuroscience, 24*(4), 878–887.

Jackendoff, R. (2002). *Foundations of Language: Brain, Meaning, Grammar, Evolution.* New York: Oxford University Press.

Jaeger, T.F., & Snider, N. (2013). Alignment as a consequence of expectation adaptation: syntactic priming is affected by the prime's prediction error given both prior and recent experience. *Cognition, 127*(1), 57–83.

Kuperberg, G.R. (2007). Neural mechanisms of language comprehension: Challenges to syntax. *Brain Research, Special Issue: Mysteries of Meaning, 1146*, 23–49.

Kuperberg, G.R., Kreher, D.A., Sitnikova, T., Caplan, D.N., & Holcomb, P.J. (2007). The role of animacy and thematic relationships in processing active English sentences: evidence from event-related potentials. *Brain and Language, 100*(3), 223–237.

Kuperberg, G.R., Lau, E.F., & Clegg, L. (2011). A Gratton effect on the syntactic P600: Evidence that syntactic processing is subject to a dynamic adjustment of executive control. Annual Meeting of the Cognitive Neuroscience Society.

Kuperberg, G.R., Sitnikova, T., Caplan, D., & Holcomb, P.J. (2003). Electrophysiological distinctions in processing conceptual relationships within simple sentences. *Cognitive Brain Research, 17*(1), 117–129.

Kutas, M., & Federmeier, K.D. (2011). Thirty years and counting: Finding meaning in the N400 component of the event-related brain potential (ERP). *Annual Review of Psychology, 62*, 621–647.

Levy, R. (2011). Probabilistic linguistic expectations, uncertain input, and implications for eye movements in reading. *Studies of Psychology and Behavior, 9*(1), 52–63.

MacDonald, M.C., Pearlmutter, N.J., & Seidenberg, M.S. (1994). The lexical nature of syntactic ambiguity resolution. *Psychological Review, 101*, 676–703.

McRae, K., Ferretti, T.R., & Amyote, L. (1997). Thematic roles as verb-specific concepts. *Language and Cognitive Processes, 12*, 137–176.

Metusalem, R., Kutas, M., Urbach, T.P., Hare, M., McRae, K., & Elman, J.L. (2012). Generalized event knowledge activation during online sentence comprehension. *Journal of Memory and Language, 66*(4), 545–567.

Myers, J.L., & O'Brien, E.J. (1998). Accessing the discourse representation during reading. *Discourse Processes, 26*(2–3), 131–157.

Paczynski M., Jackendoff, R., & Kuperberg, G.R. (2013). When events change their nature. Manuscript in review.

Paczynski, M., & Kuperberg, G.R. (2011). Electrophysiological evidence for use of the animacy hierarchy, but not thematic role assignment, during verb argument processing. *Language and Cognitive Processes, 26*(9), 1402–1456.

Paczynski, M., & Kuperberg, G.R. (2012). Multiple influences of semantic memory on sentence processing: Distinct effects of semantic relatedness on violations of real-world event/state knowledge and animacy selection restrictions. *Journal of Memory and Language, 67*(4), 426–448.

Schank, R.C., & Abelson, R.P. (1977). *Scripts, plans, goals, and understanding: An inquiry into human knowledge structures.* Hillsdale, N.J.: L. Erlbaum Associates.

Sitnikova, T., Holcomb, P.J., Kiyonaga, K.A., & Kuperberg, G.R. (2008). Two neurocognitive mechanisms of semantic integration during the comprehension of visual real-world events. *Journal of Cognitive Neuroscience, 20*, 2037–2057.

Thornhill, D.E., & Van Petten, C. (2012). Lexical versus conceptual anticipation during sentence processing: Frontal positivity and N400 ERP components. *International Journal of Psychophysiology, 83*, 382–392.

Traxler, M.J., Williams, R.S., Blozis, S.A., & Morris, R.K. (2005). Working memory, animacy, and verb class in the processing of relative clauses. *Journal of Memory & Language, 53*, 204–224.

van Berkum, J.J.A., Koornneef, A.W., Otten, M., & Nieuwland, M.S. (2007). Establishing reference in language comprehension: An electrophysiological perspective. *Brain Research, 1146*, 158–171.

van de Meerendonk, N., Kolk, H.H.J., Chwilla, D.J., & Vissers, C.T.W.M. (2009). Monitoring in language perception. *Language and Linguistics Compass, 3*(5), 1211–1224.

Van Petten, C., & Luka, B. (2012). Prediction during language comprehension: Benefits, costs, and ERP components. *International Journal of Psychophysiology, 83*(2), 176–190.

Vissers, C.T.W.M., Chwilla, D.J., & Kolk, H.H.J. (2006). Monitoring in language perception: The effect of misspellings of words in highly constrained sentences. *Brain Research, 1106*(1), 150–163.

Wittenberg, E., Paczynski, M., Wiese, H., Jackendoff, R., & Kuperberg, G.R. (2013). The difference between "giving a rose" and "giving a kiss:" A sustained anterior negativity in association with light verb constructions. Manuscript under review.

Wlotko, E.W., & Federmeier, K.D. (2012). So that's what you meant! Event-related potentials reveal multiple aspects of context use during construction of message-level meaning, *NeuroImage 62*(1), 356–366.

CHAPTER 16

# Relating Reading Comprehension to Language and Broader Reading Skills

## A Behavioral Genetics Approach

Stephen A. Petrill

Reading comprehension, defined as the ability to understand and employ text for learning, is learned and develops and grows in response to instruction and the environment (Dieterich, Assel, Swank, Smith, & Landry, 2006; Senechal, 2006; Skibbe, Justice, Zucker, & McGinty, 2008). At the same time, reading comprehension is also associated with a highly complex network of neurocognitive processes (Frost et al., 2009; Houde, Rossi, Lubin, & Joliot, 2010; Rimrodt et al., 2009) and has also been associated or linked with several regions of the genome (Paracchini et al., 2008; Petryshen & Pauls, 2009). Integrating these perspectives has important implications for understanding how reading comprehension skills develop as well as identifying the various mechanisms through which differences in reading comprehension emerge. This chapter will examine these levels of analysis through the behavioral genetics perspective. In particular, the chapter will discuss behavioral genetic studies examining reading comprehension; examine the relationship between reading and other constructs, focusing on language skills; introduce the emerging behavioral genetics literature on brain imaging and its potential use for the study of reading comprehension; and discuss implications for intervention.

## BEHAVIORAL GENETIC STUDIES OF READING COMPREHENSION

Behavioral genetic studies assume that the genetic and environmental etiology of a measured outcome can be studied by comparing family members of differing genetic relatedness (Plomin, DeFries, McClearn, & McGuffin, 2008). For example, monozygotic (MZ) twins share 100% of their inherited genes, whereas dizygotic (DZ) twins share 50% of their inherited genes (on average). If identical twins are more similar than fraternal twins on a given trait, then it is assumed that genetic influences are significant. This

---

The views expressed do not necessarily reflect the official policies of the U.S. Department of Health and Human Services. This work was supported by the *Eunice Kennedy Shriver* National Institute of Child Health and Development Grants R01HD38075, HD059215, and HD068728.

is quantified as *heritability* ($h^2$). If, on the other hand, identical twins are no more similar than fraternal twins on a given trait, then it is assumed that *shared environment* ($c^2$), such as growing up in the same home, going to the same school, or experiencing similar pre- and/or perinatal environments, is significant. Finally, the extent to which identical twins are not similar on a trait is assumed to be because of the *nonshared environment* ($e^2$), as well as error. One important aspect of $h^2$, $c^2$, and $e^2$ is that results do not refer to the proportion of genetic, shared environmental, and nonshared environmental effects in an individual. Instead, these statistics explain the etiology of differences across individuals. In other words $h^2$, $c^2$, and $e^2$, help tell us why children are different from one another, not why a particular child has a particular reading score.

Keeping this important caveat in mind, the behavioral genetics literature has provided important insights into the nature and nurture of reading comprehension. When looking at the entire range of reading comprehension skills, from very low to very accomplished reading skills, genetic influences are highly significant, ranging from $h^2$ around .40 (or 40% of the variance) to $h^2$ around .75 (or 75% of the variance), even in young children (Betjemann et al., 2008; Byrne et al., 2009; Harlaar et al., 2010; Petrill et al., 2007). This means that genetic differences between individuals account for a significant proportion of the measured differences in reading comprehension. These effects are mirrored in children with reading disability (Astrom, Wadsworth, Olson, Willcutt, & DeFries, 2012; Plomin & Kovas, 2005). Shared environmental influences are also significant in many of these studies but tend to account for smaller portions of the variance. Taken together, although arising from the environment and instruction, results suggest that the substantial differences found in children's reading comprehension are, in part, because of genetic differences.

## MULTIVARIATE GENETIC STUDIES OF READING COMPREHENSION

Behavioral genetics designs can also address the multivariate relationships between reading comprehension and other outcomes such as text decoding and language, which have shown significant and substantial genetic effects (Bishop, 2001; Byrne et al., 2009; DeThorne, Petrill, Hayiou-Thomas, & Plomin, 2005; Gayan & Olson, 2003; Harlaar, Spinath, Dale, & Plomin, 2005; Hayiou-Thomas et al., 2006; Oliver & Plomin, 2007; Olson & Byrne, 2005; Petrill, Deater-Deckard, Thompson, DeThorne, & Schatschneider, 2006). Consider the simple view of reading (Hoover & Gough, 1990), which posits that reading comprehension is the result of both text-decoding skills (reading words from a page) and language-based skills (the process of understanding what the decoded words mean; e.g., Catts, Hogan, & Adlof, 2005; Cutting & Scarborough, 2006). A central question in the reading literature is the extent to which decoding and language constitute overlapping or independent influences on reading comprehension. One can also ask this question from a multivariate genetics perspective: To what extent are genetic and environmental influences on reading comprehension related to influences associated with decoding and language? Do language and decoding contribute to reading comprehension through overlapping genetic and/or environmental sources of variance? If so, then one would expect a common set of genes or a common set of environmental circumstances related to decoding, language, and reading comprehension. On the other hand, if decoding and language demonstrate independent genetic and environmental effects on reading comprehension, then one should look to identify genetic and environmental influences that differentiate the effect of decoding and language on reading comprehension.

Keenan, Betjemann, Wadsworth, DeFries, and Olson (2006) were the first to examine this question using multivariate genetics designs. Their results suggested that the genetic influences related to decoding and language contributed both overlapping and independent sources of variance to reading comprehension. Subsequent research (Harlaar et al., 2010) extended this work in two ways. First, Harlaar et al. (2010) expanded beyond decoding and language to include phonological decoding (reading nonwords), listening comprehension, and vocabulary. Second, Harlaar et al. (2010) employed multiple measures of each construct, which meant that the multivariate genetic analysis could be conducted on latent factors, as opposed to individual measures. This approach is important because recent work has suggested that the heritability of reading comprehension varies based on the type of test employed (Betjemann, Keenan, Olson, & DeFries, 2011).

When combining results across different types of tests, researchers found reading comprehension to be highly heritable ($h^2 = .75$, $p < .05$), influenced by the shared environment ($c^2 = .23$, $p < .05$), but not by the nonshared environment ($e^2 = .02$). Harlaar et al. (2010) also examined the extent to which word recognition, phonological decoding, listening comprehension, and vocabulary accounted for the genetic and environmental influences on reading comprehension. Overlapping genetic effects accounted for $h^2 = .66$ ($p < .05$) of the heritability of reading comprehension. Beyond this general factor, reading comprehension was also explained by an independent set of genetic influences related to language (both listening comprehension and vocabulary), contributing $h^2 = .09$ ($p < .05$) to reading comprehension. It is interesting to note that shared environmental effects on reading comprehension ($c^2 = .23$, $p < .05$) were also divided between overlapping factors influencing all outcomes ($c^2 = .20$, $p < .05$) and those unique to vocabulary, but not listening comprehension ($c^2 = .03$, $p < .05$).

These results suggest that the simple view of reading comprehension is associated with genetic and environmental effects that are common to decoding, phonological processing, language skills, and reading comprehension. On the other hand, language-related outcomes were associated with reading comprehension through additional independent genetic factors (both vocabulary and listening comprehension) and shared environmental effects (vocabulary skills but not listening comprehension). This finding is important because language-based skills not only are associated with genetic and environmental overlap between decoding skills, phonological skills, and reading but also contribute additional genetic and environmental variance. Although heritable, vocabulary skills, in particular, appear to be one source of shared environmental variance associated with reading comprehension above and beyond other skills.

The studies described earlier are based on children who were unselected for reading comprehension or language deficits. However, there is also considerable evidence for comorbidity between language disability and later reading disability (Pennington & Bishop, 2009), and a portion of this comorbidity appears to be associated with shared genetic factors (Haworth et al., 2009; Logan et al., 2011; Newbury et al., 2011; Pennington & Bishop, 2009; Plomin & Kovas, 2005). For example, Logan et al. (2011) further examined the relationship between language and reading, focusing on behavioral genetic analysis of reading and language skills in extended family pedigrees, where the proband child was selected for specific language impairment. Using the same logic as in the twin studies described earlier, Logan et al. (2011) examined whether the correlation between language and reading differed across family members of different genetic relatedness. In the case of extended family pedigrees, the comparison involves siblings, parents, grandparents, cousins, uncles, aunts, and so forth, whereas in twin studies, the comparison involves identical versus fraternal twins. Using this approach, Logan et al. (2011) examined three potential mechanisms explaining the relationship between reading and language: phonological awareness, phonological memory, and auditory repetition. The results of the study suggested that genetic effects associated with phonological awareness were associated with reading and language skills, but phonological memory and auditory repetition were not.

These results have important implications for cognitive models of reading, language use, and processing. Essentially, behavioral genetic studies suggest that the distinctions found in the larger reading literature (e.g., the importance of language and decoding as described by the simple view) are reflected in distinct genetic and, to a lesser extent, shared environmental etiologies. The importance of genetic influences is not isolated to the relationship between reading and language: There is a very large behavioral genetics literature examining genetic and environmental influences on the growth of reading skills (Petrill et al., 2010) and the stability of reading skills over time (Betjemann et al., 2008; Harlaar, Dale, & Plomin, 2007; Kovas, Haworth, Dale, & Plomin, 2007; Petrill et al., 2007; Wadsworth, Corley, Hewitt, & DeFries, 2001; Wadsworth, Fulker, & DeFries, 1999). There is also a large literature examining the relationship between reading and such other outcomes as ADHD (Hart, Petrill, Willcutt, et al., 2010; Willcutt et al., 2010; Willcutt et al., 2007) and mathematics skills (Hart, Petrill, & Kamp Dush, 2010; Hart, Petrill, Thompson, & Plomin, 2009; Knopik & DeFries, 1999; Kovas et al., 2007). Taken together, this very large literature suggests not only that there are substantial individual differences in reading but also that these differences are influenced by a complex network of environmental and genetic effects that influence the development of reading and the relationship between reading with other learning outcomes.

## BRAIN IMAGING

Despite strong evidence for genetic and environmental effects, it is difficult to ascertain the biological processes though which estimates of $h^2$, $c^2$, and $e^2$ operate, given that the behavioral genetics literature on reading is almost exclusively focused on broad behavioral measures. In particular, it is unknown whether the genetic etiology of reading comprehension, as well as the covariance between reading comprehension and other skills, is driven by a small set of foundational skills, influenced by genetics, that permeate all aspects of learning disabilities, as described in the "generalist genes" hypothesis (Plomin & Kovas, 2005), or whether genetic overlap between reading comprehension and other domains results from the aggregation of a widely distributed set of neural mechanisms of potentially different genetic and environmental etiologies.

Fortunately, as noted in other chapters in this edited volume, there is a rich and extensive literature using structural and functional neuroimaging in both readers who are skilled and those who are impaired, suggesting possible neuroanatomical regions related to reading. For example, Davis et al. (2010) demonstrated that children with reading disability who did not respond to intervention (as compared to those who did) showed decreased connectivity in key white matter tracts connecting areas within the perisylvian region. In another study, Rimrodt, Peterson, Denckla, Kaufmann, and Cutting (2010) showed differences in measures of white matter integrity between controls and those with reading disability in the superior longitudinal fasiculus (SLF).

Functional imaging studies have explored the neural correlates of processing that have long been known to be critical for reading comprehension, such as sentence comprehension (Meyler et al., 2007; Rimrodt et al., 2009) and working memory (Beneventi, Tonnessen, & Ersland, 2009; Wolf et al., 2010). These studies also show abnormalities between readers who are typically developing and those with reading disability, although the areas of anomalous activation extend beyond those of traditional reading tasks, including prefrontal cortices. Other studies have been devoted to the neural correlates of word recognition and decoding. In general, neurobiological correlates of word recognition in reading disability show perisylvian region dysfunction, including underactivation of left temporo-parietal and occipito-temporal regions and greater right temporo-parietal and occipito-temporal activation compared to readers who are typically developing (Pugh et al., 2000; Rezaie et al., 2011; Richlan, Kronbichler, & Wimmer, 2009; Rumsey et al., 1997; Simos et al., 2006; Stuebing et al., 2002; Tanaka et al., 2011). Readers who are typically developing demonstrate consistent patterns of left-hemisphere perisylvian activation, in temporo-parietal and inferior frontal regions, as well as occipito-temporal activation that is especially associated with fast and efficient reading (Dehaene & Cohen, 2011; Fiez & Petersen, 1998; Georgiewa et al., 2002).

Taken together, the behavioral genetics and neurobiological literatures suggest plausible models highlighting the importance of decoding and language in understanding reading comprehension. Integrating these two bodies of work would address fundamental questions about the neurobiological structure, function, and etiology of reading comprehension. This type of work has not been conducted in reading but is feasible and has been growing in other domains. For example, in a recent twin study using a whole brain level of analysis, Chen et al. (2012) estimated all possible genetic correlations in structural imaging data, voxel by voxel, using methods similar to those described in the multivariate genetics section described earlier, but using measures of brain structure as opposed to behavioral measures. Without prior constraints, the genetic correlations largely clustered into genetically distinct regions corresponding to expected neuroanatomical regions. In another study, Blokland, de Zubicaray, McMahon, and Wright (2012) conducted a meta-analysis and found that most structural regions and functional brain-based measures (tapping cognitive development and emotional, social, and behavioral development) demonstrated significant heritability, but also significant shared environmental influences. More examples of this type of work may be found in a recent special issue in *Twin Research and Human Genetics* (2012, Volume 15, Issue 3).

Twin imaging has enormous potential for the study of reading comprehension. Consider sentence-level reading that shows activation across widely distributed brain regions and is correlated with many complex behavioral outcomes. Within a twin design, one would be able to systematically test whether functional differences in activation related to sentence-level tasks, for example, are associated with behavioral measures of reading. These genetic correlations could then be overlaid on structural imaging measures, which would allow for an elegant comparison of functional and structural correlates of reading comprehension. The same logic applies to the shared and nonshared environment and thus may yield knowledge about the boundaries of genetic and environmental vulnerability at the level of the brain, in addition to the level of behavior, both in the normal range, and in disability.

## SUMMARY AND IMPLICATIONS FOR INTERVENTION

The behavioral genetic studies described in this chapter suggest that genetic and environmental sources of variance are important to 1) reading comprehension and reading comprehension deficits, 2) the development and stability of reading comprehension over time, and 3) the relationship between reading comprehension and other domains, including decoding and language. Moreover, emerging twin-imaging designs have yet to be applied to regions and tasks derived from the large and growing reading-imaging literature. Doing so would address fundamental questions about the relationships between genes, environment, brain, and behavior.

These data lead to several implications for intervention studies. First, considering the evidence for genetic influences on reading, it is important to consider the role of family history as part of intervention studies. Doing so may offer important insight into the level of risk for nonresponse. Second, it is necessary to move past the unfortunate history of genetics in education. Because of this history, the high heritability of reading comprehension has sometimes been erroneously associated with limited opportunities for growth or deterministic outcomes. Like most complex traits, reading is influenced by multiple probabilistic genetic factors (Newbury et al., 2011).

Thus, like other domains, such as heart disease or substance use, the presence of genetic risk in reading comprehension may signal an increased need for application of early or intensive intervention, not less need. This increased need is especially true if the integration of twin designs, imaging, and reading comprehension leads to identifiable genetic or environmentally mediated biological risk factors for reading comprehension problems. It is important to begin to systematically address these possibilities. At present, by ignoring genetics, we are taking a large portion of the variance out of the discussion, which may limit the means to prevent or more quickly identify and treat reading problems.

## REFERENCES

Astrom, R.L., Wadsworth, S.J., Olson, R.K., Willcutt, E.G., & DeFries, J.C. (2012). Genetic and environmental etiologies of reading difficulties: DeFries–Fulker analysis of reading performance data from twin pairs and their non-twin siblings. *Learning and Individual Differences, 22*(3), 365–369.

Beneventi, H., Tonnessen, F.E., & Ersland, L. (2009). Dyslexic children show short-term memory deficits in phonological storage and serial rehearsal: An fMRI study. *International Journal of Neuroscience, 119*(11), 2017–2043.

Betjemann, R.S., Keenan, J.M., Olson, R.K., & DeFries, J.C. (2011). Choice of reading comprehension test influences the outcomes of genetic analyses. *Scientific Studies of Reading, 15*(4), 363–382.

Betjemann, R.S., Willcutt, E.G., Olson, R.K., Keenan, J.M., DeFries, J.C., & Wadsworth, S.J. (2008). Word reading and reading comprehension: Stability, overlap and independence. *Reading and Writing, 21*(5), 539–558.

Bishop, D.V.M. (2001). Genetic influences on language impairment and literacy problems in children: Same or different? *Journal of Child Psychology and Psychiatry, 42*(2), 189–198.

Blokland, G.A.M., de Zubicaray, G.I., McMahon, K.L., & Wright, M.J. (2012).

Genetic and environmental influences on neuroimaging phenotypes: A meta-analytical perspective on twin imaging studies. *Twin Research and Human Genetics* [Special issue], *15*(03), 351–371.

Byrne, B., Coventry, W.L., Olson, R.K., Samuelsson, S., Corley, R., Willcutt, E.G., … DeFries, J.C. (2009). Genetic and environmental influences on aspects of literacy and language in early childhood: Continuity and change from preschool to Grade 2. *Journal of Neurolinguistics, 22*(3), 219–236.

Catts, H.W., Hogan, T.P., & Adlof, S.M. (2005). Developmental changes in reading and reading disabilities. In H.W. Catts & A.G. Kamhi (Eds.), *The connections between language and reading disabilities* (pp. 25–40). Mahwah, NJ: Erlbaum.

Chen, C.-H., Gutierrez, E.D., Thompson, W., Panizzon, M.S., Jernigan, T.L., Eyler, L.T., … Dale, A.M. (2012). Hierarchical genetic organization of human cortical surface area. *Science, 335*(6076), 1634–1636.

Cutting, L.E., & Scarborough, H.S. (2006). Prediction of reading comprehension: Relative contributions of word recognition, language proficiency, and other cognitive skills can depend on how comprehension is measured. *Scientific Studies of Reading, 10*(3), 277–299.

Davis, N., Fan, Q., Compton, D.L., Fuchs, D., Fuchs, L.S., Cutting, L.E., … Anderson, A.W. (2010). Influences of neural pathway integrity on children's response to reading instruction. *Frontiers in Systems Neuroscience, 4*, 150.

Dehaene, S., & Cohen, L. (2011). The unique role of the visual word form area in reading. *Trends in Cognitive Sciences, 15*(6), 254–262.

DeThorne, L.S., Petrill, S.A., Hayiou-Thomas, M.E., & Plomin, R. (2005). Low expressive vocabulary: Higher heritability as a function of more severe cases. *Journal of Speech, Language, and Hearing Research, 48*(4), 792–804.

Dieterich, S.E., Assel, M.A., Swank, P., Smith, K.E., & Landry, S.H. (2006). The impact of early maternal verbal scaffolding and child language abilities on later decoding and reading comprehension skills. *Journal of School Psychology, 43*(6), 481–494.

Fiez, J.A., & Petersen, S.E. (1998). Neuroimaging studies of word reading. *Proceedings of the National Academy of Sciences of the United States of America, 95*(3), 914–921.

Frost, S.J., Landi, N., Mencl, W.E., Sandak, R., Fulbright, R.K., Tejada, E.T., … Pugh, K.R. (2009). Phonological awareness predicts activation patterns for print and speech. *Annals of Dyslexia, 59*(1), 78–97.

Gayan, J., & Olson, R.K. (2003). Genetic and environmental influences on individual differences in printed word recognition. *Journal of Experimental Child Psychology, 84*(2), 97–123.

Georgiewa, P., Rzanny, R., Gaser, C., Gerhard, U.J., Vieweg, U., Freesmeyer, D., … Blanz, B. (2002). Phonological processing in dyslexic children: a study combining functional imaging and event related potentials. *Neuroscience Letters, 318*(1), 5–8.

Harlaar, N., Cutting, L., Deater-Deckard, K., DeThorne, L., Justice, L., Schatschneider, C., … Petrill, S. (2010). Predicting individual differences in reading comprehension: A twin study. *Annals of Dyslexia*, 1–24.

Harlaar, N., Dale, P.S., & Plomin, R. (2007). From learning to read to reading to learn: Substantial and stable genetic influence. *Child Development, 78*(1), 116–131.

Harlaar, N., Spinath, F.M., Dale, P.S., & Plomin, R. (2005). Genetic influences on early word recognition abilities and disabilities: A study of 7-year-old twins. *Journal of Child Psychology and Psychiatry, 46*(4), 373–384.

Hart, S.A., Petrill, S.A., & Kamp Dush, C.M. (2010). Genetic influences on language, reading, and mathematics skills in a national sample: An analysis using the National Longitudinal Survey of Youth. *Language, Speech, and Hearing Services in Schools, 41*, 118–128.

Hart, S.A., Petrill, S.A., Thompson, L.A., & Plomin, R. (2009). The ABCs of math: A genetic analysis of mathematics and its links with reading ability and general cognitive ability. *Journal of Educational Psychology, 101*(2), 388–402.

Hart, S.A., Petrill, S.A., Willcutt, E., Thompson, L.A., Schatschneider, C., Deater-Deckard, K., & Cutting, L.E. (2010). Exploring how symptoms of attention-deficit/hyperactivity disorder are related to reading and mathematics performance. *Psychological Science, 21*(11), 1708–1715.

Haworth, C.M.A., Kovas, Y., Harlaar, N., Hayiou-Thomas, M.E., Petrill, S.A., Dale, P.S., & Plomin, R. (2009). Generalist genes and learning disabilities: a multivariate genetic analysis of low performance in reading, mathematics, language and general cognitive ability in a sample of 8,000 12-year-old twins. *Journal of Child Psychology and Psychiatry, and Allied Disciplines, 50*(10), 1318–1325.

Hayiou-Thomas, M.E., Kovas, Y., Harlaar, N., Plomin, R., Bishop, D.V.M., & Dale, P.S. (2006). Common aetiology for diverse language skills in 4½–year-old twins. *Journal of Child Language, 33*(2), 339–368.

Hoover, W.A., & Gough, P.B. (1990). The simple view of reading. *Reading and Writing, 2*(2), 127–160.

Houde, O., Rossi, S., Lubin, A., & Joliot, M. (2010). Mapping numerical processing, reading, and executive functions in the developing brain: An fMRI meta-analysis of 52 studies including 842 children. *Developmental Science, 13*(6), 876–885.

Keenan, J.M., Betjemann, R.S., Wadsworth, S.J., DeFries, J.C., & Olson, R.K. (2006). Genetic and environmental influences on reading and listening comprehension. *Journal of Research in Reading, 29*(1), 75–91.

Knopik, V.S., & DeFries, J.C. (1999). Etiology of covariation between reading and mathematics performance: A twin study. *Twin Research and Human Genetics, 2*, 226–234.

Kovas, Y., Haworth, C.M.A., Dale, P.S., & Plomin, R. (2007). The genetic and environmental origins of learning abilities and disabilities in the early school years. *Monographs of the Society for Research in Child Development, 72*(3), 1–144.

Logan, J., Petrill, S.A., Flax, J., Justice, L.M., Hou, L., Bassett, A.S., … Bartlett, C.W. (2011). Genetic covariation underlying reading, language and related measures in a sample selected for specific language impairment. *Behavior Genetics, 41*(5), 651–659.

Meyler, A., Keller, T.A., Cherkassky, V.L., Lee, D., Hoeft, F., Whitfield-Gabrieli, S., … Just, M.A. (2007). Brain activation during sentence comprehension among good and poor readers. *Cerebral Cortex, 17*(12), 2780–2787.

Newbury, D., Paracchini, S., Scerri, T., Winchester, L., Addis, L., Richardson, A., … Monaco, A. (2011). Investigation of dyslexia and SLI risk variants in reading- and language-impaired subjects. *Behavior Genetics, 41*(1), 90–104.

Oliver, B.R., & Plomin, R. (2007). Twins' Early Development Study (TEDS): A multivariate, longitudinal genetic investigation of language, cognition and behavior problems from childhood through adolescence. *Twin Research and Human Genetics, 10*(1), 96–105.

Olson, R., & Byrne, B. (2005). Genetic and environmental influences on reading and language ability and disability. In H.W. Catts & A.G. Kamhi (Eds.), *The connections between language and reading disabilities* (pp. 173–200). Mahwah, NJ: Erlbaum.

Paracchini, S., Steer, C.D., Lyn-Buckingham, L., Morris, A.P., Ring, S., Scerri, T., … Monaco, A.P. (2008). Association of the KIAA0319 dyslexia susceptibility gene with reading skills in the general population. *American Journal of Psychiatry, 165*(12), 1576–1584.

Pennington, B.F., & Bishop, D.V.M. (2009). Relations among speech, language, and reading disorders. *Annual Review of Psychology, 60*(1), 283–306.

Petrill, S.A., Deater-Deckard, K., Thompson, L.A., DeThorne, L.S., & Schatschneider, C. (2006). Genetic and environmental effects of serial naming and phonological awareness on early reading outcomes. *Journal of Educational Psychology, 98*(1), 112–121.

Petrill, S.A., Deater-Deckard, K., Thompson, L.A., Schatschneider, C., DeThorne, L.S., & Vandenbergh, D.J. (2007). Longitudinal genetic analysis of early reading: The Western Reserve Reading Project. *Reading and Writing, 20*(1–2), 127–146.

Petrill, S.A., Hart, S.A., Harlaar, N., Logan, J., Justice, L.M., Schatschneider, C., … Cutting, L. (2010). Genetic and environmental influences on the growth of early reading skills. *Journal of Child Psychology and Psychiatry, 51*(6), 660–667.

Petryshen, T., & Pauls, D. (2009). The genetics of reading disability. *Current Psychiatry Reports, 11*(2), 149–155.

Plomin, R., DeFries, J.C., McClearn, G.E., & McGuffin, P. (2008). *Behavioral Genetics* (5th ed.). New York, NY: Worth.

Plomin, R., & Kovas, Y. (2005). Generalist genes and learning disabilities. *Psychological Bulletin, 131*(4), 592–617.

Pugh, K.R., Mencl, W.E., Jenner, A.R., Katz, L., Frost, S.J., Lee, J.R., ... Shaywitz, B.A. (2000). Functional neuroimaging studies of reading and reading disability (developmental dyslexia). *Mental Retardation and Developmental Disabilities Research Reviews, 6*(3), 207–213.

Rezaie, R., Simos, P.G., Fletcher, J.M., Cirino, P.T., Vaughn, S., & Papanicolaou, A.C. (2011). Temporo-parietal brain activity as a longitudinal predictor of response to educational interventions among middle school struggling readers. *Journal of the International Neuropsychological Society, 17*(5), 875–885.

Richlan, F., Kronbichler, M., & Wimmer, H. (2009). Functional abnormalities in the dyslexic brain: A quantitative meta-analysis of neuroimaging studies. *Human Brain Mapping, 30*(10), 3299–3308.

Rimrodt, S.L., Clements-Stephens, A.M., Pugh, K.R., Courtney, S.M., Gaur, P., Pekar, J.J., & Cutting, L.E. (2009). Functional MRI of sentence comprehension in children with dyslexia: Beyond word recognition. *Cerebral Cortex, 19*(2), 402–413.

Rimrodt, S.L., Peterson, D.J., Denckla, M.B., Kaufmann, W.E., & Cutting, L.E. (2010). White matter microstructural differences linked to left perisylvian language network in children with dyslexia. *Cortex, 46*(6), 739–749.

Rumsey, J.M., Nace, K., Donohue, B., Wise, D., Maisog, J.M., & Andreason, P. (1997). A positron emission tomographic study of impaired word recognition and phonological processing in dyslexic men. *Archives of Neurology, 54*(5), 562–573.

Senechal, M. (2006). Testing the home literacy model: Parent involvement in kindergarten is differentially related to grade 4 reading comprehension, fluency, spelling, and reading for pleasure. *Scientific Studies of Reading, 10*(1), 59–87.

Simos, P.G., Fletcher, J.M., Denton, C., Sarkari, S., Billingsley-Marshall, R., & Papanicolaou, A.C. (2006). Magnetic source imaging studies of dyslexia interventions. *Developmental Neuropsychology, 30*(1), 591–611.

Skibbe, L.E., Justice, L.M., Zucker, T.A., & McGinty, A.S. (2008). Relations among maternal literacy beliefs, home literacy practices, and the emergent literacy skills of preschoolers with specific language impairment. *Parent–Child Interaction and Early Literacy Development, 19*(1), 68–88.

Stuebing, K.K., Fletcher, J.M., LeDoux, J.M., Lyon, G.R., Shaywitz, S.E., & Shaywitz, B.A. (2002). Validity of IQ-discrepancy classifications of reading disabilities: A meta-analysis. *American Educational Research Journal, 39*(2), 469–518.

Tanaka, H., Black, J.M., Stanley, L.M., Kesler, S.R., Reiss, A.L., Hoeft, F., ... Gabrieli, J.D.E. (2011). The brain basis of the phonological deficit in dyslexia is independent of IQ. *Psychological Science, 22*(11), 1442–1451.

Wadsworth, S.J., Corley, R.P., Hewitt, J.K., & DeFries, J.C. (2001). Stability of genetic and environmental influences on reading performance at 7, 12, and 16 years of age in the Colorado Adoption Project. *Behavior Genetics, 31*(4), 353–359.

Wadsworth, S.J., Fulker, D.W., & DeFries, J.C. (1999). Stability of genetic and environmetnal influences on reading performance at 7 and 12 years of age in the Colorado Adoption Project. *International Journal of Behavioral Development, 23*(2), 319–322.

Willcutt, E.G., Betjemann, R.S., McGrath, L.M., Chhabildas, N.A., Olson, R.K., DeFries, J.C., & Pennington, B.F. (2010). Etiology and neuropsychology of comorbidity between RD and ADHD: The case for multiple-deficit models. *Cortex, 46*, 1345–1361.

Willcutt, E., Betjemann, R., Wadsworth, S., Samuelsson, S., Corley, R., DeFries, J., ... Olson, R. (2007). Preschool twin study of the relation between attention-deficit/hyperactivity disorder and prereading skills. *Reading and Writing, 20*(1), 103–125.

Wolf, R.C., Sambataro, F., Lohr, C., Steinbrink, C., Martin, C., & Vasic, N. (2010). Functional brain network abnormalities during verbal working memory performance in adolescents and young adults with dyslexia. *Neuropsychologia, 48*(1), 309–318.

CHAPTER 17

# What We Know (or Do Not Know) About the Genetics of Reading Comprehension and Other Reading-Related Processes

Elena L. Grigorenko

These days, there is little doubt that "true" (Elliott & Grigorenko, 2012)—as opposed to garden variety (Stanovich, 1988)—reading difficulties (i.e., the atypical acquisition of reading) develop in the presence of substantial genetic risk (Fisher & DeFries, 2002). The field of scientific studies of reading and its componential processes has firmly established the importance of considering genetic factors in understanding individual differences in reading acquisition and reading performance. It is widely accepted that genetic variation among individuals accounts for a substantial amount of variance (41%–74%; Grigorenko, 2004) in virtually any process related to reading: 50%–80% for various indicators of phonological processing (Byrne et al., 2009; Byrne, Delaland, Fielding-Barnsley, & Quain, 2002), 60%–87% for various indicators of orthographic processing (Gayán & Olson, 2001, 2003), and 60%–67% for semantic processing or reading comprehension (Betjemann et al., 2008; Harlaar, Dale, & Plomin, 2007; Keenan, Betjemann, Wadsworth, DeFries, & Olson, 2006; Petrill et al., 2007). However, although these heritability estimates are substantial, reliable, and replicable, it has been difficult to "translate" them into any certain identification of the specific genetic mechanisms that underlie them. The field has generated a number of candidate genes that might be involved in these mechanisms (Grigorenko & Naples, 2009), but the profile of findings on these genes is complex, yielding both reassuring findings (Dennis et al., 2009; Paracchini et al., 2008) and nonreplications (e.g., Brkanac et al., 2007).

In interpreting this pattern of results, the field has identified a number of reasons for such "translation" difficulties. First and foremost, reading and reading-related componential processes are complex in structure and are, most likely, complex in terms of their etiological mechanisms (Smith, 2007). It is perhaps not surprising that either for all or some of its components,

The preparation of this chapter was supported, in part, by National Institutes of Health Grant R21 HD070594 to Elena L. Grigorenko. Grantees undertaking such projects are encouraged to freely express their professional judgment. This article, therefore, does not necessarily reflect the position or policies of the National Institutes of Health, and no official endorsement should be inferred. I am grateful to Mei Tan for her editorial assistance.

there are a half dozen or more genes viewed as candidate genes for typical and/or atypical reading (Skiba, Landi, Wagner, & Grigorenko, 2011). It is perhaps also not surprising that original positive findings have only been partly supported.

Second, developmental models of reading acquisition (or the development of the reading system) assume the involvement of both the formation and the engagement of multiple psychological representations (Grigorenko & Naples, 2008). Processes that sample from these representations are, by definition, highly correlated because it is these representations that permit the holistic process of reading to emerge. Yet, although multivariate models of reading are commonly found in the behavioral literature (Wagner & Torgesen, 1987), they are not so prevalent in the genetics literature on reading.

Third, it appears that given the genetic information that has been accumulated so far, genes of small-to-moderate effects underlie individual differences in reading and its components (Meaburn, Harlaar, Craig, Schalkwyk, & Plomin, 2008) and that reading is best captured as a system of related variables quantifying these components (Grigorenko, 2007). Thus, it is assumed that the power needed to identify the relevant genes requires large samples that are homogeneous genetically and well-characterized behaviorally with multivariate phenotypes.

Fourth, it has been shown that heritability estimates are differential in their magnitude at different developmental stages and are higher when estimated in samples of probands (individuals with the target disorder, disability, or difficulty) and their relatives than in population samples and that genetic influences are stronger in more severely affected probands and their relatives than in less severely affected probands (Deffenbacher et al., 2004; Francks et al., 2004).

In the remainder of this chapter, these statements are mapped onto and interpreted in light of the current situation in the field of genetic and genomic research.

## STRUCTURAL CHARACTERISTICS OF THE GENOME

In light of the assumption that typical (and atypical) reading is complex (see *First* above), it is only fair to make the supposition that the genetic and genomic mechanisms underlying the development of typical reading and the manifestation of atypical reading are no less complex. So far, the field of genetic studies of reading has focused primarily on the model postulating that reading is controlled by a genetic mechanism that follows Mendelian[1] laws (or their Fisher's extension to quantitative genetics). It has focused on the idea of finding the "risk variant"(s) that can, individually or

[1]These are the laws of dominance, segregation, and independent assortment, that is, the guiding principles for the intergenerational transmission of a hereditary trait that is controlled by a single genetic factor (i.e., a specific causal allele at a specific locus).

collectively, explain a substantial portion of the high levels of heritability mentioned previously. Yet, the idea that familial patterns of transmission of reading (dis)ability will follow or be similar to patterns of traits controlled by single genes (i.e., traits to which Medelian laws apply) is diminishing as we learn more about the structure and function of the human genome. The likelihood of the truth of this idea is decreasing with the intensification of the field's knowledge regarding the structure and function of the human genome.

For example, the last decade of genetic and genomic research has led to an explosion of studies implicating a great variety of different types of structural variation in the genome concerning the origin and manifestation of developmental disabilities (Miller et al., 2010). These types of structural variation range from large to small genomic events of different natures, among them deletions, insertions, spatial alterations (e.g., translocations and inversions), and the presence or absence of transposable[2] elements (1000 Genomes Project Consortium, 2010; Gonzaga-Jauregui, Lupski, & Gibbs, 2012; Stankiewicz & Lupski, 2010). The importance of considering these types of variation, and perhaps others, has been demonstrated for autism spectrum disorder (O'Roak et al., 2011; Sanders et al., 2011; Sanders et al., 2012), various developmental delays (Cooper et al., 2011), intellectual disabilities (Lu et al., 2007), attention-deficit/hyperactivity disorder (Lionel et al., 2011), and a number of specific genomic syndromes (Jalal et al., 2003; Roberts, Cox, Kimonis, Lamb, & Irons, 2004), many of which present with different learning disabilities. In other words, although present in individuals who are typically developing (i.e., individuals without any known neuropsychiatric disorders), structural variation in the genome of individuals with neuropsychiatric disorders appears to be present to a higher degree (e.g., more variants are observed), or of a particular type (e.g., deletions and insertions of larger size are observed), or at particular crucial locations (e.g., the deletion at 22q11.2 results in a well-known genomic syndrome, DiGeorge syndrome, one facet of which is the presentation of learning problems). There is a building literature implicating structural variation in a variety of neuropsychiatric phenotypes; its role in learning disabilities, however, has not been systematically investigated yet.

It is notable that for years, different types of structural variation have been implicated in the manifestation of reading difficulties. In fact, it is through the analyses of structural variation that a number of candidate genes for reading difficulties have been identified: *ROBO1* (Hannula-Jouppi et al., 2005), *DYX1C1* (Taipale et al., 2003), and *SEMA6D*[3] (Ercan-Sencicek

[2]A transposable element (transposon) is a DNA sequence that can change its relative position (self-transpose).

[3]Semaphorins are a large family of proteins, including both secreted and membrane-associated proteins, many of which have been implicated as inhibitors or chemorepellents in axon pathfinding, fasciculation and branching, and target selection (http://www.ncbi.nlm.nih.gov/gene/80031).

et al., 2012). All these genes have been detected through studies of isolated families (Taipale et al., 2003) or even individual cases[4] (Ercan-Sencicek et al., 2012). Systematic explorations of the importance of different types of structural variation in the field of reading have been few and, so far, on large events, for example, insertions and deletions larger than 1 MB (Girirajan et al., 2011). Yet, it is important to stress that such large structural variants are relatively rare (e.g., < 1% of the general population), and the underlying assumption here is that the identification of such rare variants will provide a clue for subsequent studies of the gene(s) affected by this structural alteration or of the pathway in which this gene(s) is/are involved. It is especially relevant to investigations of the genetic bases of such complex traits as reading abilities or disabilities. The idea is that once a rare variant is identified and associated with a particular trait (e.g., reading), there is a need to investigate common variance in the gene or region that was affected by this rare variant. In the field of reading, an example of such a transition from a rare variant to a continuous trait is the research on *ROBO1* (Bates, Luciano, Montgomery, Wright, & Martin, 2011).

The last decade of discoveries concerning the human genome has brought the realization of the importance and commonality of various genomic mechanisms to the forefront of today's studies of developmental disabilities, including reading disability. Similarly, along with the enhanced understanding of the role of structural variation in the genome, these discoveries have flagged a few more mechanisms that might be relevant to the field's understanding of the genetics of typical and atypical reading. Here, some of these mechanisms are briefly discussed.

As the accuracy of the sequence of the human genome increased, it became clear that the protein-coding sequences (i.e., genes[5]) constituted a minority in the genome compared to other types of DNA structures, for example, functional conserved noncoding elements (CNEs). There is now an accumulation of data suggesting that the differentiation of species may be driven more by innovation in CNEs than by changes in proteins (Lander, 2011). So, given that so far there are no obvious winners among the candidate genes for typical and atypical reading, it might be important not to limit the search for the genetic bases of reading to protein-coding genes only. Of note also is that the role of CNEs in reading might be directly related to the role of transposons, as many of the CNEs appear to be structurally derived from transposons (Bejerano et al., 2006).

Yet another discovery of recent years pertains to the importance of functional human nonprotein-coding RNAs. Here, two types of noncoding

---

[4]In this particular case, the proband was originally referred to the Yale Child Study Center at the age of 3 as a child with developmental language disorders; but currently, at the age of 10, he presents with a reading comprehension disorder with intact decoding skills.

[5]The current estimate of protein-coding genes is about 21,000, or 1.5% of the genome in humans (Clamp et al., 2007).

RNA are exemplified, micro RNAs (miRNAs) and large intergenic noncoding RNAs (lncRNAs). An miRNA is a short molecule that acts as a posttranscriptional regulator, which binds to complementary sequences on target messenger RNA transcripts and decreases their stability. It is estimated that the human genome encodes over 100 families of miRNA; together these miRNAs might target a large portion of human genes. It is these posttranscriptional mechanisms that might contribute to the genetic foundation of reading by modifying existing proteins, given that the creation of novel proteins is rare (and, to the best of the field's knowledge, there is no specific protein for reading). Intergenic noncoding RNAs appear to carry out a variety of functions in such processes as cell-cycle regulation, immune responses, brain processes, and gametogenesis. Moreover, and perhaps more important for the quest for the genetic bases of reading, lncRNAs may serve as "flexible scaffolds" (Zappulla & Cech, 2006) for protein complexes (i.e., combinations of protein) to elicit a specific function that is not carried out by any of the participating proteins in isolation.

## FUNCTIONAL CHARACTERISTICS OF THE GENOME

As mentioned earlier (see *Second*), it is now customary in the "behavioral corner" of the field of scientific studies of reading to consider relevant typical and atypical skills in developmental contexts. Behavior-genetic studies of typical and atypical reading and related phenotypes have indicated the presence of developmental heterogeneity in corresponding genetic bases (Byrne et al., 2009; Petrill et al., 2010). Specifically, when multiple time points of the same reading-related phenotype have been considered, the results have indicated the presence of time-general and time-specific genetic factors that contributed to the additive genetic component of the decomposed phenotypic variance (Harlaar et al., 2007). Modeling outcomes of this type have been reported for such reading-related phenotypes as phonetic-phonological processes (Coventry, Byrne, Olson, Corley, & Samuelsson, 2011), orthographic processes (Byrne et al., 2008), and vocabulary (Hart et al., 2009). Thus, it is important to investigate the impact of specific genetic risk factors not only cross-sectionally but also longitudinally; it is even more important to track, at the genetic or genomic level, the impact of effective behavioral interventions.

One relevant mechanism to consider in carrying out such developmentally and intervention-oriented research pertains to the epigenetic[6] (or epigenomic; often these terms are used interchangeably, as here) regulation of the genome. It has been observed that functionally active domains or components of the genome are characterized by specific

[6]A family of heritable events in the genome traceable through changes in gene expression or other phenotypic modifications that are not caused by structural changes in DNA (i.e., changes in what is synthesized by a particular DNA fragment that are not substantiated by changes in DNA sequence).

epigenetic marks—for example, the presence of particular molecules (Lander, 2011)—which can be recorded, cataloged, and assembled in developmental (skill acquisition) and intervention (skill reconstruction) epigenomic maps. Whereas the question of the tissue and cell specificity of these marks remains open, it has been shown (Thompson et al., 2013) that peripheral cell types (i.e., saliva or blood) provide a tremendous amount of information pertaining to the epigenomic maps differentiating behavioral groups (Naumova et al., 2012) or correlating with behavioral traits (Essex et al., 2013). There is no reason to believe that epigenomic studies will not be as useful for typical and atypical reading as they have been for other complex behavioral traits, or perhaps even more so.

It is indisputable that when various types of severe intellectual disabilities are excluded, everyone can be taught how to read. In fact, since specific reading impairment is a diagnostically distinct entity from intellectual disability, there is an explicit assumption in the very definition of this condition that any individual with this diagnosis can be taught to read. The issues are, however, the type and intensity of pedagogical intervention required and the characteristics of "mastered" reading (e.g., its accuracy and fluency). It is important to note that the literature indicates that 1) difficulties in reading per se and different reading-related processes are susceptible to intervention (Samuelsson et al., 2008); 2) the majority, if not all, of the samples currently used for genetic studies of reading impairment are ascertained with probands who have been exposed to the remedial impact of schooling; that is, with few exceptions (Byrne et al., 2002; Petrill et al., 2010), probands are recruited while in school and after their SRD has been diagnosed or at least suspected; and 3) there is reason to believe that the severity of the phenotype (or, conversely, the degree to which a learner responds to remediation efforts) is linked to the strength of the genetic findings (Deffenbacher et al., 2004; Francks et al., 2004). Thus, it seems that the success of genetic studies is conditioned on their capacity to "unscramble" the reading-related phenotypes from the type and amount of intervention received. It is especially crucial to take such previous experiences into account if epigenetic analyses are to be conducted.

## SPECIFICITY OF THE GENETIC AND GENOMIC MECHANISMS RELATED TO READING

Although the hypothesis of the possible pleiotropic nature of specific genetic alterations has been present in the field for a while (Stearns, 2010), only lately has it been verified impressively and systematically (Bilgüvar et al., 2010). With regard to the field of reading (see *Third* above), these topical findings might indicate not only that the underlying genetic mechanism of typical and atypical reading might not be reading-specific but also that it might not be connected to behavior at all, reflecting instead some more general mechanism. In fact, one such general mechanism, neuronal migration, has been collaterally associated with reading (Galaburda, LoTurco, Ramus, Fitch, & Rosen, 2006) through the analyses of the functional properties of a number of reading-related candidate genes (Ercan-Sencicek et al., 2012; Paracchini et al., 2006; Tapia-Paez, Tammimies, Massinen, Roy, & Kere, 2008).

Such nonspecificity in the search for genetic effects can, at least in part, explain the results emerging from large-scale whole-genome and genomewide association studies (GWAS) of complex behavioral traits.[7] An overview of the GWAS (Manolio, 2010) completed so far suggests that the investigated traits appear to be influenced by multiple (perhaps a large number of) loci, with the majority of the common variants at these loci being of small-to-moderate effect (i.e., increasing risk by 10%–50%, the order of magnitude characterizing the impact of many environmental risk factors), and the associated genes were those previously identified through linkage analyses as well as many not previously implicated genes (i.e., genes with specific cellular functions that might not, at least superficially, have been suspected of being relevant to the studied pathogenesis). These results (or, rather, their intermediate nature) were commented on in the context of "our near-total ignorance of [the] underlying cellular pathways" (Lander, 2011, p. 192) of complex behavioral traits; all we can do, at this point, is to continue the research with both larger samples and larger numbers of common variants.

## GROUNDING HERITABILITY

Much has been written and said lately about the so-called missing heritability problem. This issue is as relevant to reading and reading-related traits (see *Fourth*, earlier in this chapter) as to any complex phenotype. First, it is of interest that the alarm that was sounded when the problem was first announced (Manolio et al., 2009) has quieted down; with the accumulation of larger and denser GWAS, the estimates of explained heritability keep going up (Lander, 2011), ranging from 12% (for height) to 60% (for Type 1 diabetes). Second, another important caveat here is that the field seemed to be using too stringent a statistical threshold for the reproducibility of results. When the data are treated differently (Park et al., 2010; Yang et al., 2010), the missing heritability is found, at least partially, and the problem does not appear to be so alarming, or perhaps does not appear to be a problem at all. What is still missing (i.e., the unaccounted portion of heritability estimates obtained in quantitative research) might be accounted for by rare variants (Galarneau et al., 2010), but then these variants need to be identified because they are by definition rare (<1%). The trick here is that the identification of rare variants has typically occurred through single cases or families (i.e., without any statistical significance associated with

[7]It is important to note that no large-scale GWAS for reading has been comprehensively presented in the literature just yet, although relevant collateral references have been made (Becker et al., 2012).

a particular variant). To gain an appreciation of the significance of rare variants on the population scale, one needs to rely on really large samples (i.e., collective efforts across sites, countries, and continents). Third, of note also is an observation that some heritability estimates might simply contain errors (i.e., they might be overestimations), as the oft-utilized statistical techniques do not account for the nonlinear effects of such higher order interactions.

## IN LIEU OF A CONCLUSION

The most obvious conclusion to be made here is a rather lackluster one: More work needs to be done. Typical and atypical reading and reading-associated traits have been featured in both quantitative- and molecular-genetic literatures since the early 1980s as traits whose population dispersion is related to variation in the genome. The field has been active in generating interesting leads and positioning itself well for the future (i.e., by building DNA repositories with well-characterized phenotypes), and a review of the field leaves the impression that many discoveries are yet to come. Researchers in the field are hopeful that the discoveries of the Human Genome Project will both inform and inspire the field of genetics of typical and atypical reading and generate, perhaps, some unexpected but robust and replicable findings.

## REFERENCES


1000 Genomes Project Consortium. (2010). A map of human genome variation from population-scale sequencing. *Nature, 467,* 1061–1073.

Bates, T.C., Luciano, M., Montgomery, G.W., Wright, M.J., & Martin, N.G. (2011). Genes for a component of the language acquisition mechanism: ROBO1 polymorphisms associated with phonological buffer deficit. *Behavior Genetics, 41,* 50–57.

Becker, J., Czamara, D., Hoffmann, P., Landerl, K., Blomert, L., Brandeis, D., … Schumacher, J. (2012). Evidence for the involvement of ZNF804A in cognitive processes of relevance to reading and spelling. *Translational Psychiatry, 2,* e136.

Bejerano, G., Lowe, C.B., Ahituv, N., King, B., Siepel, A., Salama, S.R., … Haussler, D. (2006). A distal enhancer and an ultraconserved exon are derived from a novel retroposon. *Nature, 441,* 87–90.

Betjemann, R.S., Willcutt, E.G., Olson, R.K., Keenan, J.M., DeFries, J.C., & Wadsworth, S.J. (2008). Word reading and reading comprehension: Stability, overlap and independence. *Reading and Writing, 21,* 539–558.

Bilgüvar, K., Öztürk, A.K., Louvi, A., Kwan, K.Y., Choi, M., Tatli, B., … Günel, M. (2010). Whole exome sequencing identifies recessive mutations in severe brain malformations. *Nature, 467,* 207–210.

Brkanac, Z., Chapman, N.H., Matsushita, M.M., Chun, L., Nielsen, K., Cochrane, E., … Raskind, W.H. (2007). Evaluation of candidate genes for DYX1 and DYX2 in families with dyslexia. *American Journal of Medical Genetics (Neuropsychiatric Genetics), 144,* 556–560.

Byrne, B., Coventry, W., Olson, R., Hulslander, J., Wadsworth, S., Defries, J., … Samuelsson, S. (2008). A behaviour-genetic analysis of orthographic learning, spelling and decoding. *Journal of Research in Reading, 31,* 8–21.

Byrne, B., Coventry, W.L., Olson, R.K., Samuelsson, S., Corley, R., Willcutt, E.G., … Defries, J.C. (2009). Genetic and environmental influences on aspects of literacy and language in early childhood: Continuity and change from preschool to Grade 2. *Journal of Neurolinguistics, 22,* 219–236.

Byrne, B., Delaland, C., Fielding-Barnsley, R., & Quain, P. (2002). Longitudinal twins study of early reading development in three countries: Preliminary results. *Annals of Dyslexia, 52,* 49–73.

Clamp, M., Fry, B., Kamal, M., Xie, X., Cuff, J., Lin, M.F., ... Lander, E.S. (2007). Distinguishing protein-coding and noncoding genes in the human genome. *Proceedings of the National Academy of Sciences of the United States of America, 104,* 19428–19433.

Cooper, G.M., Coe, B.P., Girirajan, S., Rosenfeld, J.A., Vu, T.H., Baker, C., ... Eichler, E.E. (2011). A copy number variation morbidity map of developmental delay. *Nature Genetics, 43,* 838–846.

Coventry, W.L., Byrne, B., Olson, R.K., Corley, R., & Samuelsson, S. (2011). Dynamic and static assessment of phonological awareness in preschool: A behavior-genetic study. *Journal of Learning Disabilities, 44,* 322–329.

Deffenbacher, K.E., Kenyon, J.B., Hoover, D.M., Olson, R.K., Pennington, B.F., DeFries, J.C., & Smith, S.D. (2004). Refinement of the 6p21.3 quantitative trait locus influencing dyslexia: Linkage and association analyses. *Human Genetics, 115,* 128–138.

Dennis, M.Y., Paracchini, S., Scerri, T.S., Prokunina-Olsson, L., Knight, J.C., Wade-Martins, R., ... Monaco, A.P. (2009). A common variant associated with dyslexia reduces expression of the KIAA0319 gene. *PLoS Genetics, 5,* e1000436.

Elliott, J.G., & Grigorenko, E.L. (2012). *The dyslexia debate.* New York, NY: Cambridge University Press.

Ercan-Sencicek, A.G., Davis Wright, N.R., Sanders, S.S., Oakman, N., Valdes, L., Bakkaloglu, B., ... Grigorenko, E.L. (2012). A balanced t(10;15) translocation in a male patient with developmental language disorder. *European Journal of Medical Genetics, 55,* 128–131.

Essex, M.J., Boyce, W.T., Hertzman, C., Lam, L.L., Armstrong, J.M., Neumann, S.M.A., & Kobor, M.S. (2013). Epigenetic vestiges of early developmental adversity: Childhood stress exposure and DNA methylation in adolescence. *Child Development, 84,* 58–75.

Fisher, S.E., & DeFries, J.C. (2002). Developmental dyslexia: Genetic dissection of a complex cognitive trait. *Nature Reviews: Neuroscience, 3,* 767–780.

Francks, C., Paracchini, S., Smith, S.D., Richardson, A.J., Scerri, T.S., Cardon, L.R., ... Monaco, A.P. (2004). A 77-kilobase region on chromosome 6p22.2 is associated with dyslexia in families from the United Kingdom and from the United States. *American Journal of Human Genetics, 75,* 1046–1058.

Galaburda, A.M., LoTurco, J.J., Ramus, F., Fitch, R.H., & Rosen, G.D. (2006). From genes to behavior in developmental dyslexia. *Nature Neuroscience, 9,* 1213–1217.

Galarneau, G., Palmer, C.D., Sankaran, V.G., Orkin, S.H., Hirschhorn, J.N., & Lettre, G. (2010). Fine-mapping at three loci known to affect fetal hemoglobin levels explains additional genetic variation. *Nature Genetics, 42,* 1049–1051.

Gayán, J., & Olson, R.K. (2001). Genetic and environmental influences on orthographic and phonological skills in children with reading disabilities. *Developmental Neurology, 20,* 483–507.

Gayán, J., & Olson, R.K. (2003). Genetic and environmental influences on individual differences in printed word recognition. *Journal of Experimental Child Psychology, 84,* 97–123.

Girirajan, S., Brkanac, Z., Coe, B.P., Baker, C., Vives, L., Vu, T.H., ... Eichler, E.E. (2011). Relative burden of large CNVs on a range of neurodevelopmental phenotypes. *PLOS Genetics, 7,* e1002334.

Gonzaga-Jauregui, C., Lupski, J.R., & Gibbs, R.A. (2012). Human genome sequencing in health and disease. *Annual Review of Medicine, 63,* 35–61.

Grigorenko, E.L. (2004). Genetic bases of developmental dyslexia: A capsule review of heritability estimates. *Enfance, 3,* 273–287.

Grigorenko, E.L. (2007). Triangulating developmental dyslexia: Behavior, brain, and genes. In D. Coch, G. Dawson, & K. Fischer (Eds.), *Human behavior and the developing brain* (pp. 117–144). New York, NY: Guilford Press.

Grigorenko, E.L., & Naples, A. (Eds.). (2008). *Single-word reading: Biological and behavioral perspectives.* Mahwah, NJ: Erlbaum.

Grigorenko, E.L., & Naples, A.J. (2009). The devil is in the details: Decoding the genetics of reading. In P. McCardle & K. Pugh (Eds.), *Helping children learn to read:*

*Current issues and new directions in the integration of cognition, neurobiology and genetics of reading and dyslexia* (pp. 133–148). New York, NY: Psychological Press.

Hannula-Jouppi, K., Kaminen-Ahola, N., Taipale, M., Eklund, R., Nopola-Hemmi, J., Kääriäinen, H., & Kere, J. (2005). The axon guidance receptor gene *ROBO1* is a candidate dene for developmental dyslexia. *PLoS, 1,* e50.

Harlaar, N., Dale, P.S., & Plomin, R. (2007). From learning to read to reading to learn: Substantial and stable genetic influence. *Child Development, 78,* 116–131.

Hart, S.A., Petrill, S.A., DeThorne, L.S., Deater-Deckard, K., Thompson, L.A., Schatschneider, C., & Cutting, L.E. (2009). Environmental influences on the longitudinal covariance of expressive vocabulary: Measuring the home literacy environment in a genetically sensitive design. *Journal of Child Psychology and Psychiatry, 50,* 911–919.

Jalal, S.M., Harwood, A.R., Sekhon, G.S., Lorentz, C.P., Ketterling, R.P., Babovic-Vuksanovic, D., ... Michels, V.V. (2003). Utility of subtelomeric fluorescent DNA probes for detection of chromosome anomalies in 425 patients. *Genetics in Medicine, 5,* 28–34.

Keenan, J.M., Betjemann, R., Wadsworth, S., DeFries, J., & Olson, R. (2006). Genetic and environmental influences on reading and listening comprehension. *Journal of Research in Reading, 29,* 75–91.

Lander, E.S. (2011). Initial impact of the sequencing of the human genome. *Nature, 470,* 187–197.

Lionel, A.C., Crosbie, J., Barbosa, N., Goodale, T., Thiruvahindrapuram, B., Rickaby, J., ... Scherer, S.W. (2011). Rare copy number variation discovery and cross-disorder comparisons identify risk genes for ADHD. *Science Translational Medicine, 3,* 95ra75.

Lu, X., Shaw, C.A., Patel, A., Li, J., Cooper, M.L., Wells, W.R., ... Ward, P.A. (2007). Clinical implementation of chromosomal microarray analysis: Summary of 2513 postnatal cases. *PLoS ONE, 2*(3), e327.

Manolio, T.A. (2010). Genomewide association studies and assessment of the risk of disease. *New England Journal of Medicine, 363,* 166–176.

Manolio, T.A., Collins, F.S., Cox, N.J., Goldstein, D.B., Hindorff, L.A., Hunter, D.J., ... Visscher, P.M. (2009). Finding the missing heritability of complex diseases. *Nature, 461,* 747–753.

Meaburn, E.L., Harlaar, N., Craig, I.W., Schalkwyk, L.C., & Plomin, R. (2008). QTL association scan of early reading disability and ability using pooled DNA and 100K SNP microarrays in a sample of 5,760 children. *Molecular Psychiatry, 13,* 729–740.

Miller, D.T., Adam, M.P., Aradhya, S., Biesecker, L.G., Brothman, A.R., Carter, N.P., ... Ledbetter, D.H. (2010). Consensus statement: Chromosomal microarray is a first-tier clinical diagnostic test for individuals with developmental disabilities or congenital anomalies. *American Journal of Human Genetics, 86,* 749–764.

Naumova, O., Lee, M., Koposov, R., Szyf, M., Dozier, M., & Grigorenko, E.L. (2012). Differential patterns of whole-genome DNA methylation in institutionalized children and children raised by their biological parents. *Development and Psychopathology, 24,* 143–155.

O'Roak, B.J., Deriziotis, P., Lee, C., Vives, L., Schwartz, J.J., Girirajan, S., ... Eichler, E.E. (2011). Exome sequencing in sporadic autism spectrum disorders identifies severe de novo mutations. *Nature Genetics, 43,* 585–589.

Paracchini, S., Steer, C.D., Buckingham, L.L., Morris, A.P., Ring, S., Scerri, T., ... Monaco, A. (2008). Association of the KIAA0319 dyslexia susceptibility gene with reading skills in the general population. *American Journal of Psychiatry, 165,* 1576–1584.

Paracchini, S., Thomas, A., Castro, S., Lai, C., Paramasivam, M., Wang, Y., Keating, B.J., ... Monaco, A.P. (2006). The chromosome 6p22 haplotype associated with dyslexia reduces the expression of KIAA0319, a novel gene involved in neuronal migration. *Human Molecular Genetics, 15,* 1659–1666.

Park, J.H., Wacholder, S., Gail, M.H., Peters, U., Jacobs, K.B., Chanock, S.J., & Chatterjee, N. (2010). Estimation of effect size distribution from genome-wide association studies and implications for future discoveries. *Nature Genetics, 42,* 570–575.

Petrill, S.A., Deater-Deckard, K., Thompson, L.A., Schatschneider, C., Dethorne, L.S., & Vandenbergh, D.J. (2007). Longitudinal genetic analysis of early reading: The Western Reserve Reading Project. *Reading and Writing, 20,* 127–146.

Petrill, S.A., Hart, S.A., Harlaar, N., Logan, J., Justice, L.M., Schatschneider, C., ... Cutting, L. (2010). Genetic and environmental influences on the growth of early reading skills. *Journal of Child Psychology & Psychiatry & Allied Disciplines, 51,* 660–667.

Roberts, A.E., Cox, G.F., Kimonis, V., Lamb, A., & Irons, M. (2004). Clinical presentation of 13 patients with subtelomeric rearrangements and a review of the literature. *American Journal of Medical Genetics, 128A,* 352–363.

Samuelsson, S., Byrne, B., Olson, R.K., Hulslander, J. Wadsworth, S., Corley, R., ... Defries, J.C. (2008). Response to early literacy instruction in the United States, Australia, and Scandinavia: A behavioral-genetic analysis. *Learning and Individual Differences, 18,* 289–295.

Sanders, S.J., Ercan-Sencicek, A.G., Hus, V., Luo, R., Murtha, M.T, Moreno-De-Luca, D., ... State, M.W. (2011). Multiple recurrent de novo CNVs, including duplications of the 7q11.23 Williams syndrome region, are strongly associated with autism. *Neuron, 70,* 863–885.

Sanders, S.J., Murtha, M.T., Gupta, A.R., Murdoch, J.D., Raubeson, M.J., Willsey, A.J., ... State, M.W. (2012). De novo mutations revealed by whole-exome sequencing are strongly associated with autism. *Nature, 485,* 237–241.

Skiba, T., Landi, N., Wagner, R., & Grigorenko, E.L. (2011). In search of the perfect phenotype: An analysis of linkage and association studies of reading and reading-related processes. *Behavior Genetics, 41,* 6–30.

Smith, S.D. (2007). Genes, language development, and language disorders. *Mental Retardation and Developmental Disabilities, 13,* 95–105.

Stankiewicz, P., & Lupski, J.R. (2010). Structural variation in the human genome and its role in disease. *Annual Review of Medicine, 61,* 437–455.

Stanovich, K.E. (1988). Explaining the differences between the dyslexic and the garden-variety poor reader: The phonological-core variable-difference model. *Journal of Learning Disabilities, 21,* 590–604.

Stearns, F.W. (2010). One hundred years of pleitropy: A retrospective. *Genetics, 186,* 767–773.

Taipale, M., Kaminen, N., Nopola-Hemmi, J., Haltia, T., Myllyluoma, B., Lyytinen, H., ... Kere, J. (2003). A candidate gene for developmental dyslexia encodes a nuclear tetratricopeptide repeat domain protein dynamically regulated in brain. *Proceedings of the National Academy of Sciences of the United States of America, 100,* 11553–11558.

Tapia-Paez, I., Tammimies, K., Massinen, S., Roy, A., & Kere, J. (2008). The complex of TFII-I, PARP1, and SFPQ proteins regulates the DYX1C1 gene implicated in neuronal migration and dyslexia. *FASEB Journal, 22,* 3001–3009.

Thompson, T.M., Sharfi, D., Lee, M., Yrigollen, C.M., Naumova, O. Yu., & Grigorenko, E.L. (2013). Comparison of whole-genome DNA methylation patterns in whole blood, saliva, and lymphoblastoid cell lines. *Behavior Genetics, 43,* 168–176.

Wagner, R.K., & Torgesen, J.K. (1987). The nature of phonological processing and its causal role in the acquisition of reading skills. *Psychological Bulletin, 101,* 192–212.

Yang, J., Benyamin, B., McEvoy, B.P., Gordon, S., Henders, A.K., Nyholt, D.R., ... Visscher, P.M. (2010). Common SNPs explain a large proportion of the heritability for human height. *Nature Genetics, 42,* 565–569.

Zappulla, D.C., & Cech, T.R. (2006). RNA as a flexible scaffold for proteins: Yeast telomerase and beyond. *Cold Spring Harbor Symposia on Quantitative Biology, 71,* 217–224.

INTEGRATIVE SUMMARY 3

# The Neurobiology and Genetics of Reading and Reading Comprehension

Fumiko Hoeft and Chelsea Myers

Reading comprehension is a complex process involving many reading-related and more general cognitive constructs. Therefore, investigation of the neural networks of reading comprehension and its associated difficulties, as well as their genetic correlates, should be multidimensional. Chapters in this section illuminate the rapidly growing advances, challenges, and potential future directions in the fields of neuroimaging and genetics that have begun to take these approaches.

The simple view of reading, frequently referred to in this section, is one of the most commonly referenced models in the neuroscientific research of reading comprehension. In this model, word-level decoding and oral language comprehension are considered key contributors of reading comprehension. A number of studies, many using functional and structural magnetic resonance imaging (MRI), have provided evidence of a large-scale network, predominantly in the left hemisphere, which underlies these two constructs (e.g., Price, 2012; Vigneau et al., 2006). Decoding has largely been implicated in the left occipito-temporal, temporo-parietal, and prefrontal regions most commonly involved in orthographic and phonological processing, including the fusiform and inferior temporal gyri, the supramarginal and superior temporal gyri, and the inferior frontal and precentral gyri, and connectivity between these regions. On the other hand, oral language comprehension has been implicated in a somewhat different left fronto-parieto-temporal network than decoding. The temporal lobe extends more anteriorly to the temporal pole, the parietal lobe includes a more posterior angular rather than the supramarginal gyrus, and the location within the inferior frontal region is often more anterior and dorsal. This oral language comprehension network is commonly associated with semantic and syntactic processing. However, these two distributed networks overlap in key nodes such as the left inferior frontal and superior temporal regions (Vigneau et al., 2006; Cutting, Benedict, Broadwater, Burns, & Fan, Chapter 13, Figure 13.2, this volume), which may serve as transitional nodes linking the two networks.

Chapters in this section confirm and provide neurobiological evidence of decoding and language (including listening comprehension and vocabulary) as crucial constructs of reading comprehension and its associated disorders. For example, as Cutting et al. (Chapter 13) and Pugh et al. (Chapter 14) point out, word-level decoding difficulties, that is, reading disorders (RD, or developmental dyslexia) that are characterized by dysfunction in the aforementioned decoding circuitry (Maisog, Einbinder, Flowers, Turkeltaub, & Eden, 2008; Richlan, Kronbichler, & Wimmer, 2009, 2011), often lead to deficits in reading comprehension. Cutting et al. note that individuals with specific reading comprehension deficits (S-RCD) show weaknesses in such language skills as oral language, vocabulary and semantic processing. Petrill (Chapter 16) mentions evidence that early language deficiencies are associated with later RD. However, decoding and language may not be as orthogonal to each other as initially envisioned. Cutting et al. show a large amount of variance that is shared between word-level reading and language comprehension. In their respective chapters, Petrill and Cutting et al. note large overlaps in genetic and environmental influence on decoding, language, and reading comprehension (detailed below). These findings are consistent with key nodes that bridge decoding and language noted earlier.

Also highlighted in Chapters 13–15 is the awareness that there are other important factors to consider in the neurobiological bases of reading comprehension and associated disorders. For example, Pugh et al. (Chapter 14) highlight the importance of the fronto-striatal network and the medial temporal lobe in learning and consolidation in the reader profile. They suggest that this network may be related to mechanisms of early speech perception and production deficits often observed in those who later develop RD. Cutting et al. (Chapter 13) also focus on the reader profile extending beyond the typical reading-related constructs to working memory and declarative memory associated with the medial temporal lobe. They further stress the importance of considering the interaction between the reader's profile, including decoding, vocabulary, background knowledge, and executive function, and the type of text that is read, which may increase demands on these functions. They show how reader–text interaction can be tested using functional MRI. Finally, Kuperberg (Chapter 15) draws examples from work using another type of imaging—namely, event-related potential (ERP) measured with electroencephalogram (EEG)—with lower spatial but finer temporal resolution than that of MRI, and provides in detail a novel framework that shows how background knowledge constrains contexts and generates semantic, phonological, and syntactic predictions that ultimately facilitate reading comprehension. Collectively, these chapters point to the necessity of extending current neurobiological models of reading comprehension and its associated disorders to include cognitive constructs often considered outside the realm of reading comprehension.

The field of genetics in reading-related research is as or perhaps even more complex and rapidly evolving than the field of neuroimaging. An integrative approach merging these two fields is challenging and newly emergent but could lead to a quantum leap in discoveries that may advance our knowledge of the cause of reading-related disorders and potentially foster the development of personalized, early, and even preventive interventions.

In Chapter 16, Petrill discusses the large genetic influence on reading comprehension and related constructs, how imaging research may be combined with behavioral genetic approaches, known as "imaging genetics," and their implications for interventions. He emphasizes the significance of behavioral genetics, more specifically twin designs, which allows one to disentangle heritability, shared environment, and nonshared environment. Studies noted in this chapter show that heritability estimates of reading comprehension skills are high, ranging from 40% to 75%, with smaller but significant effects of shared environment (e.g., prenatal, home, and school environment typically shared by monozygotic twins) explaining approximately 23% of the variance. Consistent with the simple view of reading, decoding, phonological processing, language (listening comprehension and vocabulary), and reading comprehension constitute largely overlapping genetic and shared environmental influences accounting for the majority (66% of 75%, and 20% of 23%, respectively) of the variances. This may indicate why individuals who are affected by RD are often burdened with poor reading comprehension. On the other hand, there is a small but significant nonoverlapping (independent) genetic and shared environmental influence between language and reading comprehension. Petrill goes on to suggest that the combination of twin designs and neuroimaging will allow us to tease apart why and how there are overlaps in genetic and shared environmental influences.

Taken together, overlapping and independent genetic and shared environmental influences of reading and nonreading cognitive constructs and related disorders (including attention-deficit/hyperactivity disorder, math skills, and reading development briefly mentioned in the chapter) are important to consider carefully because they will have large impacts on developing preventive and early interventions in the future. However, it is also important to note that many of the behavioral genetic approaches, including the twin design they emphasize here, allow examination at the group but not the individual level; therefore, integration with additional approaches, such as molecular genetics, will be necessary to ultimately transition from a one-size-fits-all intervention strategy to more personalized education and intervention.

In Chapter 17, Grigorenko discusses the growing molecular genetic literature as it pertains to reading. As noted earlier, heritability estimates of reading comprehension as well as of RD are high and are thought to be 41%–74%. A number of genes such as *ROBO1, DYX1C1,* and *SEMA6D,* have been proposed as candidate genes for RD and related traits. These genes, however, account for only a small portion of variance in RD (approximately 0.5%; Meaburn, Harlaar, Craig, Schalkwyk, & Plomin, 2008). This, together with similar findings in such other complex disorders as autism and Alzheimer's disease, has led researchers to question where the remainder of the "missing heritability" lies (Manolio et al., 2009). Grigorenko points out that this missing heritability may lie in rare variants that are yet to be found; these may be found with larger samples and such technological advances as denser arrays. She also notes such factors as estimation errors and/or excessively strict statistical thresholds that may play a role. Other factors that may prove to play important roles are such mechanisms as epistasis (gene–gene interaction) and such epigenetic phenomena (changes in gene expression without change in DNA structure) as genomic imprinting (gene expression in which only one parental allele is expressed and the other is silenced).

There is a noted phenotypic variety in reading and related constructs, suggesting that one genetic alteration may have multiple phenotypic outcomes, a phenomenon known as pleiotropy. As Grigorenko explains, the genetic mechanisms dictating reading may have to do not with reading or behavior but with a more general biological mechanism. One common mechanism found in a number of the potential reading-related candidate genes is neuronal migration, which would have consequences at a variety of levels.

Also of note, Grigorenko explains that genes may be expressed differently during development and with experience or environmental influence (cf. epigenetics). These findings highlight the importance of ensuring that genetic pursuits pertaining to reading be not only cross-sectional but also longitudinal, at the same time taking into account the effect of interventions and/or schooling, which obviously influence behavioral phenotype (i.e., reading ability). These precautions also should be heeded in neuroimaging research, described earlier in this summary, where maturational changes in brain development and changes in the neural networks associated with language and literacy acquisition as well as schooling and intervention need to be addressed.

We hope that in this integrative summary, we have been able to convey the significance of examining the neurobiological and genetic correlates of reading comprehension. Understanding the degree to which genetics, epigenetics, environment, and their interactions determine brain structure, function, and connectivity is of fundamental importance and is likely to shed light on the mechanisms underlying reading comprehension and associated disorders. Likewise, such neuroimaging tools as MRI, ERP, and magnetoencephalography (MEG) are powerful and allow us to study the human brain noninvasively, linking how genes affect behavior via an intermediate phenotype, the brain. For example, studies have shown that carrying a genetic risk of RD despite being asymptomatic can show brain activation and morphometric abnormalities (e.g., Black et al., 2012; Hosseini et al., 2013; Neuhoff et al., 2012; Raschle, Chang, & Gaab, 2011; Raschle, Zuk, & Gaab, 2012). It has also been shown that there are large environmental influences (e.g., socioeconomic status) on reading-related circuits (Monzalvo, Fluss, Billard, Dehaene, & Dehaene-Lambertz, 2012; Noble, Wolmetz, Ochs, Farah, & McCandliss, 2006; Raizada, Richards, Meltzoff, & Kuhl, 2008). The recent explosion of imaging genetic studies has provided many important insights predominantly using twin designs and studies associating specific genes with language-related brain activation (Czamara et al., 2011; Lamminmäki, Massinen, Nopola-Hemmi, Kere, & Hari, 2012; Pinel et al., 2012; Roeske et al., 2011; Wilcke et al., 2012).

Looking into the future, as the authors in this section suggest, studies that integrate multiple modalities of imaging, genetics, epigenetics, and environment, including schooling and intervention effects, spanning from preliteracy to advanced literacy, will be fundamental in understanding the neurobiology of reading comprehension, its precursors, and associated disorders. These studies on *how*, together with critical studies on *when* (i.e., identification of both the timing of when deficits develop and timing of opportunity to intervene), will ultimately pave the way to the accurate diagnostic classification, subtyping, and dimensional approaches of reading and related disorders and to the development of more effective personalized education and interventions.

## REFERENCES

Black, J.M., Tanaka, H., Stanley, L., Nagamine, M., Zakerani, N., Thurston, A., … Hoeft, F. (2012). Maternal history of reading difficulty is associated with reduced language-related gray matter in beginning readers. *NeuroImage, 59*(3), 3021–3032. doi:10.1016/j.neuroimage.2011.10.024

Czamara, D., Bruder, J., Becker, J., Bartling, J., Hoffmann, P., Ludwig, K.U., … Schulte-Körne, G. (2011). Association of a rare variant with mismatch negativity in a region between KIAA0319 and DCDC2 in dyslexia. *Behavior genetics, 41*(1), 110–119. doi:10.1007/s10519-010-9413-6

Hosseini, S.M.H., Black, J.M., Soriano, T., Bugescu, N., Martinez, R., Ramen, M.M., … Hoeft, F. (2013). Topological properties of large-scale structural brain networks in children with familial risk for reading difficulties. *NeuroImage, 71*, 260–274.

Lamminmäki, S., Massinen, S., Nopola-Hemmi, J., Kere, J., & Hari, R. (2012). Human ROBO1 regulates interaural interaction in auditory pathways. *Journal of Neuroscience, 32*(3), 966–971. doi:10.1523/JNEUROSCI.4007-11.2012

Maisog, J.M., Einbinder, E.R., Flowers, D.L., Turkeltaub, P.E., & Eden, G.F. (2008). A meta-analysis of functional neuroimaging studies of dyslexia. *Annals of the New York Academy of Sciences, 1145*, 237–259. doi:10.1196/annals.1416.024

Manolio, T.A., Collins, F.S., Cox, N.J., Goldstein, D.B., Hindorff, L.A., Hunter, D.J., … Visscher, P.M. (2009). Finding the missing heritability of complex diseases. *Nature, 461*(7265), 747–753. doi:10.1038/nature08494

Meaburn, E., Harlaar, N., Craig, I., Schalkwyk, L., & Plomin, R. (2008). Quantitative trait locus association scan of early reading disability and ability using pooled DNA and 100K SNP microarrays in a sample of 5760 children. *Molecular Psychiatry, 13*(7), 729–740.

Monzalvo, K., Fluss, J., Billard, C., Dehaene, S., & Dehaene-Lambertz, G. (2012). Cortical networks for vision and language in dyslexic and normal children of variable socio-economic status. *NeuroImage, 61*(1), 258–274. doi:10.1016/j.neuroimage.2012.02.035

Neuhoff, N., Bruder, J., Bartling, J., Warnke, A., Remschmidt, H., Müller-Myhsok, B., & Schulte-Körne, G. (2012). Evidence for the late MMN as a neurophysiological endophenotype for dyslexia. *PloS one, 7*(5), e34909. doi:10.1371/journal.pone.0034909

Noble, K.G., Wolmetz, M.E., Ochs, L.G., Farah, M.J., & McCandliss, B.D. (2006). Brain–behavior relationships in reading acquisition are modulated by socioeconomic factors. *Developmental Science, 9*(6), 642–654. doi:10.1111/j.1467-7687.2006.00542.x

Pinel, P., Fauchereau, F., Moreno, A., Barbot, A., Lathrop, M., Zelenika, D., … Dehaene, S. (2012). Genetic variants of FOXP2 and KIAA0319/TTRAP/THEM2 locus are associated with altered brain activation in distinct language-related regions. *Journal of Neuroscience, 32*(3), 817–825. doi:10.1523/JNEUROSCI.5996-10.2012

Price, C.J. (2012). A review and synthesis of the first 20 years of PET and fMRI studies of heard speech, spoken language and reading. *NeuroImage, 62*(2), 816–847. doi:10.1016/j.neuroimage.2012.04.062

Raizada, R.D.S., Richards, T.L., Meltzoff, A., & Kuhl, P.K. (2008). Socioeconomic status predicts hemispheric specialisation of the left inferior frontal gyrus in young children. *NeuroImage, 40*(3), 1392–1401. doi:10.1016/j.neuro image.2008.01.021

Raschle, N.M., Chang, M., & Gaab, N. (2011). Structural brain alterations associated with dyslexia predate reading onset. *NeuroImage, 57*(3), 742–749. doi:10.1016/j.neuroimage.2010.09.055

Raschle, N.M., Zuk, J., & Gaab, N. (2012). Functional characteristics of developmental dyslexia in left-hemispheric posterior brain regions predate reading onset. *Proceedings of the National Academy of Sciences of the United States of America, 109*(6), 2156–2161. doi:10.1073/pnas.1107721109

Richlan, F., Kronbichler, M., & Wimmer, H. (2009). Functional abnormalities in the dyslexic brain: A quantitative meta-analysis of neuroimaging studies. *Human Brain Mapping, 30*(10), 3299–3308. doi:10.1002/hbm.20752

Richlan, F., Kronbichler, M., & Wimmer, H. (2011). Meta-analyzing brain dysfunctions in dyslexic children and adults. *NeuroImage, 56*(3), 1735–1742. doi:10.1016/j.neuroimage.2011.02.040

Roeske, D., Ludwig, K.U., Neuhoff, N., Becker, J., Bartling, J., Bruder, J., … Schulte-Körne, G. (2011). First genome-wide association scan on neurophysiological endophenotypes points to trans-regulation effects on SLC2A3 in dyslexic children. *Molecular psychiatry, 16*(1), 97–107. doi:10.1038/mp.2009.102

Vigneau, M., Beaucousin, V., Hervé, P.Y., Duffau, H., Crivello, F., Houdé, O., … Tzourio-Mazoyer, N. (2006). Meta-analyzing left hemisphere language areas: Phonology, semantics, and sentence processing. *NeuroImage, 30*(4), 1414–1432. doi:10.1016/j.neuroimage.2005.11.002

Wilcke, A., Ligges, C., Burkhardt, J., Alexander, M., Wolf, C., Quente, E., … Kirsten, H. (2012). Imaging genetics of FOXP2 in dyslexia. *European Journal of Human Genetics, 20*(2), 224–229. doi:10.1038/ejhg.2011.160

SECTION V

# Intervention: Addressing the Needs of Learners

CHAPTER 18

# Intervening to Support Reading Comprehension Development with Diverse Learners

Carol McDonald Connor

Proficient reading comprehension has been defined as the ability to "demonstrate [an overall] understanding of the text...to extend the ideas in the text by making inferences, drawing conclusions, and making connections to their own experiences" (National Assessment Governing Board, 2007, p. 24). Basic processes underlying reading comprehension are complex and call on the oral language system and a conscious understanding of this system, that is, metalinguistic awareness, at all levels from semantic and morphosyntactic to pragmatic awareness (Connor et al., 2011). There are also social aspects to reading comprehension, including motivation, self-regulation, self-efficacy, and reading for social reasons (e.g., the Twilight and Harry Potter series; see Meyer, 2005; Rowling, 1997). All this is portrayed in the model provided in Figure 18.1. The first assumption in our model is that the ability to read proficiently for understanding is built on children's developing social, cognitive, and linguistic systems. As these systems mature and increase in sophistication, so too does a child's ability to co-opt these systems in the service of reading. Comprehension processes may be largely automatic and unconscious *under-the-hood processes* identified in the cognitive psychology literature (Perfetti, 2008; Rapp & van den Broek, 2005) or *reflective or interrogative comprehension processes,* which include conscious efforts to reflect on, critique, and understand text more deeply, as well as social aspects of reading (e.g., book clubs), and are largely identified in the education literature (Pressley et al., 2001; Snow, Porche, Tabors, & Harris, 2007).

Because reading comprehension as a construct is so complex, researchers have attempted to break it down into critical components and study aspects of reading comprehension separately, including vocabulary, syntax, morphological awareness, inferencing, working memory, use of strategies, comprehension monitoring, and background knowledge (e.g., Cain, Oakhill, & Bryant, 2004). Recent results examining kindergartners' through fourth graders' performance on an extensive battery including these constructs indicate that many of these factors are essentially one construct and that separate factors are highly correlated (Lonigan, Schatschneider, & Connor, 2012). For preschoolers through first graders, reading is just one construct—namely, the decoding and comprehension assessments load onto just one factor. For second through fourth graders, the simple view of reading

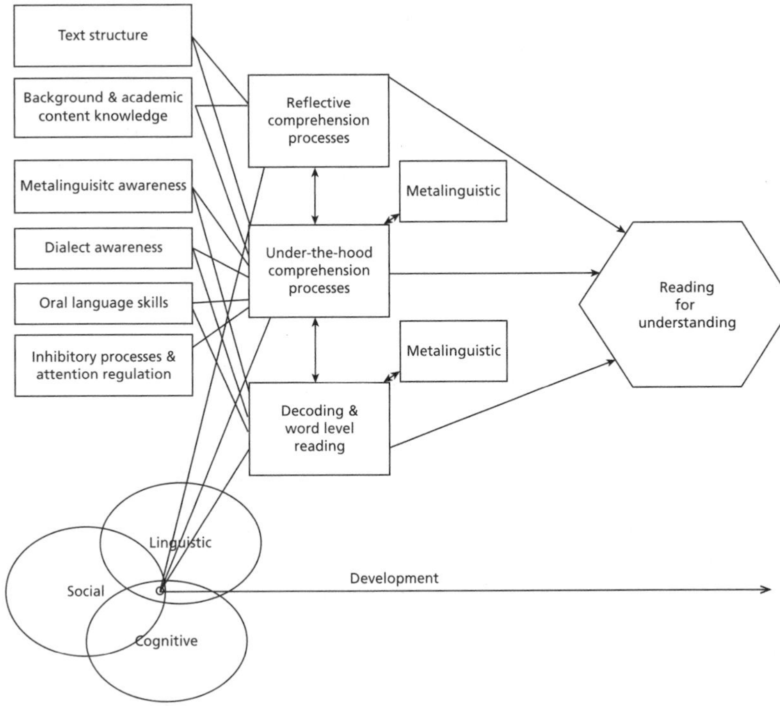


**Figure 18.1.** Component language model.

(Hoover & Gough, 1990) appears to hold. Quantile dominance analyses reveal that as second through fourth graders' reading comprehension skills get stronger, increasingly their skill is predicted more by their oral language skills and less by decoding (Schatschneider, Lonigan, & Petscher, 2012), with common variance contributing the most. Latent class analyses of the language constructs (Lonigan et al., 2012) revealed six classes that varied in overall language skill levels but not by strength or weaknesses in particular language components. Notable is that for these six classes, decoding and reading comprehension were equally affected.

Thus the language component view of reading for understanding does not appear to be supported. However, it is possible that the components that compose the language construct vary in their malleability, which has implications for intervention. There is accumulating evidence that the impact of interventions depends on children's language skills as well as their reading skills and that language skills are an important moderator of intervention effectiveness (Connor et al., 2011). Might improving component language skills also strengthen reading comprehension? There are multiple studies that suggest that this is the case (Elleman, Lindo, Morphy, & Compton, 2009). Moreover, there might be aspects of language that are more highly responsive to intervention. One way to think about this is Geary's framework of primary and secondary cognitive abilities (Geary, 2005, 2007), in which oral language, including dialect shifting, would represent primary abilities as an experience-expectant system, whereas academic knowledge (which was also loaded onto the language factor) would be a secondary ability as an experience-dependent system and hence may be more malleable. So the question becomes, by using potentially more malleable aspects of the broader language system, can we improve students' reading comprehension when their primary cognitive abilities are limited, possibly doing so by supporting potential compensatory mechanisms? And is it possible to directly intervene with primary and more under-the-hood processes by making the child more conscious of the largely unconscious skill?

To begin to answer these questions, I review results for two intervention studies focused on 1) dialect shifting (Thomas-Tate, Connor, Johnston, & Patton-Terry, in preparation) and 2) academic knowledge (Connor et al., in preparation), asking whether these interventions improve children's reading comprehension skills directly and/or indirectly. One would expect that primary under-the-hood processes, such as dialect shifting, would affect reading comprehension skills indirectly through oral language, whereas secondary and more interrogative processes, such as learning academic knowledge, would affect reading comprehension directly as well as indirectly through oral language (see Figure 18.2).

## DIALECT AWARENESS

Accumulating research reveals that Non-Mainstream American English (NMAE) use is negatively associated with students' academic achievement (Charity, Scarborough, & Griffin, 2004; Terry, Connor, Thomas-Tate, & Love, 2010), that most students who use NMAE or Home English begin to use more Mainstream American English (MAE) or School English by the end of second grade and that the more students shift their dialect to more MAE in contexts where mainstream English is expected (e.g., writing), the stronger their literacy achievement, on average (Terry, Connor, Petscher, & Conlin, 2012). Dialect shifting is generally considered to be a largely unconscious pragmatic aspect of language.

In the first of two experiments, results revealed that second-, third-, and fourth-grade students were better able to dialect shift when provided an intervention that explicitly contrasted Home English (i.e., NMAE) and School English (MAE) when compared to a no-treatment control and when compared to an alternative intervention that focused solely on the morphosyntactic features being taught with no reference to Home or School English and dialect shifting (Thomas-Tate et al., in preparation). We then investigated whether teaching children to dialect shift would improve their reading comprehension (Thomas-Tate et al., in preparation). In this study,

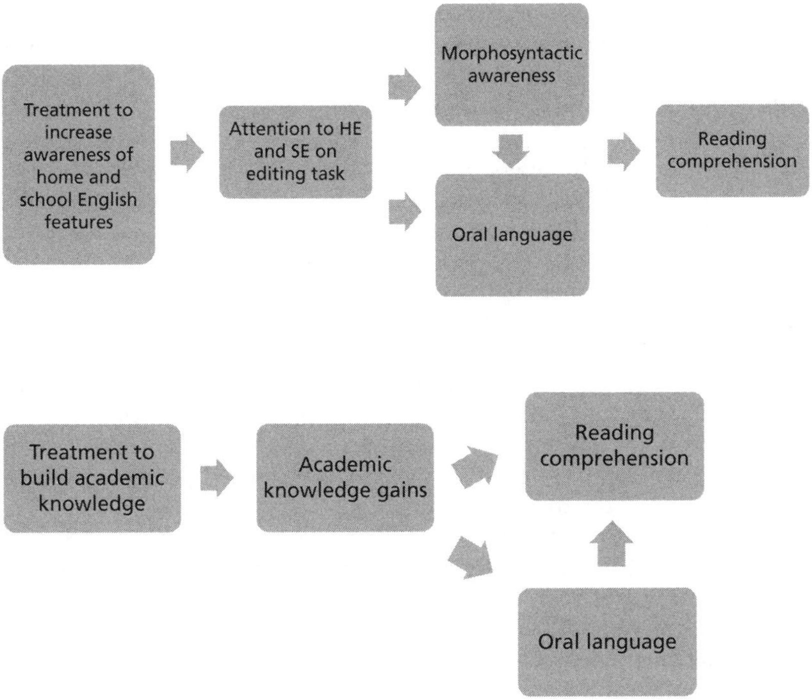


**Figure 18.2.** Theory of change for the Dialect Awareness intervention (top) and the Content Area Literacy intervention (bottom). *Key:* HE, Home English; SE, School English.

second, third, and fourth graders ($n$ = 374) who used at least one feature of NMAE in either an oral or a written task were randomly assigned within classrooms to the Dialect Awareness (DAWS) intervention or a business-as-usual control.

The DAWS intervention focuses on eight different features of NMAE that are found most frequently in written tasks and include such features as optional plural and past tense, optional copula or auxiliaries, and subject-verb agreement. Students met with interventionists in small groups of four or five students 4 days per week for 20–30 minutes/day for 8 weeks. The DAWS intervention directly addressed the idea of dialect shifting by using a formal clothing (what you would wear to a wedding) and informal clothing (what you would wear to play outside with friends) analogy. Instructional activities included Home and School English sentence-sorting tasks where student sort sentences that use Home English into one pile and those that use School English into another (e.g., "He worked hard last week" would go in the School English pile; "You should have check your work" would go in the Home English pile); paragraph completion (e.g., Yesterday I ___ cookies with my mom. We baked two dozen ___…); and writing to a picture prompt. Students were tested before and after the 8-week intervention on an editing task where they were expected to identify features of Home English and change them to School English, the Woodcock-Johnson–Third Edition Picture Vocabulary and Oral Comprehension tests (Woodcock, McGrew, & Mather, 2001), and the Test of Silent Reading Efficiency and Comprehension (TOSREC; Wagner, Torgesen, Rashotte, & Pearson, 2010). There were no differences by condition on any of the preintervention assessments. Results showed that students in the DAWS intervention improved their ability to identify features of Home English in sentences and to revise the sentences so that they utilized School English significantly better than did the students in the control group.

Using structural equation modeling (SEM; Hoyle, 1995), we then tested our theory of change (see Figure 18.2). The SEM results are provided in Figure 18.3. They show that students in the DAWS intervention, compared to the control, were better able to edit Home English sentences to School English on the editing task and that this operated indirectly on reading comprehension through oral language skills as hypothesized. However, dialect shifting also directly affected reading comprehension, which was not anticipated, though it might have been because writing (and reading) represented the context in which School English was expected and was an integral part of the intervention. Model fit was barely adequate, and the overall total direct and indirect effect size on reading comprehension was .28.

## CONTENT AREA LITERACY INSTRUCTION

Children's background and content knowledge are highly associated with their reading comprehension skills (National Institute of Child Health and Human Development [NICHD], 2000). The content area literacy instruction (CALI) intervention was developed to improve students' academic knowledge and their ability to learn from expository text and to ensure that even students with weaker comprehension skills were able to access and learn the content (i.e., take into account child characteristic by instruction interactions; Connor, 2011).

Accumulating research shows clearly that the impact of literacy and content area (e.g., science) instruction depends on the reading, language, and academic knowledge students bring to the learning task (Connor et al., 2013). For example, children with weaker academic knowledge show weaker gains in science learning when they spend more time participating in peer- and child-managed hands-on discovery science activities; yet for students with stronger academic knowledge, the reverse is the case. They are likely to learn more content when they spend more time in such activities. With this in mind, we developed CALI text and materials to be differentiated at three levels: for students with stronger, typical, and weaker reading comprehension skills. The objective was to keep the content to be learned the same for all students but to vary the extent to which learning

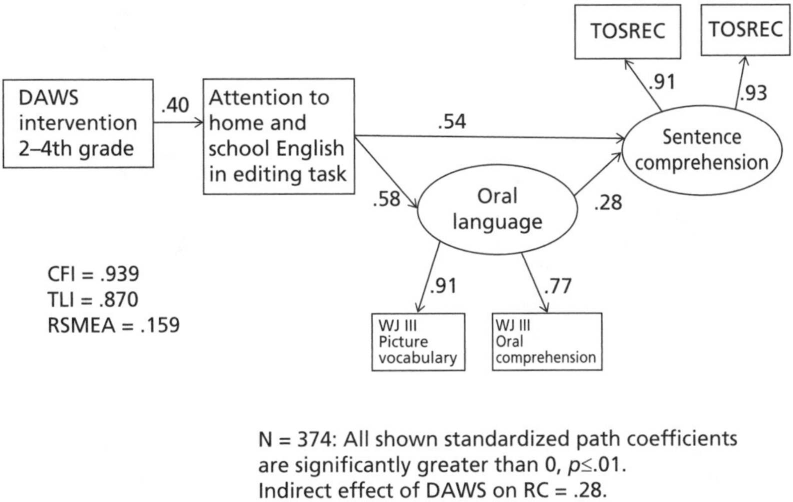


**Figure 18.3.** Structural equation modeling testing the direct and indirect effect of the Dialect Awareness (DAWS) intervention on reading comprehension. The oral language latent variable is comprised of the Woodcock-Johnson–Third Edition (WJ-III) Picture Vocabulary and Oral Language W scores. Sentence Comprehension is the Test of Silent Reading Efficiency (TOSREC).

opportunities were scaffolded (more for students with weaker skills) and to vary the difficulty of the text without removing key concepts (Connor et al., 2010). We selected topics that were less frequently taught by teachers, based on classroom observation (e.g., government and economics), part of the Florida state standards, and were aligned with the Common Core standards. The scripted lessons for each 3-week unit (two in science; two in social studies), which were conducted 4 days/week, 30 minutes per session in small groups of no more than five students, utilized a four-phase framework: *Connect; Clarify; Research; Apply.* During the *Connect* lesson, students were introduced to the content by linking it to familiar experiences. For example, in the economics unit, they brainstormed why Disney World and beaches were good for Florida's economy. In *Clarify* lessons, students read expository text on the topic (e.g., money and price), which included support through a number of comprehension strategies such as graphic organizers. Again, the texts varied in readability but not in key concepts (see Figure 18.4); in the example provided, the text on top is for first graders with stronger reading skills, and the text on the bottom is for those children with weaker reading skills. In *Research* lessons, students worked with original sources (e.g., photos from the time period) during social studies lessons and with science experiments during science lessons that were closely aligned to the unit topic. During the last phase of lessons, *Apply,* students completed a project (e.g., a lemonade stand for economics) that was designed to bring all the lessons together so that students could

## Money and Price

toys

pay

Have you ever wanted to buy a toy? Money is what we use to buy things we want and need. To buy the toy you would have to use money. You need money to buy food and clothes.

The price is what you pay. The price is not the same for all things. Some toys cost a lot of money. Other toys cost less money. To buy a ball the price would be less. To buy a car the price would be more.

## Money and Price

toys

pay

Do you like toys? Toys cost money. Money buys us things we want. We use money to pay for other things like food.

The price is what you pay. The price of cars is big. The price of a ball is small.

**Figure 18.4.** First-grade text for the economics unit with text written for students with stronger reading skills (top) and weaker skills (bottom).

integrate and apply the knowledge they had gained. For all the lessons, there were different sets of materials for students with stronger, typical, and weaker reading skills (three levels in all). Before and after the 12 weeks of lessons, students were assessed on academic knowledge, oral language, and reading, including the assessments described earlier for the DAWS intervention. The content knowledge assessments included multiple-choice and open-ended questions.

Results revealed that kindergarten through fourth grade students who participated in the CALI intervention showed significantly stronger content knowledge compared to students in the randomized untreated control group (Connor et al., in preparation); there were no differences in knowledge prior to the intervention. Effect sizes (*d*) ranged from 0.9 in kindergarten to almost 3.0 in fourth grade. Moreover, gains were not significantly different when comparing students with weaker reading and vocabulary scores with students who had stronger scores.

To test our hypothesis that CALI would affect reading comprehension directly and indirectly through oral language, SEM was conducted including only students in second through fourth grade (the same grades as the DAWS). Results are provided in Figure 18.5; there was adequate model fit. Using the same assessments as in the DAWS model, the findings do not support the hypothesis and reveal a direct effect on reading comprehension but no effect on oral language (i.e., no indirect effect), although oral language did directly affect reading comprehension. The model fit was adequate, and the total effect was 0.61.

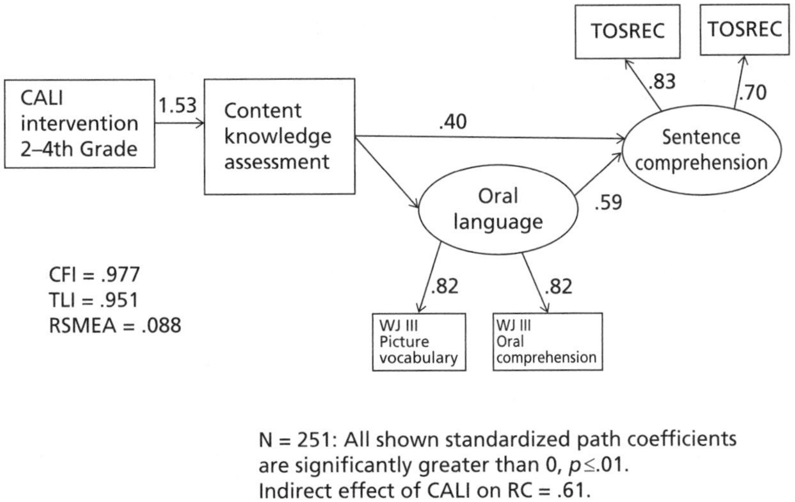


**Figure 18.5.** Direct and indirect effects of the Content Area Literacy Instruction (CALI) intervention on reading comprehension. The oral language latent variable is comprised of the Woodcock-Johnson–Third Edition (WJ-III) Picture Vocabulary and Oral Language W scores. Sentence Comprehension is the Test of Silent Reading Efficiency (TOSREC) raw scores.

## DISCUSSION

The hypotheses were supported, but only partially. The DAWS intervention did affect reading comprehension indirectly, as anticipated, but it also directly affected reading comprehension. This might have been because writing was used as the context in which School English was expected, and there is evidence that writing can support reading comprehension development (Graham, 2006). The CALI intervention did directly affect reading comprehension but did not affect it indirectly through oral language skills. In the latent profile analysis, academic knowledge clustered with all the language variables; therefore, a direct effect on oral language was anticipated. At the same time, the total effect on reading comprehension was fairly large (0.61) and more than twice as large as the effect of the DAWS intervention (0.28). Results of these two studies have a number of implications for both theory and practice, but more research is needed.

Successful dialect shifting, a largely under-the-hood process, positively predicted stronger reading comprehension, which suggests that even primary abilities are somewhat malleable. It appears that by bringing these under-the-hood processes to conscious awareness through explicit instruction, students can begin to use this awareness to achieve stronger oral language and reading comprehension.

Academic knowledge should arguably be more malleable than dialect awareness, and the correlational evidence suggests that improving academic knowledge should improve reading comprehension (Cromley & Azevedo, 2007). Human beings have adapted to learn all kinds of things (Geary, 2005). It may be that the secondary, reflective, and more malleable systems, such as knowledge acquisition, may be better targets for intervention than the under-the-hood processes. Keeping in mind that CALI was specifically differentiated to support learning for students with weak reading skills, including students with dyslexia, such interventions may help support the development of compensatory mechanisms for children with dyslexia. For example, multiple exposures to the content across the four phases may have allowed the study participants to compensate for their weak decoding skill by strengthening their knowledge of the topic.

At the same time, CALI did not affect students' oral language skills as anticipated. This result was hypothesized based on the results of the latent class analysis where academic knowledge was part of the oral language construct. It is possible that the language measures used may not have been sensitive to the changes in academic knowledge taught. However, it is also possible that intervening to build students' academic knowledge may have little or no effect on such aspects of the language system as lexical knowledge and semantics, which are considered under-the-hood processes and so likely to be less malleable. There are a number of studies that suggest that vocabulary interventions, for example, support reading comprehension without actually improving general vocabulary (Elleman et al., 2009).

The purpose of this chapter was to show how intervention studies can be used to inform both practice and theory about reading comprehension, thus helping us better understand why some children continue to struggle to comprehend even when provided with intensive interventions. Overall, the reviewed studies indicate that all children can learn when instruction is designed to accommodate their skills and weaknesses; that under-the-hood processes can be effective targets of intervention that help to improve comprehension; that building content knowledge can support comprehension; and that by testing theories using interventions studies, we can better understand how children learn to read and comprehend all kinds of texts.

## REFERENCES

Cain, K., Oakhill, J., & Bryant, P. (2004). Children's reading comprehension ability: Concurrent prediction by working memory, verbal ability, and component skills. *Journal of Educational Psychology, 96*(1), 31–42.

Charity, A.H., Scarborough, H.S., & Griffin, D. (2004). Familiarity with "School English" in African-American children and its relation to early reading achievement. *Child Development, 75,* 1340–1356.

Connor, C.M. (2011). Child by Instruction interactions: Language and literacy connections. In S.B. Neuman & D.K. Dickinson (Eds.), *Handbook on early literacy* (3rd ed., pp. 256–275). New York, NY: Guilford Press.

Connor, C.M., Kaya, S., Luck, M., Toste, J., Canto, A., Rice, D.C., … Underwood, P. (2010). Content-area literacy: Individualizing student instruction in second grade science. *Reading Teacher, 63*(6), 474–485.

Connor, C.M., Morrison, F.J., Fishman, B., Giuliani, S., Luck, M., Underwood, P., … Schatschneider, C. (2011). Classroom instruction, child X instruction interactions and the impact of differentiating student instruction on third graders' reading comprehension. *Reading Research Quarterly, 46*(3), 189–221.

Connor, C.M., Rice, D.C., Canto, A., Southerland, S.A., Underwood, P., Kaya, S., … Morrison, F.J. (2013). Child characteristics by science instruction interactions in second and third grade and their relation to students' content-area knowledge, vocabulary, and reading skill gains. *Elementary School Journal,* 113, 52–75.

Cromley, J.G., & Azevedo, R. (2007). Testing and refining the direct and inferential mediation (DIME) model of reading comprehension. *Journal of Educational Psychology, 99*(2), 311–325.

Elleman, A.M., Lindo, E.J., Morphy, P., & Compton, D.L. (2009). The impact of vocabulary instruction on passage-level comprehension of school-age children: A meta-analysis. *Journal of Research on Educational Effectiveness, 2*(1), 1–44.

Geary, D.C. (2005). *Folk knowledge and academic learning origins of the social mind: Evolutionary psychology and child development.* New York, NY: Guilford Press.

Geary, D.C. (2007). An evolutionary perspective on learning disability in mathematics. *Developmental Neuropsychology, 32*(1), 471–519. doi:10.1037/0033-2909.131.1.30

Graham, S. (2006). Strategy instruction and the teaching of writing: A meta-analysis. In C. MacArthur, S. Graham, & J. Fitzgerald (Eds.), *Handbook of writing research* (pp. 187–207). Mahwah, NJ: Erlbaum.

Hoover, W.A., & Gough, P.B. (1990). The simple view of reading. *Reading and Writing, 2*(2), 127–160.

Hoyle, R.H. (Ed.). (1995). *Structural equation modeling: Concepts, issues, and applications.* Thousand Oaks, CA: Sage.

Lonigan, C.J., Schatschneider, C., & Connor, C.M. (2012). Predicting reading comprehension: Constructs of language and decoding (working title). Presented at the Reading for Understanding Network meeting, October 2012, Washington, DC.

Meyer, S. (2005). *Twilight.* New York, NY: Little, Brown.

National Assessment Governing Board. (2007). *Reading framework for the 2007 National Assessment of Educational Progress.* Washington, DC: U.S. Department of Education.

National Institute of Child Health and Human Development (NICHD). (2000). *Report of the National Reading Panel. Teaching children to read: An evidence-based assessment of the scientific research literature on reading and its implications for reading instruction* (NIH Publication No. 00-4754). Washington, DC: U.S. Government Printing Office.

Perfetti, C.A. (2008). *Reading comprehension: A conceptual framework from word meaning to text meaning.* Paper presented at the conference on Assessing Reading in the 21st Century, Philadelphia, PA.

Pressley, M., Wharton-McDonald, R., Allington, R., Block, C.C., Morrow, L., Tracey, D., … Crenin, J. (2001). A study of effective first-grade literacy instruction. *Scientific Studies of Reading, 5*(1), 35–58.

Rapp, D.N., & van den Broek, P. (2005). Dynamic text comprehension: An integrative view of reading. *Current Directions in Psychological Science, 14*(5), 276–279.

Rowling, J.K. (1997). *Harry Potter and the sorcerer's stone.* New York, NY: Scholastic Press.

Schatschneider, C., Lonigan, C.J., & Petscher, Y. (2012). Quantile dominance analyses (working title). Presented at the Reading for Understanding Network meeting, October 2012, Washington, DC.

Snow, C.E., Porche, M.V., Tabors, P.O., & Harris, K.R. (2007). *Is literacy enough? Pathways to academic success for adolescents.* Baltimore, MD: Paul H. Brookes Publishing Co.

Terry, N.P., Connor, C.M., Petscher, Y., & Conlin, C.A. (2012). Dialect variation and reading: Is change in nonmainstream American English use related to reading achievement in first and second grade? *Journal of Speech, Language, and Hearing Research, 55*(1), 55–69.

Terry, N.P., Connor, C.M., Thomas-Tate, S., & Love, M. (2010). Examining relations among dialect variation, literacy skills, and school context in first grade. *Journal of Speech, Language, and Hearing Research, 53,* 126–145.

Thomas-Tate, S., Connor, C.M., Johnson, L., & Patton-Terry, N. (2013). Evaluating the effect of dialect awareness training: Results of an experiment with second through fourth grade students. Manuscript in preparation.

Wagner, R.K., Torgesen, J.K., Rashotte, C.A., & Pearson, N.A. (2010). *TOSREC: Test of silent reading efficiency and comprehension.* Austin, TX: Pro-Ed.

Woodcock, R.W., McGrew, K.S., & Mather, N. (2001). *Woodcock-Johnson III tests of achievement.* Itasca, IL: Riverside.

CHAPTER 19

# Why Intensive Interventions Are Necessary for Adolescents with Dyslexia

## Findings from 3-Year Intervention and Future Research

Sharon Vaughn and Michael Solis

In this chapter, through a review of data trends according to national testing results from the past 20 years, we present a rationale for providing intensive reading interventions to secondary students with dyslexia (persistent reading disabilities). We describe findings from a response to intervention model in secondary schools and provide a summary of a large-scale longitudinal research study examining reading interventions for adolescent students with severe reading difficulties. We conclude with considerations of ways to further intensify reading interventions.

Students with dyslexia, or reading disabilities, are frequently provided appropriate remediation through special programs. For many of these students, this remediation entails identification and service provided through special education. In 1996, John Merrow spent the better part of a year exploring special education to prepare a PBS documentary to address the question, What is special about special education? The many school and classroom observations, interviews with key personnel, and reviews of reports led to considerable support for the conclusion that there was not enough special about special education. Sixteen years later, members of the education community have similar concerns. Whether or not we have adequately provided robust, responsive, and data-based instruction to all students with reading disabilities remains a concern. Beyond access to the general education curriculum, students with reading disabilities need the opportunity to acquire knowledge and skills to understand and apply the meaning of text to what is being taught. That is, students with reading difficulties will continue to need access to intensive interventions in order to develop reading comprehension skills that prepare them to understand and learn from text. A review of data trends during the last 20 years underscores the need to further examine opportunities to improve reading interventions for students with dyslexia.

## TRENDS FROM NATIONAL DATA FOR STUDENTS WITH DISABILITIES

Recent data from the National Assessment of Educational Progress (NAEP; http://www.naepnet.org) provides information about the current state of education for students with disabilities. In 2011, only 46% of students identified with disabilities had completed secondary school with a regular high school diploma compared to 75% in the total population. The average reading scores for fourth graders with disabilities were lower in 2011 than 2009. For eighth graders with disabilities, average reading scores were no higher in 2011 than 2009, although average reading scores increased for students without disabilities.

As noted, although the number of students with disabilities accessing the general education classroom for the majority of the day is on the increase, the percentage of students with disabilities making gains on the NAEP reading test is on the decline. More specifically, in 2011, 68% of fourth-grade and 62% of eighth-grade students with disabilities scored below a basic proficiency level in reading. In that same year, only 29% of fourth-grade and 20% of eighth-grade students without disabilities scored below basic on the NAEP reading test. A comparison of these data raises questions about whether the instruction provided through current educational programming is sufficiently robust to promote access to reading interventions for students with reading disabilities. However, there is empirical evidence that students with reading disabilities respond to intensive and targeted reading interventions (Edmonds et al., 2009; Scammacca et al., 2007; Solis et al., 2012) and initial evidence that this is particularly the case if the interventions are extensive and take place for an extended duration (Vaughn et al., 2008).

## RESPONSE TO INTERVENTION FRAMEWORK IN SECONDARY SCHOOLS

As a result of a promising body of research on response to intervention (RTI) with primarily elementary grade students (Fuchs & Fuchs, 1998; Vaughn, Linan-Thompson, & Hickman, 2003), RTI has been considered a viable means of providing interventions to prevent reading difficulties (Fletcher & Vaughn, 2009; Vaughn & Fuchs, 2003). Through recent studies (Denton et al., 2011; Vaughn et al., 2008; Vaughn, Cirino, et al., 2010; Vaughn, Wexler, Leroux, et al., 2011), we have identified ways in which RTI is fundamentally different in secondary schools compared to elementary schools for the identification and screening process and for the tiers of intervention.

Whereas at the elementary school level a criterion-referenced test is administered to all students at the beginning of the school year, at the secondary level, universal screening can be accomplished through extant data sources (e.g., criterion-referenced tests, diagnostic tests, and high-stakes state reading tests). Some scrutiny of the extant data may be used to establish the level of performance to determine which students are at risk of reading failure at the secondary level (Vaughn & Fletcher, 2010). Then, the use of brief follow-up assessments (i.e., a reading fluency measure) can be used to identify specific reading difficulties with more detail. At the elementary grades, assignments to tiers are made to be more or less intensive based on response to progress monitoring. The uses of tiers for secondary students works differently; we can distinguish more from less impaired students and assign interventions based on their diagnostic academic profile (e.g., word reading and comprehension). In summary, RTI models used in secondary schools differ from RtI models used in elementary schools for several fundamental reasons: 1) Remediation is the focus in secondary grades, whereas prevention is the focus in elementary grades; 2) secondary level students at-risk for reading have reading problems known from past data sources, whereas the early identification of at-risk students early and prevention are the foci at the elementary grades; 3) at the secondary level, the intervention needs can be more reliably defined; and 4) there is evidence to suggest that secondary students with severe reading difficulties can be assigned to less intensive or more intensive interventions based on their current reading achievement (Fuchs et al., 2010).

## INTENSIVE READING INTERVENTIONS FOR MIDDLE SCHOOL STUDENTS WITH DYSLEXIA

Through funding from the *Eunice Kennedy Shriver* National Institute of Child Health and Human Development (NICHD) and as part of a large-scale implementation of a response to intervention (RtI) model in middle school, we conducted a 3-year study of interventions with secondary students with reading difficulties (Vaughn, Wanzek, et al., 2010; Vaughn, Wexler, Leroux, et al., 2011; Vaughn, Wexler, Roberts, et al., 2011). The RtI approach is an instructional delivery model designed to provide interventions to students who demonstrate low performance and inadequate response to research-based instruction (Vaughn & Fuchs, 2003). The essential components of RtI include initial screening of all students, schoolwide multitiered interventions of increasing intensity, progress monitoring, and data-based decision making to determine movement across the different tiers of interventions (Pyle & Vaughn, 2012). For additional information on this project, please review the primary efficacy papers located on the Texas Center for Learning Disabilities web site (http://www.texasldcenter.org).

### Screening Procedures

The reading comprehension measure of the Texas Assessment of Knowledge and Skills (TAKS) served as the screening measure to identify struggling readers. Students who did not pass TAKS (or scored within one standard error) were defined as struggling readers. Additional measures, including a fluency measure, followed the TAKS screening to further discern the specific nature of the reading problems for each student.

## Multitiered Interventions

All content area teachers received a total of 6 hours of professional development, monthly meetings, and voluntary in-class coaching as part of the Tier 1 research-based classroom instruction. The focus of the professional development and additional supports was to enhance teachers' knowledge of vocabulary and comprehension strategies and to integrate these practices within each content class (including science, social studies, math, and English or language arts).

Based on preestablished screening criteria, students identified as struggling readers were randomly assigned to a treatment condition or a comparison condition as part of a Tier 2 intervention. The Tier 2 intervention was provided by staff hired, trained, and supervised by researchers; intervention took place during a 50-minute elective class with groups of 10 to 15 students. The instruction was organized into three phases, which included instruction in all components of reading but placed emphasis on particular components. Phase I primarily focused on word study and fluency, Phase II emphasized vocabulary and comprehension, and Phase III emphasized the use of reading strategies with expository text. After 1 year of Tier 2 intervention, students who had not responded (based on a failing score on the *TAKS measure* or a standard score of less than 90 on the *Woodcock-Johnson–Third Edition Letter–Word Identification assessment* or the *GRADE Comprehension Composite* at posttest) were defined as "minimal responders." These minimal responders were then randomly assigned to receive either an individualized treatment or a standardized treatment during the following school year as part of a Tier 3 intervention. The individualized treatment provided instructors with flexibility to design and customize instruction to meet individual students' needs based on interpretation of progress monitoring and diagnostic data. The standardized Tier 3 treatment followed a standard protocol instructional approach. Both the individualized and standardized treatments were taught by the same teachers (different sections) in group sizes of approximately 4–5 students per teacher.

Students in the treatment condition (either standardized or individualized) who were minimal responders (based on criteria of continued TAKS failure), received an additional year-long intervention during Year 3, in smaller instructional groups (2 to 4 students), as part of an individualized, intensive Tier 4 intervention. Students in the comparison condition identified as minimal responders by the same criteria continued in the comparison condition for the third year. Tier 4 consisted of instructional lessons focused on students' individual needs in phonics, word reading, fluency, vocabulary, and comprehension. Teachers were trained to use biweekly progress monitoring data to adjust instruction to meet students' needs. Teachers also addressed student motivation on a regular basis by presenting opportunities for students to select text, establish learning goals, and have their parents receive positive phone calls about their participation.

## WHY INTENSIVE INTERVENTIONS ARE NECESSARY

We set out to answer a series of research questions for each of the 3 years the study was conducted. For a summary of research questions and findings, see Table 19.1. During Year 3, a compelling finding was that middle school students with significant reading disabilities who *did not* receive interventions showed substantial declines in their reading performance, whereas students receiving interventions maintained reading achievement

**Table 19.1.** Overview of findings from study of intensive interventions with secondary students

| Year | Research question(s) | Finding |
|---|---|---|
| 1 | 1. What are the relative effects of a secondary intervention (Tier 2) provided in relatively large groups (10–15 students) on the reading-related outcomes of individuals with reading difficulties? | Small effects (median $d = 0.16$) in favor of treatment students on measures of decoding, fluency, and comprehension. |
| | 2. Do students who are assigned to small-group ($n = 5$ students) instruction outperform students in large-group ($n = 10$ students) instruction? | No statistically significant differences between students in small-group and large-group instruction. |
| 2 | 1. What are the relative effects of a tertiary intervention (Tier 3) provided in an individualized versus a standardized approach in groups of five students on reading-related outcomes of individuals with reading difficulties? | No statistically significant differences between students participating in the standardized or the individualized treatment. |
| | 2. What are the relative effects of a tertiary intervention (Tier 3) provided in groups of two to four students on the reading-related outcomes of individuals with reading difficulties? | Statistically significant differences favoring students in the treatment condition on a reading comprehension measure. |
| 3 | What are the effects of an intensive, individualized intervention (Tier 4) provided in groups of two to four students on the reading outcomes of students with significant reading difficulties who had demonstrated very low growth in 2 years on previous small-group reading intervention, relative to low-growth students in a comparison condition, who received whatever instruction was typically provided to low-performing readers in their schools? | Large effects found in favor of the treatments students found on reading comprehension ($ES = 1.20$) and medium effects found on word identification ($ES = 0.49$), although treatment students continued to fall below grade-level proficiency. |

*Note*: Research questions and findings cited in Vaughn, Cirino et al., 2010; Vaughn, Wexler, Leroux et al., 2011; and Vaughn, Wexler, Roberts et al., 2011.

at levels commensurate with their peers and did not experience decline in performance. By intervention students' maintaining their initial reading achievement, there was no acceleration in performance; thus when compared to typically achieving peers, intervention treatment students did not close the gap of performance. By Year 3, we reported medium and large effects for word reading (*ES* = 0.49) and comprehension (*ES* = 1.20) in favor of the treatment students.

This finding is of major importance to policy makers, practitioners, and researchers and provides a strong rationale for remediating secondary students with reading difficulties. Struggling readers in the secondary grades need different levels of intensity of instruction in all reading components: word study, fluency, vocabulary, and comprehension. This large-scale RtI study clearly indicates the need for intensive evidence-based interventions as a part of instructional programming for secondary students with reading difficulties to prevent further decline in performance. Multiyear interventions and an increase in research-based strategies across general education instruction should be considered. Further work is needed to explore methods for improving and intensifying interventions for secondary students with reading difficulties.

## INTERVENTIONS FOR ADOLESCENTS WITH DYSLEXIA AND READING DISABILITIES

As we refine and further develop interventions, one objective is to better understand how to improve curricula and instruction to intensify treatments for students with dyslexia and reading disabilities. This can be done through a focus on two areas: 1) integrating strategies that support cognitive processes (e.g., memory, self-regulation) within reading instruction in order to align learners' need with reading progress and 2) making instruction explicit and systematic.

### Integrating Strategies that Support Cognitive Processes

Early research on executive functions and self-regulation examined processing problems based on the neurological models of learning of individuals with brain injuries (Johnson & Myklebust, 1967; Kirk & Kirk, 1971). One underlying assumption of this early work was that students with learning disabilities had cognitive processing problems similar to individuals who suffered brain trauma. A second assumption was that treatment of underlying cognitive processing problems was not only possible but also essential prior to academic learning. Although some students with learning disabilities have cognitive processing problems, and we do not dispute the potential importance of many of these cognitive processes, the current base of research does *not* support the practice of identifying processing problems (e.g., auditory processing) and treating them separately from and in isolation of academic learning (e.g., training auditory processing apart from academic learning for students; Lyon, 1985; Mann, 1979). Furthermore, specifically identifying these problem processes reliably has continued to be challenging.

Unlike this earlier research, however, the current research on cognitive processing, including executive functions and self-regulation, has improved educators' understanding of learning in two important ways. First, current understanding of executive functions and self-regulation is grounded in theoretical frameworks supported by a robust empirical base (e.g., Pintrich, 1995). Second, conceptualization of these constructs has been integrated as a part of academic instruction rather than taught in isolation prior to academic learning.

Some students with difficulties in reading demonstrate difficulties with cognitive processing that impair their reading performance. These difficulties include such executive functions as self-regulation, memory, attention, and strategy selection and use. These constructs, often conceptualized as "control processes" that influence goal direction for learning, integrate with other cognitive and behavioral processes, including language, short-term memory, processing speed, and nonverbal reasoning. We focus our discussion of cognitive processing difficulties on executive functions and self-regulation based on a growing research base that associates executive functions with learning in reading (Booth, Boyle, & Kelly, 2010; Locascio, Mahone, Eason, & Cutting, 2010) and with general academic outcomes (Barnett et al., 2008; Blair & Razza, 2007: Diamond, Barnett, Thomas, & Munro, 2007).

Difficulties with students' poor executive functioning and self-regulation abilities can be observed in how well they set learning goals, monitor success in goal acquisition, use language to self-talk through difficult tasks, and regulate language and memory to promote learning. For example, a recent study (Pike, Barnes, & Barron, 2010) revealed that a student's working memory serves as a predictor of the individual's ability to make inferences from short and long portions of text. Working memory and inferencing ability each make unique contributions to reading comprehension performance. Students with reading difficulties often have problems with all memory tasks; such pervasive memory problems are associated with poor performance in both basic reading skills (e.g., phonological awareness, word reading) and reading comprehension (Swanson, Zheng, & Jerman, 2009). Previous studies indicate that students who have difficulty regulating their thinking and behavior consistently demonstrate lower academic learning and cognitive and motivational processes (Dembo & Eaton, 2000; Krouse & Krouse, 1981). In addition, students who improve self-regulatory skills show gains in academic achievement and increased self-efficacy (Zimmerman, Bonner, & Kavach, 1996; Zimmerman & Risemberg, 1997).

Attribution, an individual's beliefs about the causes of his or her failures and successes, is highly relevant to self-regulation. A student with maladaptive attribution may believe that failure is a result of fixed, internal causes that cannot be altered and that success is a result of such unexplainable causes as luck or chance. Robertson (2000) reviewed 20 studies that indicated that accurate attribution is associated with small to moderate improvements in outcomes for students with learning difficulties. In studies designed specifically to improve reading comprehension by providing attribution training (the connection between effort and learning outcomes), small benefits were reported (Berkeley, Mastropieri, & Scruggs, 2011; Chan, 1996). Yet if attribution training is not included as part of instructional practices, students may experience low motivation to perform well academically (Fulk & Mastropieri, 1990). In summary, for students with significant learning difficulties, many of whom are prone to maladaptive attribution styles, integrating attribution training within reading interventions seems promising.

## Explicit and Systematic Instruction

A meta-analysis of intervention studies conducted by Swanson, Hoskyn, and Lee (1999) concluded that interventions delivered through a combination of direct instruction and strategy instruction yielded the highest effects. Key components of these interventions included explicit instruction, systematic instruction, and opportunities for student response and feedback. Explicit instruction means clearly teaching the steps or processes necessary to comprehend a concept, apply a strategy, or complete a task. Teachers start by presenting new information through teacher modeling, demonstrations, and step-by-step instructions of what is expected of students in the learning task. This is followed by opportunities for students to practice the new material with feedback provided by the teacher after each step of the learning task. It is essential that teacher feedback relate to the specific learning task and that the teacher provide opportunities for students to discuss and deepen their understanding of the concepts. Finally, students are given opportunities to practice and apply the material independently. Research on interventions incorporating explicit instruction for students with learning difficulties has shown improved outcomes for both basic skills and higher-level concepts (Biancarosa & Snow, 2004; NICHD, 2000; Swanson, 2000).

Research findings on interventions incorporating systematic instruction for students with learning difficulties have shown improved learning outcomes (Coyne, Kame'enui, & Simmons, 2001; Swanson, 2000; Torgesen, 2002). Systematic instruction refers to breaking down complex tasks into smaller "chunks" or discrete pieces of information that are more manageable and effective; this approach requires careful consideration of how these discrete skills relate to the overall learning goal. Through sequencing discrete chunks of information from easier to more difficult, systematic instruction utilizes scaffolds and temporary supports to manage the level of difficulty throughout the learning process. Complex learning tasks are broken down into multiple steps or processes with discrete skills taught to mastery before bringing together the entire learning process. Systematic phonics instruction, progressing from smaller to larger units and sequenced from easier to more difficult sounds and words was more effective in increasing word reading than was less systematic instruction (NICHD, 2000). Interventions that combine explicit and systematic instruction yield the highest outcomes across content areas (Fletcher, Lyon, Fuchs, & Barnes, 2007; Swanson et al., 1999).

As we continue to develop and refine interventions for adolescents with dyslexia and reading difficulties, we recognize the importance of providing opportunities for students to have consistent practice reading and responding to text. Cunningham and Stanovich (1998) reported a not surprising connection between students' reading percentile and the number of words read: Students who read considerably more are likely to be better readers. This provides a message for what educators can do to support improved reading. Students with difficulties need extensive opportunities to practice independently reading text of an appropriate difficulty level and to practice reading more challenging text but with additional supports provided by teachers. For students in middle school and beyond, compared to the elementary grades, both the complexity and quantity of text must be taken into account. Students who enter the middle school grades with severe reading difficulties have struggled with text requirements for many years; these struggles may decrease the likelihood that students develop adequate habits in the use of text evidence to support learning. While we acknowledge the need for effective instruction as a key component of intensive interventions, we also note that the opportunities for students to work with and grapple with more complex text for longer portions of time over the duration of interventions must be considered.

## REFERENCES

Barnett, W.S., Jung, K., Yarosz, D.J., Thomas, J., Hornbeck, A., Stechuk, R., & Burns, S. (2008). Educational effects of the Tools of the Mind curriculum: A randomized trial. *Early Childhood Research Quarterly, 23*(3), 299–313. doi:10.1016/j.ecresq.2008.03.001

Berkeley, S., Mastropieri, M.A., & Scruggs, T.E. (2011). Reading comprehension strategy instruction and attribution retraining for secondary students with learning and other mild disabilities. *Journal of Learning Disabilities, 44*(1), 18–32. doi:10.1177/0022219410371677

Biancarosa, G., & Snow, C.E. (2004). *Reading next—A vision for action and research in middle and high school literacy: A report to Carnegie Corporation of New York.* Washington, DC: Alliance for Excellence in Education.

Blair, C., & Razza, R.P. (2007). Relating effortful control, executive function, and false belief understanding to emerging math and literacy ability in kindergarten. *Child Development, 78*(2), 647–663. doi:10.1111/j.1467-8624.2007.01019.x

Booth, J.N., Boyle, J.M., & Kelly, S.W. (2010). Do tasks make a difference? Accounting for heterogeneity of performance of children with reading difficulties on tasks of executive function: Findings from a meta-analysis. *British Journal of Developmental Psychology, 28*(1), 133–176. doi:10.1348/026151009X485432

Chan, L.S. (1996). Combined strategy and attributional training for seventh grade average and poor readers. *Journal of Research in Reading, 19*(2), 111–127. doi:10.1111/j.1467- 9817.1996.tb00092.x

Coyne, M.D., Kame'enui, E.J., & Simmons, D.C. (2001). Prevention and intervention in beginning reading: Two complex systems. *Learning Disabilities Research and Practice, 16*(2), 62–73. doi:10.1111/0938-8982.00008

Cunningham, A.E., &, Stanovich, K.E. (1998). What reading does for the mind. *American Educator, 22*, 8–15.

Dembo, M.H., & Eaton, M.J. (2000). Self-regulation of academic learning in middle-level schools. *Elementary School Journal, 100*(5), 473–490. doi:10.1086/499651

Denton, C.A., Cirino, P.T., Barth, A.E., Romain, M., Vaughn, S., Wexler, J., … Fletcher, J.M. (2011). An experimental study of scheduling and duration of "Tier 2" first-grade reading intervention. *Journal of Research on Educational Effectiveness, 4*(3), 208–230. doi:10.1080/19345747.2010.530127

Diamond, A., Barnett, W.S., Thomas, J., & Munro, S. (2007). The early years: Preschool program improves cognitive control. *Science, 318*(5855), 1387–1388. doi:10.1126/science.1151148

Edmonds, M.S., Vaughn, S., Wexler, J., Reutebuch, C., Cable, A., Tackett, K.K., & Schnakenberg, J.W. (2009). A synthesis of reading interventions and effects on reading comprehension outcomes for older struggling readers. *Review of Educational Research, 79*(1), 262–300. doi: 10.3102/0034654308325998

Fletcher, J.M., Lyon, G.R., Fuchs, L.S., & Barnes, M.A. (2007). *Learning disabilities: From identification to intervention*. New York, NY: Guilford Press.

Fletcher, J.M., & Vaughn, S. (2009). Response to intervention: Preventing and remediating academic difficulties. *Child Development Perspectives, 3*(1), 30–37. doi:10.1111/j.1750- 8606.2008.00072.x

Fuchs, L.S., & Fuchs, D. (1998). Treatment validity: A unifying concept for reconceptualizing the identification of learning disabilities. *Learning Disabilities Research & Practice, 13*, 204–219.

Fuchs, L., Geary, D.C., Compton, D.L., Fuchs, D., Hamlett, C.L., Seethaler, P.M., … Schatschneider, C. (2010). Do different types of school mathematics development depend on different constellations of numerical versus general cognitive abilities? *Developmental Psychology, 46*(6), 1731–1746. doi:10.1037/a0020662

Fulk, B., & Mastropieri, M.A. (1990). Training positive attitudes: "I tried hard and did well!" *Intervention in School and Clinic, 26*(2), 79–83.

Johnson, D.J., & Myklebust, H.R. (1967). *Learning disabilities: Educational principles and practice*. New York, NY: Grune & Stratton.

Kirk, S.A., & Kirk, W.D. (1971). *Psycholinguistic learning disabilities: Diagnosis and remediation*. Urbana: University of Illinois Press.

Krouse, J.H., & Krouse, H.J. (1981). Toward a multimodal theory of academic achievement. *Educational Psychologist, 16*(3), 151–164. doi:10.1080/00461528109529237

Locascio, G., Mahone, E.M., Eason, S.H., & Cutting, L.E. (2010). Executive dysfunction among children with reading comprehension deficits. *Journal of Learning Disabilities, 43*(5), 441–454. doi:10.1177/0022219409355476

Lyon, G.R. (1985). Neuropsychology and learning disabilities. *Neurology and Neurosurgery, 5*, 1–8.

Mann, L. (1979). *On the trail of process*. New York, NY: Grune & Stratton.

Merrow, J. (1996). What's so special about special education? Documentary developed by the Public Broadcasting Service.

National Institute of Child Health and Human Development (NICHD). (2000). *Report of the National Reading Panel. Teaching children to read: An evidence-based assessment of the scientific research literature on reading and its implications for reading instruction* (NIH Publication No. 00-4754). Washington, DC: U.S. Government Printing Office.

Pike, M.M., Barnes, M.A., & Barron, R.W. (2010). The role of illustrations in children's inferential comprehension. *Journal of Experimental Child Psychology, 105*(3), 243–255. doi:10.1016/j.jecp.2009.10.006

Pintrich, P.R. (1995). Understanding self-regulated learning. *New Directions for Teaching and Learning, 63*(3), 3–12. doi:10.1002/tl.37219956304

Pyle, N., & Vaughn, S. (2012). Remediating reading difficulties in a response to intervention model with secondary students. *Psychology in the Schools, 49*(3), 273–284. doi:10.1002/pits.21593

Robertson, J.S. (2000). Is attribution theory a worthwhile classroom intervention for K–12 students with learning difficulties? *Educational Psychology Review, 12*(1), 111–134.

Scammacca, N., Roberts, G., Vaughn, S., Edmonds, M., Wexler, J., Reutebuch, C.K., … Torgesen, J.K. (2007). *Interventions for adolescent struggling readers: A meta-analysis with implications for practice.* Portsmouth, NH: RMC Research Corporation, Center on Instruction.

Solis, M., Ciullo, S., Vaughn, S., Pyle, N., Hassaram, B., & Leroux, A. (2012). Reading comprehension interventions for middle school students with learning disabilities: A synthesis of 30 years of research. *Journal of Learning Disabilities, 45*(4), 327–340.

Swanson, H.L. (2000). What instruction works for students with learning disabilities? Summarizing the results from a meta-analysis of intervention studies. In R.M. Gersten, E.P. Schiller, & S. Vaughn (Eds.), *Contemporary special education research: Syntheses of the knowledge base on critical instructional issues* (pp. 1–30). Mahwah, NJ: Erlbaum.

Swanson, H.L., Hoskyn, M., & Lee, C. (1999). *Intervention for students with learning disabilities: A meta-analysis of treatment outcomes.* New York, NY: Guilford Press.

Swanson, H., Zheng, X., & Jerman, O. (2009). Working memory, short-term memory, and reading disabilities: A selective meta-analysis of the literature. *Journal of Learning Disabilities, 42*(3), 260–287. doi:10.1177/0022219409331958

Torgesen, J.K. (2002). The prevention of reading difficulties. *Journal of School Psychology, 40*(1), 7–26. doi:10.1016/S0022-4405(01)00092-9

Vaughn, S., Cirino, P.T., Wanzek, J., Wexler, J., Fletcher, J.M., Denton, C.A., … Francis, D.J. (2010). Response to intervention for middle school students with reading difficulties: Effects of a primary and secondary intervention. *School Psychology Review, 39*(1), 3–21.

Vaughn, S., & Fletcher, J.M. (2010). Thoughts on rethinking RTI with secondary students. *School Psychology Review, 39*(2), 296–299.

Vaughn, S., Fletcher, J.M., Francis, D.J., Denton, C.A., Wanzek, J., Wexler, J., … Romain, M.A. (2008). Response to intervention with older students with reading difficulties. *Learning and Individual Differences, 18*(3), 338–345. doi:10.1016/j.lindif.2008.05.001

Vaughn, S., & Fuchs, L.S. (2003). Redefining learning disabilities as inadequate response to instruction: The promise and potential problems. *Learning Disabilities Research & Practice, 18*(3), 137–146. doi:10.1111/1540-5826.00070

Vaughn, S., Linan-Thompson, S., & Hickman, P. (2003). Response to instruction as a means of identifying students with reading/learning disabilities. *Exceptional Children, 69*(4), 391–409.

Vaughn, S., Linan-Thompson, S., Kouzekanani, K., Bryant, D.P., Dickson, S., & Blozis, S.A. (2003). Grouping for reading instruction for students with reading difficulties. *Remedial and Special Education, 24*(5), 301–315. doi:10.1177/07419325030240050501

Vaughn, S., Wanzek, J., Wexler, J., Barth, A., Cirino, P.T., Fletcher, J.M., … Francis, D. (2010). The relative effects of group size on reading progress of older students with reading difficulties. *Reading and Writing, 23*(8), 931–956. doi:10.1007/s11145-009-9183-9

Vaughn, S., Wexler, J., Leroux, A., Roberts, G., Denton, C., Barth, A.E., & Fletcher, J. (2011). Effects of intensive reading intervention for eighth grade students with persistently inadequate response to intervention. *Journal of Learning Disabilities.* doi:10.1177/0022219411402692

Vaughn, S., Wexler, J., Roberts, G., Barth, A.A., Cirino, P.T., Romain, M.A., … Denton, C.A. (2011). Effects of individualized and standardized interventions on middle school students with reading disabilities. *Exceptional Children, 77*(4), 391–407.

Woodcock, R.W., McGrew, K.S., & Mather, N. (2001, 2007). Woodcock-Johnson III. Itasca, IL: Riverside.

Zimmerman, B.J., Bonner, S., & Kovach, R. (1996). *Developing self-regulated learners: Beyond achievement to self-efficacy.* Washington, DC: American Psychological Association.

Zimmerman, B.J., & Risemberg R. (1997). Self-regulatory dimensions of academic learning and motivation. In G.D. Phye (Ed.), *Handbook of academic learning: Construction of knowledge* (pp. 105–125). San Diego, CA: Academic Press.

INTEGRATIVE SUMMARY 4

# Intervention

## Addressing the Needs of Learners

Heikki J. Lyytinen and Peggy McCardle

Most of the research into reading acquisition and reading difficulties and disorders has focused on the early stages of reading. It is encouraging that researchers' attention is increasingly focusing toward the next steps in reading. The final goal of research is not only to understand all stages of the reading acquisition process but also to apply the results to help individuals acquire the necessary skills for knowledge acquisition, independent of the difficulties faced in their learning. The final goal of reading is comprehension, which plays a central role in guaranteeing a child's future success, and we are finally approaching this important goal. In the last section of this volume, the authors address intervention, which is critical to that goal. These two highly informative chapters are good examples of necessary steps toward this important goal. The authors describe results of intervention studies intended to help struggling readers during primary (Connor) and middle (Vaughn and Solis) school.

Connor (Chapter 18) summarizes the basic processes underlying reading comprehension and how these can be supported among readers who have recently acquired basic reading skills. Connor highlights a complex set of components that comprise reading comprehension; these tend to be highly integrated and, in empirical analyses, have been shown to form just a single factor associated strongly with spoken language skills for children in the early elementary grades. Connor and colleagues (Connor et al., 2011) evaluated interventions focusing on oral language, specifically dialect shifting and academic content knowledge. They found that explicit contrast of Home English and School English helped children in grades 2–4 to dialect shift, with both indirect and direct effects on reading comprehension. In addition, Connor and colleagues documented that practice (via Connect, Clarify, Research, and Apply activities) using familiar experiences related to the content areas had a direct (not language skill–mediated) effect on reading comprehension larger than the separate effects via oral language skill mentioned earlier. These effects were independent of initial reading level and were found across a wide grade range (kindergarten to fourth grade). This chapter highlights the malleability of even some tacit abilities, which Connor refers to as "under-the-hood" processes, and the value for all children of tailored interventions.

Vaughn and Solis (Chapter 19) review investigations of interventions intended to improve reading comprehension among middle-school students with severe reading disabilities. The main message is that the support functions should be intensive when reading disabilities have been shown to be persistent. The authors show that a multitiered intervention of increasing intensity with progress monitoring and data-based decision making can improve literacy skills, but that with older severely affected students the duration of intervention is much longer than is usually required for younger students. Two foci were given special attention in building the interventions: 1) cognitive processes were supported in an integrated way and implemented as part of academic instruction providing support to executive functions, self-regulation, memory and strategy selection, and goal-directed learning; 2) interventions were systematic and explicit, proceeding step-by-step and consistently. Concentration on treating in isolation such specific problems as auditory processing is not supported by available recent data. An important observation is the importance of intervening earlier to avoid maladaptive behaviors.

Both chapters support the importance of an analytical approach to the multistep learning route along which children proceed in learning to read. Earlier skills mastery affects the opportunity to be successful in the most important final stage, successfully gaining meaning from the written word. Decoding and developing reading fluency are foundational, but integration of other aspects of reading is also crucial.

In addition, learning requires willingness to practice as a starting point. This is why it is important to maintain student motivation and also try to optimize engagement to keep students focused on the task; both motivation and engagement are supported by positive experiences associated with learning, and they may be even more important in older students, who have struggled longer. Vaughn and Solis document the need to address not only reading comprehension strategies but also issues of self-regulation and goal-directed learning. Lovett, Lacerenza, De Palma, and Frijters (2012) have similarly commented on the difficulty of remediating older struggling readers, and they too emphasize integration of basic- and higher level reading skills and strategies with engaging students in interesting and enjoyable texts, positive group dynamics around reading instruction, and improved self-perception of one's own improvement. The introduction and maintenance of an enjoyable experience associated with reading-related activities has been a guiding principle in the development of Graphogame (Lyytinen, Erskine, Kujala, Ojanen, & Richardson, 2009; Richardson, Aro, & Lyytinen, 2011; see Grapho Learning Initiative at http://Grapholearn.info), which introduces basic reading skill via a computer game designed to maintain interest and reinforce success. Results have shown this approach to be more effective than face-to-face remedial instruction among struggling early readers, irrespective of the type of cognitive bottleneck or whether reading accuracy or fluency is the target skill (Saine, Lerkkanen, Ahonen, Tolvanen, & Lyytinen, 2010, 2011).

The emerging possibilities that stem from new technology fuel optimism for possibilities to support goal-directed learning, as can be seen in Connor's work (Connor et al., 2011; Chapter 19, this volume) and that of Lyytinen and colleagues (Lyytinen, Erskine, Kujala, Ojanen, & Richardson, 2009; Richardson, Aro, & Lyytinen, 2011). In addition, Connor, Vaughn (e.g., Vaughn et al., 2008; Chapter 19, this volume), Lyytinen, Lovett (e.g., Lovett, Lacerenza, De Palma, & Frijters, 2012), and others highlight the importance of interventions being systematic and carefully designed based on what is known about the progression and integration of language and reading skills from prior research. The studies presented demonstrate our ability to potentially assist many more struggling readers to succeed in reading comprehension. The types of interventions discussed in this section and those under development by many researchers are reassuring that progress is being made toward solving the complex problem of how best to improve reading comprehension.

## REFERENCES

Connor, C.M., Morrison, F.J., Fishman, B., Giuliani, S., Luck, M., Underwood, P., … Schatschneider, C. (2011). Classroom instruction, child X instruction interactions and the impact of differentiating student instruction on third graders' reading comprehension. *Reading Research Quarterly, 46*(3), 189–221.

Lovett, M.W., Lacerenza, L., De Palma, M., & Frijters, J.C. (2012). Evaluating the efficacy of remediation for struggling readers in high school. *Journal of Learning Disabilities, 45,* 151–169. doi:10.1177/0022219410371678.

Lyytinen, H., Erskine, J., Kujala, J., Ojanen, E., & Richardson, U. (2009). In search of a science-based application: A learning tool for reading acquisition. *Scandinavian Journal of Psychology, 50,* 668–675.

Richardson, U., Aro, M., & Lyytinen, H. (2011) Prevention of reading difficulties in highly transparent Finnish. In P. McCardle, B. Miller, J.R. Lee, & O.J.L. Tzeng (Eds.), *Dyslexia Across Languages* (pp. 62–75). Baltimore, MD: Paul H. Brookes Publishing Co.

Saine, N.L., Lerkkanen, M.-K., Ahonen, T., Tolvanen, A., & Lyytinen, H. (2010). Predicting word-level reading fluency outcomes in three contrastive groups: Remedial and computer-assisted remedial reading intervention, and mainstream instruction. *Learning and Individual Differences, 20,* 402–414.

Saine, N.L., Lerkkanen, M.-K., Ahonen, T., Tolvanen, A., & Lyytinen, H. (2011). Computer-assisted remedial reading intervention for school beginners at-risk for reading disability. *Child Development, 82*(3), 1013–1028.

Vaughn, S., Fletcher, J.M., Francis, D.J., Denton, C.A., Wanzek, J., Wexler, J., … Romain, M.A. (2008). Response to intervention with older students with reading difficulties. *Learning and Individual Differences, 18*(3), 338–345.

# Future Directions in Reading Comprehension Research

Peggy McCardle, Laurie E. Cutting, and Brett Miller

A major theme throughout the symposium and this volume about reading comprehension is the effort to make the implicit explicit: for researchers to more clearly understand and be able to explicate those "under-the-hood" processes and inner workings that control, enable, enhance, or impede the development of reading comprehension, and to be able to make instructional processes sufficiently explicit that what must become implicit or automatized can do so, to take what we consider implicit processes and be able to have teachers and educators as well as researchers see ways to make them explicit to support learning.

As outlined throughout by the contributing authors, such an endeavor involves a range of complexities that unfold over time, including at its heart the interplay between stages of reading at the phoneme and word level and at such higher levels as inferencing, which all form part of what we call reading comprehension. Such an endeavor should be sensitive to shifting emphases as some skills become automatized and are then used in developing higher level abilities within this multicomponential construct.

There are several key areas where additional research is needed to enable us to make the implicit explicit, both for research and for practice, and these parallel by design the major sections in this volume. Identification and classification are an ongoing focus of work among learning disabilities researchers and among reading researchers in particular. Historically, reading disabilities classification work has focused heavily on identification of word identification or other word-level problems consistent with common definitions of dyslexia. In Chapter 2, this volume, Morris illustrates some of the challenges faced in identifying and classifying reading comprehension deficits. Given data that suggest difficulties in reading comprehension with and without clear word-level problems, these two divergent but likely dimensional subgroup profiles have led to recognition of the increased complexity in early identification and classification of individuals with reading disabilities and in determining whether various subtypes of reading difficulties are consistent with traditional definitions of dyslexia.

We also need to clearly understand where the reading process can and does break down for some individuals (Section II), as well as how we can measure, model, and understand all these factors individually and in combination (Section III). Researchers continue to seek keys to why some students struggle with reading and what biological bases might account for their difficulty (the neurobiology and genetics, Section IV). Such issues as technology and sharing of data and measures will be important to future research in the field in all these areas. And finally, the foundational understanding developing from these lines of inquiry will be necessary for successful identification, classification, and, critically, remediation efforts, which are the focus of the intervention section (V), where the authors investigate what we can do about reading comprehension difficulties.

## CLASSIFICATION

Continued work on classification is needed. Early work addressed possible subtypes of reading difficulty and was based mainly on reading at the decoding level. Although work is still needed on those issues, classification must include reading comprehension more directly. We must better understand the heterogeneous population of individuals with comprehension problems, which may or may not meet traditional definitions of dyslexia.[1] Evidence supports neurobiological and genetic mediation of reading comprehension independent of word recognition (Betjemann, Keenan, Olson, & Defries, 2011; Cutting et al., 2013 Harlaar et al., 2010) and is broadly consistent with the supposition that there could be a significant group with specific comprehension problems that are genetically based. In practice, this group may have comorbid problems, so these individuals are generally mixed together with others who have similar symptoms but potentially different etiologies. This admixing creates a need to determine classification for both research purposes and clinical purposes. And this is not a once-and-done task. Classification is a dynamic picture (Catts, Compton, Tomblin, & Bridges, 2012); as children progress, the manifestation of their difficulties will also change (Scarborough, 2001), and other characteristics or areas of difficulty may arise over time. So as we seek to establish classification metrics, we must consider not only what the student's profile of skills is at one point in time but also what it will become. A better enumeration of the longitudinal nature of individuals' profiles and the stability and predictive value of profiles over time will be important to refine our attempts at more efficacious, early identification, classification, and intervention and, more generally, to justify service provision. This enhanced knowledge would facilitate molecular genetics study of reading comprehension by providing clear behavioral phenotypes to link to biological measures with the long-term hope of better understanding the underlying etiology and perhaps helping guide our development and tailoring of interventions.

---

[1]Reading disabilities may or may not be termed dyslexia, depending on whether one's definition requires decoding problems; see especially the chapter by Catts in this volume (Chapter 7) addressing late-emerging reading difficulties.

## READING COMPREHENSION BREAKDOWN, OR PRESSURE POINTS

Understanding the many points at which comprehension can break down is not a straightforward task. We know woefully little about the specificity of reading comprehension compared to, for example, decoding. As we unpack the construct of reading comprehension, we find that we need to better understand the language components—the depth of vocabulary (its syntactic and semantic aspects), phrasal and sentential syntax, and semantics—and how these relate to executive control and attention allocation. We also need a deeper understanding of reading at the cognitive level, and we need to be able to communicate that to teachers for intervention.

A lynchpin of understanding reading comprehension is to examine the on-line processes as children succeed and as they fail. It is important to understand that reading comprehension is a process that yields an outcome. In building models of the biological bases of reading and seeking to know the degree of predictability or malleability, we must look at these processes as probabilistic rather than as specific causalities. And we must try to determine which are malleable and which are not; the importance of a focus on malleable factors cannot be understated. Trying to change those things that are not open to change is frustrating for both student and teacher or clinician and, critically, is an ineffective use of precious learner time and school resources. We must also be able to recognize compensatory mechanisms; given that there are many subprocesses, if one is lost, unavailable, or malfunctioning, can you use others to compensate? Such information could inform the development of interventions that could take the implicit and make it explicit. For example, to pull meaning from text, one individual may rely more heavily on background knowledge, another on the word base, and yet another may lean more on syntax. Recognizing these subtleties may enable us to offer supportive interventions tailored to the individual.

## MEASUREMENT

Comprehension is a dynamic process. It occurs at different levels, and at least some of the on-line processing occurs incrementally as each word comes in; the reader builds up understanding, creating the context within which to understand other things. Our ability to track and understand how this process happens is limited by our measures. For example, if a measure is heavily loaded on decoding, we will not be able to understand why a child whose reading difficulties are not primarily mediated by word recognition problems has reading comprehension problems. To understand why some children have downstream reading comprehension difficulties, why some have difficulties related to word level, and why some exhibit problems that emerge at higher levels, we need more finely tuned measures.

Good measures of both reading and listening comprehension could better enable us to unpack the simple model of reading more explicitly to perhaps better understand the common shared variance even in typically developing individuals; such measures might allow more precision in defining phenotypes across traditional diagnostic categories. Good measures of reading comprehension must address the multiple components of reading comprehension (see Sabatini & O'Reilly, Chapter 9, this volume) and consider the various demands of different types of texts (see Cutting, Benedict, Broadwater, Burns, & Fan, Chapter 13, this volume). Finally, capitalizing on other design, measurement, and analytic approaches may not have an immediate yield for reading comprehension measurement but could help refine the way we think about measurement (see Compton, Miller, Gilbert, & Steacy, Chapter 12, this volume; Reichle, Chapter 10, this volume; and Zevin & Yang, Chapter 11, this volume).

## GENETICS AND NEUROBIOLOGY

Currently we base interventions and their timing on what we know of behavioral manifestations of risk, difficulty, and academic failure. But it is not that difficult to imagine that one day we might be able to intervene earlier based on genetic risk factors; we can at present consider preventive intervention based on family history of dyslexia, an inherited risk; preventive action based on family risk is an easily implementable change. There are also studies of genetic variants that may eventually inform early intervention attempts by unraveling or unpacking complicated etiologies or guiding possible directions for such meaningful intervention targets as the work on *DYXY1C1* (Marino et al., 2007, 2012), which is associated with working memory deficits. We also need to continue work on phenotypes. Persistent inability to respond to reading comprehension interventions could be a very important phenotype from an intervention perspective; identifying possible genetic profiles that correlate with a lack of response could signal efforts for early and intensive interventions (e.g., Keltikangas-Järvinen, et al., 2010; Petrill & Justice, 2007). This foundational understanding of intervention response and its possible genetic bases is an important piece of the puzzle, along with environmental mediators of response, to improve successful identification, classification, and, critically, remediation efforts. This type of agenda could lay the groundwork for research that could enable earlier and more targeted interventions and is likely to become more feasible as a future component of our educational tool arsenal as genotyping continues to become less expensive, particularly in comparison to the administration of in-depth neuropsychological batteries. We are not advocating dropping in-depth neuropsychological testing, but if genetic information could be used to identify individuals at risk, it would be cost effective in identifying if and when such testing is most appropriate and could allow for wider scale assessment of risk in a way that is not economically feasible with extensive, in-depth testing.

In addition, based on accumulating neurobiological work, we appear to be moving from primarily explanatory tools to predictive utilization of tools, including electroencephalography (e.g., Espy, Molfese, Molfese, & Modglin, 2004; Leppänen et al., 2012), magnetoencephalography (Rezaie et al., 2011), and magnetic resonance imaging (Barquero, Burns, Davis, Dove, & Cutting, 2012; Hoeft et al., 2011). Neurobiological information combined with state-of-the-science analytic techniques holds the promise of informing our understanding of who will be in need of preventive interventions as well as their likelihood of responsiveness. To do this, we will also need better utilization of advanced analytic approaches for neuroimaging data and validation of tasks and protocols with increasingly younger children. At the same time, it is critical that we obtain enhanced data on behavior and the developmental trajectories of individuals at risk and on the malleability of certain behaviors that underlie or contribute to the construct of reading comprehension, such as working memory and other aspects of executive control. We must remember, however, that even if we can identify at-risk individuals very early in life, using genetic or neuroimaging biomarkers, family history, or behavioral assessments, the context in which the child lives, grows, and is educated is critical to the success of any intervention and to future learning and life success.

## SHARING MEASURES AND DATA

The need for new and improved measures to be used for research is clear. There is a need for a broad toolkit of measures in order to capture the various aspects of how a construct as complex as reading comprehension is conceptualized. It is very unlikely that we can fully understand the many facets of how reading comprehension is developed or built within an individual; how, when, and where it breaks down; or how well an instructional program or intervention works purely by relying on standardized measures. We also need to have carefully experimentally constructed items that hone in on the constructs dictated by theory. Tasks and study-specific instruments are needed to achieve these goals and should be made responsibly available to other researchers such that their potential value can be fully realized and limitations fully recognized.

We also need to broaden the range of what we consider data and to develop efficient systems for capturing, utilizing, and integrating the information. For example, can we devise and take to scale a flexible system that can efficiently examine large quantities of data to give us feedback about what is working for whom. If we can obtain clinical data about students in schools, about where they succeed and where they have problems, and relate that to data on brain imaging and genetics, perhaps we can accelerate the speed of discovery and intervention development. It is true that with multivariate complex data structures, we risk making inflexible models. However, iteratively studying those interventions that seem to be effective could reveal ways to identify more intervention approaches that are effective. We should be sharing more about what is actually happening in schools and comparing across studies and schools as well as examining genetics and imaging data to find some higher order correlations to see how they replicate across samples.

Some such efforts exist, but there seems to be no centralized or easily accessible means of knowing which research teams or labs have relevant measures, information on how the measures have been used to date (including publications if relevant), and information about the researchers' willingness to share them. There is a need for a centralized access point or network of information sharing on unpublished, experimental measures or a bank of investigator-developed measures with documentation and guidance, as well as ways to know who is currently using them. The field could benefit greatly from such collaborative and collegial sharing.

Existing exemplars are emerging in three categories: school databases, research databases, and grantees sharing data or measures. The U.S. Department of Education has provided grant support to 47 states and the District of Columbia, Puerto Rico, and the Virgin Islands to establish data systems.[2] One example of collaboration using this system is the Florida Progress Monitoring and Reporting Network (PMRN) database, which shares measures that were recommended by researchers within the state with the developers and with the state department of education. The Center for Applied Linguistics (http://www.cal.org), which focuses on bilingualism and second- or additional language learning, offers information and instructional materials as well as experimental measures.[3] Examples of more general research resources sponsored by the National Institutes of Health include the Neuroimaging Informatics Technology Initiative (NIfTI),[4] the Biomedical Informatics Research Network (BIRN),[5] and an independent research data repository, the Inter-University Consortium for Political and Social Research (ICPSR).[6]

---

[2]Statewide Longitudinal Data Systems Grant Program, http://nces.ed.gov/programs/slds/stateinfo.asp.

[3]Measures for use with English learners, developed under a past research consortium funded jointly by the NICHD and the U.S. Department of Education, are available on their web site (http://www.cal.org/acquiringliteracy/assessments/index.html).

[4]NIfTI is meant to work with the tool-user and tool-developer communities to address these needs. Thus, the primary goal of NIfTI is to provide coordinated and targeted service, training, and research to speed the development and enhance the utility of informatics tools related to neuroimaging. The National Institute of Mental Health and the National Institute of Neurological Disorders and Stroke are joint sponsors of this initiative. See http://nifti.nimh.nih.gov.

[5]BIRN is a national initiative to advance biomedical research through data sharing and online collaboration. Funded by the National Institute of General Medicine Sciences, NIH; it provides data-sharing infrastructure, software tools, strategies, and advisory services, all from a single source. See http://www.birncommunity.org.

[6]ICPSR is an interuniversity consortium housed at the University of Michigan, which provides membership-based research and instructional data for the social sciences. The data archives include a range of disciplines, with searchable data archives, and offer more than a half million data files. See http://www.icpsr.umich.edu/icpsrweb/landing.jsp.

## TECHNOLOGY

Clearly, technology is already critical to research in traditional ways. We can now analyze huge data sets rapidly, and data sets large and small can be shared and accessed globally with ease and efficiency. Technology has made more sophisticated types of modeling possible. The very creation of data sets has been revolutionized in that it is now possible to construct systems such that researchers could use online databases that track students at every level and could be linked to schools around the world to find subsets of students responding to treatments in ways that we could not possibly guess. This potential to pool data can enable us to more rapidly and efficiently test, scale up, and individualize interventions.

Technology is also ubiquitous in schools, both intentionally (e.g., SMART boards in classrooms, digital course materials, and school-issued devices) and unintentionally (e.g., students' own smart phones). Just as telework is delinking jobs from standard office buildings and specific locations, and virtual classes delink university students from specific geographic regions or campuses, technology can also allow us to unhinge students from specific educational settings (e.g., virtual learning communities), thus reducing the limitations to the delivery of interventions. The role of technology in education in the future will certainly include uses for assessment, instruction, and content delivery, including virtual and enhanced peer-to-peer interactions, professional development, and other education-related uses, but it will also include uses we have yet to imagine, which may enhance the abilities of all students to learn and to use what they learn. In research too, it may enable us to capture, code, and analyze data in ever more efficient and creative ways that will help all of us to learn and use what we learn to improve learning for students.

## INTERVENTION

It is important in considering targets of intervention to know what is amenable to intervention and how to measure it. Also important is to clearly indicate which of the constructs of reading comprehension are accessible to teachers, and of these which are most malleable. Indeed, this endeavor is where neurobiological and genetic information may prove to be particularly helpful—namely, in understanding which processes will require more intensive intervention to move and which are generally more resistant to movement.

In addition to helping children who are struggling, we need to use intervention research to evaluate and inform our theories of reading development. It will be important to expand how we think about, design, and test interventions. This work can begin before entering the classroom: Preliminary work to inform targets of intervention can be done using computational modeling to model the aspects of skill development that are most critical and perhaps those that are potentially sensitive to change at a particular time point, aspects which could then be tested formally in an intervention context. This approach could be an efficient process to get us to effective interventions more quickly than we do at present, an approach similar conceptually to the use of design experiments to reify and iteratively modify aspects of an intervention to enhance impact.

Examining predictors such as preschool language abilities and linking these to later reading outcomes has been productive and continues to be explored. Using such efforts, as well as detailed assessments of learning trajectories into the early grades, linked to genetic and neuroimaging information to isolate protective factors could also guide work on intervention. Such efforts may yield usable information and occur in tandem with the difficult work of determining etiologies. Both directions of inquiry are important, but the immediacy of the need for intervention drives a parallel rather than a sequential research trajectory.

Which intervention, for whom, under what conditions? It is important to understand, appreciate, and be sensitive to the similarities and potential differences of learners. These differences encompass a range of dimensions (e.g., severity of impact, age of learner) and have implications for how to most efficiently and effectively intervene. Attention should be paid to when and where comprehension breaks down and the impact that has on the learning progression; for students with problems at the most severe end of the continuum, much more concentrated, individualized effort is needed over longer periods of time. Many strategies that work with struggling younger students do not work as well with older students and those with more severe problems. For the most severely affected students, we have the greatest need to develop effective interventions, and to do this we must not only understand more deeply how reading comprehension develops but also understand language and know how to remediate aspects of language in ways that will affect reading comprehension.

The timing, focus, and structure of interventions is important, and so we are often reluctant to move forward with interventions when we have not fully determined the optimal conditions for them. Yet we have children needing intervention. There is a need to share what we do know while continuing to solve all the problems and unearth all that we do not know. Doing so often raises new and interesting questions. If we become involved with schools and study what is being implemented to help readers who are struggling, we could offer innovative interventions to address obvious student needs and thereby make unexpected overall gains in student outcomes as well as in research knowledge. In addition, examining parent profiles might enable us to predict children's needs.

## CONCLUSION

To more completely understand how individuals learn to read, we must deepen and broaden our understanding of the construct and the process of reading comprehension. We need to examine in depth the cognitive processes that are our focus. For example, comprehension may be problematic because of executive function issues; however, we need to fully explore language abilities at a higher level, including those language functions and problems that have an impact or reciprocal influence on executive function. Such investigations will also be useful in developing etiologies and classifications, which are critical for developing appropriate interventions. We must explore biological mechanisms, including genetics and the structure and function of the brain. It will be important to determine which online processes—be they explicit or implicit—are malleable and whether we can indeed make what appears implicit to us explicit for intervention and instructional purposes in order to enable the target process to become implicit or automatized for more efficient learning. For serious work that can reach our goals regarding the next generation of intervention for reading comprehension problems, we need to realize that we are tackling a complex task that will require new approaches. Further development of multidisciplinary teams and sharing of data will become increasingly important; the fields of education, psychology, speech and language, cognitive neuroscience, genetics, and computation combined with emerging and innovative technologies could each bring a higher level of understanding to inform the process. To fully tackle this issue, we need to increase our work developing and enhancing theory and conceptualization of reading comprehension and related processes, to continue to find creative ways to intervene, and to study and improve the effectiveness of those interventions; we also must prepare researchers to collaborate and communicate fluently across disciplines. Clearly, research on reading comprehension continues to be a frontier that we have not yet conquered, but it is one toward which we are making strides in ways that hold great promise.

## REFERENCES

Barquero, L.A., Burns, S.S., Davis, N., Dove, D., & Cutting, L.E. (2012, July). *Neurobiological correlates predicting responsiveness to reading intervention in children with RD.* Poster presented at the annual meeting of the Society for the Scientific Study of Reading, Montreal, Canada.

Betjemann, R.S., Keenan, J.M., Olson, R.K., & Defries, J.C. (2011). Choice of reading comprehension test influences the outcomes of genetic analyses. *Scientific Study of Reading, 15*(4), 363–382.

Catts, H.W., Compton, D., Tomblin, J.B., & Bridges, M. (2012). Prevalence and nature of late-emerging poor readers. *Journal of Educational Psychology, 104*(1), 166–181.

Pugh, K.R., Burns, S., Cao, A., Pekar, J., Davis, N., & Rimrodt, S.L. (2013). Not all reading disabilities are dyslexia: Distinct neurobiology of specific comprehension deficits. *Brain Connectivity, 3*(2), 199–211.

Espy, K.A., Molfese, D.L., Molfese, V.J., & Modglin, A. (2004). Development of auditory event-related potentials in young children and relations to word-level reading abilities at age 8 years. *Annals of Dyslexia, 54*(1), 9–38.

Harlaar, N., Cutting, L.E., Deater-Deckard, K., Dethorne, L.S., Justice, L.M., Schatschneider, C., … Petrill, S.A. (2010). Predicting individual differences in reading comprehension: A twin study. *Annals of Dyslexia, 60*, 265–288.

Hoeft, F., McCandliss, B.D., Black, J.M., Gantman, A., Zakerani, N., Hulme, C., …

Gabrieli, J.D. (2011). Neural systems predicting long-term outcome in dyslexia. *Proceedings of the National Academy of Sciences of the United States of America, 108,* 361–366.

Keltikangas-Järvinen, L., Jokela, M., Hintsanen, M., Salo, J., Hintsa, T., Alatupa, S., & Lehtimaki, T. (2010). Does genetic background moderate the association between parental education and school achievement? *Genes, Brain, and Behavior, 9,* 318–324.

Leppänen, P.H., Hämäläinen, J.A., Guttorm, T.K., Eklund, K.M., Salminen, H., Tanskanen, A., … Lyytinen, H. (2012). Infant brain responses associated with reading-related skills before school and at school age. *Neurophysiology Clinics, 42*(1–2), 35–41.

Marino, C., Citterio, A., Giorda, R., Facoetti, A., Menozzi, G., Vanzin, L., … Molteni, M. (2007). Association of short-term memory with a variant within *DYX1C1* in developmental dyslexia. *Genes Brain and Behavior, 6,* 640–646.

Marino, C., Meng, H., Mascheretti, S., Rusconi, M., Cope, N., Giorda, R., … Gruen, J.R. (2012). DCDC2 genetic variants and susceptibility to developmental dyslexia. *Psychiatric Genetics, 22,* 25–30.

Petrill, S., & Justice, L. (2007). Bridging the gap between genomics and education. *Mind, Brain, and Education, 1*(4), 153–161.

Rezaie, R., Simos, P.G., Fletcher, J.M., Cirino, P.T., Vaughn, S., & Papanicolaou, A.C. (2011). Engagement of temporal lobe regions predicts response to educational interventions in adolescent struggling readers. *Developmental Neuropsychology, 36*(7), 869–888.

# Index

Page numbers followed by *t*, *f*, and *n* indicate tables, figures, and notes, respectively.